TURKEY'S NEW STATE IN THE MAKING

TURKEY'S NEW STATE IN THE MAKING

TRANSFORMATIONS IN LEGALITY, ECONOMY AND COERCION

Edited by Pınar Bedirhanoğlu, Çağlar Dölek, Funda Hülagü and Özlem Kaygusuz

ZED

LONDON · NEW YORK · OXFORD · NEW DELHI · SYDNEY

Zed Books
Bloomsbury Publishing Plc
50 Bedford Square, London, WC1B 3DP, UK
1385 Broadway, New York, NY 10018, USA
29 Earlsfort Terrace, Dublin 2, Ireland

BLOOMSBURY and Zed Books are trademarks of Bloomsbury Publishing Plc

First published in Great Britain 2020

This paperback edition published 2022

Copyright © Pınar Bedirhanoğlu, Çağlar Dölek, Funda Hülagü, Özlem Kaygusuz 2020

Pınar Bedirhanoğlu, Çağlar Dölek, Funda Hülagü and Özlem Kaygusuz have asserted
their rights under the Copyright, Designs and Patents Act, 1988, to be identified
as editors of this work.

For legal purposes the Acknowledgments on p. xix constitute
an extension of this copyright page.

Cover designed by Terry Woodley
Cover image © Ozan KOSE/AFP/Getty Images

A catalogue record for this book is available from the British Library.

A catalogue record for this book is available from the Library of Congress.

ISBN: HB: 978-1-7869-9870-5
PB: 978-1-7869-9871-2
ePDF: 978-1-7869-9873-6
eBook: 978-1-7869-9872-9
mobi: 978-1-7869-9874-3

Typeset in Plantin by Swales and Willis Ltd, Exeter, Devon

To find out more about our authors and books visit
www.bloomsbury.com and sign up for our newsletters.

CONTENTS

TABLES

FIGURES

ABBREVIATIONS AND ACRONYMS

AA	*Anadolu Ajansı* / Anatolian Agency
AKP	*Adalet ve Kalkınma Partisi* / Justice and Development Party
ANAP	*Anavatan Partisi* / Motherland Party
AYM	*Anayasa Mahkemesi* / Constitutional Court
BAK	*Barış için Akademisyenler* / Academics for Peace
BDDK	*Bankacılık Düzenleme ve Denetleme Kurumu* / Banking Regulation and Supervision Agency
BMI	Barro's Misery Index
BSV	*Bilim ve Sanat Vakfı* / Foundation for Sciences and Arts
CBT	*Coğrafi Bilgi Taraması* / Geographic Information System
CHP	*Cumhuriyet Halk Partisi* / Republican People's Party
CHS	*Cumhurbaşkanlığı Hükümet Sistemi* / presidential system of government
CIA	Central Intelligence Agency
DGM	*Devlet Güvenlik Mahkemeleri* / State Security Courts
DİTİB	*Diyanet İşleri Türk-İslam Birliği* / Turkish–Islamic Union of Religious Affairs
ECFR	European Council for Fatwa and Research
ECHR	European Court of Human Rights
ESAM	*Ekonomik ve Sosyal Araştırmalar Merkezi* / Economic and Social Research Centre
EU	European Union
FDI	foreign direct investment
FED	Federal Reserve System
FETÖ	*Fethullahçı Terör Örgütü* / Fethullahist Terrorist Organization
FX	foreign exchange
GBT	*Genel Bilgi Taraması* / General Information Check
GDP	gross domestic product
GNP	gross national product

GONGO	government-organized non-governmental organization
HDP	*Halkların Demokratik Partisi* / People's Democratic Party
IMF	International Monetary Fund
ISIS	Islamic State
KCK	*Koma Civakên Kurdistan* / Kurdistan Communities Union
KESK	*Kamu Emekçileri Sendikaları Konfederasyonu* / Confederation of Public Employees' Trade Unions
KGF	Credit Guarantee Fund / Kredi Garanti Fonu
KHK	*Kanun Hükmünde Kararname* / decree with the force of law
KOSGEB	*Küçük ve Orta Ölçekli İşletmeleri Geliştirme ve Destekleme İdaresi Başkanlığı* / Small and Medium Enterprises Development Organization
MERNIS	*Merkezi Nüfus İdaresi Sistemi* / Population Registration System
MGK	*Milli Güvenlik Kurulu* / National Security Council
MHP	*Milliyetçi Hareket Partisi* / Nationalist Movement Party
MİT	*Milli İstihbarat Teşkilatı* / National Intelligence Organization
MOBESE	*Mobil Elektronik Sistem Entegrasyonu* / Mobile Electronic System Integration
MP	member of parliament
MÜSİAD	*Müstakil Sanayici ve İşadamları Derneği* / Independent Association of Industrialists and Businessmen
NASA	National Aeronautics and Space Administration
NATO	North Atlantic Treaty Organization
NEP	New Economic Programme
OSCE	Organization for Security and Co-operation in Europe
PDY	*Paralel Devlet Yapılanması* / parallel state organization
PKK	*Partiya Karkerên Kurdistanê* / Kurdish Workers' Party
PPL	Public Procurement Law
PWC	Post-Washington Consensus

PYD	*Partiya Yekîtiya Demokrat* / Democratic Union Party
REIT	real-estate investment trust
SAR	Scholars at Risk
SETA	*Siyaset, Ekonomi ve Toplum Araştırmaları Vakfı* / Foundation for Political, Economic and Social Research
SME	small and medium-sized enterprise
SPK	*Sermaye Piyasaları Kurulu* / Capital Markets Board
SSB	*Savunma Sanayii Başkanlığı* / Presidency of Defence Industries
TAK	*Teyrêbazên Azadiya Kurdistan* / Kurdistan Freedom Hawks
TBB	*Türkiye Barolar Birliği* / Turkish Bar Association
TCK	*Türk Ceza Kanunu* / Turkish Penal Code
TCMB	*Türkiye Cumhuriyeti Merkez Bankası* / Central Bank of the Republic of Turkey
TDV	*Türk Diyanet Vakfı* / Turkish Diyanet Foundation
TMMOB	*Türk Mühendis ve Mimar Odaları Birliği* / Union of Chambers of Turkish Engineers and Architects
TMSF	*Tasarruf Mevduatı Sigorta Fonu* / Savings Deposit Insurance Fund
TOKİ	*Toplu Konut İdaresi Başkanlığı* / Mass Housing Administration
TRT	*Türkiye Radyo ve Televizyon Kurumu* / Turkish Radio and Television Corporation
TRY	Turkish lira
TTB	*Türk Tabipler Birliği* / Turkish Medical Association
TURKSTAT	Turkish Statistical Institute
TÜSİAD	*Türk Sanayicileri ve İşadamları Derneği* / Turkish Industry and Business Association
TVF	*Türkiye Varlık Fonu* / Turkey Wealth Fund
UE	urgent expropriation
UN	United Nations
UR	urban regeneration
US	United States
US$	United States dollar
YAŞ	*Yüksek Askeri Şura* / Supreme Military Council

CONTRIBUTORS

Ahmet Akkaya is a doctoral candidate in Political Science at Middle East Technical University in Ankara, Turkey. He received his BA and MA in International Relations there and has written a master's thesis on Turkey's anti-terror legislations after 9/11. He is currently working on a PhD dissertation on military politics in Turkey during the early Cold War period. He conducts transdisciplinary research in security studies, Turkish politics and international relations.

Ali Rıza Güngen is a political scientist and a Carnegie Mellon University Distance Fellow at the Committee on Human Rights (CHR), US National Academies of Sciences, Engineering, and Medicine. His articles have appeared in *The Journal of Peasant Studies* and *New Political Economy*. He co-edited the 2019 book *The Political Economy of Financial Transformation in Turkey* (Routledge) and is the co-author of *Financialization, Debt Crisis and Collapse: The Future of Global Capitalism* (in Turkish, 3rd edition, Notabene, 2019). His research currently focuses on dependent financialization, sovereign debt management across the global South, and financial inclusion in Turkey.

Behlül Özkan received his PhD from Fletcher School of Law and Diplomacy, Tufts University in 2009. He is currently an associate professor in the Department of International Relations at Marmara University in Istanbul. He is the author of *From the Abode of Islam to the Turkish Vatan: Making of a National Homeland in Turkey* (Yale University Press, 2012). He has also contributed op-eds to *The New York Times*, *Huffington Post*, *Birgün* and the Open Democracy website. Recently, his academic studies have focused on political Islam in Turkey and Europe.

Çağlar Dölek received his PhD in Sociology with a collaborative specialization in Political Economy from the Department of Sociology and Anthropology at Carleton University in Ottawa, Canada in 2019. He has a BA in International Relations (2008), a Minor Diploma in

Sociology (2008) and an MA in Political Science (2011) from Middle East Technical University in Ankara. He has had articles published in *Science and Society*, *Critical Sociology* and *Austrian Journal of Development Studies*. His research reflects a transdisciplinary engagement with critical criminology, urban sociology, political economy and police science from a comparative-historical perspective of the global South. He is currently working on a book project with the tentative title of 'Thieves, *Kabadayıs*, and Revolutionaries on the Margin: A Social History of the Police in the Altındağ Slums in Ankara, Turkey (1920s–1970s)'.

Çağlar Kurç is an adjunct instructor in the Department of International Relations at Bilkent University in Ankara. He was a postdoctoral fellow at the Center for Foreign Policy and Peace Research in Bilkent in 2018. Between 2015 and 2017, he was a visiting postdoctoral scholar at the Arnold A. Saltzman Institute of War and Peace Studies at Columbia University, New York. In 2012–13, he was a Fulbright Fellow on the MIT Security Studies Program. He has a BA in International Relations from Bilkent University, an MA in War Studies from King's College London, and a PhD in International Relations from Middle East Technical University. His research focuses on defence industrialization in emerging countries, arms transfers and global arms production networks. His work has appeared in journals such as *European Security*, *Comparative Strategy*, *Defense Studies* and *Defense One*.

Fuat Ercan received a BA from the Department of Public Administration and an MA in Politics and Social Sciences at Marmara University in Istanbul. He completed his PhD in Economic Development and International Economics there in 1996. He was awarded a postdoctoral research scholarship by the Turkish Academy of Sciences in 2001, which he used for a year of research at SOAS. In 2005–06 he was a visiting scholar at York University in Toronto. In 2015, he was forced to retire from the Department of Economics at Marmara University, where he worked as a professor of Development Economics, due to political pressure at the university. He is the author of *Para ve Kapitalizm* (*Money and Capitalism*, Devin, 1997), *Modernizm, Kapitalizm ve Azgelişmişlik* (*Modernism, Capitalism and Underdevelopment*, Bağlam, 2000), *Eğitim ve Kapitalizm* (*Education and Capitalism*, Bilim, 1998) and *Toplumlar ve Ekonomiler* (*Societies and Economies*, Bağlam,

2001) and editor of a series of books on political economy. His articles have been published in Turkish and international journals.

Funda Hülagü works as a research associate at the Department of Political Science, Philipps University of Marburg, Germany. After receiving her MA in Political Theory from University of Ottawa (2005) and a PhD in International Relations at Middle East Technical University (2011), she worked as an assistant professor in different universities in Turkey. Since 2015, she has been living and teaching in Germany. She has several publications in the fields of critical political economy of security, state theory and critical theories of international relations. She is currently working on a monograph provisionally entitled 'Police Reform in Turkey: Human Security, Gender and Political Violence under Erdoğan'. Her current research interests include feminist international political economy, feminist state theory, and restructuring of the state in Turkey.

İlhan Uzgel is a professor of International Relations. He received his MA and PhD from Ankara University, and an MPhil from University of Cambridge. He worked at the Department of International Relations of Ankara University, where his last position was as head of the department. He was a recipient of Chevening, Jean Monnet and Fulbright scholarships/fellowships. He has conducted research at American University and Georgetown University in Washington DC and was a short-term visiting scholar at Oklahoma City University. His research interests are Turkish foreign policy, international relations theories and US foreign policy. He is currently an op-ed contributor on foreign affairs to the online newspaper *Gazete Duvar*.

Melehat Kutun is a Philipp Schwartz fellow at the University of Kassel in Germany. She was dismissed from Mersin University as she was one of the signatories to the Peace Declaration from the Academics for Peace in 2016. Her publications mostly focus on critical state theories, Turkish politics and contemporary political theory. She is currently studying for her habilitation thesis on 'The "humanitarian face" of the state: refugee integration, labor regime, and state restructuring in Germany'. She is on the editorial board of *Praksis*, a refereed quarterly journal of social sciences embracing the rich tradition of historical materialism in Turkey.

Oya Aydın has been a practising lawyer for 20 years as a member of the Ankara Bar Association and the Berlin Bar Association. She studied law at Ankara University and wrote her master's thesis in Women's Studies at the Institute of Social Sciences at Ankara University. She is currently a PhD candidate in General Public Law at Ankara University, and a visiting scholar at the Centre for Socio-Legal Studies at Oxford University. Her articles on Turkey's legal framework and human rights violations and gender issues have been published in various journals, magazines and books.

Özlem Çelik is a postdoctoral researcher in Development Studies at the Helsinki Institute of Sustainability Science, University of Helsinki, where she is part of the team working on Social Sustainability of Urban Transformations in the Global South. Her research concerns the political economy of urban development and change, including the politics of urban economic relations, housing, state interventions, rescaling of the state, and urban social movements. She has published on various issues, such as the right to the city, the spatiality of the state, the financialization of housing, and social movements and commoning practices in Turkey. She is currently completing a book on 'The Political Economy of Urban Transformation in Istanbul'; editing a special issue of *Housing Studies* that brings together a set of papers examining the financialization of housing and the violation of housing rights at a time of crisis; and coordinating the Urban and Regional Political Economy Working Group in the International Initiative for Promoting Political Economy. She is a recipient of a Swedish Institute postdoctoral scholarship and Raoul Wallenberg Institute research funding, among other awards. She has previously worked at Lund University, Yaşar University, Middle East Technical University and University of Sheffield, after obtaining a PhD in Urban Studies and Planning, an MA in Sociology and a BA in Urban and Regional Planning.

Özlem Kaygusuz is an associate professor in the Department of International Relations at Ankara University. She studied International Relations at Middle East Technical University and completed her PhD in political science at Bilkent University. She was a visiting scholar at Georgetown University in 2003–04 and at Stanford University in 2012. She teaches undergraduate and graduate courses on globalization, international relations theory, critical security, democratization and

Turkey–EU relations. Her articles and works in these areas have appeared in various academic journals and books, in both Turkish and English.

Pınar Bedirhanoğlu is an associate professor in the Department of International Relations at Middle East Technical University in Ankara. She is currently a visiting professor in the Department of Politics at York University in Toronto. She received her PhD in International Relations from University of Sussex in 2002. She has published in English and Turkish, and has had articles translated into German and French, on neoliberal state transformation, state–capital relations, privatizations and financialization in Turkey; the political economy of corruption and neoliberal anti-corruption policies; and the politics of capitalist transformation in Russia. Her most recent research addresses the neoliberal transformation of state security structures and state transformation within and through financialization with a focus on Turkey and the global South.

Şebnem Oğuz is a professor of Political Science at Başkent University in Ankara. She received her PhD in Political Science from York University in Toronto in 2008 with her dissertation 'Globalization and the contradictions of state restructuring in Turkey'. Her research interests include state theory, political economy, Marxism and Turkish politics. She is the author of 'Rethinking globalization as internationalization of capital: implications for understanding state restructuring' (*Science and Society*, 2015) and 'The developmental state as an institutional construct: a historical and theoretical critique' (*Review of Public Administration*, 2013), and co-author (with Fuat Ercan) of 'From Gezi Resistance to Soma Massacre: capital accumulation and class struggle in Turkey' (*Socialist Register*, 2015), 'Rethinking anti-neoliberal strategies through the perspective of value theory: insights from the Turkish case' (*Science and Society*, 2007) and 'Rescaling as a class relationship and process: the case of public procurement law in Turkey' (*Political Geography*, 2006). She is a member of the Socialist Register editorial collective.

Zana Çitak is an associate professor in the Department of International Relations at Middle East Technical University in Ankara. She has a BSc from Middle East Technical University, an MSc from the London School of Economics, and a PhD from Boston University. She was a visiting fellow at the Kroc Institute for International Peace Studies at University of Notre Dame, Indiana in 2011. Her research interests are nationalism, comparative state–religion relations and Islam in Europe. She has contributed several book chapters in Turkish, English and French as well as articles that have appeared in *Middle Eastern Studies, Journal of Ethnic and Migration Studies, Journal of Church and State, Annuaire Droit et Religions, Cahiers de l'obTic, International Journal of Discrimination and the Law* and *Global Networks: A Journal of Transnational Affairs.*

Zeynep Alemdar is a professor of Political Science and International Relations at Okan University, Istanbul, where she also heads the department and the EU Research Centre. Her research interests involve human rights, democratization and civil society, and gender issues in Turkey. While her work on freedom of speech, citizenship perceptions and the privatization of security issues in Turkey, as well as on Turkey–EU relations, has been published in academic outlets, she also writes research reports, policy papers and booklets on similar topics for various research and policy institutions and media outlets. She also works on women, peace and security issues, as both an academic and an activist. She founded the Women in Foreign Policy Initiative (WFP14), which encourages and promotes women's participation in foreign policy. She has taught International Politics in various capacities and was a visiting professor at the Mark O. Hatfield School of Government at Portland State University. She spent her sabbatical leave as a Next Generation Hurford Fellow as part of the Euro-Atlantic Security Initiative at the Carnegie Endowment for International Peace in Washington DC. She earned her BA in Economics from Galatasaray University, her MA from the Patterson School of Diplomacy, and her PhD in Political Science at University of Kentucky.

Zeynep Gönen is an assistant professor at Framingham State University in the Department of Sociology. Her research is on penal formations, processes of criminalization and practices of security from a global and historical perspective, and she has been recently working on how contemporary policing in Turkey transforms the so-called common crimes. Her book *The Politics of Crime in Turkey* (I. B. Tauris, 2016) explores the practices and discourses of criminalization of the racialized urban poor, the new policing strategies of the Izmir Police, and the restructuring of policing in Turkey within the context of neoliberal transformations. Through her work, she explores the different ways in which Turkey's authoritarian state formation relies on the expansion of prisons, the police and criminal justice interventions. In turn, she locates her work on Turkey within a global scholarship that aims to understand the growing penal state around the world in relation to neoliberalism.

ACKNOWLEDGEMENTS AND BEYOND

This book is the outcome of a two-day workshop entitled 'Turkey's New Neoliberal State in the Making?', convened on 11–12 October 2018 at Middle East Technical University in Ankara. It brought together critical scholars from Turkey and asked them to make sense of the recent wide-ranging political and economic transformations that had ultimately culminated in a deep state crisis in Turkey by 2018. The participants were invited to tackle various sub-questions, including the changing global and geopolitical context of state crisis and transformation in Turkey; the political impasses brought about by the growing financialization of Turkish capitalism; the redefinition and/or the erosion of the rule of law; and the domination strategies developed by the Justice and Development Party (*Adalet ve Kalkınma Partisi* or AKP) governments to tame political opposition and social dissent in the country.

However, this basic information from the workshop remains very limited if its political context is not taken into consideration. The chaotic state transformation that the workshop questioned was taking place hand in hand with a purge in academia, which had direct implications for the lives of the workshop participants. At the time of the workshop, of the 21 participants, 14 were 'Peace Academics'; six had lost their academic positions and their right to work in public service due to emergency rule decrees; most were facing administrative investigations and/or criminal prosecutions on accusations of terrorist activity; three were in exile abroad while five were unable to leave the country because their passports had been cancelled; about half were young critical academics with little prospect of a secure job in Turkey, primarily because of their political views; and all were depressed by the traumatic events and threats surrounding them. Hence, rather than being a standard academic exchange, these dynamics inevitably turned this workshop into an act of resistance against political pressure on any critical intellectual activity, and a moment to revitalize 'the optimism of the will' à la Gramsci.

These difficult conditions prevented some of the workshop participants and conveners from contributing to the final product. We are grateful to them all – namely, Fuat Özdinç, Hülya Kendir, İsmet Akça and Duygu Kabak – for their participation, contributions and presentations to the workshop. We must express our special gratitude to Fuat Özdinç, who launched the project, for his invaluable effort and his insistence on pursuing this academic conversation under social, economic and political conditions that mostly make us question its very meaning. We also thank the discussants at the workshop – İlhan Uzgel, Filiz Zabçı, Ebru Voyvoda and Menderes Çınar – for their stimulating reflections on the papers. One of them, İlhan Uzgel, kindly accepted our invitation to prepare a chapter for the book and joined us.

INTRODUCTION: PUTTING THE AKP-LED STATE TRANSFORMATION IN ITS NEOLIBERAL HISTORICAL CONTEXT

Pınar Bedirhanoğlu, Çağlar Dölek, Funda Hülagü and Özlem Kaygusuz

Introduction

The debates on the neoliberal-authoritarian character of the state in Turkey are not new. In fact, the bloody *coup d'état* of 12 September 1980 (hereafter, 12 September[1]) and the military rule that followed it for three years have always been analysed by critical leftist scholars as the victory of the ruling capitalist classes. The junta restored their power over the working class, pacified labour militancy, and initiated a wholesale neoliberal transformation in the country.[2] Indeed, these early debates on neoliberal authoritarianism helped critical scholars in Turkey not to be fascinated by the AKP's so-called first democratic phase, and to problematize the latter in continuity with the authoritarianism of the 12 September military regime.

Nevertheless, the general attitude within and abroad until the 2010s was to perceive the AKP as the representative of the 'peripheral' masses who had long been oppressed by the patronizing Kemalist cadres at the 'centre', and as a political actor that would ensure liberalization, restoration of human rights, and even 'revolutionary' democratization in Turkey.[3] It is true that the AKP in its early years in power tried to send the military back to the barracks and initiated some reform processes within the context of the European Union (EU) membership process. Indeed, state violence in the early 2000s was not as pervasive as it had been in the 1990s, enabling the AKP's alliance with the liberal intellectuals, then fierce critics of the brutal policies of the Turkish state. The AKP promised to investigate state atrocities committed under the so-called 'military tutelage' and make a new social contract with the excluded of

Turkey, namely the Kurds, Alevis and Romas, among others. Some argued that even if the Islamists of the AKP might not be sincere in their promises, the path they had pragmatically opened up would urge them to become 'forced democrats'.[4] The course of events, however, has drastically proved the opposite. By the beginning of the 2010s, along with the new direction Turkish foreign policy took in the Syrian War and especially after the 2013 Gezi Uprising, state violence was resurrected, the military returned through the back door, and the police became the new custodian of the AKP regime.[5]

The mainstream/liberal approaches have responded to this sea change by developing a periodization that differentiates between two supposedly distinct and opposite phases of the AKP's rule. Defining the new period as one of 'de-democratization', 'electoral authoritarianism', 'competitive authoritarianism' and/or 'unconsolidated democracy',[6] they contrast the AKP's earlier image of a democratizing agent with its post-Gezi standing as a regressive one that has been directing the country away from democracy towards some kind of hybrid regime.[7] The sharp authoritarian shift in AKP rule has been attributed mainly to Erdoğan's changing political stand, shaped also in relation to autocratic tendencies elsewhere and international developments such as the Arab Spring, or the rise of China as a global power and Russia as a regional one.

This book is an attempt to analyse the drastic oppressive and coercive drive in Turkish politics in the 2010s without taking for granted this widespread reading of the AKP's and Erdoğan's two distinct periods.[8] It problematizes the political developments of the last decade in continuity with the AKP's earlier neoliberal policies and in relation to the party's general Islamist character. This is to say that the state in Turkey has introduced new strategies and instruments to govern the social as well as the state crisis in the country in the 2010s, whereas these new fixtures were indeed implanted within the very developments that characterized the so-called first period of AKP rule: full political and financial support provided by international and global circles for the implementation of neoliberal reforms, the institutionalization of neo-patrimonial relations, weakening of the political opposition, and the effective silencing of social forces, especially working-class movements – the best example of which was the dissolution of the TEKEL resistance[9] that pretty much shook the political power in 2009.

Within the continuity of neoliberal social transformations, however, the rupture is identified at the level of the state. As the AKP developed new strategies and instruments to tame and manage the social and political contradictions of neoliberal transformations that the party itself has been part of, the institutional setting and power configuration of the Turkish state have also been redefined. Hence, the main hypothesis of the book is that, despite its still unfolding, contradictory and crisis-prone character, there is a *new neoliberal state in the making* in Turkey, and the oppressive and coercive policies of the AKP regime have been constitutive of this new state. The novelty of the 2010s therefore lies not in the change in the attitude of political power, but in the changing political form of the state as the culmination of the four decades-long neoliberal social transformation in the country, a transformation that has acquired a specific direction with the Islamist AKP coming to power in 2002. The emergent characteristics of Turkey's new neoliberal state in the making can be identified for the moment as the privatization and personification of state power, the rise of coercion, discretionary economic management, and the crippling of basic modern state institutions through processes such as deconstitutionalization and Islamization, while the historically specific global and domestic determinants of these tendencies have to be duly problematized.

Why not a simple regime change? Bringing back the state transformation in critical analyses on neoliberalism

The main arguments and findings of the book can be challenged on the grounds that there is indeed nothing new in these tendencies, since they have been identified in the institutional character of the state in Turkey since its establishment in the 1920s. Three points need to be clarified to respond to such an objection. First, although many strategies and instruments used by political power in Turkey can be conceived with reference to the institutionalist regime analyses developed in the field of Middle Eastern studies, a pure regime analysis would stay short of conceptualizing the ongoing state transformation in Turkey. The Middle Eastern regime analyses mostly concentrate on political leaders, their mechanisms of political co-optation and their lust for political power due to their liberal individualistic methodology. Moreover, most of the time, the resilience of authoritarian regimes is explained with reference to the main characteristics of those regimes: a robust coercive apparatus and a neo-patrimonial political setting.[10] Every change or reform introduced in or by those regimes are conceptualized as specific strategies to further the authority of the autocrats. Despite being beneficial in recording domestic events and short-term developments in detail, such a theoretical position would be limited in understanding the scale of the ongoing state transformation in Turkey. The Turkish state has never been caught in the dilemma of many Middle Eastern states: being fierce in terms of state practices, but weak in terms of infrastructural reach.[11] A historical sociological perspective would easily show that the state in Turkey was fierce but also quite strong in terms of its infrastructural capacity and institutional matrix.[12] Therefore, in order to qualify the current transformation of the state in Turkey, it is necessary to understand the logic of state decomposition and recomposition under AKP rule without losing sight of the main characteristics of the republican state formation in the country during the first half of the twentieth century, which arose on the basis of one of the most developed and far-reaching examples of a late bourgeois revolution in the European periphery.[13]

Second, the ongoing state crisis-cum-transformation in Turkey should not be perceived as an exception. Turkey is not an outlier state, not even under the rule of the political Islamists. A focus on neoliberalism – understood as the restoration of capital's *private* power over *the public* – has its own merits for it warns us not to reduce historical political transformations to the interventions of single actors such as the AKP, Erdoğan and/or the Kemalists, but to locate their agency within wider social relations. Such a starting point would help retrieve the global social determinants of the ongoing state transformation in the country, for the rise of authoritarian/autocratic/fascist/populist states all over the world implies the existence of similar constitutive social dynamics at work in different places.[14] The AKP's Turkey, once hailed in the West as the model moderate-Islamist middle-range capitalist country, can be considered one of the first examples of right-wing populism, which appears to curse neoliberal capitalism but, in practice, deeply endorses it. However, AKP-defined populism in Turkey, rather than defining the political strategies only of Erdoğan as the political leader or of the AKP as the political party, has had transformative effects on the political form of the state. For those who are familiar with the history of neoliberalism, Chile is accepted as the first laboratory for the implementation of neoliberal shock doctrines. We argue in a similar fashion that Turkey under AKP rule can be conceived as the first laboratory for the making of the new political form of global capitalism, although this historical process, like that of neoliberal social transformations, will be a contingent and long one that will be continually redefined by class and political struggles, adventurous political moves, and costly political and economic crises.

Third, besides its global determinants, the ongoing state transformation in Turkey needs to be problematized within the context of the historical specificities of AKP rule since 2002. The longevity of AKP rule is notable in this sense, given the deteriorating political consequences of neoliberalism on both conservative and social-democratic mass parties in power elsewhere in the world over the last two decades. The AKP's coming to power after the political and economic destruction of the 2001 crisis in Turkey has always been highlighted as the initial basis of the party's rise to hegemony in the 2000s, an argument that is also shared by the authors of this book. We contribute to this discussion by highlighting additionally the role of financialization in lengthening the AKP's life in power. Another historical specificity of AKP rule in Turkey that has been effective in the ongoing state transformation is the party's Islamist incentives. The AKP's Islamism, besides redefining the content and working of state institutions as well as strategic state policies targeting women, intellectuals and masses, is also important in understanding the party's dedicated implementation of the neoliberal agenda in its first years in office. This dedication strengthened the AKP vis-à-vis the secular establishment of the Turkish state in the party's most vulnerable early years in power by ensuring the financial, political and ideological support of international actors.

Critical debates on neoliberal state transformation in Turkey

Thanks to the AKP coming to power as an Islamist and neoliberal actor, there has been a lively intellectual debate among leftist circles on the historical potentials of an AKP-led state transformation in Turkey from as early as 2002. The liberal left circles' earlier calls for the establishment of a 'Second Republic' in Turkey – one that would really bring people to power by putting an end to the capture of the state by the Kemalist cadres – resonated well with the AKP's self- and liberal promotion as a revolutionary democratic agent at that time.[15] Also alerted by the implications of this rapprochement on the strengthening of the AKP's neoliberal hegemony in Turkey, different versions of the left have criticized this liberal-leftist optimism on political and methodological grounds since then through detailed and focused analyses of the capitalist state in general and the Turkish state in particular, mostly from Gramscian and Poulantzasian perspectives.[16]

If critical investigations on the state in Turkey – a topic that has always been central to leftist analyses of neoliberal transformation due to its launch by a military coup – acquired a first impetus around a Turkey-specific regime debate by the AKP's coming to power, the accelerated move of AKP rule towards coercion and oppression in the 2010s has provided state debates with their second impetus. The leftist investigations on neoliberal state transformation have been further enriched in this decade by analyses of 'authoritarian statism', 'the exceptional state', 'fascism', 'constitutional dictatorship', 'Bonapartism', 'Rabiism', 'Sunni nation formation' and/or 'the neoliberal sultanate', through which the analytical capacities of almost all critical Marxist conceptualizations on the state are utilized comprehensively to make sense of the drastic political transformations taking place in the country.[17] They have converged on the neoliberal and class bases of the AKP-led political transformations while diverging from each other on their differing approaches to the internal–external divide (read as imperialism), the importance of the Kurdish issue for socialist struggle in Turkey, the AKP's relation to capital, and the mobilization capability of the masses, among other issues.

The analyses in this book are certainly nourished by this rich and rigorous corpus of research on neoliberal state transformation in Turkey. Still, its initial motivation has been to pay due attention to the concrete historical developments of the last decade, and not to take for granted that our critical Marxist conceptual toolbox is sufficient to problematize the recent ruptures in neoliberal political transformations in Turkey.[18] To this end, the authors of the book, from different critical traditions, have been invited to rethink the contradictory, contingent and complex domestic political developments of the 2010s within their global context, and to differentiate the global, domestic and AKP-specific determinants of the ongoing

transformations. We hope that some critical questions we have ultimately posed in relation to the emergent political trends and state
strategies in contemporary Turkey will pave the way for new theoretical and methodological inquiries to understand the ongoing political
and state transformations within neoliberal capitalism elsewhere.

Towards a new political form for Turkey's capitalist state

Making proper and full sense of the rapid and significant political
transformations the Turkish state has been passing through is definitely impossible as it is a continuously contested process in motion.
A quick look at the major domestic developments in the last decade
speaks for itself. There was possibly no single person or institution
in the country that was not affected by the accelerated processes
of political conflict, confrontation, realignment and transformation
during this period. The chapters in this book have tried to make
sense of these processes within a global context, so that a critical
distance from the events surrounding us can be constructed. At the
time of the completion of this book, people in Chile, Bolivia, Hong
Kong, Lebanon, Iraq and Iran were concurrently on the streets,
objecting to the lives granted to them within neoliberal capitalism,
and displaying different forms and strategies of resistance and solidarity. The collection of essays in this book help link those struggles
to the authoritarian and coercive historical tide defining politics all
over the world by attracting attention to the specificities of Turkish
neoliberal state transformation within the totality of global social
complexity.

The first part of the book problematizes the *global political context of state transformation in Turkey* and brings together four studies
reinforcing each other's arguments. The first chapter by Pınar
Bedirhanoğlu, 'Social constitution of the AKP's strong state through
financialization: state in crisis, or crisis state?', questions the implications of the AKP-led financialization process in the 2000s on the
state in Turkey, and argues that this process has increased the subordination of the state by capital while also increasing its political
room for manoeuvre vis-à-vis domestic and international actors.
Having identified some specific class contradictions precipitated in
Turkey by the Islamist AKP rule through household indebtedness,
she maintains that, if not contested by social struggles, the ongoing
transformations would imply the consolidation of a personalized,

non-transparent and discretionary crisis state that would continually reproduce itself through financial, political and social crises. The legal implications of this crisis are demonstrated in detail by Özlem Kaygusuz and Oya Aydın in their chapter 'Deconstitutionalization and the state crisis in Turkey: the role of the Turkish Constitutional Court and the European Court of Human Rights'. By means of a critical exposition of three significant turning points – namely, the enactment of the Internal Security Law in May 2015, the lifting of immunity for opposition parliamentarians in June 2016, and the declaration of the state of emergency in July 2016 – they argue that, through processes of what they call 'political deconstitutionalization', AKP rule has radically eroded the regulatory role of the separation of powers principle, which is considered a necessary founding principle of modern statehood. By showing how the Turkish Constitutional Court and the European Court of Human Rights have been ineffective in and incapable of using their higher judicial authority to prevent these moves, they also point to the wider processes at work in political deconstitutionalization. The chapters by İlhan Uzgel and Çağlar Kurç present a rigorous empirical demonstration of the rather unfounded, albeit highly contradictory, character of the AKP's *apparently* anti-Western foreign policy agenda that is generally associated with a possible 'shift of axis'. Uzgel, in his chapter 'Turkey's double movement: Islamists, neoliberalism and foreign policy', first problematizes how the Europeanization process during 2002–07 facilitated the AKP's takeover of the state. Having later warned of the illusion created by the AKP over its anti-Western position, Uzgel shows the continuing force of gravity the West possesses in the resilience of AKP rule in Turkey. Grounded in a critique of the politics of defence procurement, Kurç's chapter, 'A shift of axis or business as usual? Turkey's S-400 procurement decision and defence industry', demonstrates one of the material reasons that make the AKP dependent on the West, and assesses the AKP's search for alternative global allies as 'irrational', even from the perspective of state security.

The second part of the book on the *politics of economic management* questions the changes in the AKP's economic management strategies within the totality of capital accumulation dynamics and class relations in Turkey. The first problematization in this regard is provided by Fuat Ercan and Şebnem Oğuz in their chapter titled 'Understanding the recent rise of authoritarianism in Turkey in terms of the structural contradictions of the process of capital accumulation'. Identifying the structural roots of the recent move towards authoritarianism in Turkey within the historical impasses of the capital accumulation process, they argue that many strategies that the AKP endorses today can be defined as strategies of buying time, as Turkish capitalism is incapable of reproducing itself through an increase in relative surplus value production. Ali Rıza Güngen's chapter, 'Turkey's financial slide: discipline by credit in the last decade of the AKP's rule', shows how this postponement strategy has become systematic in the financial field. Depicting the processes that have disciplined households and SMEs in the last decade through renewed cycles of debtfarism, Güngen demonstrates that if discipline by credit has succeeded as a strategy in the making of the new neoliberal state in Turkey, it has done so only at the expense of deepening the contradictions inherent in financialized capitalism. Melehat Kutun's contribution, 'The AKP's move from depoliticization to repoliticization in economic management', provides a critical analysis of the institutional transformations in economic management of the last decade. Mapping the historical stages of the AKP's shift from depoliticization to repoliticization in the management of the economy, she problematizes how the decomposition of state power in economic management has been instrumental in the centralization and personification dynamics that characterize the new neoliberal state in Turkey. Finally, Özlem Çelik's chapter in this part on 'The AKP's income-differentiated housing strategies under the pressure of resistance and debt' perfectly illustrates the AKP's class-sensitive strategies in the housing sector, which are constantly redefined in response to changes in market conditions as well as resistance. Çelik's field study in three important districts of *gecekondu* transformation in Istanbul demonstrates how the management of class confrontations is conducted by the AKP on a case-by-case basis and at the expense of nature in the final analysis.

The third part of the book aims to problematize the *politics of domination* defining state–society relations in the AKP's Turkey by focusing on four different topics. In her chapter entitled 'The transformation of the state–religion relationship under the AKP: the case of the Diyanet', Zana Çitak powerfully demonstrates the central, increasing and transnational role of the Directorate of Religious Affairs in the politics of de-secularization in Turkey under AKP rule. Challenging the popularized arguments on post-Islamism, she shows not only the return of the theological into the political scene in Turkey but also the elimination of the modern separation of religion and state. The next contribution by Ahmet Akkaya problematizes the historical agency of liberals in the making of authoritarianism in Turkey. His chapter, 'From military tutelage to nowhere: on the limitations of civil–military dualism in making sense of the rise of authoritarianism in Turkey in the 2010s', underlines the poverty of the liberal conception of 'military tutelage', which was once a central political argument to praise the democratizing potential of the Islamists against the Kemalist establishment. His overview of the politics of military transformation since the late 2000s also provides a summary of the intra-state controversies of the AKP's rule. The following chapters by Zeynep Alemdar and Behlül Özkan depict the desperate state of intellectuals in Turkey in the 2010s. Alemdar, in 'Courtrooms as solidarity spaces and trials as sentences: defending your rights and asking for accountability in Turkey', shows how unsubstantiated legal processes, in some cases ending in years of imprisonment for academics, journalists and Gezi protestors, turn into actual punishment in the 2010s. She argues that these trials, which also reflect the transformations taking place in judicial practices, must be rethought in relation to the AKP's anti-intellectualism, which aims to criminalize, degrade and paralyze the intellectual capacity of progressive circles. Anti-intellectualism, as a decisive instrument in the politics of domination, is also coupled with the production of 'the vulgar' in everyday life and in political discourse. In his chapter 'SETA: from the AKP's organic intellectuals to AK-paratchiks', Özkan demonstrates the poverty of the intellectual hegemony of the AKP with a focus on the party's organic intellectuals in SETA, a rich conservative think tank with offices in many parts of the globe. This contribution provides a critical perspective on the ongoing inability of the Turkish Islamists to consolidate their power in the struggle over intellectual production.

The last part of the book, on the *politics of coercion*, aims to contribute to the problematization of different dimensions, accumulated tensions and inherent contradictions of the AKP's quest to fabricate a new social order and its corresponding interventions in the coercive capacities of the state. In her chapter 'Domesticating politics, de-gendering women: state violence against politically active women in Turkey', Funda Hülagü argues that the new patriarchal AKP state is selective in its domination strategies, where different groups of women are subject to different forms of gender-based state violence. This selective governance, however, does not operate in a void but takes shape amidst contradictions emanating from the competition between different gender ideologies in Turkey. Zeynep Gönen's chapter, titled 'War on drugs: a view from Turkey', tackles the same question but with a particular focus on a rather under-researched topic. Based on a rigorous survey of Turkey's narcotics police, Gönen vividly demonstrates how the criminalization of common crimes, which also helps in disciplining the Kurdish population, has reinforced and diversified the trajectory of authoritarian state formation in Turkey. Çağlar Dölek contributes to this discussion in his chapter '"The law of the city?": Social war, urban warfare and dispossession on the margin'. Dölek's analysis attempts to expose organic links between the 'social war' rooted in the violence of capital accumulation, dispossession and marginalization of the proletariat with the 'urban warfare' waged against political dissent in the country. According to Dölek, the policing strategies formulated amidst this twin warfare on the margins have become generalized as the dominant police order in the 2010s.

The chapters' detailed investigation into the strategies and instruments the AKP has applied to manage the social contradictions of neoliberal transformation in Turkey and the party's specific interventions in the institutional materiality of the state highlight the mutually reinforcing paths constructed by the AKP between the neoliberal class project and its own Islamist agenda. The AKP's success in turning the crises of financialized Turkish capitalism into an opportunity for the fulfilment of its own political Islamist concerns has been conditioned, in addition to its strategic policy choices, by the active support of Western states and finance, and the general weakening of labour within neoliberal transformations worldwide. As the analyses on financialization indicate, even though the implementation of this specific neoliberal agenda has structurally redefined the class contours of the Turkish state in favour of capital, it has also provided the AKP with an enhanced political room for manoeuvre to manage the social and economic crises in conformity with its Islamist priorities.

The emergent tendencies in state transformation towards the privatization and personification of the state, the rise of discretionary economic and coercive political management, and the erosion of basic modern state institutions by processes of deconstitutionalization and Islamization can be seen as products of the AKP's strategic agency forcing the new structural and political limits of the Turkish neoliberal state for its own ends. However, as shown by Turkey's initially hyper-reactionary relations but ultimately appeasement with the West and the latter's accommodation of this approach, these limits are not fixed but also continually redrawn within global and international configurations of power. Hence, the AKP's adventures to define a new political form of state capable of better managing the current financialized contradictions of Turkish capitalism are conditioned within a global context, which is itself subject to change through highly complex processes of crisis, social upheavals and accompanying political strategies of containment and repression at multiple scales.

Overall, Turkey's new neoliberal state in the making is characterized by a radical displacement or dismantling of 'public power' as the historical legacy of modern state formation in Turkey. As the analyses in the following chapters show from many different angles, this means a historical development that involves more than just the privatization of once state-provided public services, but requires a questioning of the public character of the state, with all its basic modern qualities, as it has been defined since the early twentieth century in Turkey. Those who have an inclination to see this as a Turkey-specific development should start thinking about what it is that prevents their modern liberal democratic institutions from facing a similar fate after four decades of fundamental neoliberal transformations in their social bases.

APPENDIX: THE COURSE OF EVENTS
IN THE 2010s IN TURKEY

This appendix aims to provide readers with limited knowledge of contemporary Turkish history with a short overview of the course of events in the 2010s. This will be done by highlighting different turning points proposed by different political views in order to understand the reasons for the recent drastic move of the AKP governments towards authoritarianism and coercion. Of course, the most memorable of these turning points is the Gezi Uprising in June 2013, during which millions of people took to the streets for days and nights to demand the resignation of the AKP government. The Gezi Uprising brought together many different voices in society, ranging from secularist social-democrats and socialists to liberals and nationalists. Remarkable too was the extensive participation of marginalized urban populations, including the Alevi and Kurdish youth, dissenting women and white-collar workers. Based on the composition of the protestors, the events that triggered the public reaction that culminated in the Gezi Uprising can be traced back to 2007–08, although this is a highly contested issue in political debates in Turkey.

The period 2007–08 was a significant turning point because of the negative impact of the global capitalist crisis on Turkey's financialized economy, which faced a sharp decline in total foreign inflows despite Erdoğan's counterclaims that the crisis had had only a 'tangential' effect on the economy.[19] Additionally, 2007 was the year when, for the first time in Turkish political history, a First Lady wearing a headscarf took part in state protocol as one of the founders of the AKP, Abdullah Gül, was elected President. From this date, the secular–religious divide started to deepen. Parts of the state establishment that were still living under the legacy of Kemalism hit back via large-scale public meetings to save the republic. A court case in 2008 asked for the closure of the ruling AKP based on the charge that the party violated the principle of the separation of religion and state in Turkey. The AKP, with the help of Gülenist state cadres, located mostly in internal security and the judiciary, retaliated with the *Ergenekon* trials, targeting military officers, journalists and opposition lawmakers, all alleged members of a suspected secularist clandestine organization, who were accused of plotting against the Turkish government. The trials resulted in lengthy prison sentences for most of the accused.

The 2010 referendum on a set of constitutional amendments that were arguably designed to increase parliamentary control over the army and judiciary must be mentioned as another crucial turn. At the time, many progressive intellectuals hailed the 12 September 2010 referendum as an important step in getting rid of the authoritarian legacy of the military elites and of a constitution that bears their mark. Many opposition groups and parties, however, countered the so-called constitutional reform, seeing it as an attempt to empower the executive, and hence to replace military tutelage over politics with a civilian-majoritarian tutelage under the AKP.[20]

The 2010 referendum ended with the victory of the AKP, followed by the party's resounding win in the June 2011 general elections. Erdoğan embarked on a third term in office as Prime Minister. The same year, Turkey's stance on the Syrian uprisings crystallized. The AKP regime declared Syrian President Bashar al-Assad 'a bloody dictator' and started to support armed opposition groups across the border. In relation to the new ambitious and expansionist foreign policy agenda, a new round of nationalist ideology and politics started determining the internal politics of Turkey. The rise of the security state also accelerated as the conflict with the Kurdish Workers' Party (*Partiya Karkerên Kurdistanê* or PKK) escalated in 2011, turning into an intense intra-regional war with internal, regional and international determinants.

After the 2013 Gezi Uprising put the legitimacy of the AKP governments in question, the ruling bloc started to dismantle. In December 2013, the government sacked numerous police chiefs over the arrests of pro-government public figures on corruption charges. This was one of the initial moments in the AKP's ongoing power struggle with Fethullah Gülen, a US-based Islamist cleric and an AKP ally at the time. Erdoğan started the purge within security institutions, which included many Gülenists. Furthermore, the government proposed a new internal security law both to facilitate the purges within the security sector and to augment the sector's powers. Despite widespread opposition, the law was enacted. The post-Gezi turmoil within politics and society and the increasing authoritarianism that followed can be considered one significant turning point in the recent political history of Turkey. Erdoğan won the first direct popular election for the presidency in 2014 within such a tense political context.

Another historical point that accelerated the coercive and authoritarian drive of the state in Turkey came with the general elections on 7 June 2015, when the pro-Kurdish People's Democratic Party (*Halkların Demokratik Partisi* or HDP) entered parliament, passing the 10 per cent electoral threshold and hence depriving the governing AKP of its majority. The elections were renewed and rescheduled; a short-lived ceasefire with the PKK crumbled under the weight of political tensions in Turkey and geopolitical issues in the region. The government not only put pressure on HDP-affiliated politicians but also initiated a new round of violent repression in the Kurdish-populated regions that caused the death, injury and forced displacement of hundreds of people and violations of fundamental human rights, including the rights to life, liberty, security, housing, health, access to effective legal means, and prohibition from inhuman and degrading treatment. The Kurdish-populated regions of Şırnak/Cizre, Şırnak/Silopi, Şırnak/İdil, Mardin/Nusaybin, Hakkari/Yüksekova and Diyarbakır/Sur were greatly affected during this process.[21]

In the same period, the Islamic State (IS) became very active in Turkey. In July 2015, an IS suicide bomber killed 32 young activists at a rally in Suruç on the Syrian border. In October 2015, IS attacked the Ankara peace rally, killing 102 people and leaving many injured. During 2015 and 2016, political violence reached a peak in Turkey. In addition, Kurdish groups involved in political violence, such as *Teyrêbazên Azadiya Kurdistan* (Kurdistan Freedom Hawks or TAK), retaliated with suicide bomb attacks that killed both military personnel and civilians in Ankara and Istanbul.

July 2016 is another essential juncture in the recent historiography of Turkey. On 15 July, a faction within the military and police forces, mostly associated with the Gülenists, initiated a coup attempt. The putsch was aborted. In the aftermath, the authorities detained thousands of soldiers and judges on suspicion of involvement in the coup attempt. The government declared a state of emergency and started to govern the country with decrees having the force of law. As Erdoğan himself openly declared, the coup attempt provided the AKP with 'a God's gift' for engineering its political agenda pertaining to state transformation. Decrees with the force of law, a historical legacy from 12 September, quickly became a decisive instrument for the AKP to instigate a major restructuring of the political decomposition and institutional architecture of the state. Positions in various state departments were cleared through numerous purges that dismissed about 150,000 people from public institutions. It has also been argued that the public offices emptied by these purges have been filled with the cadres of various political groups, as well as religious sects, reflecting the ongoing power bargaining and struggles within the state. On the other hand, it was through the emergency decrees that the basic institutional, political and legal architecture of the *sui generis* presidential system of government was formed between July 2016 and June 2018.[22] Henceforth, the protracted emergency rule was proved to be politically conducive for the decomposition and recomposition of the new neoliberal state in Turkey.

During this process, although Erdoğan has seemed to lose electoral support, he has managed to overcome the crisis by way of a more aggressive and suppressive consolidation of his personalized rule. In April 2017, he narrowly won the referendum to extend his powers. In June 2018, he was re-elected for the presidency while the credibility of the electoral system in Turkey became more and more questionable. This victory signalled the official end of the emergency period, which was prolonged seven times after its initial inception in July 2016. During the process, the AKP has been relatively successful in building a coalition campaign with the Nationalist Movement Party (*Milliyetçi Hareket Partisi* or MHP), and has managed to keep the Republican People's Party (*Cumhuriyet Halk Partisi* or CHP) within the main parameters of its own policies. This has been evident in the nationalist-cum-Islamist mobilization around the Kurdish issue, both within and outside the country.

Finally, just before the contributors to this volume met for the October workshop, in August 2018, the Turkish lira sank to record lows, having lost more than 40 per cent of its value against the dollar in a month. The US-imposed sanctions linked to Ankara's refusal to release a jailed US pastor exacerbated the crisis. Although the local elections of June 2019, in which a social democratic candidate was elected as the new mayor of Istanbul, opened a hole in Erdoğan's success story, the AKP regime has succeeded in rallying its supporters around an Islamist-nationalist-populist rhetoric until very recently.

Notes

1. This is how the *coup d'état* is referred to in public and academic debates in Turkey.
2. Tünay 1993; Öngen 2002; Savran 2016a.
3. Barkey and Çongar 2007; Hale and Özbudun 2010; İnsel 2003; Öniş 2006.
4. Ü. Kıvanç (2015) 'Çünkü ben aptalım', *Radikal*, 25 June.
5. See the appendix following this introductory chapter for a brief overview of the political and economic developments in Turkey after 2007.
6. Öniş 2016; Taş 2015; Özbudun 2015; Esen and Gümüşçü 2016; Aydın-Düzgit and Keyman 2013; Arbatlı 2014.
7. Tansel 2018.
8. For critical studies that accept a similar periodization, although within a neoliberal historical analysis, see Tansel 2018; Bozkurt-Güngen 2018; Kaygusuz 2018.
9. Yalman and Topal 2017.
10. Bellin 2004; Holger and Schlumberger 2004.
11. See Mann 1984. For a historically sensitive institutionalist analysis of the question of corruption in Turkey, see Jacoby 2010.
12. For a similar call for the advancement of a historical sociological approach to state formation in the Middle East, see Hinnebusch 2010.

13. On state formation in the Middle East, see Bromley 1994; Kansu 1997; Owen 2006 [1992]; Düzgün 2012.
14. Among the ever-growing literature, see Peters 2018; Jessop 2019; Yalvaç and Joseph 2019; Ehmsen and Scharenberg 2018.
15. These calls dated back to the early 1990s. See M. Altan (1992) '2. Cumhuriyet nedir, ne değildir?', *Derkenar*. For a detailed discussion of this perspective with a specific emphasis on the explanatory limits of its 'military tutelage' argument, see Akkaya (Chapter 10).
16. Yalman 2009; Uzgel 2009; Bedirhanoğlu 2009; Akça et al. 2014; Oğuz 2016.
17. Benlisoy 2017; Berksoy 2017; Kaygusuz 2018; Oğuz 2016; Savran 2016b; Tuğal 2016; Yaşlı 2014; Yıldırım 2013.
18. For a similar critical concern, see Akça et al. 2017a: 189.
19. See Bedirhanoğlu (Chapter 1), Ercan and Oğuz (Chapter 5) and Güngen (Chapter 6).
20. See Akkaya (Chapter 10).
21. See TMMOB (2019) *Yıkılan Kentler Raporu*, https://www.tmmob.org.tr/sites/default/files/tmmob_yikilan_kentler_raporu.pdf.
22. Akça et al. 2017b.

References

Akça, İ., A. Bekmen and B. A. Özden (eds) (2014) *Turkey Reframed: Constituting Neoliberal Hegemony*. London: Pluto Press.

Akça, İ., A. Bekmen and B. A. Özden (2017a) 'Antinomies of authoritarian neoliberalism in Turkey: the Justice and Development Party era' in C. B. Tansel (ed.), *States of Discipline, Authoritarian Neoliberalism and*

the Contested Reproduction of Capitalist Order. London and New York, NY: Rowman and Littlefield, pp. 189–210.

Akça, İ., S. Algül, H. Dinçer, E. Keleşoğlu and B. A. Özden (2017b) *When State of Emergency Becomes the Norm: The Impact of Executive Decrees on Turkish Legislation*. Cologne: Heinrich Böll Stiftung.

Arbatlı, E. (2014) 'Türkiye'nin yeni yolu, seçimlere dayalı otoriterizmin yükselişi', *ResearchTurkey*, 26 December.

Aydın-Düzgit, S. and F. Keyman (2013) 'EU–Turkey relations and the stagnation of Turkish democracy' in S. Aydın-Düzgit, A. Duncker, D. Huber, E. F. Keyman and N. Tocci (eds), *Global Turkey in Europe: Political, Economic and Foreign Policy Dimensions of Turkey's Evolving Relations with the EU.* Rome: Edizioni Nuova Cultura, pp. 103–64.

Barkey, H. J. and Y. Çongar (2007) 'Deciphering Turkey's elections: the making of a revolution', *World Policy Journal 24* (3): 63–73.

Bedirhanoğlu, P. (2009) 'Türkiye'de neoliberal otoriter devletin AKP'li yüzü' in İ. Uzgel and B. Duru (eds), *AKP Kitabı: Bir Dönüşümün Bilançosu.* Ankara: Phoenix, pp. 40–64.

Bellin, E. (2004) 'The robustness of authoritarianism in the Middle East: exceptionalism in comparative perspective', *Comparative Politics 36* (2): 139–57.

Benlisoy, F. (2017) 'Plebisiter Bonapartismin Sınıfla Yaklaşan İmtihanı', *Evrensel*, 16 July.

Berksoy, B. (2017) '2010'larda Türkiye'de "güvenlik devleti" "olağanüstü devlet" biçimine evrilirken', *Birikim*, *335*: 11–26.

Bozkurt-Güngen, S. (2018) 'Labour and authoritarian neoliberalism: changes and continuities under the AKP government in Turkey', *South European Society and Politics 23* (2): 219–38.

Bromley, S. (1994) *Rethinking Middle East Politics.* Austin, TX: University of Texas Press.

Düzgün, E. (2012) 'Class, state and property: modernity and capitalism

in Turkey', *European Journal of Sociology / Archives Européennes de Sociologie 53* (2): 119–48.

Ehmsen, S. and A. Scharenberg (2018) *The Far Right in Government: Six Cases from across Europe.* New York, NY: Rosa Luxemburg Stiftung, http://www.rosalux-nyc.org/wp-content/files_mf/farrightingovernmenten_web.pdf.

Esen, B. and Ş. Gümüşçü (2016) 'Rising competitive authoritarianism in Turkey', *Third World Quarterly 37* (9): 1581–606.

Hale, W. and E. Özbudun (2010) *Islamism, Democracy, and Liberalism in Turkey: The Case of the AKP.* New York, NY: Routledge.

Hinnebusch, R. (2010) 'Toward a historical sociology of state formation in the Middle East', *Middle East Critique 19* (3): 201–16.

Holger A. and O. Schlumberger (2004) 'Waiting for Godot: regime change without democratization in the Middle East', *International Political Science Review 25* (4): 371–92.

İnsel, A. (2003) 'The AKP and normalizing democracy in Turkey', *South Atlantic Quarterly 102* (2–3): 293–308.

Jacoby, T. (2010) 'Turkey and Europe: culture, capital and corruption', *Review of International Studies 36*: 1–22.

Jessop, B. (2019) 'Authoritarian neoliberalism: periodization and critique', *South Atlantic Quarterly 118* (2): 343–61.

Kansu, A. (1997) *The Revolution of 1908 in Turkey.* Leiden: Brill.

Kaygusuz, Ö. (2018) 'Authoritarian neoliberalism and regime security in Turkey: moving to an "exceptional state" under AKP', *South European Society and Politics 23* (2): 281–302.

Mann, M. (1984) 'The autonomous power of the state: its origins, mechanisms, and results', *European Journal of Sociology 25* (2): 185–213.

Oğuz, Ş. (2016) 'Yeni Türkiye'nin siyasal rejimi' in T. Tören and M. Kutun (eds), *Yeni Türkiye? Kapitalizm, Devlet, Sınıflar*. Istanbul: SAV, pp. 81–127.

Öngen, T. (2002) 'Political crisis and strategies of crisis management: from "low intensity conflict" to "low intensity instability"' in N. Balkan and S. Savran (eds), *The Politics of Permanent Crisis: Class, Ideology and State in Turkey*. Huntington, NY: Nova Science Publishers, pp. 55–84.

Öniş, Z. (2006) 'İslam'ın Ekonomi Politiği ve Türkiye'de Demokrasi: Refah Partisi'nden AKP'ye', *Avrasya Dosyası 12* (2): 121–52.

Öniş, Z. (2016) 'Turkey's two elections: the AKP comes back', *Journal of Democracy 27* (2): 141–54.

Owen, R. (2006 [1992]) *State Power and Politics in the Making of the Modern Middle East*. London and New York, NY: Routledge.

Özbudun, E. (2015) 'Turkey's judiciary and the drive toward competitive authoritarianism', *The International Spectator 50* (2): 42–55.

Peters, M. A. (2018) 'The end of neoliberal globalization and the rise of authoritarian populism', *Educational Philosophy and Theory 50* (4): 323–5.

Savran, S. (2016a) *Türkiye'de sınıf mücadeleleri*. 4th edition. Istanbul: Yordam Kitap.

Savran, S. (2016b) 'Faşizm mi, Rabiizm mi?', *Devrimci Marksizm 27*: 19–68.

Tansel, C. B. (2018) 'Authoritarian neoliberalism and democratic backsliding in Turkey: beyond the narratives of progress', *South European Society and Politics 23* (2): 197–217.

Taş, H. (2015) 'Turkey: from tutelary to delegative democracy', *Third World Quarterly 36* (4): 776–91.

Tuğal, C. (2016) 'In Turkey, the regime slides from soft to hard totalitarianism', *Open Democracy*, 17 February.

Tünay, M. (1993) 'The Turkish New Right's attempt at hegemony' in A. Eralp, M. Tünay and B. Yeşilada (eds), *The Political and Socioeconomic Transformation of Turkey*. Westport, CT: Praeger, pp. 11–30.

Uzgel, İ. (2009) 'AKP: Neoliberal Dönüşümün Yeni Aktörü' in İ. Uzgel and B. Duru (eds), *AKP Kitabı: Bir Dönüşümün Bilançosu*. Ankara: Phoenix, pp. 11–39.

Yalman, G. (2009) *Transition to Neoliberalism: The Case of Turkey in the 1980s*. Istanbul: Bilgi University Press.

Yalman, G. and A. Topal (2019) 'Labour containment strategies and working-class struggles in the neoliberal era: the case of TEKEL workers in Turkey', *Critical Sociology 45* (3): 447–61.

Yalvaç, F. and J. Joseph (2019) 'Understanding populist politics in Turkey: a hegemonic depth approach', *Review of International Studies 45* (5): 786–804.

Yaşlı, F. (2014) *AKP, Cemaat, Sunni-Ulus: Yeni Türkiye Üzerine Tezler*. Istanbul: Yordam Kitap.

Yıldırım, D. (2013) 'Rejim Dönüşümünü Sınıfsal Zemin Üzerine Yerleştirerek Analiz Etmeliyiz', *Muhalefet*, 5 January.

PART I

GLOBAL POLITICAL CONTEXT OF STATE TRANSFORMATION

1 | SOCIAL CONSTITUTION OF THE AKP'S STRONG STATE THROUGH FINANCIALIZATION: STATE IN CRISIS, OR CRISIS STATE?

Pınar Bedirhanoğlu

Introduction: Turkey's political and legal impasse

Neoliberal state transformation in Turkey, which entered into a historically specific phase after the AKP came to power in 2002, reached a political and legal impasse in the late 2010s. Politically, the country has been divided into two electoral halves: about 50 per cent of the population, predominantly not well-educated, old and pious, often with a rural background, opposes the other 50 per cent, which is mainly urban, educated, young and secular.[1] This division has been reflected in all the recent critical electoral results: the AKP received 49.49 per cent of the votes in the general elections on 1 November 2015; the referendum on 16 April 2017 on the AKP's political project of transition to Turkish-style presidentialism was approved by 51.41 per cent; the Presidential Alliance formed by the AKP and the MHP got 49.50 per cent of the votes in the general elections on 24 June 2018; and Erdoğan received 52.59 per cent in the presidential elections conducted on the same day and was elected the first all-powerful President of the 'New Turkey'.[2] These two halves are also in opposition every day through conventional media channels as well as on social media on almost all the burning social problems of the country, such as child abuse, rape, murders of women, suicides and even the exclusion of the disabled.[3] The government never misses the chance to be part of this verbal violence while also intervening in the legal handling of individual cases according to its immediate needs.[4] President Erdoğan, who is also head of the AKP, is systematically constructing a binary opposition between the two halves by defining the former as 'homegrown and national' and the latter as 'Western mimics' at best and 'terrorists' at worst. Interestingly, it is only when there is a perceived foreign threat or humiliation that these two halves seem to approach each other politically, showing that it is only through nationalistic mobilization that they are brought together.[5] However, whether this makes the Turkish social space a 'society' is questionable, as Necmi Erdoğan has rightly asked.[6]

Legally, the *sui generis* presidential system of government (*Cumhurbaşkanlığı Hükümet Sistemi* or CHS), which was approved by the 2017 referendum and put into practice in July 2018 immediately after the end of a three-year state of emergency, is merely the 'legal' transgression of the rule of law, due to its discretionary and personalized character and implementation.[7] This is strange, as this new 'system' is apparently the product of years-long constitutional debates as well as numerous changes to the still valid 1982 Constitution.[8] While the purported aim of this whole enterprise was the establishment of a more democratic, transparent and free society, the outcome has been an oppressive, non-transparent and centralized one in which the violent disciplining of free speech by humiliation, criminalization and imprisonment has become an everyday practice.

The general mood of the 50 per cent in opposition seems to be one of 'waiting' for a breaking point to end this impasse,[9] be it a financial collapse, a terminal clash of interests between the AKP and the big powers in foreign policy, the rise of a miraculous, heroic figure to challenge President Erdoğan, or even civil strife. These hopes reflect the inability of the moribund modern bourgeois institutions – including parliament, political parties, state institutions, professional bodies, trade unions and civil society organizations – to produce ways out of this impasse in Turkey. No one talks anymore about the institutional capacities of the Turkish state or society to handle the current situation, as all such hopes were lost some time between 2015 and 2018. Put simply, the old is already dead but there is nothing new on the horizon.[10] The worst scenario would be Erdoğan totally eliminating elections, turning the de facto practice[11] into a 'constitutional' fix.

This impasse implies some substantial historical transformations in capitalist social relations in Turkey within which the state reproduces itself. However, the currently available political institutions, based on the modern public conception of the state, are no longer capable of managing these transformed social relations.

Rather, material private interests and crude political and economic negotiations seem to define current political processes. The fact that this development is not confined to Turkey but is also observed elsewhere[12] suggests that there are some global dynamics at work in the constitution of such trends, although Turkey seems to represent a case where they have become more generalized.

Problematizing all the political, social, economic and ideological tensions and contradictions that led to the current impasse would be beyond the scope of an academic essay. This chapter thus aims to focus on its constitution through the processes of financialization under AKP rule since 2002. Suggesting an Open Marxist analytical framework, it looks for answers to two questions: how has financialization redefined capital–labour relations in Turkey within a crisis-ridden historical process, one in which the AKP's specific Islamist orientation has played a significant role? And how has this social transformation affected the Turkish state's conditions of reproduction within financialized capitalism in the 2010s? The emphasis on 'reproduction' here requires the development of a non-reductionist analysis which accepts that the capitalist state is continuously contested as well as reproduced within class and political struggles in contingent and historically specific ways, hence within open-ended processes in which everyday encounters between capitalists and labourers define only one line of constitutive confrontation. The emphasis on 'reproduction', however, also reminds us of the class limits or boundaries the capitalist state form imposes on individual states, as it requires the need to make sense of states within the totality and globality of the capital accumulation process.[13] As Clarke argues:

> The mediations between capital and the state do not determine that the state intervene to act in the 'best interests' of capital, or even that a particular government will not use the levers at its disposal to undermine altogether the reproduction of capital. Thus, the state is not simply a tool of capital, it is an arena of class struggle. But the form of the state is such that if the political class struggle goes beyond the boundaries set by the expanded reproduction of capital, the result will be not the supersession of the capitalist mode of production but its breakdown, and with it the breakdown of the material reproduction of society.[14]

On the other hand, ensuring the material reproduction of society within the global conditions of capital accumulation does not free the state from tensions and contradictions, since society's material reproduction is inevitably at odds with its social reproduction within capitalist relations of production. States then can only manage, rather than overcome, these contradictions through various strategies of dislocation in time and space, depending on their differentiated as well as changing historical, ideological, political and economic capacities. Following Bonefeld, the capitalist states' form-limited but dynamic, persistent and contingent reproduction within class and political struggles will be defined here as their 'social constitution'.[15]

The chapter's focus on 'financialization' recognizes the present critical role played by finance in the reproduction of both capitalist social relations and states. Financialization is understood here as the historical outcome of financial liberalization, expansion, deepening and inclusion policies implemented worldwide since the 1980s as part of the neoliberal assault on labour. Besides class struggles, it has also been shaped by the US strategy to preserve the country's dominant position within world capitalism.[16] Today's financial relations can be differentiated from those in the earlier periods, first by the reduced capability of states to manage financial markets and flows in a definitive way. This argument, which is true for many Southern states, also defines the position of the US. So, even though the US seems to be the most powerful and capable country in giving direction to global financial flows, this capability has its own relatively narrower limits today. The second feature of financialization is the systematic expansion of finance into the processes of individual and social reproduction through the increased indebtedness of working populations worldwide.[17] Increased household indebtedness became a general trend after the 2001 dot.com crisis in the US, which led the country to move towards expansionary monetary policies. This trend accelerated after the 2007–08 global capitalist crisis. As will be discussed below, both characteristics of global finance have had direct implications for the processes of state transformation in Turkey under AKP rule.

In problematizing the implications of financialization on the reproduction of states, we should also note finance's general role in the postponement and deepening of the inherent contradictions of capital accumulation. Bonefeld and Holloway define the temporary relieving effect of credit on capital–labour relations as a 'gamble on the future', for, while credit provides capital with extra time to 'decompose and recompose' labour for the latter's effective exploitation, capital's inability to do this would risk its own material reproduction.[18] Furthermore, regardless of the result of the gamble, credit expansion increases the inherent crisis tendencies of capital accumulation at the macro-level as well as providing capital with time and flexibility in eliminating obstacles in the path of accumulation.[19] Today, the redefinition of global credit relations through financialization suggests that the world has turned into a site of permanent gamble, the destructive political and class implications of which need to be managed by states that are themselves highly indebted. Within the combined and unequal historical development of capitalism, this results in the persistent political and economic dislocation of capitalist crises in time and space within a contested international and global context. Historically, the US's concern with managing the effects of the 2007–08 crisis on its hegemonic position through monetary expansionism has created new challenges as well as opportunities for states elsewhere for over a decade. In this process, states also implanted new financialized class and political contradictions, while the US's cautious attempt to put an end to quantitative easing policies after 2013 has meant the end of this period and has led to these contradictions surfacing on both global and domestic levels.

In their endeavours to reproduce themselves within the aggravated tensions and contradictions of financialized capitalism, Southern states such as Turkey have been pushing against the limits of their own capitalist form to free themselves hopelessly from the socially destructive effects of their subordination by capital.[20] The honeymoon period of simultaneous material and social reproduction of states under conditions of monetary glut has ended, forcing them to prioritize their material reproduction at the expense of the latter, facing the threat of a crisis of legitimacy at best and total breakdown at worst.

It is indeed notable that, until 2013, AKP rule in Turkey overlapped with a period that enabled the party to reproduce itself within extraordinarily favourable global monetary and financial conditions. This chapter associates the AKP's move towards oppressive, non-transparent, centralized, personalized and discretionary state

practices after 2013 with the surfacing of the class and political contradictions of AKP-managed financialization in Turkey. It argues
that, in order to avoid the severe political challenges it faces, the
AKP has had to free itself from the political limits imposed by the
modern parliamentary form of the Turkish state through trial and
error. The two sections that follow are based on historical periodization, recognizing the importance of changing global financial
dynamics in the social constitution of the AKP-led state transformation. Hence, the first section focuses on the 2002–13 period, while
the second looks at political transformations from 2013 to 2019.
The conclusion clarifies the political meaning of the historically
specific interventions the AKP has made in the decomposition and
recomposition of labour in Turkey.

Formation of the AKP's strong neoliberal state through financialization: 2002–13

This section underlines the neoliberal character of AKP rule in
Turkey by problematizing how the AKP has redefined the social
constitution of the Turkish state in favour of capital and has formed
Turkey's strong state through financialization – hence a state which
is stronger vis-à-vis labour, but more subordinate, thus weaker,
vis-à-vis capital.[21]

Indeed, the 2001 crisis, which prepared the conditions for the
AKP's rise to power, was the outcome of earlier coalition governments' inability to do this, leading to the labelling of the 1990s as
the 'lost decade' in Turkey.[22] This is because financial liberalization had already reached an advanced level by the 1990s, setting
the conditions for the Turkish state to be disciplined by finance due
to its high public borrowing requirements from global markets,[23]
but the established centre-right and centre-left parties proved to
be politically incapable of taking the necessary action to comply
with the dictates of finance. The AKP, which came to power with a
neoliberal Islamist programme, could avoid similar political limitations with the help of the global monetary glut, which defined the
party's first ten years in power. This global tide provided the AKP
with very favourable material conditions in which to manage the
politically deteriorating social implications of neoliberal constitutionalism, while also trying to reframe Turkish society through its
Islamist ideology.[24] Neoliberal 'reforms' the AKP effected during

the 2000s included some politically risky ones such as the privatization of large-scale profitable state enterprises and the imposition of
new social security and labour market laws, as well as relatively more
'technical' but definitely highly political changes such as the financial regulatory reforms in favour of the depoliticization of economic
management.[25]

Having been rewarded by financial investors due to its loyal
implementation of the neoliberal agenda, the Turkish economy reg-
istered growth at 7.3 per cent of real GDP in 2003–07[26] and 4.9 per
cent in 2002–14, despite the negative impact of the 2007–08 global
capitalist crisis and the subsequent Eurozone crisis.[27] However, the
emphasis on the availability of funds should not obscure the fact that
the AKP used these funds strategically to strengthen the state in a
way that served its own Islamist political agenda as well. This meant
more than simply the transfer of funds to a select group of companies loyal to the AKP through the burgeoning construction sector,
or the provision of support in kind to poor AKP electorates through
municipalities.[28] Longer-term historical changes were introduced to
the state's relation to capital and labour through the specific challenges as well as the opportunities provided by financialization in
the 2000s.

The trajectory of financialization during AKP rule was initially
set by the International Monetary Fund (IMF) standby agreement
signed in 1999. The AKP embraced the basic macro-economic targets of this agreement by ending the use of the exchange rate as a
nominal anchor and targeted a high primary surplus (6.5 per cent
of GDP) in the government budget through cuts in social spending
and privatizations. Moreover, as the 2001 crisis involved a banking
sector crisis as well, the post-crisis measures included a thorough
restructuring of the banking sector with widespread bankruptcies.[29]
These were considered to be confidence-building steps that enabled
the strong inflow of finance to Turkey in the early 2000s. Ultimately,
these policies brought about a very vulnerable economy, the fate of
which has become increasingly dependent on the persistent supply
of short-term financial inflows. Appreciation of the national currency, deteriorating current account deficits, cheap foreign credit,
relatively high real interest rates, a low inflation rate and the resulting de-industrialization defined the post-2002 Turkish economy,
with a growth pattern of 'jobless growth'.[30]

The crisis-generating implications of financial liberalization, together with the state's need to reproduce itself within this process, set the stage for the AKP's move towards financialization in Turkey, leading simultaneously to a shift from public to private indebtedness throughout the 2000s. This meant, besides the increased indebtedness of domestic capital,[31] the systematic and speedy inclusion of labourers in the violence of financial markets. Thus, the household debt ratio rose from 3 per cent of GDP in 2003 to 23.8 per cent in 2013. In the same decade, the ratio of debt to households' usable income jumped from 7.4 to 55.2 per cent.[32] Under conditions of stagnating real wages and precarious working conditions, household debt has helped substitute wages, and thus has been spent mainly for subsistence.[33] Even though the household indebtedness/GNP ratio is still relatively low in Turkey compared with other Southern countries, Turkey differs from the latter due to the speed of the rise of household indebtedness. The difference between the household indebtedness/GNP ratio in 1997–2007 and in 2008–15 is 329.8 per cent, while the same rate is 34.7 per cent for South Korea, 27.6 per cent for Thailand, and 151.8 per cent for Hungary,[34] meaning that the AKP has particularly made household indebtedness one of its central strategies to reproduce its rule.

What about the state?

The AKP-managed financialized turn in capital–labour relations has also had implications for state–capital and state–labour relations. Apparently, there was an overlap between the AKP's concern with relieving the state of the direct disciplinary pressures of finance – hence the public debt burden – and the interest of financial circles in 'including' wider populations within financial markets, leading to the wholesale subjection of society to financial commodification through financialization. Moreover, the shift from public to private indebtedness in Turkey has redefined the position of the state as the 'saviour of last resort', meaning that the state now lets the financialized discipline of the capitalist market 'civilize' the population in its own terms, and enters the picture only when most needed as a 'saviour'. This implies the formation of a hierarchy in state–society relations, no longer defined according to the provisions of the 'social contract'.

This is another way of saying that capitalist social relations' wholesale disciplining by the excesses of the financialized capitalist market has increased the political room for manoeuvre of the state in Turkey. While the state's subordination by capital has deepened – although this has become visible only in times of monetary contraction – its political capacities have increased within the limits set out by finance. This explains why the so-called Istanbul bourgeoisie, which used to be more influential in state policies, no longer enjoys this privilege, although the Turkish Islamists' dislike of them also played a role in their declining influence. As long as the AKP-led state managed to attract financial flows to the Turkish economy, it acquired greater freedom in the domestic political arena vis-à-vis societal actors, including business groups and representatives. The argument that this is indeed a reflection of the shift in the economic base of the AKP from the so-called Istanbul bourgeoisie to the Anatolian one should be made with caution. The AKP's policies towards the SME-dominated Anatolian bourgeoisie can be interpreted better in relation to the party's strategic politico-electoral choices as SMEs in Turkey account for 73.5 per cent of total employment,[35] a figure that does not take into account their informal employment practices. Therefore, their importance lies in their action's direct effects on the lives of the poor labouring masses, who constitute the AKP's main electoral base.

On the other hand, the political opportunities financialization has provided to the Islamist AKP have possibly paved the way for a historically specific decomposition and recomposition of the labouring population in Turkey. The availability of cheap credit to finance AKP rule throughout the 2000s has enabled the party to provide its poor electoral base with an enhanced consumption capability through indebtedness, giving these people the chance to be included in modern and urban lifestyles in a rather short period of time. Erdoğan's provocative discourse based on the centre–periphery dichotomy[36] has also defined their new identity as an assertive, demanding but humiliated new population,[37] situated by the AKP in opposition to the Gezi 'traitors'. It is questionable whether any other conservative government without an Islamist revisionist mission would pursue such a fearless class project, and awaken a hitherto pacified mass. The road that splits society down the middle – as pictured in the introduction – has therefore been constructed by the AKP's decomposition and recomposition of labour by financialization in such a politically risky way.

A closer look at the rise of household indebtedness, with the encouragement of state regulations in Turkey, suggests that the AKP responded to the crucial political and class challenges to its rule by extending financialization at significant historical junctures. As Akçay shows, household indebtedness persistently rose from 2002 to 2016 but experienced two moments of acceleration and deceleration, in 2009 and 2013 respectively.[38] Renewed impetus given by the state to household indebtedness can be interpreted as a political management strategy, as the first of these years, 2009, was the year of the start of TEKEL workers' mass resistance to precarity with a very successful political campaign in the centre of Ankara;[39] and the second, 2013, was the year of the Gezi Uprising in Turkey. The AKP's adherence to this strategy, despite the US's possibility of moving towards higher interest rates after May 2013, can be explained by both the party's confidence in attracting money to Turkey after a decade of 'success' and its desperation due to the absence of any other economic escape route.[40] The next section of the chapter problematizes the political adventures the AKP has had recourse to in response to this global challenge, as well as to the accompanying domestic ones.

State transformation after 2013 in the grip of financial breakdown

Turkey's move from a neoliberal 'wonderland' to an atrocious state of order in the 2010s cannot be understood without problematizing the role of the Gezi Uprising, or the ending of the AKP's so-called Kurdish Opening, leaving the ground once more to militarized and para-militarized actors and ending up with the country being bogged down in the Syrian Civil War, or the 15 July 2016 coup attempt. But it cannot be fully grasped without taking into consideration the changes in the global monetary context either. The Eurozone crisis in 2009, the US Federal Reserve's cautious steps in rising interest rates after 2013, and the election of Donald Trump as the new US President in November 2016 have led to a general tendency for capital flight from the Southern countries, with direct implications for Turkey. There was a threefold devaluation in the Turkish lira (TRY) from 2013 to 2019, reaching sky-high levels during the August 2018 crisis,[41] but such economic figures do not really reflect the severe implications of this global sea change for the political impasse the AKP faces. This impasse is due to the surfacing of class and political contradictions after the shrinking of credit channels, contradictions introduced during the AKP-managed financialization of the 2000s.

Indeed, the initial responses of the AKP to the emergent global risks are instructive about the class nature of the problem. First, despite a brief attempt at restrictive policies relating to household indebtedness from 2014 to 2016,[42] consumption through private indebtedness was further encouraged through financial inclusion policies, as mentioned above.[43] Second, harmonizing the AKP's Islamist priorities with those of capital, a neoliberal educational reform with an Islamist face was launched,[44] which turned the religious *Imam Hatip* schools into a necessary substitute for vocational schools on the one hand, and paved the way for the exploitation of child labour through vocational schools in the form of compulsory training on the other.[45]

On the financial 'regulation' terrain, retreat from depoliticization in favour of repoliticization has become prevalent through Erdoğan's aggressive calls to TCMB to lower the interest rates, starting in 2014.[46] The government even intervened in the numbers when the Turkish Statistical Institute revised its national accounting system in December 2016, arguably claiming to harmonize it with EU standards. This revision has substantially improved the macro-economic indicators of Turkey on paper and constituted a notable example of the politicization of statistics. Another response of the AKP to the post-2013 financial challenges was to establish a sovereign wealth fund (*Türkiye Varlık Fonu*/Turkey Wealth Fund or TVF) with the declared aim of increasing the state's financial capacity. TVF was founded by an emergency rule in 2016 with an initial capital of US$50 billion.[47] The government attempted to counteract the obvious problem of establishing such a fund in a country with high current account deficits by transferring to the TVF the country's most lucrative state-owned banks and enterprises, such as Ziraat Bank and Turkish Airlines. As the TVF was founded as a private management corporation, this meant the de facto privatization of Turkey's biggest state-owned companies.[48] After transition to the CHS, President Erdoğan was made the chairman of the company with his son-in-law appointed as the deputy chair.[49]

The non-transparent, unaccountable, centralized, personalized and privatized form of the TVF signalled the new historical form of Turkey's capitalist state, as these characteristics started to redefine the whole institutional structure of the state after the transition to the CHS. It would be futile to draw up long and detailed analyses of the new administrative architecture of the CHS, as practically it has meant the centralization of all power and state money in the hands of President Erdoğan. Despite the detailed schemes proposed on paper for the internal working of various offices, policy committees or ministries, the real hierarchy has been set by internal power struggles taking place in the Presidential Palace (*Külliye*), with the ultimate decision made by Erdoğan.[50]

It is interesting to note that similar trends define the government's conduct of foreign relations. This can be powerfully illustrated by the August 2018 crisis, the severe currency crisis that tested the resilience of the CHS immediately after its introduction in July 2018. The TRY/US$ exchange rate, which was 4.53 on 9 July 2018, rose close to 7.00 in mid-August, dropping to 5.50 on 30 October 2018.[51] Besides the challenges prevailing in global financial markets at that time, liberal critics associated the crisis with Turkey's own mistakes, such as not completing the structural reforms needed.[52] On the other hand, President Erdoğan, contrary to such comments, politicized the crisis by interpreting it as a war waged by the US against Turkey due to the detention of an American pastor, Andrew Brunson, on charges of working for the Gülenists. Other tensions in US–Turkey relations, such as the trial of Halkbank General Director in the US on claims of breaking the sanctions against Iran and Turkey's plans to purchase S-400 missiles from Russia, were also brought onto the agenda,[53] turning the crisis into a catastrophic encounter between Erdoğan and Trump. Following a showdown, the US first imposed sanctions on 2 August with regard to the Minister of Justice Abdülhamit Gül and Minister of Interior Affairs Süleyman Soylu by freezing their assets in the US, and then doubled the tax on steel and aluminium imports from Turkey on 10 August. The crisis continued with Erdoğan inviting people to boycott electronic devices of US origin, slowed down with Pastor Brunson being put under house arrest, and finally ended with his release and return to the US on 12 October. It is not possible to know what negotiations were conducted behind the scenes during this complicated scenario. About a year later, however, in another US–Turkey confrontation, this time relating to Turkey's military operation in northern Syria, Trump threatened Erdoğan by saying that he would devastate the Turkish economy again like he had done before.[54] The development and the handling of the August 2018 crisis suggest that theatrical foreign policy encounters, conducted via social media, have been made into strategic crisis management tools by both Erdoğan and Trump. Within the novel context of the financialized subordination of states by capital, however, the crisis can also be rethought as a political encounter in which the two states tested the limits of their political and economic room for manoeuvre vis-à-vis each other.

Conclusion: the class nature of Turkey's political impasse

All of these tense political transformations can be understood as aspects of the AKP's search for a way out of the dilemmas within Turkey's financialized capitalism that it was stuck in after 2013 – either to start implementing the set of measures demanded by global finance, including austerity measures and the commodification of land, or to avoid these Western finance-set limits by searching for alternative sources of money and survival. Both options have their own tragic implications. The first is the conventional neoliberal method, which the AKP has already started trying, but this leads to a political weakening for Erdoğan that might ultimately bring about his fall from power. This is because the neoliberal package requires an inevitable deterioration in the AKP's relations with the labouring masses as a whole, including its relations with its own constituency of the poor. The second, non-conventional approach has led to debates on the shift of axis in Turkey's international alliances, and an accidental failure in this regard would lead to the material breakdown of the society, together with the state. Since 2013, the AKP has been making political experimentations in all directions by hitting the capitalist limits of the state form, or the AKP's own political limits in Turkey as a neoliberal Islamist party, and moving from one crisis to another. The CHS has been a product of these attempts, and its resilience, if not powerfully contested with a coordinated rejection by labouring people, will prove its ability to manage the current class contradictions of Turkey's financialized capitalism. The resilience of the CHS, with its privatized, personalized and coercive characteristics, would also prove its potential to be the new political form of the capitalist state.

What currently differentiates the Turkish political experiment from others elsewhere is related to the AKP's somewhat 'irresponsible' use of the period of global monetary glut by revitalizing the demands for equality of a populous, precarious and indebted mass in an attempt to create its own loyal political constituency.

The question of how their impossible expectations will be managed is the challenge faced today not only by the AKP but by the whole Turkish political establishment as these people will not just return to their silent precarity if their hopes of the AKP are dashed. And their reactions might not be as peaceful as those of the Gezi 'marauders'. The AKP, by severing the class contradictions of Turkish capitalism in this way through financialization in the 2000s, has created the conditions of its own crisis, while also promoting itself as the only power capable of managing it. The political management of Turkey's financialized capitalism today requires the AKP to prevent the two social halves mentioned in the introduction from coming together, by manufacturing crises and confrontations of all possible sorts. This means that the strength of the AKP's neoliberal state depends on its continuous reproduction as a crisis state. The alternative would be that people realize the liberty, equality and fraternity claims that are currently frozen in the modern bourgeois state by radically redefining them.

Notes

1. B. A. Uncu, *Konda Seçmen Kümeleri, Ak Parti Seçmenleri*, May 2018, http://konda.com.tr/wp-content/uploads/2018/05/KONDA_Secmen Kumeleri_AkParti_Secmenleri_Mayis2018.pdf. This, of course, does not mean that the AKP has no urbanized, educated, young and secular voters, but when compared with the average age, sex, education, place of birth and belief distribution of the total electorate in Turkey, the AKP attracts relatively more people with the opposite characteristics. An interesting finding from the election survey is the AKP's positive score in attracting more women voters, particularly housewives. This requires a closer look at the AKP's policies relating to women (see Chapter 13 by Hülagü).

2. Even though the emphasis on the 'New Turkey' existed in the early years of AKP rule, it was popularized after the election of Erdoğan as president by popular vote on 10 August 2014.

3. One of the worst recent cases is of four siblings who committed suicide by taking cyanide. Their suicide was interpreted as an outcome of their precarity by some people, who also noted their humanistic concern for others: they put a sign on their door saying 'Attention: cyanide!' The tragedy was promoted as having nothing to do with their poverty or precarity by others, who even attempted to devalue them due to a book in their house that arguably proved their unfaithfulness (i.e. their not being good Muslims at best and their being atheists at worst).

4. The death of 11-year-old Rabia Naz is one such example. During the investigations, only the father and two left-wing journalists were detained. See 'Journalists and father detained for investigating child's suspicious death', *Duvar English*, 14 November 2019.

5. Two such recent moments were Trump's humiliating letter to Erdoğan,

and the Operation Peace Spring conducted by Turkey in Syria.

6. N. Erdoğan (2015) 'Türkiye bir toplum mu?', *Birgün Fikir*, 18 October.

7. The contradiction of constituting unlawfulness through law is also covered by Kaygusuz and Aydın (Chapter 2).

8. See Kaygusuz and Aydın (Chapter 2).

9. It appears that 'waiting' is not a mood that defines only Turkish society. For a similar argument on Iran, proposed from an anthropological perspective, see Khosravi 2017.

10. K. Can (2019) 'Tehlikenin farkında mısınız?', *Gazete Duvar*, 2 November; Kaygusuz and Aydın (Chapter 2). The statement is a revised version of one by Gramsci (see Gramsci 1971: 175). See also Fraser 2019.

11. The arrest and detention of Kurdish elected mayors and their removal from their positions by the government-appointed trustees after the local elections in March 2019 are examples of such practices.

12. This is reflected in the way in which the refugee question is handled in Turkey–EU relations. See also Uzgel (Chapter 3) and Kaygusuz and Aydın (Chapter 2).

13. Clarke 1990–91: 452–3. In response to some possible reductionist and economistic readings of the concept of 'capital accumulation', it is important to note that it refers to a globally, nationally and locally shaped process in which capital tries to overcome all the natural, technical, social and historical limits it faces within capitalist competition through the persistent commodification and effective exploitation of labour and the commons in a crisis-ridden and contingent way.

14. Clarke 1991: 195.

15. Bonefeld 1992.

16. Albo et al. 2010: 19, 121; Fine 2010: 19; Bryan et al. 2009; Panitch and Gindin 2005, 2014; Gowan 1999, 2009.

17. Fine 2010: 18.

18. Bonefeld and Holloway 1996: 211–12.

19. Clarke 1990–91: 460–2.

20. For a detailed discussion on the implications of financialization on state transformation in the South, see Bedirhanoğlu (forthcoming).

21. Gamble 1979; Bonefeld 2017.

22. Yeldan 2002: 1.

23. Köse and Yeldan 1998: 70.

24. Gill 2002.

25. Angın and Bedirhanoğlu 2012; Bozkurt-Güngen 2018; Kutun (Chapter 7); Yılmaz-Akın 2018. For a detailed analysis of the AKP's implementation of the neoliberal agenda in this period, see Bedirhanoğlu and Yalman 2010. For the concept of 'depoliticization of economic management' and the fate of depoliticized economic management in Turkey during AKP rule, see Burnham 2000 and Kutun (Chapter 7) respectively.

26. Boratav 2015: 141.

27. Benlialper et al. 2015: 5–7.

28. Çarıkçı 2017; Çelik and Karaçimen 2017.

29. Bedirhanoğlu et al. 2013: 93.

30. Bakır and Öniş 2010: 96; Yeldan and Ünüvar 2015: 12–13.

31. See Güngen (Chapter 6).

32. Bağımsız Sosyal Bilimciler 2015: 169.

33. Karaçimen 2015: 762–4.

34. Karwowski and Stockhammer 2016: 40.

35. Topal 2019: 221.

36. See Özkan (Chapter 12) and Akkaya (Chapter 10).

37. A memorable example of this attitude was a woman expressing her love to Erdoğan by proudly saying in an AKP public meeting on 16 June 2013 that she was the 'hair on Erdoğan's arse'.

38. Akçay 2017: 69.

39. See Yalman and Topal 2019 for a detailed discussion of the whole process.

40. Bedirhanoğlu 2019b.

41. While the TRY/US$ exchange rate was around 1.7 in January 2013, it rose to around 5.7 in November 2019. During the August 2018 crisis, it climbed to 6.68. See the TCMB statistics at https://www.tcmb.gov.tr.

42. Bakır and Öniş 2010: 99–100; Kahraman 2017: 116–22.

43. Güngen 2018. See also Güngen (Chapter 6).

44. See Çitak (Chapter 9).

45. Şaşmaz 2013.

46. See Kutun (Chapter 7).

47. Law no. 6741.

48. Even Yeltsin's share-for-loans privatization scheme for the sale of profitable Russian oil giants was not as creatively destructive as this.

49. 'Varlık Fonu'nun başına kendi geçti, damadını yardımcılığına getirdi', *Birgün*, 13 September 2018.

50. For a detailed analysis of economic management under CHS, see Bedirhanoğlu 2019a.

51. See the TCMB statistics at https://www.tcmb.gov.tr.

52. O. Uluagay (2018) 'Yanlışımızı kabul etmeden krizi aşamayız', *Dünya*, 5 September.

53. For a detailed discussion of the S-400 problem, see Kurç (Chapter 4).

54. 'Trump: Türkiye'nin ekonomisini yok ederim', *Dünya*, 7 September 2019.

References

Akçay, Ü. (2017) 'Finansallaşma, Merkez Bankası Politikaları ve Borcun "Özelleştirilmesi"' in P. Bedirhanoğlu, Ö. Çelik and H. Mıhçı (eds), *Finansallaşma Kıskacında Türkiye'de Devlet, Sermaye Birikimi ve Emek.* Istanbul: Notabene, pp. 45–80.

Albo, G., S. Gindin and Panitch, L. (2010) *In and Out of Crisis: The Global Financial Meltdown and Left Alternatives.* Oakland, CA: Spectre PM Press.

Angın, M. and P. Bedirhanoğlu (2012) 'Privatization processes as ideological moments: the privatization of large-scale state enterprises in Turkey in the 2000s', *New Perspectives on Turkey 47*: 139–67.

Bağımsız Sosyal Bilimciler (2015) *AKP'li Yıllarda Emeğin Durumu.* Istanbul: Yordam.

Bakır, C. and Z. Öniş (2010) 'The regulatory state and Turkish banking reforms in the age of post-Washington Consensus', *Development and Change 41* (1): 77–106.

Bedirhanoğlu, P. (2019a) 'Cumhurbaşkanlığı Hükümet Sistemi ve Türkiye'de Ekonomi Yönetiminin Dönüşümü: Neoliberalizmin Sonu mu?' in E. Karaçimen, M. Yaman, N. Özkaplan, Ö Akduran and Ş Oğuz (eds), *Nuray Ergüneş için Yazılar: Finansallaşma, Kadın Emeği ve Devlet.* Istanbul: SAV, pp. 211–32.

Bedirhanoğlu, P. (2019b) 'Finansallaşma, Yeni Sınıfsal Çelişkiler ve Devletin Dönüşümü', *Çalışma ve Toplum 60* (1): 371–87.

Bedirhanoğlu, P. (forthcoming) 'Financialization, household indebtedness and state transformation in the global South' in E. Babacan, M. Kutun, E. Pınar and Z. Yılmaz (eds), *Authoritarianism and Resistance in Turkey: Contestations, Setbacks and Possibilities.* Abingdon: Routledge.

Bedirhanoğlu, P. and G. L. Yalman (2010) 'State, class and the discourse: reflections on the neoliberal transformation in Turkey' in A. Saad-Filho and G. L. Yalman (eds), *Economic Transitions to Neoliberalism in Middle-income Countries*. Abingdon: Routledge, pp. 107–27.

Bedirhanoğlu, P., H. Cömert, İ. Eren, I. Erol, D. Demiröz, N. Erdem, A. R. Güngen, T. Marois, A. Topal, O. Türel, E. Voyvoda, G. Yalman and E. Yeldan (2013) 'Comparative perspective on financial systems in the EU: country report on Turkey', *FESSUD Studies in Financial Systems* 11.

Benlialper, A., H. Cömert and G. Düzçay (2015) '2002 sonrası Türkiye ekonomisinin performansı: Karşılaştırmalı bir analiz', *ERC Working Papers in Economics 15* (4): 1–44.

Bonefeld, W. (1992) 'Social constitution of the form of the capitalist state' in W. Bonefeld, R. Gunn and K. Psychopedis (eds), *Open Marxism. Vol. I: Dialectics and History*. London: Pluto Press, pp. 93–132.

Bonefeld, W. (2017) *The Strong State and the Free Economy*. London and New York, NY: Rowman and Littlefield.

Bonefeld, W. and J. Holloway (1996) 'Conclusion: money and class struggle' in W. Bonefeld and J. Holloway (eds), *Global Capital, National State and the Politics of Money*. London: Palgrave Macmillan, pp. 210–27.

Boratav, K. (2015) *Dünyadan Türkiye'ye, İktisattan Siyasete*. Istanbul: Yordam.

Bozkurt-Güngen, S. (2018) 'Labour and authoritarian neoliberalism: changes and continuities under the AKP government in Turkey', *South European Society and Politics 23* (2): 219–38.

Bryan, D., R. Martin and M. Rafferty (2009) 'Financialization and Marx: giving labor and capital a financial makeover', *Review of Radical Political Economics 41* (4): 458–72.

Burnham, P. (2000) 'Globalisation, depoliticization and modern economic management' in W. Bonefeld and K. Psychopedis (eds), *The Politics of Change: Globalization, Ideology and Critique*. London: Palgrave, pp. 9–30.

Çarıkçı, Ç. (2017) '2001 krizi sonrası Türkiye'de büyük ölçekli kentsel yatırım projeleri: İstanbul örneği' in P. Bedirhanoğlu, Ö. Çelik and H. Mıhçı (eds), *Finansallaşma Kıskacında Türkiye'de Devlet, Sermaye Birikimi ve Emek*. Istanbul: Notabene, pp. 103–28.

Çelik, Ö. and E. Karaçimen (2017) 'Türkiye'de gayrimenkul ve finansın derinleşen ve yeniden yapılanan ilişkisi' in P. Bedirhanoğlu, Ö. Çelik and H. Mıhçı (eds), *Finansallaşma Kıskacında Türkiye'de Devlet, Sermaye Birikimi ve Emek*. Istanbul: Notabene, pp. 83–102.

Clarke, S. (1990–91) 'The Marxist theory of overaccumulation and crisis', *Science and Society 54* (4): 442–67.

Clarke, S. (1991) 'State, class struggle and the reproduction of capital' in S. Clarke (ed.), *The State Debate*. London: Palgrave Macmillan, pp. 183–203.

Fine, B. (2010) 'Neoliberalism as financialisation' in A. Saad-Filho and G. Yalman (eds), *Economic Transitions to Neoliberalism in Middle-income Countries: Policy Dilemmas, Crises, Mass Resistance*. London: Routledge, pp. 11–23.

Fraser, N. (2019) *The Old Is Dying and the New Cannot Be Born*. London and New York, NY: Verso.

Gamble, A. (1979) 'The free economy and the strong state: the rise of the social market economy' in R. Miliband and J. Savile (eds), *The*

Socialist Register. London: Merlin Press, pp. 1–25.

Gill, S. (2002) 'Constitutionalizing inequality and the clash of globalizations', *International Studies Review 4* (2): 47–65.

Gowan, P. (1999) *The Global Gamble: Washington's Faustian Bid for World Dominance.* London and New York, NY: Verso.

Gowan, P. (2009) 'Crisis in the heartland', *New Left Review 25:* 5–29.

Gramsci, A. (1971) *Selections from the Prison Notebooks.* Translated by Q. Hoare and G. N. Smith. New York, NY: International Publishers.

Güngen, A. R. (2018) 'Financial inclusion and policy making: strategy, campaigns and microcredit *a la Turca*', *New Political Economy 23* (3): 331–47.

Kahraman, E. (2017) 'The management of household indebtedness: changing forms of state intervention in Turkey in the post-2001 period'. MSc thesis in International Relations, Middle East Technical University, Ankara.

Karaçimen, E. (2015) 'Interlinkages between credit, debt and the labor market: evidence from Turkey', *Cambridge Journal of Economics 39* (3): 751–67.

Karwowski, E. and E. Stockhammer (2016) 'Financialization in Emerging Economies: A systematic overview and comparison with Anglo-Saxon economies'. *Economics Discussion Papers 2016/11.* London: Kingston University.

Khosravi, S. (2017) *Precarious Lives: Waiting and Hope in Iran.* Philadelphia, PA: University of Pennsylvania Press.

Köse, A. H. and E. Yeldan (1998) 'Turkish economy in the 1990s', *New Perspectives on Turkey 18* (Spring).

Oğuz, Ş. (2012) 'Türkiye'de kapitalizmin küreselleşmesi ve neoliberal otoriter devletin inşası', *Türk Tabibler Birliği, Mesleki Sağlık ve Güvenlik Dergisi 45/46:* 2–48.

Panitch, L. and S. Gindin (2005) 'Superintending global capital', *New Left Review 35:* 101–23.

Panitch, L. and S. Gindin (2014) 'Political economy and political power: the American state and finance in the neoliberal era', *Government and Opposition 49* (3): 369–99.

Şaşmaz, A. (2013) 'To which direction does the education policy of AK Party change?', *ResearchTurkey 2* (2): 40–7.

Topal, A. (2019) 'The state, crisis and transformation of small and medium-sized enterprise finance in Turkey' in G. L. Yalman, T. Marois and A. R. Güngen (eds), *The Political Economy of Financial Transformation in Turkey.* London and New York, NY: Routledge, pp. 221–42.

Yalman, G. and A. Topal (2019) 'Labour containment strategies and working-class struggles in the neoliberal era: the case of TEKEL workers in Turkey', *Critical Sociology 45* (3): 447–61.

Yeldan, A. E. and B. Ünüvar (2015) 'An assessment of the Turkish economy in the AKP era', *Research and Policy on Turkey 1* (1): 11–28.

Yeldan, E. (2002) 'On the IMF-directed disinflation program in Turkey' in N. Balkan and S. Savran (eds), *The Ravages of Neoliberalism: Economy, Society and Gender in Turkey.* New York, NY: Nova Science Publishers, pp. 1–20.

Yılmaz-Akın, B. G. (2018) 'Turkish individual pension system: from voluntary basis to automatic enrolment', *Research and Policy on Turkey 3* (2): 201–16.

2 | DECONSTITUTIONALIZATION AND THE STATE CRISIS IN TURKEY: THE ROLE OF THE TURKISH CONSTITUTIONAL COURT AND THE EUROPEAN COURT OF HUMAN RIGHTS

Özlem Kaygusuz and Oya Aydın

Introduction

Since the Gezi Uprising, scholarly debate on Turkey's neoliberal transformation has been accompanied by a parallel debate on the transformations in the constitutional order of the country, mostly framed as a regime transformation.[1] Both debates, however, acquired a new direction after the 7 June 2015 general elections, in which the AKP lost its parliamentary majority and was forced to form a coalition government for the first time in its previously one-party rule. The traumatic events that followed, culminating ultimately in the 15 July 2016 coup attempt, not only deepened the political crisis but also equipped President Recep Tayyip Erdoğan with exclusive political-legal instruments to further transform the constitutional foundations of the state. This chapter argues that these widespread political-institutional transformations have reached a phase that can be characterized as *deconstitutionalization*, reflecting a state crisis in Turkey, rather than a crisis in the country's political regime. In other words, since 2015, the scope of these transformations has gone well beyond regime transformation, so they should be discussed within the framework of state transformation. 'State transformation' here refers to deeply rooted, essential and persistent changes taking place in the very foundations and institutional/administrative setting of the state rather than a change in the governmental system of the country, discussed mostly as regime transformation.

The AKP's recent political initiatives did not emerge all at once. As early as mid-2014, after his first election to the presidency, Erdoğan started disregarding the constitutional norms that used to regulate the impartial status of the President, especially those

limiting his authority.[2] Between 2013 and 2016, his disregard for
constitutional norms increased, with the implementation of deliberate authoritarian practices based on two pillars. First, feeling
relatively secure in his new political coalition with the ultranationalists, Erdoğan started transforming relations among state powers,
especially between the executive and the judiciary, and targeted
constitutional-institutional mechanisms of checks and balances to
free the government from judicial control under the pretext of the
struggle against the so-called 'parallel state organization' (*Paralel
Devlet Yapılanması* or PDY) and rising violence following the end
of the peace process with the Kurds.[3] Second, in order to remain in
power, he also targeted social checks and balances, especially those
provided by the democratic and critical opposition of the media, civil
society organizations and universities.[4] His ability to do this has to
be questioned within the wider context of changing social relations,
something that this volume tries to address. Ultimately, the construction of an authoritarian/oppressive regime reached its peak with the
declaration of a state of emergency after the July 2016 coup attempt;
this enabled a very narrow group of Islamist, far-right and ultranationalist politicians led by Erdoğan to establish almost full control
over all state powers, especially against the parliament and over the
judiciary. The move to a presidential system in June 2017 under
emergency rule was the end point of this steady transformation.

This chapter argues that a particular form of deconstitutionalization – that is, *political deconstitutionalization*, which is proposed here as
a term to describe the profound changes to Turkey's constitutional
order – is now leading to state transformation. Deconstitutionalization
is defined in the academic literature as the violation of existing constitutional norms by making them practically ineffective and void,[5] a
process that has been underway since Erdoğan's first election to the
presidency in July 2104. By redefining the term as political deconstitutionalization, this chapter aims to make sense of the much more
radical processes at work that seem to target the idea of constitutional rule and the foundations of the Turkish state. The following
discussion identifies three significant turning points after the 7 June
elections that progressively upgraded and accelerated the previous
deconstitutionalization into a 'political' one: the enactment of the
Internal Security Law in May 2015; the lifting of the immunity
of opposition MPs in June 2016; and the declaration of a state of

emergency on 20 July 2016, which paved the way to the formation of an unprecedented system of government – that is, a regime of emergency decrees (KHK regime), and then a *sui generis* system of presidential government approved by a constitutional referendum in April 2017 by a slim margin. By effectively rejecting the constitutional essence of the republican state through overt and deliberate deconstitutionalization after each of these turning points, the AKP initiated a political transformation that has gone well beyond regime transformation.

The analysis also shows that, after each of these critical junctures, two constitutional control mechanisms – one domestic and one international, namely the Turkish Constitutional Court (*Anayasa Mahkemesi* or AYM) and the European Court of Human Rights (ECHR) – that had the power to restrain Erdoğan's desire for executive centralization, in violation of the constitution, did not use that power but in fact paved the way first for the gradual eradication of existing constitutional norms and then for the deliberate elimination of the constitutional foundations of the state in Turkey. In other words, both of these constitutional control mechanisms have played a critical 'political role' in the deconstitutionalization process before and after emergency rule. To substantiate these arguments, the chapter first problematizes the proposed concepts within the context of constitutional developments before and during the AKP years. Then, it analyses the AKP-led process of political deconstitutionalization in the 2010s in relation to AYM and ECHR decisions in three appeals from Turkey that worked as significant catalysts in this process.

Turkey's tradition of authoritarian constitutionalism and deconstitutionalization

In the constitutional history of Turkey, authoritarian constitutionalism is a concept that expresses the determinative position of the army and high-level military bureaucracy in the constitution-making process through military coups, and the continuation of military tutelage over civil politics after the coups via military-imposed norms and institutions in the country's constitutions. In broad terms, this concept shows that constitutions have traditionally protected not individual rights and freedoms but state power and the Kemalist ideology.[6] The 1982 Constitution, the example par excellence of authoritarian constitutionalism in Turkey, institutionalized military tutelage by including emergency rule and martial law regulations that are unacceptable in standard liberal/democratic constitutions and by suppressing basic rights and freedoms that a constitution is supposed to protect. This is why the 1982 Constitution is said to have made authoritarian constitutionalism the permanent paradigm of Turkey's politics since the 1980s.[7] Although its undemocratic regulations were smoothed out to some degree with amendments in the pre-AKP and AKP periods, its authoritarian spirit and the political rationale that the constitution is the main instrument for establishing tutelage rule remained largely intact.[8]

Similarly, the AKP resorted to the authoritarian constitutionalism of periods of military rule to restore its hegemony, which was shaken especially in the post-Gezi period, and to re-establish the power it lost after the 7 June elections. It started to construct a new political order, targeting the democratic, pluralistic and secular constitutional order through the imposition of a political Islamist and ultranationalist agenda. Erdoğan, by relying on the logic of constitutional authoritarianism, managed to implant and guarantee the exceptional powers he acquired during the state of emergency between 2016 and 2018 in constitutional amendments that established a presidential system;[9] he also introduced the 'Authorization Law',[10] which was passed before the end of the state of emergency. In other words, he established a civil tutelage that is very similar to military tutelage. Nevertheless, the concept of authoritarian constitutionalism is inadequate to understand the constitutional transformation of the later AKP rule. Therefore, we suggest 'deconstitutionalization' in place of authoritarian constitutionalism, further modifying it as 'political deconstitutionalization'.

Why is authoritarian constitutionalism inadequate to make sense of the constitutional transformations of the post-2015 election period? First, the authoritarian practices of AKP rule and the corresponding legal/constitutional amendments have been implemented by civil rather than military rule, making the constitution a tool for an oppressive regime. Here, instead of the army or high-level judicial bodies (which are extra-political actors), an elected civil authority has established an authoritarian regime of tutelage with the help of judicial bodies that it has taken into its extensive political control. Second, the 1982 Constitution had shaped public power in favour of the state at the expense of individual rights and freedoms, whereas the 2017 constitutional amendments have redefined public power in favour of almost unchecked personal rule operating at the expense of the supreme principle of the separation of powers and an independent judiciary. In other words, the basic constitutional norm violated by the 1982 Constitution was the protection of basic rights and freedoms by the state, with very limited restrictions under exceptional cases; the deconstitutionalization of the AKP targets, in addition to that, two basic norms of the constitutional foundation of the state: the legislative supremacy of parliament established through democratic processes and the duty of an independent high court to control the actions of the executive.[11] Finally, the military tutelage of the 1982 Constitution had basically aimed to establish the dominance of Kemalist ideology within the state, and reflected not only the will of the army but also the consensus of the entire establishment, which traditionally meant the military, judiciary, universities and bureaucracy. However, today's deconstitutionalization does not reflect such a widespread paradigmatic consensus in the establishment; on the contrary, it aims to guarantee Erdoğan's leadership, whose ideational and paradigmatic hegemony weakens as it becomes more and more authoritarian. What, then, is deconstitutionalization?

Deconstitutionalization: definition and conceptual framework

Deconstitutionalization is generally understood as the lack or removal of existing constitutional norms in a given public policy area. More specifically, it can be defined as non-compliance with the provisions of the constitution, which therefore loses its efficacy. Much more critically, however, deconstitutionalization means the complete abandonment of all constitutional mechanisms to limit non-compliant acts by the executive to the extent that the constitution in force becomes ineffective and void.[12] In this sense, it is a form of power extremism. This last dimension in particular pertains to the institutional configuration of state powers, which results in damage to the very idea and essence of constitutionalism – that is, the supreme principles of separation of powers, judicial independence and the rule of law. In terms of the level this has reached in Turkey, and the mechanisms that have made it 'politically' possible during the recent phase of Erdoğan's regime, this study proposes a differentiation between *legal* and *political* forms of deconstitutionalization.

Legal deconstitutionalization and the normalization of
emergency practices in Turkey

Legal deconstitutionalization refers to rulers' lack of compliance with the constitutional provisions and institutions in force and their inactivation, but the continuation of political life is not seen as a problem.[13] As state officials continue to violate various articles of the constitution, the higher-level constitutional norms mentioned above – the separation of powers, judicial independence and the rule of law – are severely damaged; these are the foundational norms that make the executive accountable according to constitutional norms. Legal deconstitutionalization in this sense is widely observed in today's rising authoritarian regimes in the post-2008 global crisis context, and it refers to democratic backsliding, the erosion of the rule of law, and the rise of the (neoliberal) security state.[14] In many national contexts, we see neoliberal authoritarian states legalizing their authoritarian, extra-juridical practices by hurriedly making relevant laws, thus formally keeping the norm of the rule of law. Therefore, legal deconstitutionalization is a process that takes place within the possibilities of the existing legal order. It can be defined as a political order fabricated as an exceptional one, which suspends the constitution in force while becoming normalized due to its legalization.

The rise of an authoritarian regime in Turkey, especially in the post-Gezi period, is generally perceived in this way.[15] Several constitutional law experts who have adopted this perspective define the ruling government's de facto and continuous violations of the existing constitutional norms[16] and the legalization of unconstitutional actions as deconstitutionalization. İbrahim Kaboğlu, for instance, points to this aspect of Erdoğan's leadership and defines deconstitutionalization as essentially an arbitrary and unruly governing practice.[17] Another constitutional lawyer, Kemal Gözler, defines deconstitutionalization as the inactivation of current constitutional articles with bad faith by either the executive or the judiciary; this causes them to fall into disuse, as, in practice, many laws that were enacted in accordance with the 1982 Constitution have not been in force since 2014.[18]

An essential characteristic of legal deconstitutionalization is that the current constitution exists but is not applied; hence, by reactivating the unapplied constitutional articles, it would be possible to end this form of deconstitutionalization.[19] In this sense, legal deconstitutionalization refers to a regime and/or a democracy crisis. If the actors exercising public authority start complying with the constitution again, the regime crisis would come to an end.[20] In this kind of deconstitutionalization, sometimes the executive first acts against the constitution and then legalizes its unconstitutional acts by enacting new – and mostly unconstitutional – laws. This process ends with the normalization of the exceptional or emergency practices carried out unconstitutionally. This is what happened in the post-Gezi period in Turkey, as the government legalized its unconstitutional practices by making the exceptional normal.[21]

This discussion, although relevant, does not help us to grasp the novel and deepening dimensions of the ongoing deconstitutionalization process, which has acquired qualitatively different and irreversible features. This turn has developed out of the AKP's response to its loss of power in the June 2015 elections. As the subsequent political crisis deepened, legal deconstitutionalization developed into a political deconstitutionalization, particularly after a state of emergency was declared as a result of the 15 July coup attempt. The deconstitutionalization has ceased to be a regime or democracy crisis; it has become a state crisis signalling that the institutional configuration of state powers has been not only disregarded but radically transformed, to the extent that the constitutional foundation of the state has almost been dismantled. But what is political deconstitutionalization, and in what sense is it different from legal deconstitutionalization?

Political deconstitutionalization and beyond the permanent emergency rule

In this chapter, the concept of political deconstitutionalization is used to define the process through which the constitution, beyond the invalidation of its basic norms, is openly and substantially ruled out, with no institutional or political control mechanism able to limit this process. Political deconstitutionalization should be differentiated from legal deconstitutionalization, since it involves not only the invalidation of current constitutional norms. In other words, this is not a situation that can be reversed by the reactivation of constitutional norms. In that sense, it is not a regime crisis, but a phase in state crisis.

As a concept derived from the Turkish experience, political deconstitutionalization refers to a situation in which not only the basic constitutional norms but also the very idea of constitutional rule with regard to the institutional foundations of the state – at both national and local administrative levels – are overturned. First, the supreme norms of the separation of powers, judicial independence, the subjection of executive action to judicial control and the rule of law – all of which exist in legal deconstitutionalization as well – are invalidated through the use of emergency decrees and constitutional amendments. Hierarchical order and balance among and within executive and juridical bodies at local and national levels are degraded, resulting in an unpredictable administrative order. Second, with judicial independence and impartiality impaired, starting with the erosion of the rights to a fair trial and to freedom of expression, all basic individual rights and freedoms – rights that have long been protected by modern constitutions, including by the Turkish constitutions to a certain degree – are seriously and permanently restricted because of the decisions and practices of an executive acting outside the realm of constitutional control. Third, political deconstitutionalization includes making regulations and implementing practices using means that were unforeseen in the constitution and that are deeply harmful to the idea of constitutional rule. In other words, new norms, legal forms and procedures are invented that seriously damage the essence of constitutional rule. And finally, political deconstitutionalization puts an end to law making as we know it, deactivating the supreme legislative power of parliament and violating the 'legality of state acts'.[22]

Most critically, the adjective 'political' in our term denotes that, in the post-2015 election period, the *political power relations* established by the AKP at home and abroad are what have enabled the violation of the current constitution and the damage to the idea and foundations of constitutional rule through executive decisions. The two constitutional control mechanisms – the AYM and the ECHR – that are meant to control or end the ongoing deconstitutionalization process are unable or unwilling to use their authority. In the rest of this chapter, we question the critical role they played in this process as higher-level courts with the authority to intervene in political deconstitutionalization. They have made deconstitutionalization politically possible – the AYM by taking decisions in line with the expectations of political power, and the ECHR by rejecting individual applications against the emergency decrees and other political and legal decisions of those in power, delaying their judgements, prolonging lawsuits and taking pro-government decisions. The following section discusses the scope of the political deconstitution-alization and why it relates to a state crisis rather than a regime crisis in Turkey by using three specific cases.[23]

Political deconstitutionalization in Turkey through AYM and ECHR decisions

The process of political deconstitutionalization went through certain turning points. At these points, the ongoing deconstitution-alization essentially moved forward due to the decisions or attitudes of the AYM and ECHR, which did not fulfil their function of check-ing the power of the executive. Here, we provide an overview of these critical decisions that gave the AKP and President Erdoğan further room to continue with their political deconstitutionalization.[24]

Internal security law and curfews: relations between the executive and the judiciary

The first and most striking example that demonstrates the role of AYM and ECHR decisions in political deconstitutionalization is the enactment of the Internal Security Law No. 6638 on 4 April 2015 and the declaration of a curfew based on this law. The law has been widely questioned due not only to its uncertain articles, which would severely limit basic individual rights and freedoms or eliminate them altogether, but also to its erosion of the supreme constitutional norms of judicial independence and the separation of powers. We highlight here two basic dimensions of deconstitu-tionalization revealed by this law and its application. The first is the deconstitutionalization that resulted from the curfew declared based on the law. According to the constitution, curfew is regulated by Martial Law No. 1402 and the State of Emergency Law No. 2935, and is a measure exclusive to these two specific situations only.[25] Despite this, the Internal Security Law granted provincial and dis-trict governors the authority to declare a curfew using a problematic reference to the current Law of Provincial Administration;[26] the new law also gave them the power to prevent the exercise of some con-stitutional rights and freedoms.[27] It is important to note that, even though the government could have used its constitutional power to declare a state of emergency – and therefore a curfew – under

Article 120 of the 1982 Constitution, it preferred not to do so as this would ensure parliamentary and judicial supervision of the curfew. Second, this law, which granted the power of criminal investigation to the executive's appointed representatives, exhibited a very serious deconstitutionalization practice that ruled out the principles of judicial independence and judicial control of all actions of the executive at the local level; the power to order a criminal investigation is actually a power held by the independent judiciary, and specifically by the office of the public prosecutor. Constitutionally speaking, granting this power to local representatives of the executive – outside emergency rule – means handing over juridical power to an executive body, which is an explicit and severe violation of the supreme principle of the separation of powers.

This violation was not prevented by the AYM or ECHR. The curfew that started in the Kurdish-majority cities of south-east Turkey in August 2015 caused the death, injury and forced displacement of hundreds of people and led to violations of basic human rights including the rights to life, liberty, security, housing and health, the right to apply to effective legal representation and all other legal instruments, and prohibition from inhuman or degrading treatment.[28] Individuals' applications to the AYM and ECHR to stop these violations were rejected, and even secondary actions such as the effective investigation of violations were not implemented.[29] In other words, the AYM found the declaration of curfew based on the Law of Provincial Administration lawful – although it was considered explicitly unconstitutional in the doctrine – thereby contributing to the process of deconstitutionalization.[30] With this decision, the AYM remained blind not only to the violation of the separation of powers, but also to the complete deactivation of the legislature: according to the constitution, the declaration of curfew, which is an authority intrinsic to a state of emergency, needs to be approved by the Council of Ministers and by the legislature. The exercise of this power by a district governor in an unlimited way and for an undefined period of time is also against the principle of the separation of powers, given the hierarchical relations between the executive and the judiciary at the local level. The AYM also ignored the constitutional requirements that the exercise of powers relating to a state of emergency is exceptional and should be clearly and explicitly limited.[31]

Following the rejection of their applications to the AYM, the applicants filed applications with the ECHR. The ECHR requested a defence from Turkey for the first time on 31 December 2015, asking about the legal grounds of the curfew, whether basic goals had been achieved or not, and whether measures to protect the basic right to life had been implemented. This request was positively welcomed by the democratic opposition in Turkey,[32] but unfortunately the ECHR ultimately stated in a press release dated 13 January 2016 that it was aware of the severity of the situation, but rejected interim measures on the *belief* that the government would take the necessary measures.[33] Later, the need for interim measures was accepted for five applicants among the many severely injured people trapped in a basement in Cizre, although none of these measures were applied by the Turkish government, and four applicants lost their lives.[34] The ECHR stated on 5 February 2016 that it rejected the remaining applications, noting the AYM's willingness to monitor the applicants' situation.[35] About a year later, in a press release on 15 December 2016, the ECHR stated that 43 applicants whose applications had been rejected had lost their lives during the curfew. The ECHR declared that it had decided to give priority to examining the complaints about the interim measures in essence based on Rule 41 (the order in which cases are dealt with) of the court's rules.[36] However, after three years, it again rejected all the applications, stating that the AYM is an effective domestic legal remedy and that domestic remedies had not been exhausted.

It is also important to note the inconsistency of the ECHR's attitude towards the curfews in Turkey compared with its earlier decisions on similar cases. For instance, in the applications of Georgia, Crimea and Ukraine against Russia, the ECHR had called upon the parties to refrain from taking any measures, particularly military actions, that might entail breaches of the rights of the civilian population and put their lives and health at risk, and to comply with their engagements under the convention.[37] For some reason, a similar attitude was not adopted with regard to these applications from Turkey.

This indicates a process of political deconstitutionalization in which the principles of the separation of powers, judicial independence and rule of law were de facto eliminated by the ruling authority. During the applications against the unconstitutional curfew decisions, the hierarchical order and balance among and within the executive and judicial bodies at the local level was severely degraded. Moreover, with impaired judicial independence and impartiality, the fundamental human rights of the people living in provinces under curfew were violated, including the right to access the courts. All the decisions and practices of the local governors, as well as of the government, remained beyond the realm of constitutional control and therefore the AYM and ECHR were ineffective in avoiding deconstitutionalization in this case.

Lifting parliamentary immunity: relations between the legislature and the executive

Another significant turning point in the political deconstitutionalization is the lifting of parliamentary immunity through a provisional amendment made to the constitution in 2016; this was followed by the arrests of a number of opposition MPs, pushing them out of the political realm. As prominent constitutional experts of the country emphasized, the removal of parliamentary immunity took place in a very questionable and unconstitutional manner.[38] Even the main opposition party leader, who approved the amendment, had to admit this.[39]

Following the amendment, which came into force on 8 June 2016, the co-chairs and MPs of the HDP, who were voicing strong opposition to the transition to the AKP-imposed presidential system of government, were arrested. Two MPs from the main opposition party were also arrested in this process. The allegations against the HDP co-chairs and CHP parliamentarians involved their speeches delivered in the context of their political activities. Therefore, with this amendment to parliamentary immunity, a basic constitutional norm securing legislative action – namely, parliamentarians' non-liability and chair immunity – was violated. In a democratic parliamentary constitutional order, MPs' freedom to conduct political debate and to express the opinions of the people they represent are considered key aspects of a functioning legislative power.[40]

Even though 70 members of the legislature filed an annulment action with the AYM, the court rejected it. From a constitutional perspective, the amendment meant that the article of the constitution regulating the lifting of immunity was suspended using a provisional article, and a differentiated regulation was enacted for a group of people for a certain period of time.[41] In this way, the basic legal procedural assurance regarding the way in which a rule may be amended was disregarded with the consent of the Constitutional Court.[42]

The individual application of Selahattin Demirtaş, a co-chair of the HDP, regarding his arrest, was considered first by the AYM and then by the ECHR. The AYM rejected Demirtaş's individual application. However, in a previous decision regarding the applications of Mehmet Haberal and Mustafa Ali Balbay, who were elected to parliament as CHP MPs after their arrests, the AYM had stated that the courts, while taking decisions regarding the continued detention of elected members of parliament, should provide evidence that there was a greater value to be protected than both the individual right to liberty and security and the right to stand for election and political activity.[43] In contradiction with this evaluation, and despite the fact that Demirtaş was not only a member of parliament but also a party chair and a presidential candidate, his application was examined a year and a month later and rejected on 21 December 2017.[44] The AYM thus disregarded its own evaluation and prevented Demirtaş from exercising his right to stand for election and to political activity.

Following this rejection, Demirtaş applied to the ECHR and the court ruled that it was a breach of his rights, without discussing the legislative immunity and non-liability issues. In other words, the ECHR established some elements of political deconstitutionalization, pointing to the adverse effects of Selahattin Demirtaş's continued detention on the democratic regime and a pluralistic political order, particularly at a time of presidential elections that also involved possibly the most significant constitutional amendment in the history of the republic – that is, the transition to the presidential system of government.[45] In its decision, the ECHR called attention to the acceleration of these investigations after the President stated: 'I do not find the closure of political parties right. But, I am also saying that the chairs of this party must pay for this issue. One by one, individual by individual.' Referring to the statements of the Council of Europe Commissioner for Human Rights, the ECHR made it clear that the prevailing political climate, especially during the state of emergency, put political pressure on national courts and judges, and that judicial bodies in Turkey had lost their independence.[46] With this decision, the ECHR abandoned its former attitude of giving the government room to manoeuvre. Moreover, the court stated that the violation of the rights of Demirtaş, a significant political opposition figure, was linked to the erosion of the pluralistic democratic political system as a whole, and, with this decision, Turkey was drifting away from the Western liberal constitutional system regarding the supreme principle of an independent judiciary. [47]

Once again, the ECHR decision was not taken into consideration by the AKP government. One might have expected the Committee of Ministers of the Council of Europe to impose some measures on Turkey to force the country's recognition of the ECHR decision, but this did not happen. Ultimately, the Council of Europe, which used to be considered the bastion of Western democratic values and human rights, refrained from imposing its main mission on the AKP government during a period of historical political transformations in Turkey, and hence contributed to the country's move towards deconstitutionalization.

The state of emergency, the KHK regime and the Turkish presidential system: relations among the legislation, judiciary and executive

The declaration of a state of emergency on 21 July, following the coup attempt, constitutes a historical moment in the transformation from regime crisis to state crisis in Turkey.[48] The governmental order established during the state of emergency between July 2016 and July 2018 endowed Erdoğan's government with unlimited power, unprecedented even during coups.[49] The government exercised its power by issuing emergency decrees, which are normally limited to issues relating to a state of emergency, in areas not related to the state of emergency, deliberately defying the constitution. Moreover, it passed permanent regulations that would continue to be valid after the state of emergency. Some of these regulations deliberately altered the constitutional foundations of the state in many respects.[50]

Overall, the emergency decrees that destroyed the constitutional foundations of the state, the 2017 constitutional amendments that created the presidential system of government and the Authorization Law introduced before the end of the state of emergency constituted the third, but most crucial, turning point in the political deconstitutionalization process that had been taking place since 2014 in Turkey. With all these transformations, the late rule of the AKP completely abolished the supreme norm of the separation of powers, and especially parliament's supremacy in law making – specifically the norm that the legislature constructs the executive. During the KHK regime, the government moved to a new state order by entirely exceeding the limits of the state of emergency regime as defined by the constitution. During the unconstitutional emergency rule, the powers of the legislature were taken over, the right to apply to legal means was eliminated and all basic rights and freedoms were over-turned, defying even the state of emergency conditions regulated by the 1982 Constitution.[51] Ultimately, the KHK regime during the state of emergency and the presidential system of government that was made possible through subsequent constitutional amendments ensured the superiority of the power of a single person over all state powers.[52] In this process, the AYM gave consent to the most severe examples of deconstitutionalization by defying its own jurisprudence.

The AYM, in a former jurisprudence related to this issue, had investigated the location, time and content of a case to determine whether a certain emergency decree was compatible with Article 121 of the constitution.[53] However, this time the AYM ruled to reject the applications on the grounds that it did not have the power of judi-cial review over emergency decrees that could make amendments in issues and laws that were not related to the state of emergency, based on Article 148 of the constitution.[54] Meanwhile, emergency decrees issued during the state of emergency were quickly legislated in parliament. All applications filed by the CHP to the AYM were rejected.[55] As stated in these application files, regulations that were not related to and outside the scope and duration of the state of emergency were envisaged in this process: that is, general and per-manent amendments were made in several laws that were currently in force.[56] The emergency decrees, although they were not discussed in parliament within 30 days, as foreseen in its internal regulations, thus lost their quality as emergency decrees but were still legalized. Moreover, the approval of an emergency decree by an assembly res-olution also meant the takeover of legislative power. Defying all such objections, however, the AYM ruled again to reject the applications.

On seeing that the AYM was not an effective domestic legal remedy against unconstitutional emergency decrees, individual applications were filed with the ECHR. At the beginning, the applicants were mainly individuals dismissed from their public posts due to emer-gency decrees and whose passports were seized. The ECHR rejected these applications despite reports from the Venice Commission and drafted by the Council of Europe Commissioner for Human Rights that covered the issues mentioned above. On this specific issue, the AYM and the ECHR continuously conducted talks. As a result, a 'State of Emergency Commission' was established in Turkey as a body to which dismissed public employees could apply.[57] In this way, a new domestic legal process was created, relieving the ECHR from the heavy load of files from Turkey. Even though the problem was resolved for the ECHR pragmatically, significant legal, procedural and ethical questions were left unresolved, leaving aside the erosion of fundamental democratic principles. For instance, it was not clear in what capacity the State of Emergency Commission would review and annul a regulation.

The ECHR had been complaining of its heavy workload for a long time, looking for measures that would decrease the number of applications on behalf of states; indeed, the 'pilot judgment' procedure was promoted as a tool to deal with this problem. Even though there was such an option, however, the ECHR did not give a 'pilot judgment' in the applications from Turkey and ruled to reject all of them on a problematic pretext that domestic legal remedies were not exhausted.[58] In fact, the Venice Commission reports indicated that the attitude of the AYM was wrong.[59] The AYM's avoidance of making a decision by keeping files waiting for a long time was also an indication that it was avoiding a judicial review of the state of emergency regime; in other words, the High Court at the domestic level was not acting independently of political power. The ECHR rejected applications after the establishment of the State of Emergency Commission on the grounds that the commission was an effective internal remedy. In this way, the court has basically violated or ignored a previous decision on the exhaustion of internal remedies that it took in a similar case.[60]

The move towards an exceptional state in Turkey?

The deconstitutionalization process that started with the election of Erdoğan as President in 2014 accelerated following the general elections when the AKP lost power in 2015, a process that still continues today after passing through various critical turning points in the late 2010s. Given its persistence, it is clear that the rise of authoritarianism in Turkey is not a regime problem any more. As several political scientists and analysts have argued, what has been going on in Turkey is the construction of an *exceptional state*, in which the total elimination of all practical and constitutional control mechanisms has left political power completely unchecked.[61] If the basic characteristic of the modern constitutional establishment is the restriction of individual power by means of constitutional norms and institutions, the deconstitutionalization of Turkey has reached a phase in which the constitutional establishment itself has started to dismantle, with no domestic and international constitutional control mechanism having the capability or willingness to stop this. One might wish to think that this has been a process specific to Turkey, but the fact that the same incapability can also be identified in the ECHR shows that the problem has global and international determinants. Moreover, until the 2010s, the political/constitutional order in Turkey used to function, despite its limitations and historical ups and downs, within the framework and confines of a state-society model, based on Western capitalism and liberal democracy. If Turkey's membership of the Council of Europe has been one indication of this, another has been the military's reconstruction of the basic norms and institutions of this model, such as parliamentary democratic institutions, the constitutional protection of basic rights and freedoms and the rule of law. But today, a civilian political power seems to be challenging this Western-originated normative political order by making the system non-functional through deliberate interventions. The inability of the domestic and international high courts to use their legal authority to reverse this tide shows that the problem of authoritarianism cannot be reduced to the intentions of single actors but has wider roots. It may be that what has been discussed in this chapter as political deconstitutionalization refers to a crisis not only in the Turkish state, but also in the Western normative and political order.

Notes

1. Akça et al. 2014; Oğuz 2016; Berksoy 2017; Esen and Gümüşçü 2016; Iğsız 2014; Kaygusuz 2016; Somer 2016; Tansel 2018.

2. After his election to the presidency, Erdoğan effectively took hold of the policymaking power of the Council of Ministers, losing his impartial position and acting as a de facto prime minister, defying Articles 101, 109 and 112 of the constitution until the move to a presidential system in 2017. See Gözler 2016: 10–14.

3. Özbudun 2015: 46–7; Oğuz 2016: 98–9, 101–2; Kaygusuz 2018: 293. The 17/25 December corruption investigations organized by the Gülenist prosecutors were the decisive moment

after which the AKP government effectively re-regulated the organization of the judiciary and considerably increased its power over the judges. Another significant step was the passage of the Internal Security Law, which is analysed later in detail.

4. Bilgiç 2018; Akdeniz and Altıparmak 2018, see also Alemdar (Chapter 11).

5. Gözler 2016; Acar 2016; İ Kaboğlu (2017), 'Acil Gündem: Anayasal Kamuoyu', *Gazeteduvar*, 9 January; Kaboğlu 2017b.

6. See Tanör 1986, 1994; Arato 2010a; Belge 2006; Isiksel 2013; Parla 2016.

7. Isiksel 2013: 716.

8. The constitutional amendments of 2010 in particular were a critical turning point paving the way for the politicization of the judiciary under AKP rule. See Arato 2010b; Bali 2013, 2016.

9. Kaboğlu 2019. In its opinion, the Venice Commission stressed the dangers of degeneration of the proposed presidential system towards an authoritarian regime because of the excessive powers that the President would have. See Venice Commission (2017) 'Turkey: Opinion on the amendments to the constitution adopted by the Grand National Assembly on 21 January 2017 to be submitted to a national referendum on 16 April 2017', 13 March.

10. 'Meclis'ten geçti: OHAL'i "Olağan" hale getirdiler', *Cumhuriyet*, 25 July 2018.

11. Ibid.

12. Gözler 2016: 51-2.

13. Ibid., p. 51. The adjective 'legal' might seem elusory at first glance. We use 'legal' to characterize the inactivation of the laws in force and/or the constitution in force. There is no better expression to contrast this type of deconstitutionalization with the 'political' one in the context of this analysis.

14. Bruff 2014; Hallsworth and Lea 2011; Boukalas 2015; Bermeo 2016; Tansel 2017.

15. Taş 2015; Somer 2016; Kaygusuz 2016; Oğuz 2016; Berksoy 2017.

16. Against the AYM's ruling with regard to two journalists, recognizing the violation of their rights, Erdoğan openly stated in February 2016 that he did not abide by the decision or respect it, and that the courts of first instance may also not abide by it. This is considered a typical example of deconstitutionalization. See 'Turkey's President Erdogan rejects court ruling to free journalists', *Independent*, 28 February 2016.

17. Kaboğlu 2017a: 17; see also Demirkent 2014.

18. Gözler 2016: 55-6.

19. This is particularly Gözler's interpretation about the post-2014 deconstitutionalization process. Other constitutional experts cited are possibly critical of such an interpretation but they still use the term within the confines of legality.

20. According to Gözler, one of the most significant examples of deconstitutionalization was the curfew decisions made as an application of the Internal Security Law No. 6638, dated 4 April 2015. These were emergency decisions taken in the context of rising violence in the Kurdish-populated provinces after the summer of 2015 that were applied unconstitutionally by provincial governors as representatives of the executive, based on the Law of Provincial Administration. However, according to the constitution, governors can declare curfew only under a state of emergency, based on the state of emergency law. Gözler suggests the declaration of a state of emergency complying with the constitution to end this deconstitutionalization practice. See Gözler 2016: 76-7.

21. Altıparmak 2015; Aydın 2015; Kaygusuz 2016; Berksoy 2017.

22. Altıparmak et al. 2018a; IHOP 2018. See also Venice Commission (2016) 'Turkey: Opinion on Emergency Decree Laws Nos 667–676 adopted following the failed coup of 15 July 2016', 9–10 December.

23. All cases examined in this chapter contain more than one dimension of deconstitutionalization, but we prefer to focus on the most striking dimension in each.

24. In the period this study focuses on, there were several decisions, political practices and interventions by the AKP that led towards deconstitutionalization, but here we particularly selected cases in which the AYM and ECHR intervened to establish our argument.

25. Article 3 of Martial Law No. 1402 and Article 11 of State of Emergency Law No. 2935.

26. In fact, Article 11/c of the Law of Provincial Administration No. 5442, through which the Internal Security Law connects the curfew, did not grant this power to provincial and district governors. For this reason, an amendment was made in the Law of Provincial Administration in 2018, granting these powers to provincial and district governors.

27. Gözler 2016; Ardıçoğlu 2015; Aydın 2015.

28. See UN-OHCHR (2017) 'Report on the human rights situation in Turkey: July 2015–December 2016'; Human Rights Watch (2016) 'Turkey: state blocks probes of southeast killings', 11 July.

29. All individual applications to the Constitutional Court filed in December 2015 and January 2016 relating to the deaths of people in Cizre and the need of emergency healthcare for dozens of injured people were quickly rejected by the court. For AYM

decisions 2015/15266, 2015/20376, 2015/20218 and 2016/1652, see https://kararlarbilgibankasi.anayasa.gov.tr. (accessed 19 September 2019).

30. See http://www.kararlaryeni.anayasa.gov.tr/BireyselKarar/Content/cc3b7777-aaaf-49a0-9197-3e1ba1fa6a29?wordsOnly=False. For a critique of the AYM decisions, see Yokuş 2016.

31. Ibid.

32. 'AİHM Türkiye'den savunma istedi', T24, 2 January 2016; 'AİHM eski yargıcı Türkmen: AİHM sokaga çıkma yasaklarıyla ilgili tedbir kararı alacak', *BirGun*, 1 January 2016.

33. ECHR (2016) 'Requests for lifting of curfew measures in south-eastern Turkey', press release, 13 January.

34. See https://anayasagundemi.com/2016/12/19/ihamin-sokaga-cikma-yasaklariyla-ilgili-34-basvuruda-verdigi-kararlarin-ozet-cevirisi/.

35. ECHR (2016) 'Curfew measures in south-eastern Turkey: court decides to give priority treatment to a number of complaints', press release, 5 February. Lawyer Ramazan Demir, acting as the representative of the majority of the applicants following the rejection of interim measures (who himself was detained after the applications), points out that this attitude of the ECHR followed the visits of heads and members of the Constitutional Court, Supreme Court and Council of State. See 'Tutuklu avukat Ramazan Demir: Mahkemede tahliye talep etmeyeceğim, yaparsam cübbeyi bir daha giymem', T24, 20 June 2016. The president of the Supreme Court at the time, in a speech delivered at the opening ceremony of the 2016–17 court year, justified these talks with his statement: 'We exchanged views on terrorism in Turkey with the President of the ECHR' (https://www.yargitay.gov.tr/documents/acilisKonusma/2016-2017.pdf).

36. ECHR (2016) 'European Court of Human Rights looks into complaints about curfew measures in Turkey', press release, 15 December.

37. See https://www.ECtHR.coe. int/Documents/FS_Interim_measures_ ENG.pdf.

38. İ. Kaboğlu (2016) 'Anayasaya Aykırı Anayasa Değişikliği', *Birgün*, 28 April; H. S. Türk (2016) 'Dokunulmazlıkları Kaldıran Anayasa Değişikliği-1/2', *Milliyet*, 18–19 April.

39. 'Turkish opposition backs immunity bill that Kurdish MPs say targets them', *Reuters*, 14 April 2016.

40. Can and Şimşek 2019.

41. See Venice Commission (2016) 'Turkey: Opinion on the suspension of the second paragraph of Article 83 of the Constitution (Parliamentary Inviolability)', 14 October.

42. AYM decisions E.2016/54 and K.2016/117 of 3 June 2016; see http://www.anayasa.gov.tr/media/3875/2016-117.pdf.

43. See http://www.kararlaryeni. anayasa.gov.tr/BireyselKarar/ Content/143efb4c-4d11-4d16-aa12-5195968201ce?wordsOnly=False; http:// kararlaryeni.anayasa.gov.tr/Bireysel Karar/Content/fa075be0-4161-4abf-b90a-bc772518dd12?wordsOnly=False.

44. See https://kararlarbilgibankasi. anayasa.gov.tr/BB/2016/25189?Basvur uAdi=SELAHATT%C4%B0N+DEM%C4 %B0RTA%C5%9E.

45. ECHR (2017) 'The case of Selahattin Demirtaş V. Turkey', application no. 14305/17, 20 February, https://hudoc.echr.coe.int/eng#{%22ite mid%22:[%22001-187961%22]}.

46. Ibid.

47. Ibid.

48. A detailed analysis of the KHK regime and the presidential system is beyond the scope of this analysis. This part analyses the files opened in the AYM and ECHR in relation to the emergency decrees to show their role in political deconstitutionalization.

49. For an extensive analysis of the state of emergency period, see IHOP (2018).

50. Altıparmak et al. 2018a, 2018b; Akça, et al. 2017.

51. Altıparmak et al. 2018a; Günday 2017; Gözler 2016; Metin Günday (2017) 'Son KHK ile TBMM fiilen lağvedildi, anayasa değişikliği yürürlük tarihi öne çekildi', T24, 25 August.

52. 'Venedik Komisyonu Üyesi Aydın: Anayasasız Bir Dönem Başladı', *Cumhuriyet*, 23 April 2017.

53. AYM decisions E.1990/25, K.1991/1, E.1991/6, K.1991/20, E.1992/30, K.1992/36, E.2003/28 and K.2003/42; General Board Decision of the Council of State for Unified Decisions of Supreme Courts regarding the validity of decisions taken in martial law only during martial rule: 1988/6 and 1989/4.

54. For an example of similar AYM decisions, see 2018/114 and 2018/91 at http://kararlaryeni.anayasa.gov.tr/ Karar/Content/3787eeb5-2a71-4875-93b1-d3f7f0286267?excludeGerekce=Fal se&wordsOnly=False.

55. For an example of similar AYM decisions, see 2018/42 and 2018/48 at http://kararlaryeni.anayasa.gov.tr/ Karar/Content/5bfa864b-94f0-4243-a5bc-85b12eadbb90?excludeGerekce=Fa lse&wordsOnly=False.

56. M. Günday (2017) 'Son KHK ile TBMM fiilen lağvedildi, anayasa değişikliği yürürlük tarihi öne çekildi', T24, 25 August.

57. Secretary General of the Council of Europe, Thorbjørn Jagland, stated that they were in collaboration with the Turkish authorities. See 'Avrupa Konseyi Genel Sekreteri Jagland: Türkiye'den yapılan başvurular konusunda AİHM muhtemelen pilot

karar verecek', *MemurlarNet*, 22 January 2018.

58. Application No. 59061/16, Akif Zihni versus Turkey decision, http://hudoc.echr.coe.int/eng?i= 002-11459.

59. Venice Commission (2016) 'Turkey: Opinion on the Emergency Laws Nos 667–676 adopted following the failed coup of 15 July 2016', 12 December.

60. Application No. 70478/16, Gökhan Köksal versus Turkey, https://hudoc.echr.coe.int/eng#%7B.

61. Space does not allow us to explain Poulantzas's concept of 'exceptional state' to elaborate the new authoritarian features of the state in Turkey. For discussions on the emerging exceptional state in Turkey, see Kaygusuz 2018; Oğuz 2016; Karahanoğulları and Türk 2018.

References

Acar, A. (2016) 'De-constitutionalism in Turkey?', *I-CONnect: Blog of the International Journal of Constitutional Law*, 19 May, http://www.iconnectblog.com/2016/05/deconstitutionalism-in-turkey/.

Akça, İ., A. Bekmen and B. A. Özden (eds) (2014) *Turkey Reframed: Constituting Neoliberal Hegemony*. London: Pluto Press.

Akça, İ. et al. (2017) 'Olağanlaşan OHAL / KHK'ların yasal mevzuat üzerindeki etkileri'. Cologne: Heinrich Böll Foundation.

Akdeniz, Y. and K. Altıparmak (2018) 'Turkey: freedom of expression in jeopardy', English PEN, 28 March, https://www.englishpen.org/campaigns/turkey-freedom-of-expression-in-jeopardy/.

Altıparmak, K. (2015) 'İçinden "İç Güvenlik Paketi" Geçen Kabus Senaryosu', *Bianet*, 29 January, http://bianet.org/kurdi/insan-haklari/161898-icinden-ic-guvenlik-paketi-gecen-kabus-senaryosu.

Altıparmak, K., D. Demirkent and M. Sevinç (2018a) 'Atipik KHK'ler ve Daimim Hukuksuzluk: Artik Yasalari İdare mi İptal Edecek' in *Olağanüstü Hal ve Uygulamaları Bilgi Notu 2018/1*. Ankara: IHOP.

Altıparmak, K., D. Demirkent and M. Sevinç (2018b) 'Atipik KHK'ler ve Daimi Hukuksuzluk: OHAL KHK'si ile Kadını Erkek, Erkeği Kadın Yapamazsınız' in *Olağanüstu Hal ve Uygulamaları Bilgi Notu 2018/2*. Ankara: IHOP.

Arato, A. (2010a) 'Democratic constitution-making and unfreezing the Turkish process', *Philosophy and Social Criticism* 36 (3–4): 473–87.

Arato, A. (2010b) 'The constitutional reform proposal of the Turkish government: the return of majority imposition', *Constellations* 17 (2): 345–50.

Ardıçoğlu, A. (2015) 'Hukuka Uygun Olmayan Sokağa Çıkma Yasağı Hukuka Aykırı Mıdır?', *Birikim*, 27 November.

Aydın, O. (2015) 'İç güvenlik yasa tasarısı: Anayasal düzene son', *Birikim*, 20 January.

Bali, A. (2013) 'Courts and constitutional transition: lessons from the Turkish case', *International Journal of Constitutional Law* 11 (3): 666–701.

Bali, A. (2016) 'Shifting into reverse: Turkish constitutionalism under the AKP', *Theory and Event* 19 (1), https://muse.jhu.edu/article/610221.

Belge, C. (2006) 'Friends of the court: the republican alliance and selective activism of the constitutional court

of Turkey', *Law and Society Review*
40 (3): 653–92.

Berksoy, B. (2017) '2010'larda Türkiye'de
"güvenlik devleti" "olağanüstü
devlet" biçimine evrilirken', *Birikim*
335: 11–26.

Bermeo, N. (2016) 'On democratic
backsliding', *Journal of Democracy*
27 (1): 5–19.

Bilgiç, A. (2018) 'Reclaiming the
national will: resilience of Turkish
authoritarian neoliberalism after
Gezi', *South European Society and
Politics 23* (2): 259–80.

Boukalas, C. (2015) 'Class war-on-terror:
counterterrorism, accumulation,
crisis', *Critical Studies on Terrorism
8* (1): 55–71.

Bruff, I. (2014) 'The rise of authoritarian
neoliberalism', *Rethinking Marxism
26* (1): 113–29.

Can O. and A. D. Şimşek (2019)
'Venedik Komisyonu Raporları
Işığında Anayasa'nın Geçici
20. Maddesi ve Yasama
Dokunulmazlığı Enis Berberoğlu
Kararı' in A. Kendigelen and S.
Yüksel (eds), *Ord. Prof. Dr. Ali
Fuad Başgil'in Anısına Armağan.*
Istanbul: 12 Levha, pp. 417–64.

Demirkent, D. (2014) 'Liberallerin
Dinmeyen Özlemi: Anti Ceberrut,
Anti-Derin, Anti-Paralel Devlet ya
da Sadece Devlet', *Ayrıntı Dergi 4*
(12 May).

Esen, B. and Ş. Gümüşçü (2016) 'Rising
competitive authoritarianism in
Turkey', *Third World Quarterly 37*
(9): 1581–606.

Gözler, K. (2016) '1982 Anayasası Hala
Yürürlükte mi? Anayasasızlaştırma
Üzerine Bir Deneme', http://
www.anayasa.gen.tr/
anayasasizlastirma-v4.pdf.

Günday, M. (2017) 'OHAL, İhraç KHK'leri
ve Hukuki Durum', *Ankara Barosu
Dergisi 2017/1*: 29–38.

Hallsworth, S. and J. Lea (2011)
'Reconstructing Leviathan:
emerging contours of the security
state', *Theoretical Criminology 15*
(2): 141–57.

Iğsız, A. (2014) 'Brand Turkey and the
Gezi protests: authoritarianism
in flux, law and neoliberalism' in
U. Özkırımlı (ed.), *The Making of
a Protest Movement in Turkey
#occupygezi.* Basingstoke: Palgrave
Macmillan, pp. 22–49.

IHOP (2018) *Updated Situation Report:
State of Emergency in Turkey, 21
July 2016–20 March 2018.* Ankara:
IHOP.

Isiksel, T. (2013) 'Between text and
context: Turkey's tradition of
authoritarian constitutionalism',
*International Journal of
Constitutional Law 11* (3): 702–26.

Kaboğlu, İ. Ö. (2017a) *15 Temmuz
Anayasası.* Istanbul: Tekin.

Kaboğlu, İ. Ö. (2017b) 'Sunuş
Yazısı: Anayasa Fetişizmi ve
Anayasasızlaştırma İkilemi', *Anayasa
Hukuku Dergisi 2* (4): 7–8.

Kaboğlu, İ. Ö. (2019) *Anayasasızlaştırma
ve Demokrasi Umudu.* Istanbul:
Tekin.

Karahanoğulları, Y. and D. Türk (2018)
'Otoriter Devletçilik, Neoliberalizm,
Türkiye', *Mülkiye 42* (3): 403–48.

Kaygusuz, Ö. (2016) 'Bir siyasal idare
tekniği olarak güvenlik ve AKP
dönemi'nde ulusal güvenlik devleti',
Praksis 40: 85–119.

Kaygusuz, Ö. (2018) 'Authoritarian
neoliberalism and regime security in
Turkey: moving to an "exceptional
state" under AKP', *South European
Society and Politics 23* (2): 281–302.

Oğuz, Ş. (2016) 'Yeni Türkiye'nin siyasal
rejimi' in T. Tören and M. Kutun
(eds), *Yeni Türkiye? Kapitalizm,
Devlet, Sınıflar.* Istanbul: SAV,
pp. 81–127.

Özbudun, E. (2015) 'Turkey's judiciary and the drive toward competitive authoritarianism', *The International Spectator 50* (2): 42–55.

Parla, T. (2016) *Türkiye'de Anayasalar: Tarih, İdeoloji, Rejim.* Istanbul: Metis.

Somer, M. (2016) 'Understanding Turkey's democratic breakdown: old vs. new and indigenous vs. global authoritarianism', *Southeast European and Black Sea Studies 16* (4): 1–23.

Tanör, B.(1986) *Osmanlı-Türk Anayasal Gelişmeleri: 1798–1098.* Istanbul: Yapı Kredi.

Tanör, B. (1994) *Türkiye'nin İnsan Hakları Sorunu.* Istanbul: BDS.

Tansel, C. B. (ed.) (2017) *States of Discipline: Authoritarian Neoliberalism and the Contested Reproduction of Capitalist Order.* London: Rowman and Littlefield International.

Tansel, C. B. (2018) 'Authoritarian neoliberalism and democratic backsliding in Turkey: beyond the narratives of progress', *South European Society and Politics 23* (2): 197–217.

Taş, H. (2015) 'Turkey: from tutelary to delegative democracy', *Third World Quarterly 36* (4): 776–91.

Yokuş, S. (2016) 'Türkiye'den Avrupa İnsan Haklarına Mahkemesi'ne Başvuruda İç Hukuk Yolu Olarak Anayasa Şikayeti', *İstanbul Kemerburgaz University Journal of Social Sciences 1* (2): 33–50.

3 | TURKEY'S DOUBLE MOVEMENT: ISLAMISTS, NEOLIBERALISM AND FOREIGN POLICY

İlhan Uzgel

Introduction

The last two decades of Turkey's political scene have been defined by transformations in the nature of the state, society, class relations, politics and foreign policy, along with the rise of identity politics and shifting alliances of the AKP in the domestic sphere. With its uninterrupted incumbency, the AKP has been at the nexus of these multiple transformations. The party was established in 2001 when a younger generation of Islamists, as an offshoot of the Turkish Islamist movement, broke up with the old generation and initiated an ideological transformation from an Islamist, developmentalist and anti-Western to a conservative democrat (i.e. moderate/post-Islamist), neoliberal and Western-oriented position. Once they came to power, their swift adaptation and reckless implementation of neoliberal principles without serious backlash from the lower classes, and their shrewd tactics to forge various alliances in order to dismantle the military-centred establishment, transform the secular character of the state and project their cause to the broader Middle East have been notable developments that have determined the course of political life in Turkey in the years that followed.

There is a myriad of academic and popular works that have analysed almost all aspects of the AKP's rule so far. Most of these studies attributed high hopes to the party's democratization efforts in the 2000s,[1] while several works displayed a critical stand towards the AKP as early as that decade.[2] In the 2010s, however, the literature took a dramatic turn towards analyses of 'authoritarianism', along with developments inside and outside Turkey. Most of these studies started acknowledging that the AKP has moved in an authoritarian direction, but with some Turkish/Islamist characteristics,[3] while some have continued to trace the roots of AKP authoritarianism to the early 2000s.[4] Although a persistent authoritarian drive can be identified within neoliberalism in relation to the conditions of capital accumulation and its crises,[5] a periodization may still be required in the Turkish case – not necessarily because the AKP used to be a genuinely democratizing agent, but because the Turkish state, its institutional structure and its almost unchanged Cold War mindset in terms of securitization and its position vis-à-vis globalization have made it necessary for the AKP to engage in a restructuring of the Turkish state–society complex in two successive phases.

This chapter argues that, in the first phase of neoliberal restructuring, the AKP's political mission was to expand neoliberalism inclusively through a newly formed hegemonic bloc, incorporating the conservative/Islamist sections of society within it, and to instigate an aggressive privatization programme. In the second phase, after 2011, its main mission has been to contain the adverse effects of neoliberalism through coercive measures which it deems necessary to guarantee its survival. The chapter also argues that throughout these two successive and complementary processes, the AKP has skilfully intertwined its political survival with the needs of global and domestic capitalist interests as well as the political priorities of the Western world; this also explains its long incumbency. Following this argument, the chapter challenges those perspectives that see the possibility of a shift of axes in Turkish foreign policy away from its Western orientation.[6] Although divergences exist in policies regarding the purchase of the S-400 missile system from Russia and US support for the PYD (Kurdish Democratic Union Party) in Syria, these issues are confined to the usual bickering of intra-alliance ties. In the first phase, the AKP, with the strong support of the domestic and external components of the hegemonic bloc, gradually embarked upon dismantling the statist, obsessively secular and occasionally Western-sceptic, if not altogether anti-Western, military/judiciary-dominated bureaucratic tutelage, which had developed an anti-globalization attitude starting from the late 1990s.[7] In the second phase, it has moved towards authoritarian rule with the personification of power, criminalization of the opposition, curtailment of freedom of expression, erosion of the established institutions and the rule of law, and militarization of foreign policy.

The AKP's pro-Western position has been critically significant in terms of building a broader hegemonic bloc that can produce (external) legitimation and (domestic) consent, and in restructuring the state along with the requirements of internationalized circuits of capital accumulation. These two consequential and complementary moments are two reflections of different phases in the neoliberal restructuring of the state. In the first phase, identity politics prepared the ground for the Islamists to come to power and to reform the state through a newly emerged hegemonic bloc; in the second phase, now that the AKP has consolidated its power and Erdoğan has entrenched his personality cult, it has become easier to move towards a new authoritarian establishment that would successfully manage the crises of neoliberalism.

The AKP governments' multiple functions in terms of state restructuring, such as being a democratic model for the broader Middle East and opening up venues for identity politics, combined with their critical role in developing a hegemonic discourse on the benefits of neoliberalism that would incorporate the conservative masses into the neoliberal scheme. After all, neoliberalism is not only about the markets and the states, but also about how to administer a society that lives with declining wages, higher consumerism and a huge increase in consumer debt. Statistical data reveals that there has been a tremendous sevenfold rise in household debt from 2003 to 2012 in Turkey, which has reached 49 per cent of disposable income.[8] Therefore, what Turkey has gone through is beyond a mere state transformation; it has been an inclusive process involving society, various factions of the bourgeoisie and the state. The great successes of the AKP regime in both periods have been the inclusion of the subordinate classes in the commodification of social relations and the emergence of a conservative/Islamist middle class, mostly through their ties to local and central government subsidies,[9] while at the same time accommodating the needs of domestic and global capital and absorbing social discontent.

Identity politics as democratization and the agent of transformative diplomacy

Although it was the previous hegemonic bloc, which was composed of the military, centre-right politics and an Istanbul-based bourgeoisie, that had imposed neoliberal reforms in the early 1980s, when it came to the 1990s this bloc proved to be incapable of carrying out the neoliberal agenda due to its internal skirmishes and weaknesses, while the military–judicial establishment was reluctant to implement state restructuring since it would mean its loss of power in Turkish politics.

With the ascent to power of the AKP in 2002, a new hegemonic bloc was promoted that powerfully brought together both the external and domestic capitalist circles, including the big bourgeoisie organized around TÜSİAD, the conservative business represented by MÜSİAD, the Nakşi, Gülen and other religious brotherhoods, the US and the EU with their capitalist and geopolitical interests, and the Gulf countries with their surplus capital. This newly emergent hegemonic bloc marginalized the once-powerful Kemalist establishment and incrementally dislocated it from the state institutions, diminishing its power despite failed counterattacks by disgruntled secular Kemalists and/or nationalists.

Particularly noteworthy was the consensus in the centres of world capitalism regarding the need for a fresh and untainted new agent, willing to implement the neoliberal agenda and carry out the long-overdue transformation of the Turkish state. In fact, the rise of Islamist politics in the late 1990s coincided with the US policy of promoting moderate Islam in the broader Middle East. The US – and, concomitantly, the EU – began to foster what later came to be called the 'moderation-inclusion thesis'[10] and post-Islamism.[11] These theses suggested that if Islamists were allowed to enter normal politics and absorbed into democratic political processes, they would in return modify their discourse and goals and would be legitimate agents on the democratic playing field.[12] Instead of pursuing an Islamist agenda, they would prioritize democratization and human rights, embrace neoliberal principles, and drop their anti-Western discourse. Thus, in the early 2000s, the US started urging its allies in the Middle East to open up political space for pluralism, which would enable the Islamists to be legitimate political actors. While the experts and academics on the Middle East focused on the demographic changes and the controversial relationship between Islam and democracy, the US administration declared a new policy dubbed 'forward strategy of freedom';[13] this envisaged engaging Islamists and urging them to change their political language and position vis-à-vis the West. The National Security Advisor of the

Bush administration, Condoleezza Rice, explicitly stated that the US was asking for a transformation in the Middle East and was launching a new policy of 'transformational diplomacy', whereby US diplomats would adopt the mission of promoting governments for reforms.[14] The new generation of Turkish Islamists led by Recep Tayyip Erdoğan and Abdullah Gül were ready to make a deal and they held negotiations before and after they set up the AKP. In one of his tours in the US, Erdoğan met with Wall Street bankers, expressed the changes in his world view at Washington's conservative think tanks, such as the Jewish Institute for National Security of America and American Enterprise Institute, and ensured the US that he and his party enthusiastically embraced privatization, were attached to free-market principles, and would be a good friend of the US.[15] It is interesting to note that many Turkish experts, such as Graham Fuller, Morton Abramowitz, Henri Barkey and David Philips, who had an influence on Washington's Turkish policy, were critical of the Kemalists at that time and provided their full support to the transformative promise of the Turkish Islamists.[16] Meanwhile, the European Stability Initiative was praising the emergence of what it called 'Islamic Calvinists' in Turkey's rural Anatolia who were becoming more individualistic and embracing more pro-business attitudes over time.[17]

It should also be stated that the AKP governments initiated a critical policy change in Turkish foreign policy during this first period. Not only Turkey's foreign policy discourse but also its approach to some of the critical and intractable foreign and security issues such as the Cyprus problem and the Kurdish issue underwent a radical break with previous policy. Turkey, under AKP rule, took a conciliatory position in Cyprus by conceding the withdrawal of Turkish troops stationed on the island and the dissolution of the Northern Turkish Cypriot Republic as envisaged under the Annan Plan in 2004.[18] The AKP worked with the active support of the hegemonic bloc, which helped it to stave off the nationalist backlash from the Kemalist establishment at home and could thus sideline Rauf Denktaş, the founding president of the Turkish Cypriot Republic and the leading proponent of the Cyprus case. Several openings in the Kurdish issue, such as the recognition of the 'Kurdish problem' by a prime minister for the first time, the inauguration of a Kurdish-language channel on Turkish state TV and the removal of emergency rule in Kurdish areas, were among the steps taken by the AKP government. As important as those radical initiatives were, the AKP government, at the height of its liberal undertaking, was bold enough to initiate a reconciliation process with its neighbour, Armenia, and signed two protocols in October 2009 that envisaged the opening of the border and normalization of relations.[19]

The AKP's transformative character was also highlighted in its ties with the EU. Traditionally, the Turkish Islamists despised the EU, defining it a 'Christian club', and they urged the formation of a Muslim common market.[20] The new generation of Islamists, however, strongly embraced the EU's promotion of democracy, not because they were genuinely committed to democracy but because the AKP instrumentalized EU leverage in order to transform the state and to diminish the power of the Kemalist establishment. The EU conditionality, especially the harmonization packages, together with the start of the accession process in 2004, gave a new boost to the comprehensive political reforms. The so-called 'Europeanization' – i.e. employing EU conditionality, financial incentives and putative measures, if necessary, to impose European institutional organization, norms and practices – was utilized by the AKP to reorganize the state along neoliberal lines. Critically important was the restructuring of the National Security Council and its General Secretariat, which used to have the power to limit the actions of elected governments. Most of its functions, such as following up decisions on behalf of the prime minister, were abrogated with the Seventh Reform Package in 2003.[21] The prevalent discourse in EU and US circles and among pro-Western liberals in Turkey was to ask for a 'divorce' between Kemalism and the state, a split between (moderate) Islamism and nationalism, and thus an abandonment of the Turkish–Islamic synthesis of the early 1980s. The progress report prepared by the European Parliament stated that Kemalism was an obstacle on the way to Turkey's membership, although this had to be revised due to criticism coming from secular sections.[22] The leading US experts on Turkey explicitly stated that the country should overcome the Kemalist, statist ideology and give way to the AKP experiment, which was expected to project its own transformation to the broader Middle East.[23] Turkey's transformation in critical areas was hence hailed both domestically and internationally.[24] It was suggested that Turkey under AKP rule shifted its Hobbesian logic to a

Kantian one,[25] its foreign policy understanding was 'Europeanized', it moved from a national security state to liberal trading state, and it was transformed from a hard to a soft power.[26]

The 'liberal turn' in foreign policy, like other areas of political and judicial reforms, was indeed designed not to pursue a problem-solving and reconciliatory policy but to break the obstinacy of the establishment. For the ruling moderate Islamists, making Turkey a democratic country was never an ideational motivation.[27] Not a single change in foreign and security policy, such as Cyprus, the Kurdish and Armenian issues, yielded any result, and in the 2010s Turkey reverted to its traditional foreign and security policy discourses and practices.

On the economic front, the AKP governments continued the IMF-dictated austerity programme signed by the previous coalition government after the economic crisis of 2001. The incoherent three-party coalition government was in disarray and its prime minister was weak and incapable of both carrying out the IMF programme and managing the rising discontent of the subordinate and middle classes. Moreover, the secular sections of society and the bureaucracy had gradually become anti-EU, considering Turkey's EU accession process as inimical for the future and national sovereignty of the country.[28]

The AKP, on the other hand, after coming to power, made significant strides in furthering neoliberal structuring in at least three critical areas. First, it implemented an aggressive privatization campaign, which the previous Kemalist regime had been recalcitrant in implementing. In fact, the military was meddling with several privatization initiatives that it deemed security-sensitive, such as in the telecom sector. Consequently, Turkey saw a privatization spree that involved mostly the bloc sales of some of the biggest public enterprises to Turkish and Turkish–foreign conglomerates.[29] Of all the privatizations that had started in 1984, 88 per cent were realized under AKP governments, a figure that AKP circles continue to boast about. Revenue reached US$68 billion, although this was consumed in paying domestic and foreign debts.[30] Second, taking advantage of the quantitative easing policies of the 2000s, which continued up until 2013, the AKP governments allowed the private sector and the banks to borrow foreign currency at low interest rates, which Yeldan and Ünüvar called 'debt-driven accumulation',[31] thus increasing the foreign debt burden to US$453.4 billion as of 2018.[32] And third, this policy also opened the way for more mergers and acquisitions, leading to a change of ownership in many sectors and with half the banking sector being acquired by foreign companies either through direct sales or the purchasing of shares. In addition, dollarization of the economy reached new levels, and total savings in foreign currency surpassed savings in Turkish lira.[33] It is apparent that the AKP's economic policies have deepened Turkey's financial and economic integration into globalization and dependency on Western capitalism. During AKP rule, Turkey paid around US$157 billion in interest rates to international financial institutions.[34] What is more important is that, even though the AKP enthusiastically pursued neoliberal policies, it was also able to conceal its apparent class character and was successful in branding its pursuit of reckless neoliberalism as genuine national developmentalism peculiar to the AKP period. In the first period, the AKP was capable of absorbing possible class tensions through various mechanisms of distribution to the lower classes[35] via municipalities and government subsidies. Second, the AKP in this period resorted to full-scale identity politics, promoting itself as an anti-elitist democratizing agent and authentic representative of the nation. This helped it to reframe and appease the possible reactions of the discontented masses within a discourse of polarization between the Islamists and secularists.

In the first period, the hegemonic bloc built around the AKP as its political agent worked in harmony in the restructuring of the state–society complex, economy and politics. While the new constitutional and institutional arrangements diminished the role and place of the military in politics, the Kemalist elite's counter-attacks in 2007 in the form of issuing a threatening memorandum against the government and bringing a closure case against the AKP failed. With the start of the *Ergenekon* and *Balyoz* trials, in which leading military commanders were charged of planning a coup against the government, the establishment lost not only its power but also its legitimacy, and was eventually marginalized.[36] In this process, not only the new generation of Islamist political elites and businesses but also the newly emergent Islamist/conservative middle classes and lower classes were incorporated into the neoliberal agenda under AKP rule, which produced legitimacy through its developmentalist discourse, skilful manipulation of identity politics, rhetorical anti-elitism and coalition-building capability. The liberal turn in foreign policy both in discourse, such as the one claiming 'zero problems with neighbours', and in deeds, such as the radical change in the Cyprus issue, helped the AKP garner the support of Western liberal circles and provided external legitimacy.

The second phase of transformation

The second phase of the AKP-led transformation of the state began roughly after the 2011 elections, which brought the AKP a decisive victory. Erdoğan's dismissal of the liberals by overtly declaring that he did not need their support any more[37] and his subsequent break-up with the Gülen movement in the early 2012 led to the reconfiguration of the hegemonic bloc, preparing the ground for Erdoğan's authoritarian trajectory. From that time on, Erdoğan has taken advantage of every opportunity to entrench his authoritarian rule. The Gezi revolts marked another breaking point, although the coup attempt in 2016 led to the institutionalization of authoritarian rule during the two-year state of emergency and the personalization of power with the ensuing constitutional changes.

The dynamics and causes of the transition from a flawed democratic system to authoritarian governance are controversial issues that involved the early signals of the economic crisis, the idiosyncrasies of Erdoğan, and collision between him and the statist, security-centred circles in Turkish politics. This took Turkey to an authoritarian trajectory that has meant backsliding to a statist political tradition due to the AKP's own concerns of political survival, cajoling capital with coercive measures against workers and returning to heavy-handed oppression with regard to the Kurdish problem. This transition can be related to the AKP's own concerns for regime security[38] as well as to the growing strains in the implementation of neoliberalism.[39]

After the failed coup attempt in July 2016, the AKP government, in alliance with the nationalists, developed a new rhetoric of associating the Gülen movement (which is now designated a terrorist organization) with the PKK as a 'cocktail' threat controlled by foreign powers. As Boukalas has argued, 'counterterrorism pertains to a restructuring of the state so that it can manage economic crisis'.[40] The ensuing state of emergency enabled the AKP to restructure the state by empowering the executive, declaring war on terror domestically and externally, silencing the opposition, and curbing workers' rights. The report prepared by a dissenting workers' union reveals the anti-labour character of the state of emergency, during which the government closed down 19 workers' unions and postponed strikes that involved 150,000 workers.⁴¹ Indeed, Erdoğan was rather bold in declaring the class dimension of the prolonged state of emergency by saying that 'we are employing the state of emergency so that the business world can work more comfortably'.⁴²

It is not mere coincidence that the AKP took advantage of a rising global trend towards authoritarianism. Rather, it has been a meticulously worked-out policy in domestic politics for consolidating and concentrating power through a reshuffling of allies and by developing hegemonic discourses and coercive measures when necessary.

Whereas the AKP allied with the liberal circles and the Gülen movement in the first period in order to dismantle the statist structure and its hegemony, this second round of authoritarian restructuring was made possible thanks to the alliance of nationalists. This does not necessarily mean that the AKP was not capable of instituting an authoritarian regime alone; rather, the alliance has been instrumental in both ensuring legitimacy through a new, more nationalist political discourse and controlling the legislative branch with the support of the nationalist MHP. The gradual move of the political system towards authoritarianism took its final shape after the failed coup attempt, and it manifested itself most severely in the remilitarization of the Kurdish issue and in the adventurous conduct of foreign policy in Syria. Unlike the first period, during which the AKP represented itself as a democratizing agent, in this period the Erdoğan regime has resorted to a polarizing discourse, declaring that it is fighting those external powers and their domestic extensions that are trying to undermine Turkey. In its first phase, the AKP, through a new configuration of allies, was able to transform the state, while in its second phase it is being merged with the state, whose authoritarian and repressive character it has constructed itself.

Domestic and global circumstances are conducive to this move towards authoritarianism. Economic growth is slowing down, the income gap is growing, and the West is no longer interested in the moderation of the Islamists and their reformist agenda. This culturally Islamist, politically authoritarian, economically neoliberal and security-oriented militarist model has taken hold despite the new strains, social and political polarization and an ailing economy. The AKP government aims to continue with its neoliberal programme while at the same time gaining the consent of the conservative/Islamist/ nationalist middle and lower classes for its authoritarian turn. Erdoğan today is not only riding the rising authoritarian wave but also promises to be an early contributor to a globally entrenched trend.

The US, Trump and the tacit support for Turkey's authoritarianism

In the early 2010s, unlike in the previous phase, the external elements of Turkey's hegemonic bloc – the US and the EU – abandoned their policy of moderation of the Islamists, encouraging further reform of the Turkish political system. The fall of the moderate Islamist Ennahda-led coalition government in Tunisia and the military coup that ousted the Islamist Morsi government in Egypt in 2013 marked a silent end to the moderation–inclusion thesis. Both the US and the EU had minimal and mild reactions to the overthrow of Morsi and the cruel suppression of Islamists, and they promptly recognized the Sisi government despite the deteriorating situation in terms of human rights violations against opposition groups, and especially against members of the Muslim Brotherhood in Egypt.[43] US support given to the Sisi regime in Egypt as well as to Mohammad bin Salman, the strongman of Saudi Arabia, and the slide into chaos and instability in Libya, Syria and Yemen put an end to the popularity of debates on the moderation of Islamists and themes such as the compatibility of Islam and democracy in academia, think tanks and policymaking circles after 2013.

Therefore, the international and regional circumstances in the 2010s set the stage for an authoritarian turn for the ruling Islamists in Turkey. In particular, the election of Trump and the negligence of the EU represented two key turning points in providing the external conditions for the authoritarian slide of the AKP. The outgoing Obama administration had had some criticisms of the Erdoğan government, which were manifest in various influential think tank reports,[44] while Obama himself did not hide his disappointment with Erdoğan.[45] But the Trump administration was not only inattentive of transformative diplomacy, but also took further steps to pull back from the promotion of human rights and democracy,[46] and the US itself withdrew from the UN Human Rights Council, which highlighted its negligence of democratic reforms.[47] Trump himself expressed his admiration for authoritarian leaders such as Duterte of the Philippines, Putin of Russia, al-Sisi of Egypt and Erdoğan,[48] although the US media and Congress have maintained a negative view of Erdoğan. The support given to rising right-wing populist and authoritarian leaders should not be read as Trump's personal preference for strong leaders; rather, it is more of a structural turn with the deepening contradictions of capitalist reproduction that have led to the rise of populist, xenophobic, right-wing politics and authoritarianism. Indeed, Trump was part and parcel of the rise of a populist right-wing wave in the US that was represented by the Tea Party-type movements that emerged after the 2008 global capitalist crisis.[49]

The EU and a disgraceful bargain over refugees

Like the US, the EU has long lost its interest in furthering Turkey's democratic restructuring, especially once it became clear that the remnant of the Cold War statist establishment had lost its determining place in the echelons of the state. With the rise of racist/ xenophobic and Islamophobic movements, the anti-Turkey rhetoric became the order of the day in European politics, while both Brussels and individual EU members and successive AKP governments ceased to pursue an integration process. Instead, Erdoğan acquired the upper hand due to the Syrian migration issue and was strong enough even to blackmail German Chancellor Merkel and the EU to flood Syrian refugees into the EU, a threat he repeated intermittently and that led eventually to the signing of a refugee deal between Turkey and the EU in March 2016.[50] The refugee deal envisaged the return of some of the migrants from Greece to Turkey and stricter control of the refugee flow from Turkey in return for a disbursement of €3 billion from Brussels.[51] In fact, the EU, apart from paying for a small portion of the expenses of nearly 3.6 million Syrian refugees in Turkey, took a conciliatory position against the rolling back of many of the reforms it had urged the AKP government to implement in the previous period. Officially, the EU Commission's 2019 report continued to criticize Turkey's 'serious backsliding' on implementing its recommendations regarding human rights, reiterating its decision to keep Turkey's accession talks on hold. Interestingly, the same report still praised Turkey's dialogue and cooperation in the field of migration, stating that

'Turkey made good progress in the area of migration and asylum policy and remained committed to the effective implementation of the March 2016 EU–Turkey Statement'.[52] Hence, the EU's reactions to the Erdoğan regime's gradual move to authoritarianism and its growing human rights abuses have been confined to its reports with no concrete measures taken.

In short, while the US provided tacit support for Erdoğan's authoritarian regime mostly through Trump's personal contacts, the EU's 'malign neglect' provided the external conditions for the authoritarian restructuring of the state under AKP rule.

Conclusion: towards a new form of the state

The AKP managed to dismantle the national security state of the 1990s in Turkey, which was a remnant of the Cold War era, although after a short period of democratic reforms it reverted to authoritarianism again. The post-2011/post-2013 authoritarianism, however, has been different from the national security state of the 1990s, despite their commonalities in terms of militarism and expansionism. Turkey used to be a dependent peripheral country inside the Western capitalist system whose main characteristics were laicism, capitalism and a national security state under the tutelage of the military/civilian sections of the bureaucracy. The recent transition, undertaken by two successive hegemonic blocs, in both of which the Islamists occupied a central place, has integrated Turkish capitalism, contrary to the government's claims, in a more dependent way within global capital accumulation processes, increasing its economic and financial vulnerabilities, turning the state into a less secular, more Islamist/nationalist and belligerent security state in foreign and security policies.

The Islamists in general and Erdoğan in particular have played a prominent role in these two critical turns, tying their political fortunes to the exigencies of the reproduction of capital and engaging in an authoritarian state transformation, a growing tendency of capitalism's political form. Their political shrewdness has allowed them to pursue an unswerving neoliberal policy, while turning the conservative sections of society into consumers on the one hand, and producing the consent of the subordinate classes that made them an asset for both domestic and global capitalism on the other. The peculiarity of Erdoğan has lain in his ability to make critical transformations that are conducive to prolonging the span of his incumbency, while at the same time restructuring the state in line with capitalist and Western interests. The Western governments, despite their apparent critical stand towards the AKP, have been highly aware of this.

Notes

1. İnsel 2003; Hale 2005.
2. Tuğal 2009; Uzgel and Duru 2009; Coşar and Yücesan-Özdemir 2012.
3. Tansel 2018; Akkoyunlu and Öktem 2016.
4. Akça 2014: 34.
5. See Jessop 2019.
6. For a critical discussion on this question with a focus on defence industrial relations, see Kurç (Chapter 4).
7. Many of the left- and right-wing nationalists, together with a group inside the military, developed an anti-Western attitude starting from the late 1990s. For instance, the infamous statement by the Secretary-General of the National Security Council, General İlhan Kılınç: 'Turkey should consider the Russian and Iran alternatives', *Hürriyet*, 13 March 2002. See also İlhan 2000.
8. Karaçimen 2014: 163.
9. Akçay 2018.
10. Schwedler 2011.
11. Dağı 2004.
12. Rabasa et al. 2004: xxii–xxvi.
13. The White House (2003) 'Fact sheet: President Bush calls for a "forward strategy of freedom" to promote democracy in the Middle East', 6 November, https://georgewbush-whitehouse.archives.gov/news/releases/2003/11/20031106-11.html.
14. Condoleezza Rice (2006) 'Transformational diplomacy', Georgetown University, 18 January, https://2001-2009.state.gov/secretary/rm/2006/59306.htm.
15. Uzgel 2009: 19.
16. Fuller 2007.
17. 'Islamic Calvinists: change and conservatism in central Anatolia', *European Stability Institute*, 19 September 2005, https://www.esiweb.org/pdf/esi_document_id_69.pdf.
18. Fırat 2009.
19. 'Armenia–Turkey protocols: one year on', *Carnegie Europe*, 6 October 2010, https://carnegieeurope.eu/2010/10/06/armenia-turkey-protocols-one-year-on-event-3050.
20. Özbudun and Hale 2010: 6.
21. Güney and Karatekelioğlu 2005: 456.
22. I. Oostlander, '2003 regular report on Turkey's progress towards accession', ab.gov.tr. See also Uzgel 2009: 12.
23. Abramowitz and Barkey (2009).
24. Ibid.; D. Howden (2008) 'The world's most important political project', *The Independent*, 29 July.
25. 'Turkish foreign policy: from status quo to soft power', European Stability Initiative (ESI), April 2009, https://www.esiweb.org/pdf/esi_pict ure_story_-_turkish_foreign_policy_-_april_2009.pdf.
26. Oğuzlu 2010; Tocci 2005.
27. Özpek and Yaşar 2018: 201.
28. Kalaycıoğlu 2011: 273.
29. Angın and Bedirhanoğlu 2013.
30. 'Özelleştirmeden geldi, borçlara gitti', *Birgün*, 16 March 2018.
31. Yeldan and Ünüvar 2016.
32. Ministry of Treasury and Finance, 'Gross and net external debt stock of Turkey', https://en.hmb.gov.tr/duyuru/gross-and-net-external-debt-stock-of-turkey-as-of-31-march-2019.
33. A. Yıldırım (2019) 'Bankalarda yabancı rüzgarı esiyor', *Bloomberght*, 5 September.

78 | ILHAN UZGEL

34. 'Türkiye'nin Kaybı 157 milyar dolar', *Haber7*, 26 May 2016.
35. Akça 2014: 31.
36. See Akkaya (Chapter 10).
37. K. Okuyan (2011) 'İslamcılardan Liberal Elitistlere Nanik!', *Sol*, 31 January.
38. Kaygusuz 2018.
39. Akçay 2018.
40. Boukalas 2015: 56.
41. 'OHAL ve Başkanlık Emeğe Zararlıdır', *DİSK*, 21 July 2018, p. 5.
42. 'Erdoğan'dan itiraf: OHAL'den istifade ederek grevlere anında müdahale ediyoruz', *Cumhuriyet*, 12 July 2017.
43. 'The White House and the strongman', *The New York Times*, 27 July 2018.
44. Abramowitz and Edelman 2013.
45. J. Goldberg (2016) 'The Obama doctrine', *The Atlantic*, April.
46. S. Margon (2018) 'Giving up the high ground: America's retreat on human rights', *Foreign Affairs*, March–April.
47. G. Harris (2018) 'Trump administration withdraws the US from the UN Human Rights Council', *The New York Times*, 19 June.
48. T. Roylance (2018) 'As global democracy declines, Trump embraces dictators', *Freedom House*, 18 January.
49. Kiely 2019: 132.
50. 'Erdoğan'dan AB'ye Mülteci Tepkisi: Alnımızda Enayi Yazmıyor', BBC Türkçe, 11 February 2016.
51. European Council (2016) 'EU–Turkey statement', 18 March, https://www.consilium.europa.eu/en/press/press-releases/2016/03/18/eu-turkey-statement/.
52. European Commission 2019.

References

Abramowitz, M. and H. Barkey (2009) 'Turkey's transformers: the AKP sees big', *Foreign Affairs 88* (6): 118–28.
Abramowitz, M. and E. Edelman (2013) *From Rhetoric to Reality: Reframing US Turkey Policy*. Washington, DC: Bipartisan Policy Center.
Akça, İ. (2014) 'Hegemonic projects in post-1980 Turkey and the changing forms of authoritarianism' in İ. Akça, A. Bekmen and B. A. Özden (eds), *Turkey Reframed: Constituting Neoliberal Hegemony*. London: Pluto Press.
Akçay, Ü. (2018) 'Neoliberal populism in Turkey and its crisis'. Berlin: Institute for International Political Economy.
Akkoyunlu, K. and K. Öktem (2016) 'Existential insecurity and the making of a weak authoritarian regime in Turkey', *Southeast European and Black Sea Studies 16* (4): 505–27.
Angın, M. and P. Bedirhanoğlu (2013) 'AKP Döneminde Türkiye'de Büyük Ölçekli Özelleştirmeler ve Devletin Dönüşümü', *Praksis 30–31*: 75–95.
Boukalas, B. (2015) 'Class war-on-terror: counterterrorism, accumulation, crisis', *Critical Studies on Terrorism 8* (1): 55–71.
Coşar, S. and G. Yücesan-Özdemir (eds) (2012) *Silent Violence*. Ottawa: Red Quill Books.
Dağı, I. D. (2004) 'Rethinking human rights, democracy, and the West: post-Islamist intellectuals in Turkey', *Critique: Critical Middle Eastern Studies 13* (2): 135–51.
European Commission (2019) *Turkey 2019 Report*. Commission Staff Working Document. Brussels: European Commission, https://ec.europa.eu/neighbourhood-enlargement/sites/near/files/20190529-turkey-report.pdf.

Fırat, M. (2009) 'AKP Hükümetinin Kıbrıs Politikası' in İ. Uzgel and D. Duru (eds), *AKP Kitabı: Bir Dönüşümün Bilançosu*. Ankara: Phoenix, pp. 439–60.

Fuller, G. (2007) *The New Turkish Republic: Turkey as a Pivotal State in the Muslim World*. Washington, DC: United States Institute of Peace.

Güney, A. and P. Karatekelioğlu (2005) 'Turkey's EU candidacy and civil-military relations: challenges and prospects', *Armed Forces and Society 31* (3): 439–62.

Hale, W. (2005) 'Christian democracy and the AKP: parallels and contrasts', *Turkish Studies 6* (2): 293–310.

İlhan, S. (2000) *Avrupa Birliği'ne Hayır*. Istanbul: Ötüken Yayınları.

İnsel, A. (2003) 'The AKP and normalizing democracy in Turkey', *South Atlantic Quarterly 102* (2–3): 293–308.

Jessop, B. (2019) 'Authoritarian neoliberalism: periodization and critique', *South Atlantic Quarterly 118* (2): 343–61.

Kalaycıoğlu, E. (2011) 'The Turkish–EU odyssey and political regime change in Turkey', *South European Society and Politics 16* (2): 265–78.

Karaçimen, E. (2014) 'Financialization in Turkey: the case of consumer debt', *Journal of Balkan and Near Eastern Studies 16* (2): 161–80.

Kaygusuz, Ö. (2018) 'Authoritarian neoliberalism and regime security in Turkey: moving to an exceptional state under AKP', *South European Society and Politics 23* (2): 281–302.

Kiely, R. (2019) 'Locating Trump: paleoconservatism, neoliberalism, and anti-globalization', *The Socialist Register*, pp. 126–49.

Oğuzlu, T. (2010) 'Turkey and Europeanization of foreign policy?', *Political Science Quarterly 125* (4): 657–83.

Özbudun, E. and W. Hale (2010) *Islamism, Democracy and Liberalism in Turkey: The Case of the AKP*. London: Routledge.

Özpek, B. B. and N. Yaşar (2018) 'Populism and foreign policy in Turkey under the AKP rule', *Turkish Studies 2*: 198–216.

Rabasa, A. M. et al. (2004) *The Muslim World After 9/11*. Santa Monica, CA: Rand Corporation.

Schwedler, J. (2011) 'Can Islamists become moderates? Rethinking the inclusion-moderation hypothesis', *World Politics 63* (2): 347–76.

Tansel, C. B. (2018) 'Authoritarian neoliberalism and democratic backsliding in Turkey: beyond the narratives of progress', *South European Society and Politics 23* (2): 197–217.

Tocci, N. (2005) 'Europeanization in Turkey: trigger or anchor for reform?', *South European Society and Politics 10* (1): 73–83.

Tuğal, C. (2009) *Passive Revolution: Absorbing the Islamic Challenge to Capitalism*. Stanford, CA: Stanford University Press.

Uzgel, İ. (2009) 'AKP: Neoliberal Dönüşümün Yeni Aktörü' in İ. Uzgel and B. Duru (eds), *AKP Kitabı: Bir Dönüşümün Bilançosu*. Ankara: Phoenix, pp. 11–39.

Uzgel, İ. and B. Duru (eds) (2009) *AKP Kitabı: Bir Dönüşümün Bilançosu*. Ankara: Phoenix.

Yeldan, E. and B. Ünüvar (2016) 'An assessment of Turkish economy during the AKP era', *Research and Policy on Turkey 1* (1): 11–28.

4 | A SHIFT OF AXIS OR BUSINESS AS USUAL?: TURKEY'S S-400 PROCUREMENT DECISION AND DEFENCE INDUSTRY

Çağlar Kurç

Introduction

Turkey's decision to buy the Russian S-400 air defence system was another blow in the already strained relationship between Turkey and its Western allies. The relationship had been under stress for some time, as Turkey and the US were unable to bridge their differences on the issues of combating ISIS and PKK, the future of Syria, solving the refugee crisis, and foreign policy approaches towards Russia and Iran, while the arrests of an American pastor, a NASA employee and two Turkish employees of the US State Department in Turkey deeply scarred the relationship.[1] Despite the strained relations and continuous warnings about the procurement of a non-NATO air defence system, Turkey's decision surprised many observers.

Turkey's fixed position on the S-400 decision reignited the old shift of axis debate, as well as discussions on the possible US reaction to Turkey's decision among experts. Some view this as Turkey moving away from its traditional allies. When Turkey chose the Chinese FD-2000 (the export version of the HQ-9 air defence system) in 2013, this decision was also perceived as a flirtation with China and a pivot to the East.[2] In the face of growing problems, Daniel Pipes argued at that time that sustaining the alliance becomes increasingly difficult if Turkey does not try to align its foreign policy with that of its allies.[3] This time, Lisel Hintz commented: 'I wouldn't even call Turkey an ally. An ally doesn't behave the way in which Turkey has been behaving.'[4] Richard Haass and Steven Cook perceive the present differences as the beginning of the end for the alliance between Turkey and the West. They contend that the differences between the two states are reflections of structural changes in the international system, such as the disappearance of the anti-Soviet glue that used to hold the two together.[5] Haass puts the blame on the AKP government, while Cook thinks that the relationship has altered so significantly that a change in the government would no longer matter. According to the latter, as Turkey constructed more collaborative relations with Russia, Iran and China, the nature of the relationship needed to be adapted to these changes, thus making it a transactional one.[6] Departing from the transactional relationship, Max Hoffman argues that if Turkey deploys S-400 systems, the US should downgrade its security ties with Turkey through actions to curtail Turkey's access to American military technology, reduce the US's and NATO's footprint, and stop NATO's security investments.[7] Hence, these experts see Turkey's recent foreign and security policy moves as signs of the widening gap between Turkey and its allies.

Others disagree with the shift of axis perspective. While they recognize the differences and problems between Turkey and its allies – especially the US – they do not think that they signify a shift of axis. For them, the differences emerge from the changing dynamics of international politics and Turkey's growing desire to follow autonomous foreign policy rather than a wish to break the country's ties with the West.[8] For example, even though Turkey strives to establish good relations with Russia and Iran, it also has a NATO missile shield radar in Malatya Kürecik, with the aim of countering ballistic missile threats from Iran.[9] It is argued that there might be disagreements and differences in policies between allies as Turkey seeks to upgrade itself from 'junior partner' to 'regional power'.[10] The way to resolve these differences is for Turkey and its allies to recognize their responsibility in creating and perpetuating these problems, and to work together to find solutions that are acceptable to both sides through constructive dialogue.[11] However, even the more optimistic observers recognize the possibility of a breakdown in the relationship if both sides do not reach a compromise on the S-400 deal. Kasapoğlu and Ülgen[12] argue that the uncompromising stances of both Turkey and the US on the S-400 and F-35 damage their relationship, and that this could result in Turkey sleepwalking out of the alliance. If the US pushes Turkey away, this would only serve the interests of Russia.[13] Consequently, the future of the relationship depends on the tough choices each side should make.

Taking the latter perspective on Turkey's concern to follow autonomous foreign policy seriously, this chapter questions whether the purchase of the Russian S-400 system would provide Turkey with such an opportunity. I do this by rethinking this concern within the context of Turkey's defence-industrial development dynamics. To this end, I first problematize whether Turkey has gained anything concrete so far by its insistence on the purchase. Then, in the next part, the possible costs of this insistence on the future of the Turkish defence industry are highlighted, with a specific emphasis on the sector's high dependence on Western technology. Questioning what this purchase ultimately tells us about the quality of the decision-making process behind it, the conclusion underlines that this decision is likely to decrease rather than increase Turkey's already limited autonomy in the defence industry and that its rationality is highly dubious.

Decoding the S-400 procurement decision

There is no clear explanation why Turkey chose the S-400 system and insisted on sticking to this decision. What we know is that the S-400 decision is the result of negotiations between the two presidents, Vladimir Putin and Recep Tayyip Erdoğan, rather than a formal tender process.[14] Throughout the negotiations and following the declaration of the procurement decision, however, the Turkish government sought to hide the personalized nature of the decision by justifying it on four grounds: (1) transfer of technology; (2) superiority of the system; (3) urgent need; and (4) the US's unwillingness to sell Patriot systems to Turkey. These arguments do not hold up under critical evaluation.

Transfer of technology has been presented as the main reason that shaped Turkey's decision to buy the S-400 system from Russia. The Turkish government argued that its US and European allies failed to meet the country's transfer of technology concerns and this forced Turkey to search for other deals that included better transfer of technology offers.[15] During the S-400 negotiations, President of the Defence Industries Ismail Demir said: 'We are ready to negotiate with any country, Russia included, who would like to cooperate with us to develop a long-range air defence system.'[16] On 27 July 2017,[17] İbrahim Kalın, the then presidential spokesperson and current Special Adviser to the President of Turkey, said the purchase of the

S-400 system 'will not only meet Turkey's security needs but also bring about the transfer of this technology. This [aspect] has been put very openly in our agreement with the Russians and in talks held by our President with Putin.'[18] However, Vladimir Kozhin, Russian Presidential Aide on military-technical cooperation, declared on 29 September 2017 that there would not be any technology transfer.[19] Although the Turkish Minister of Foreign Affairs Mevlüt Çavuşoğlu still insisted that the S-400 deal involved joint production provision, and that '[i]f Russia doesn't want to comply, we'll make an agreement with another country',[20] Turkey ultimately signed the procurement contract, at least for the first two systems, without a technology transfer.[21] President Erdoğan then proposed that Turkey and Russia would jointly develop the new generation air defence system, S-500;[22] but Dmitry Peskov, the press secretary for the Russian President, mentioned technology transfer only for the S-400s.[23] In the following month, however, the CEO of Rostec Corporation Sergey Chemezov said that the negotiations were still continuing.[24] On 14 July 2019, President Erdoğan stated that optional follow-on procurement of the third S-400 system would involve indigenization and technology transfers,[25] but the Russian side argued that these issues were still being negotiated.[26] In short, neither the claim for the co-production of S-500s nor the one regarding the production of S-400 parts has been substantiated to date.

The Turkish government has persistently argued that S-400s are necessary to meet Turkey's capability gap in a high-altitude air defence system, and that this was the only solution because the West was too slow to respond to Turkey's request. Foreign Minister Çavuşoğlu said: 'Since we do not have our own missile defence system, we urgently needed this. Due to the Congress's reservations, we experienced difficulties in buying even rifles. We had to buy them from somewhere. If the US government assures us about the Congress approval, we would buy the Patriot system.'[27] President Erdoğan also argued: 'We have been demanding them [air defence systems] for years, but the answer given to us has been "The [US] Congress does not allow." We are tired of this.'[28] Various observers also stress this point. They contend that the US Congress put up various obstacles for the acquisition of armed drones and attack helicopters when Turkey needed them most, and that it does not allow technology transfer.[29] Consequently, the argument is that Turkey was 'forced' to buy the S-400 system. Its acquisition, which started in mid-July 2019 and continues in successive phases, would meet this security gap efficiently.[30] Both the government's and the observers' arguments, however, are misleading.

First, the S-400 system would be used as a stand-alone system in Turkey. It would not be integrated into Turkey's radar systems, which is part of the NATO radar network, because NATO is concerned about possible security breaches. When an air defence system is not integrated into an overall radar network, which would allow the system to see its blind spots, its effectiveness in countering missile and cruise threats decreases significantly. This means that the expected benefits of the S-400 system would not be achieved under the current conditions.[31]

Second, both the US and European countries offered good transfer of technology packages during the S-400 procurement process. The US even provided assurance of Congress approval if Turkey cancelled the process and chose to buy Patriots. However, the Turkish government rejected the US's final Patriot system offer, which came, they argued, at a very late stage – too late for Turkey to move away from the S-400 deal.[32] On the other hand, even if the US proved to be a very difficult supplier, Turkey could have always opted for the European system rather than the S-400. Indeed, it had already done so: in 2018, Turkey concluded a study programme on the joint development of a high-altitude air and ballistic missile defence system, SAMP-T, with Eurosam,[33] which included various options that could satisfy Turkey's demands.

Finally, despite the differences and problems with NATO, it continues to support Turkey's defence. NATO approved the deployment of air defence units on 4 December 2012, and Dutch, German and US units were deployed in January 2013.[34] Currently, Italian and Spanish air defence units are deployed in the south-east of Turkey.[35] NATO provided assistance to deal with the missile threat and did not leave Turkey unprotected. All in all, Turkey's decision to buy S-400s is hard to justify on the basis of a technical security gap argument.

The weakness of the government's justifications for the S-400 decision has led many observers to link the decision to other factors. Some argue that the S-400 decision could be a 'coup-proofing' measure to protect the airspace around key government installations from high-performance aircraft in the case of another coup attempt.[36] According to Stein, this could explain why Turkey is also collaborating with Eurosam[37] – S-400 against internal threats, SAMP-T against external threats. However, this argument does not seem to hold true: if there were a coup, the plotters would ultimately find a way to control the S-400 system as well. Others link the issue to Turkey's Syria policy and argue that the S-400 would allow Turkey a breathing space and accommodate resurgent Russia in the region.[38] The recent Russian–Syrian encirclement of the Idlib pocket controlled by Turkish forces proves that the link between the two is not very secure.[39] Ultimately, these are all attempts to make sense of the rationality behind a rather opaque decision-making process, which not only defines defence policy but also other policy fields. The main problem is that Turkey's foreign policy lacks consistency and is full of contradictions, and given the opaque nature of foreign policymaking, it is hard to clearly identify the process at work. However, no matter why this decision was taken, it is clear that it puts defence-industrial relations between Turkey and the West, as well as Turkey's previous security strategies, at risk. The next section problematizes the possible adverse implications of the S-400 purchase on Turkey's defence-industrial development trajectory.

At risk: defence-industrial cooperation and integration between Turkey and the West

Partnerships with foreign defence companies have been considered critical in Turkey since the 1980s, with the anticipation that these would ensure the acquisition of military technology and know-how, and facilitate the development of local production with export capabilities. To name some examples, Rolls-Royce (UK) and the Kale Group established TAEC Engine Company (Rolls-Royce 51 per cent; Kale 49 per cent) for the development of an engine that will be used in the national fighter plane (TF-X) project. The Kale Group formed another joint venture with Pratt & Whitney (US) to provide maintenance for the F-35 engines. In the land systems sector, FMC Corporation (US) (now BAE Systems (UK)) and Nurol established FNSS as a joint venture to produce tracked and wheeled armoured vehicles, combat engineering vehicles and turrets.[40]

As Turkish companies acquired capability in integrating different subsystems and components as well as designing indigenous platforms, the content of cooperation with foreign companies has become more complex. Otokar, for instance, acquired technical support from Hyundai Rotem (South Korea) during the development phase of the Altay main battle tank and integrated both the engine (MTU) and transmission package (Renk) from Germany.[41] The T-129 attack and reconnaissance helicopter uses a CTS800-4A turboshaft engine from LHTEC (USA).[42] Besides joint ventures for locally produced weapons systems, Turkish defence companies have started taking part in the international arms trade and running collaborative projects through subcontracting agreements.

The Presidency of Defence Industries (*Savunma Sanayii Başkanlığı* or SSB) encourages Turkish defence companies' international cooperation, especially with Western companies, as a state policy in various official policy documents. Both the 2012–16 Strategic Plan and 2017–21 International Cooperation and Export Strategy Document express the significance of establishing cooperative relations within Western security structures. The 2012–16 Strategic Plan states: 'We believe that membership in European procurement agencies, such as the European Defence Agency and OCCAR [Organisation for Joint Armament Cooperation], provides a fertile ground for joint-production project development and collaboration ... We sought to increase the share of Turkish defence companies in NATO procurement projects and organize the relationship between defence companies and NATO agencies.'[43] In similar fashion, the 2017–21 International Cooperation and Export Strategy Document states: 'Departing from a holistic approach, we aim to increase the active participation of Turkish companies in NATO ... and increase the effect of NATO cooperative armaments programmes in the industrialization process.'[44] Thus, collaborations, particularly with Western companies, are considered important in the provision of military technology and export revenues.

Indeed, Turkish defence companies' participation in collaborative production and procurement projects has made the defence industry increasingly integrated into the production networks of the West, creating complex linkages of dependency.[45] For example, Turkish companies participated in an OCCAR project producing vehicles such as the A400M tactical and strategic cargo plane. Roketsan became the subcontractor of Raytheon (USA) for the production of a key component in the international sales of the

Patriot Guidance-Enhanced Missile-Tactical (GEM-T) system in 2009. Furthermore, ten Turkish companies (Alp Aviation, Aselsan, Ayesas, Fokker Elmo, Havelsan, Kale Aerospace, Mikes, Roketsan, TUBITAK-Sage and TAI) participated in the F-35 programme.[46] This enabled them to take an active role in both the production and lifecycle phases (logistics and maintenance services) of the F-35, thereby creating long-term integration into global production networks and the flow of income. According to the SASAD *Defense and Aerospace Industry Performance Report,* the US is the leading customer (at US$698 million) of Turkish defence companies, followed by Europe (US$521 million).[47] Exports to the US and Europe are the results of offset agreements (a return on Turkey's procurement of Western weapons systems) rather than simply of exports of Turkish-made weapons systems.

Turkey continues to procure major weapons systems and major subsystems (such as engines) from Western suppliers in order to continue production in the defence industry. Western companies are also the main source of arms. Between 2012 and 2016, Turkey's major arms suppliers have been as follows: USA (63.31 per cent), Italy (11.59 per cent), Spain (9.26 per cent), South Korea (8.05 per cent), the Netherlands (3.01 per cent), Germany (2.25 per cent), Israel (0.87 per cent), China (0.74 per cent), France (0.49 per cent), Canada (0.28 per cent) and Denmark (0.19 per cent).[48] Therefore, Turkey depends heavily on Western sources to continue its defence industrialization, increase its production capabilities, acquire military technology, sustain its defence-industry companies through collaborative projects, and strengthen its defence base. This dependency, especially on the US and European countries, acts as a limiting factor in Turkey's foreign relations and defence policy.

It was this integrated and dependent nature of defence-industrial relations between Turkey and the West that made experts expect Turkey to reverse its S-400 decision, as it had done before in relation to the procurement of the Chinese FD-2000 system.[49] Indeed, following the declaration of Turkey's interest in the S-400, the US offered various alternatives such as the Medium Extended Air Defense System (MEADS)[50] and a renewed and better Patriot deal to Turkey. Yet, these yielded no results.[51] The US's initial response has been a delay in the delivery of F-35s and a threat to impose sanctions on Turkey, according to the Countering America's Adversaries

Through Sanctions Act (CAATSA).[52] On 1 April 2019, the US halted the shipment of F-35 parts to Turkey,[53] which was followed by the suspension of the F-35 training programme for Turkish pilots and technical staff.[54] Despite these open warnings, Turkish policy-makers possibly believed that the US was bluffing, so they repeatedly mentioned that Turkey was an integral part of the F-35 project. They argued that, if Turkey was removed from the project, the F-35 production would fail; that there was indeed no legal basis for the country's removal; and thus that the US could not remove Turkey from the programme.[55] However, following the delivery of the S-400s, the US removed Turkey from the F-35 programme.[56] While there is still a slight chance for Turkey to return to the programme, currently this removal has severe implications for the country.

First, from the perspective of Turkey's defence and security needs, removal from the F-35 project would alter the country's force planning. Turkey has been planning to replace its ageing F-4E 2020s with F-35As from 2020 onwards. If the delivery of F-35As is delayed significantly or cancelled altogether, it will put more pressure on Turkey's F-16s, as they also need to fill the gap created by retirement of the F-4E 2020s. Furthermore, Turkey was planning to procure the F-35B short take-off/vertical landing variant. The removal of Turkey from the F-35 project means that the multi-purpose amphibious assault ship (LHD) TCG *Anadolu* will be left without a fighter wing because there are no other short take-off and vertical landing aircraft available in the international market.[57] For the air force, Turkey is now searching for interim solutions, ranging from modernization of the F-16 fleet (which requires US coopera-tion) to buying aircrafts from Russia.[58]

Second, the removal would negatively affect the Turkish defence companies that participated in the F-35 programme. There are ten different defence companies working in the F-35 project as well as numerous small and medium-sized enterprises that work with these major companies. According to Lockheed Martin, the total value of Turkey's industrial participation in the F-35 programme was estimated to reach more than US$12 billion.[59] Turkey's removal from the programme means a significant loss of work and profit for the participating Turkish companies and their local sup-pliers. Furthermore, under the original plans, Turkey was going to produce its own Pratt & Whitney F135 engines and host the first regional engine overhaul depot, which would mean additional income for Turkish companies.[60] Yet this has also vanished with the removal decision.

If the US chooses to extend the suspension of defence-industrial cooperation with Turkey, it will inhibit certain procurement programmes that have American inputs in the short term, such as the T-129 ATAK helicopter, S-70 utility helicopter and MilGem corvette. Despite the political tensions, Turkey is still heavily reliant on its NATO allies and its firms remain deeply enmeshed in Western production networks, as mentioned above. If the US slows down the sale of components, including engines, armaments and spare parts, or if other deals, such as offset contracts, are cancelled, Turkey's defence industry could find itself facing a supply crisis, at least in the short run.[61] On the other hand, this would be counterproductive for the US as Turkey might switch to other suppliers, such as Russia and China, while deepening the rift between the US and Turkey.

Conclusion

While the S-400 procurement is a critical juncture in Turkish foreign policy and defence policy, it does not represent a shift of axis by itself mainly because it does not alter the continuing dependence of Turkey on Western suppliers. Turkey's long-lasting defence-industrial cooperation with the West has produced a specific dependency relation for Turkey. As long as the dependencies continue, Turkish foreign policy will continue to be somewhat aligned with the West in order to protect defence-industrial cooperation. If the shift of axis is really happening, we would expect to see a substantial change in Turkey's defence-industrial relations. At the time of writing, we observed neither a significant change in defence-industrial relations nor a desire for such a change, insofar as the SSB's strategic planning implies.

Yet Erdoğan's decision to buy the S-400, taken arguably for the sake of defence autonomy, would have significant counterproductive implications as it could seriously harm the development of the Turkish defence sector, at least in the short term. Turkey's decision could also yield unintended consequences, such as breaking long-established defence-industrial relations and creating a new dependency on Russia and a significant change in Turkish foreign policy.

Given that none of the available defence-industrial explanations for why Turkey opted for the Russian S-400 system seem logical – or, at best, are highly risky – I conclude that this purchase can only make sense if understood as an outcome of a personalized and opaque decision-making process, revealing the increasingly authoritarian character of the regime in Turkey. This is a decision that has underestimated the US's response, overlooked the dependency of the Turkish defence industry on the West, and ignored the risks of a Russia-dependent security structure. Whatever its motivations, it has ultimately narrowed rather than enhanced Turkey's capacity to follow autonomous foreign policy and weakened its negotiation power vis-à-vis the US in other foreign policy matters.

Notes

1. E. Edelman and J. Sullivan (2018) 'Turkey is out of control: time for the US to say so', *Politico*, 13 February.

2. C. Hoyos and A. Amann (2013) 'Turkey builds domestic defence industry', *Financial Times*, 9 October; C. Sidar (2013) 'Turkey's unwise pivot to the East', *Bloomberg*, 7 October.

3. D. Pipes (2014) 'Who lost Turkey?', *The Weekly Standard*, 13 October.

4. Cited in A. Ward (2019) 'How America's relationship with Turkey fell apart', *Vox*, 11 April.

5. Cook 2018; Haass 2018.

6. Cook 2018.

7. Hoffman 2019.

8. S. Ünay (2017) 'Is Turkey's foreign policy axis shifting toward Eurasia?', *Daily Sabah*, 27 October.

9. 'Turkey to site Nato missile shield radar in its south-east', *The Guardian*, 14 September 2011.

10. Kibaroğlu and Sazak 2015: 108–9.

11. M. Singh and J. F. Jeffrey (2018) 'The US alliance with Turkey is worth preserving', *Foreign Policy*, 19 March; Kibaroğlu and Sazak 2015; S. Sazak (2018) 'The US–Turkey relationship is worse off than you think', *Foreign Policy*, 11 September; S. Sazak and Ç.

Kurç (2018) 'Turkey's slow-cooking crisis with its allies is coming to a boil', *Defense One*, 22 June; A. Sloat (2018) 'The United States and Turkey should fix their relationship – before it's too late', *Foreign Policy*, 14 February.

12. Kasapoğlu and Ülgen 2018.

13. Kirişci and Köstem 2018.

14. 'Rusya: Türkiye'ye hava savunma sistemi sevkiyatı gündemde', *Sputnik*, 7 November 2016; 'Putin and Erdoğan discuss S-400 missile system deliveries to Turkey', TASS: Russian News Agency, 3 May 2017; 'Russia ready to supply advanced S-400 air defense missile systems to Turkey', TASS: Russian News Agency, 1 June 2017.

15. C. Kasapoğlu (2019) 'How Turkey's NATO allies "successfully" advertised S-400?', Anadolu Agency, 20 March.

16. 'Rusya'yla uzun menzilli hava savunma sistemini görüşmeye hazırız', *Sputnik*, 8 November 2016.

17. President Erdoğan announced the S-400 deal with Russia on 25 July 2017. See 'Erdoğan announces deal with Russia on S-400 air defense missile systems', TASS: Russian News Agency, 25 July 2017.

18. 'Russia agreed to transfer technology along with S-400 missile systems', *Hürriyet Daily News*, 28 July 2017.

19. 'Россия не передаст Турции технологии в рамках поставки С-400', Interfax.ru, 29 September 2017.

20. B. E. Bekdil (2017) 'Turkish procurement saga weighs Russian S-400 deal against pleasing the West', *Defense News*, 6 November.

21. 'Сделай там. Коммерсантъ', *Kommersant*, 10 October 2017.

22. 'Erdoğan: Putin'le S-500 görüşmelerimiz de oldu, işi S-400'lerle bitirmeyi düşünmüyoruz', *Sputnik*, 13 October 2017.

23. 'Kremlin: S-400 anlaşması, Türkiye'ye kısmi teknoloji transferini öngörüyor', *Sputnik*, 29 June 2019.

24. 'S-400'lerin belirli parçaları Türkiye'de üretilebilir', *Gazete Duvar*, 22 July 2019.

25. Directorate of Communications 2019.

26. 'Rusya: Türkiye'ye S-400'ün tüm unsurlarının sevkiyatı yapıldı', *Sputnik*, 23 October 2019.

27. 'Mevlüt Çavuşoğlu'ndan S-400 açıklaması', *Kokpit Aero*, 11 May 2019.

28. 'Turkey–Russia S-400 deal in response to US threats', PressTV, 16 June 2018.

29. C. Kasapoğlu (2019) 'How Turkey's NATO allies "successfully" advertised S-400?', Anadolu Agency, 20 March; Kibaroğlu 2019.

30. 'Turkey–Russia S-400 deal in response to US threats', PressTV, 16 June 2018.

31. Egeli 2018: 85–8.

32. S. Hacaoğlu and F. Kozok (2019) 'Turkey rejects latest US offer to sell Patriot missiles', Bloomberg, 1 March.

33. P. Tran and B. E. Bekdil (2018) 'Turkey goes European for indigenous air defense system,' *Defense News*, 8 January.

34. NATO 2013.

35. 'Spain extends air defense system deployment in Turkey', *Daily Sabah*, 18 June 2019; 'Italy extends duration of missile system in SE Turkey', *Hürriyet Daily News*, 5 July 2019.

36. A. Stein (2017) 'Ankara's look East: how Turkey's warming ties with Russia threaten its place in the transatlantic community', *War on the Rocks*, 27 December; B. Zilberman (2017) 'The S-400: Erdoğan's fail-safe', *FDD*, 3 November.

37. A. Stein (2017) 'Ankara's look East: how Turkey's warming ties with Russia threaten its place in the transatlantic community', *War on the Rocks*, 27 December.

38. Kardaş 2019; Sedat Ergin (2019) 'S-400'lerin hangi yönü daha baskın, askeri mi, yoksa siyasi mi?', *Hürriyet*, 13 August.

39. H. Barkey (2019) 'Putin plays Erdoğan like a fiddle', *Foreign Policy*, 3 September.

40. See http://www.fnss.com.tr.

41. 'Otokar Altay MBT: land warfare platforms: armoured fighting vehicles', https://janes-ihs-com.ezproxy.cul.columbia.edu/Janes/Display/1494423.

42. 'TAI (AgustaWestland) T129 ATAK' in *Jane's All the World's Aircraft*. The Lakes, UK: Jane's. Also see Kurç 2017.

43. SSM 2009: 64.

44. SSM 2017: 8.

45. Kurç 2017.

46. C. Akalın (2018) 'Lockheed Martin opens F-35 JSF production base to Turkish journalists', *Defence Turkey Magazine* 84.

47. The share of the rest of the world is US$969 million. See SASAD 2019.

48. Blanchfield et al. 2017.

49. G. Tsiboukis (2015) 'Turkey scraps HQ-9/FD-2000 Chinese air defence system after two years of negotiations', *DCSS News*, 18 November.

50. B. E. Bekdil (2017) 'New terms offered for a Turkish MEADS missile-defense system', *Defense News*, 8 February.

51. S. Hacaoğlu and F. Kozok (2019) 'Turkey rejects latest US offer to sell Patriot missiles', Bloomberg, 1 March.

52. A. Hanna (2017) 'Cardin, Turkey's purchase of Russian missile system may trigger sanctions', *Politico*, 14 September.

53. C. Clark (2019) 'US halts F-35 parts shipments to Turkey', *Breaking Defense*, 1 April.

54. B. Starr, Z. Cohen and N. Hodge (2019) 'US air force halts Turkish F-35 pilot training amid Russia dispute', CNN, 11 June.

55. D. Reid (2019) 'F-35 jet program will fail without Turkey's support, President Erdoğan says', CNBC, 30 April; M. Sofuoğlu (2019) 'Turkey thinks that the US cannot kick Ankara out from the F-35 deal', TRT World, 23 May.

56. A. Williams (2019) 'Trump formally expels Turkey from F-35 programme', *Financial Times*, 17 July.

57. S. Kahraman (2019) 'F-35 suspension reveals fake defence reports in Turkish media', *Ahval*, 23 July.

58. R. Aboulafia (2019) 'Turkey after the F-35: choice for alternative fighter will help shape country's future', *Forbes*, 21 July.

59. C. Akalın (2018) 'Lockheed Martin opens F-35 JSF production base to Turkish journalists', *Defence Turkey Magazine* 84.

60. S. Sazak and Ç. Kurç (2018) 'Turkey's slow-cooking crisis with its allies is coming to a boil', *Defense One*, 22 June.

61. Ibid.

References

Blanchfield, K., P. D. Wezeman and S. T. Wezeman (2017) 'The state of major arms transfers in 8 graphics', Stockholm International Peace Research Institute, 22 February, https://www.sipri.org/commentary/blog/2017/state-major-arms-transfers-8-graphics.

Cook, S. A. (2018) 'Trump is the first president to get Turkey right', Council on Foreign Relations blog, 13 August, https://www.cfr.org/blog/trump-first-president-get-turkey-right-0.

Directorate of Communications (2019) 'Cumhurbaşkanı Erdoğan: "S-400'leri alarak barışı ve kendi milli güvenliğimizi garanti altına almaya çalışıyoruz"', Presidency of the Republic of Turkey, Directorate of Communications, https://www.iletisim.gov.tr/turkce/haberler/detay/cumhurbaskani-erdogan-s-400leri-alarak-barisi-ve-kendi-milli-guvenligimizi-garanti-altina-almaya-calisiyoruz/.

Egeli, S. (2018) 'Making sense of Turkey's air and missile defense merry-go-round', *All Azimuth 8* (1): 69–92.

Haass, R. N. (2018) 'The West must face reality in Turkey', Project Syndicate, 15 August, https://www.project-syndicate.org/commentary/turkey-broken-relationship-with-the-west-by-richard-n--haass-2018-08.

Hoffman, M. (2019) 'Responding to Turkey's purchase of Russia's S-400 missile system', Center for American Progress, 21 March, https://www.americanprogress.org/issues/security/reports/2019/03/21/467518/responding-turkeys-purchase-russias-s-400-missile-system/.

Kardaş, S. (2019) 'Turkey's S400 vs. *F35 conundrum and its deepening strategic partnership with Russia*', German Marshall Fund of the

United States, 28 May, http://www.gmfus.org/publications/turkeys-s400-vs-f35-conundrum-and-its-deepening-strategic-partnership-russia.

Kasapoğlu, C. and S. Ülgen (2018) 'Is Turkey sleepwalking out of the alliance? An assessment of the F-35 deliveries and the S-400 acquisition'. *Foreign Policy & Security 2018/6*. Istanbul: EDAM.

Kibaroğlu, M. (2019) 'On Turkey's missile defense strategy: the four faces of the S-400 deal between Turkey and Russia'. SAM Papers 16. *Ankara: Center for Strategic Research, Republic of Turkey Ministry of Foreign Affairs*, http://sam.gov.tr/wp-content/uploads/2019/04/SAM-Papers-No.-16.pdf.

Kibaroğlu, M, and S. C. Sazak (2015) 'Business as usual: the US–Turkey security partnership', *Middle East Policy 22* (4): 98–112.

Kirişci, K. and S. Köstem (2018) 'Don't let Russian S-400s peel Turkey away from the West',

Brookings, 18 December, https://www.brookings.edu/blog/order-from-chaos/2018/12/18/dont-let-russian-s-400s-peel-turkey-away-from-the-west/.

Kurç, Ç. (2017) 'Between defence autarky and dependency: the dynamics of Turkish defence industrialization', *Defence Studies 17* (3): 260–81.

NATO (2013) 'NATO support to Turkey: background and timeline', NATO, 19 February, http://www.nato.int/cps/en/natohq/topics_92555.htm.

SASAD (2019) *SASAD Performans Raporu 2018*. Ankara: Savunma ve Havacılık Sanayii İmalatçılar Derneği.

SSM (2009) *2009–2016 Savunma Sanayii Sektörel Strateji Dokümanı* [2009–16 Defence Industry Sector Strategy Document]. Ankara: SSM.

SSM (2017) *2017–2021 Uluslararası İşbirliği İhracat Stratejik Plan* [2017–21 International Cooperation Export Strategic Plan]. Ankara: SSM, https://www.ssb.gov.tr/Images/Uploads/MyContents/F_2017052 315200118882.pdf.

PART II

POLITICS OF ECONOMIC MANAGEMENT

5 | UNDERSTANDING THE RECENT RISE OF AUTHORITARIANISM IN TURKEY IN TERMS OF THE STRUCTURAL CONTRADICTIONS OF THE PROCESS OF CAPITAL ACCUMULATION

Fuat Ercan and Şebnem Oğuz[1]

Introduction

The recent turn towards authoritarian state practices in Turkey and globally has been the subject of numerous scholarly studies. What makes the Turkish case particularly difficult to analyse is the pace and unpredictability of the political developments, which constantly invalidate the concepts used to define the process. In this context, one needs to be even more cautious of characterizations based on hasty generalizations of short-term tendencies. This chapter tries to overcome this difficulty by confining its focus to the long-term, structural roots of the recent move towards authoritarianism in the contradictions of the process of capital accumulation.[2] In doing this, it will differentiate between the two types of causal dynamics for nation states in the face of global capitalism: first, the necessity to internalize and reproduce the requirements of the global capital accumulation process; and second, the more contingent forms through which this necessity is realized historically and through country-specific political and class actors.[3] The most important short-term actors in this regard are political parties in power, which contingently use the long-term state mechanisms necessary for the reproduction of capital accumulation. The total reproduction of capitalist societies requires the reproduction of capital accumulation, the state and the ruling parties.[4] Since the reproduction of all these components does not take place at the same time, contradictions among them as well as between these components and global dynamics lead to non-synchronous problems. To demonstrate this process, we need to look at the changing functioning of all these components over time. In late capitalist countries, the process of reproduction of the conditions of accumulation is realized in two phases. In the first, the conditions necessary for the creation of surplus value must be constructed, and in the second the conditions for the rapid expansion of surplus value through internationalization and the transition to relative surplus value production must be secured. Thus, in this second phase, the ruling parties must secure the conditions of both surplus value creation and relative surplus value production for different sections of capital that participate in the global accumulation process at different speeds.

In the Turkish case, these two phases correspond to the decades from the 1950s to the late 1970s and the post-1980 period respectively. As will be demonstrated below, the inability to make the transition to increased relative surplus value production in the second phase has been the most important weakness of Turkish capitalism, with important implications for the state form. The AKP's rise to power in 2002 was based on the expectation that it would expedite this transition as well as secure the conditions of surplus production for all sections of capital, and therefore the total reproduction of capitalist society. As the AKP failed to secure these conditions, particularly in the 2010s, it increasingly resorted to authoritarian measures to maintain its political power, preparing the ground for its own tendency to collapse that culminated in the 2018 economic crisis and its defeat in the March 2019 local elections. From this perspective, the AKP's rule can be roughly divided into three periods: (1) adoption of policies aiming at internationalization through increased relative surplus value production and the restructuring of state economic apparatuses (2002–10); (2) failure to increase relative surplus production and further authoritarian transformation of the state so as to create new financial resources to postpone crisis dynamics (2010–18); and (3) crisis of postponement mechanisms and the AKP's move towards collapse (2018 onwards). In what follows, we will explain how this happened.

Capital accumulation in late capitalist countries: 'structural change' and 'change within the structure'

In a late capitalist country such as Turkey, the contradictions of capital accumulation and the changing form of the state in response to these contradictions need to be discussed through an analysis of the changing phases of accumulation, which we call 'structural change' and 'change within structure'. 'Structural change' refers to the transition from an agricultural-based pre-capitalist society to a capitalist one, and 'change within the structure' refers to the changes within capitalist society through the differentiation of accumulation processes. In late capitalist countries, the 'structural changes' and 'changes within structure' generally occur simultaneously and in interaction with the dynamics of the international accumulation process, so the relationship between the state and capital takes hybrid forms. The fact that capital accumulation in Turkey takes place in the context of a changing global accumulation process as well as pre-capitalist relations of production leads to problems not only in the sphere of accumulation but also in the total reproduction of society. Different phases of intensification and deepening of capital correspond to different forms of integration within the global accumulation process. Unlike advanced capitalist countries, late capitalist countries face crisis dynamics in the realization sphere in the form of decreasing exports if they cannot supply foreign exchange for the import of capital goods. Thus, the articulation of global capital circuits leads to different power conflicts on the part of advanced and late capitalist states. It is in this context that Poulantzas has rightfully argued that, 'given the deepening division between dominant and dominated countries of the imperialist chain – a result of the internationalization of capitalist relations – we cannot engage in general theorization about the contemporary State covering transformations of these countries as a whole'.[5] In late capitalist countries such as Turkey, production starts in labour-intensive sectors and capital goods must be imported in order to produce consumption goods. As production increases in labour-intensive sectors, more imports of capital goods and therefore more foreign exchange are needed. This limitation can be overcome only through a transition to increased relative surplus production, which in turn necessitates a series of structural changes such as a transformation of the education system for the training of qualified labour power as well as investment in research and development activities. However, although this is a necessity for the collective interests of capital and the long-term plans of states, individual capitalists or political parties in power act according to their own short-term interests. Therefore, instead of making the structural changes necessary for increasing relative surplus production, political parties in power might resort to a series of mechanisms for postponing the crisis dynamics.

This has been the case for the capital accumulation process in Turkey in the post-1980 period. Short-term opportunities posed by integration with global capital circuits were used for obtaining foreign exchange, first through the internationalization of commercial capital in the 1980s, and then through the internalization of money capital in the 1990s. As these mechanisms failed to secure the total reproduction of society, a new attempt to increase relative surplus value through structural changes known as Post-Washington Consensus (PWC) reforms was initiated after the 2001 crisis in line with the demands of global and internationalized domestic capitals. The AKP came to power in this context, but its policies failed to meet these demands in the long term. This is because the increase in constant capital in certain sectors was realized through imports of necessary inputs without a change in the organic composition of capital. As the return on exports was limited, this led to a deadlock in production, in a pattern described by Hirschman as the major setback of developing countries.[6] So, positive economic growth and exports went together with negative balance of payments deficits and unemployment, leading to a crisis of both the reproduction of accumulation and the ruling party. As a response, the AKP increased its mechanisms of control over labour through restrictions on trade union rights, the precarization of labour and increased absolute surplus value production. In the absence of an improvement of productive forces, however, these mechanisms could not secure the expansion of value necessary for the total reproduction of society. The AKP therefore resorted to other mechanisms such as the commodification of nature and public services. This was made possible through an increasing concentration of power within the executive branch, adoption of the presidential system, and the personalization of power in the hands of Erdoğan, initiating a move towards collapse, the signals of which are discussed below.

Signals of contradictions in the accumulation process

In late capitalist countries, structural change and change within the structure are revealed at two different levels: signals such as prices, which are reflections of class relations; and visible social outcomes such as unemployment and poverty levels. Among the major signals of the accumulation process are: commodity prices (inflation or deflation); wages as the price of labour power; interest rates as the price of money (producer–consumer credit); exchange rates as the price of national currencies vis-à-vis foreign currencies (these are weaker in late capitalist countries); the prices of public services provided by the state; and taxes as the share the state gets from the total wealth created. All these prices are determined by a series of inner connections in the process of total reproduction of society mentioned above. The failure of the total reproduction of society can become visible in outcomes such as an increase in producer and consumer debt, a decline in production, an increase in unemployment rates and the state cutting back financial resources. The most important among these outcomes, from the perspective of the general population, is the increase in poverty. Analysis of these indicators is important for understanding the transformation of political regimes. For instance, we can see that all military coups in Turkish political history were preceded by large currency devaluations. Although this correlation between devaluations and military coups seems like a repetition, each of these devaluations corresponded to different periods of change within the structure. Thus, despite the similarities between the conditions preceding the 1960 and 1980 military coups, we can see that they corresponded to different phases of capital accumulation.

The devaluation of the Turkish lira is not only related to imports and exports but also to the structural constraints of production in late capitalist countries such as Turkey. Thus 'financial dependency' is not only a result of external dynamics but a direct extension of these structural constraints. When we look at signals only (devaluation of the Turkish lira, increasing interest rates and balance of payments deficits), we can observe a continuity in all economic crises since the 1960s. But we can also see that there is a differentiation of accumulation dynamics and restructuring of state apparatuses as well as an inability to overcome some structural problems.[7] For instance, there are important parallels between the signals of the 2001 crisis that brought the AKP to power and the signals of the 2018–19 crisis that accelerated its decline. Signals of the 2001 crisis included the rise of inflation to 55 per cent, devaluation of 50 per cent and the decline in real wages by 20 per cent. These were followed by social outcomes such as the rise of the unemployment rate to 10 per cent, decline of the growth rate from 6.4 per cent in 1984–87 to 1.6 per cent in 1988–89, the rise of the poverty rate to 42 per cent in agriculture,

50 per cent in the construction sector, 60 per cent among temporary workers, and 38 per cent among the self-employed in the trade sector.[8] When we look at the annual inflation rate today, we see that it rose from 17.90 per cent to 24.52 per cent between 2002 and 2019, and we are now witnessing a peak.[9] The Central Bank had managed to hold down interest rates in response to political pressure from Erdoğan, who long criticized the 'interest rate lobby'. This policy ended when the Central Bank increased interest rates from 17.25 per cent to 24 per cent. There was also a devaluation of 57 per cent between January and August 2018.[10] Turkey's external debt rose from US$386 billion in 2002 to US$4,932 billion in the second half of 2018.[11] The similarity between the signals of the two crises shows the nature of unresolved structural problems of accumulation. These signals also show why the AKP rapidly used the repressive and ideological apparatuses of the state to increase its capacity for manoeuvre in the face of these unresolved problems. Thus, understanding the relation of price signals and social outcomes to contradictions of the accumulation process and the role of the state in managing those contradictions will help us explain the political economy of the move towards authoritarianism.

The AKP's failure to perform some basic functions of capitalist states

There are three main functions that capitalist states must perform for the total reproduction of society: (1) maintaining the general conditions of production; (2) securing the conditions for the improvement of productive forces, particularly relative surplus value production; and (3) providing a favourable investment climate for capital operating at the global scale and making the necessary institutional changes for the internationalization of domestic capital and the internalization of global capital.[12] As the AKP failed to perform these three functions, it adopted policies that would decrease its financial burden and create new resources for the material reproduction of the state. So, let us have a closer look at how it failed to do this.

When the AKP government came to power following the 2000–01 crisis, it articulated the need for structural reforms of capital operating at the global scale and took steps in implementing such reforms. However, in time it increasingly turned to the 'contingent necessity' of prioritizing the demands of those sections of capital that could not articulate with the global accumulation process and shifted its emphasis to the promotion of labour-intensive sectors, and more recently began to use a discourse of supporting 'domestic and national production' through a critique of the 'interest rate lobby', 'foreign exchange lobby' and European capital. Mainstream or institutionalist economists approach this problem through concepts such as the 'middle-income trap' or 'early deindustrialization'[13] and put the blame for failure in this area on the wrong economic policies. From a Marxist perspective, however, the failure to make a transition to increased relative surplus value production must be explained through the inner contradictions of capital accumulation. The transition to relative surplus value requires a shift away from labour-intensive sectors such as textiles and construction, and thereby means an increase in the organic composition of capital. However, this requirement cannot be met because of both the insufficiency of capital and the government's preference for keeping these sectors (especially the construction sector) alive so that it can use them for employment and patronage relationships.[14]

Despite this, the AKP government was relatively successful in terms of economic growth between 2002 and 2011, with a growth rate of 4–6 per cent. This was made possible through the inflow of foreign money capital due to the policies of high interest rates and the overvalued Turkish lira, the major class preference of big internationalized capital groups. However, this growth was not accompanied by a transition to relative surplus value production, or 'high value-added' industries in mainstream terms. As Yükseler notes, the ratio of total value added to production in the manufacturing industry declined from 34 per cent in 2003 to 29.4 per cent in 2013.[15] Between 2003 and 2014, there was a decline in the number of capitalist enterprises, wage labourers and total value added, as seen in the Table 5.1.

The AKP also failed to complete the necessary institutional changes known as PWC reforms for the internationalization and internalization of capital, which were initiated in 2001. Following the 2001 crisis, the new institutionalist paradigm, which reflected the interests of global and internationalized big domestic capital, also offered recipes for late capitalist countries such as Turkey. The vigorous funding provided by the IMF and World Bank not only served the transformation of the Turkish state apparatus in line with these

TABLE 5.1 The ratio of the manufacturing industry in the Turkish economy (per cent)

	2003	2014
Percentage of enterprises	13.48	12.45
Percentage of employees	32.55	26.79
Percentage of salary-wage earners	40.86	29.74
Salary-wage payments	41.68	32.55
Total value added	39.75	34.44
Production value	51.11	43.91

Source: Yükseler (2016).

recipes but also helped overcome the state's financial constraints. Kemal Derviş, the minister responsible for the economy at the time, used the expression 'we will prepare the ground, and you will score a goal' to describe this process. The creation of new institutions such as independent regulatory agencies and the strengthening of existing ones led to the concentration of power in the executive branch, thereby consolidating what Poulantzas called 'authoritarian statism'.[16] These institutional changes initially increased the AKP governments' capacity to manoeuvre, but at the same time they unleashed a series of conflicts within capital, as they primarily served the interests of big internationalized capital groups. This is an important problem area in state–capital relations in late capitalist countries. Internationalized capital needs not only proper price mechanisms but also institutions that regulate those mechanisms, such as a central bank. This necessity is a source of conflict between newly growing domestic capital and internationalized capital, which is actively mediated by the state. When the AKP came to power, it appealed to all sections of capital. As it made attempts to facilitate the integration of Turkish capitalism in the global accumulation process, however, the conflicts between big internationalized capital groups and the newly growing small and medium-sized enterprises (SMEs) increased and the AKP chose to adopt policies supporting the latter.[17]

Despite the huge amount of support it gave to these capital groups, the bulk of the total surplus value in Turkey was still created by big internationalized capital, which demanded regulations facilitating the acceleration of the transition to increased relative surplus value production. As the AKP failed to make this transition, the structural necessity for foreign exchange in order to import capital goods increased. As indicated above, a policy of an overvalued Turkish lira and high interest rates was necessary in order to secure the inflow of foreign exchange. This policy harmed the SMEs that formed AKP's support base. So, as the AKP had to continue surplus value creation through the import of capital goods, it also attempted to secure the support of SMEs that were adversely affected by this process by decreasing interest rates at the expense of the elimination of the independence of the Central Bank. In the same vein, in 2011, the AKP government issued a series of decree laws that would make substantial changes in central administration whereby all regulatory agencies would be politically controlled by their respective ministries through a process that has been called the 're-politicization of economic management'. Thus, by 2011, it had already retreated from the 'depoliticized' economic management initiated after the 2001 crisis.[18]

Having said that, the AKP governments used the increased institutional capacity provided by the PWC reforms not for the structural transformation of the accumulation model towards relative surplus value production but for making regulations that would facilitate the creation of new spheres of commodification to please all sectors of capital and the wider sections of society that formed the AKP's support base, as well as raise revenue for the party. As the AKP failed to reproduce the conditions of capital accumulation and the state, it tried to reproduce its own power position in the 2010s. From 2010 onwards – specifically after the constitutional referendum in 2010 and AKP's landslide electoral victory in June 2011 – the regime started to move from what Poulantzas called 'authoritarian statism' towards an 'exceptional state form' marked by a profound restructuring of the relations between ideological and repressive state apparatuses[19] as well as by an increase in the relative autonomy of the state and economic apparatuses so as to create revenues and control the sphere of production and circulation.[20] The enhanced institutional capacity for creating new revenues made it possible for the AKP to increase its relative autonomy from global and big domestic capital and from imperial powers such as the US and the EU, with which it had strong economic ties in areas such as the import of intermediate and capital goods, the inflow of capital in the form of foreign currency and exports. This was seen more clearly in the aftermath of the 2008 crisis, when the AKP used its increased autonomy to turn towards the Middle East in response to the decline in European demand for Turkish export goods, and when it increasingly cooperated with Gulf capital, which gave it a temporary financial source of relief with no need for accountability.[21]

It should be noted that the necessity to orient all production capacity to exports in order to obtain foreign exchange, coupled with the curbing of internal demand in order to increase exports, also accelerated the dissolution of pre-capitalist relations of agriculture and crafts and their insertion into the circuits of capital, thereby leading to a rather harsh articulation of 'structural change' and 'change within structure' as mentioned above. However, the inclusion of dispossessed peasants and artisans within the circuits of capital did not lead to an intensification of accumulation either. Rather, the labour power of these peasants and artisans, as well as the money capital provided from abroad, were used in labour-intensive sectors such as construction and services.[22] Thus, the dissolution of the peasantry and its articulation within the circuit of commercial and money capital did not make a significant contribution to the expanded reproduction of capital. Therefore, what is termed 'construction-based' or 'finance-led' growth regimes[23] were in fact postponement mechanisms used in the face of contradictory class demands. Thus, conceptualizations such as 'construction-based accumulation', 'a rentier economy' or 'finance-led growth' do not help us reveal the inner dynamics of accumulation, but they do give hints about the mechanisms used by the AKP to postpone the negative effects of its failures in securing the conditions of accumulation.[24] The next section takes a closer look at these mechanisms.

The AKP's postponement mechanisms

The AKP governments used several postponement mechanisms to increase revenue for the total reproduction of society. It also resorted to religious and traditional norms and symbols in order to embed itself in the world of the masses and sustain their material reproduction through social assistance programmes. However, the sustainability of these programmes was also based on the capacity of the AKP to create new financial resources, and therefore it made a tremendous effort in this direction, using mechanisms that created new conflicts while overcoming some of the existing ones. Some of the major postponement mechanisms under the AKP rule were as follows: (1) increased control over labour without an upgrading of workers' skills and technology; (2) the promotion of labour-intensive sectors such as construction and services; (3) the commodification of nature and public services; (4) the internalization of international money capital; and (5) the transfer of some of the newly created resources to the poorest sections of society through social assistance programmes.[25]

The so-called construction-based or finance-led growth regime can be understood through an analysis of the inner links between the postponement mechanisms mentioned above. The AKP governments' frequent use of decree laws, regulations such as 'Urgent Expropriation' (UE) and numerous amendments made to the Public Procurement Law (PPL) were aimed at creating value that was not supplied through the capital accumulation process. These regulations provided the state under AKP rule with two important resources (the promotion of labour-intensive sectors and the commodification of nature) and two mechanisms (transformation of the delivery of public services through public–private partnerships and the creation of new spheres of commodification, such as land, energy, mining, water and housing). And all these spheres were mobilized through the deepening of financial instruments at the national and international level. In order to raise revenue, the AKP transformed the financial content of public services through public–private partnerships. These new forms of state–capital relationship, which emerged especially in education, health and infrastructure investments, were also used in construction and construction-related investments such as energy, housing and infrastructure.

Under AKP rule, control over labour was increased without a change in productivity. In line with Salama's earlier arguments,[26] the dissolution of peasants and artisans created a huge reserve army of labour for capital and the AKP promoted their employment in labour-intensive sectors such as construction and mining without having to cover the costs of upgrading their skills.[27] In the same vein, the Syrian refugee crisis was turned into an opportunity for capital, through the informal employment of Syrian workers, which led to an enormous reduction in the cost of reproduction of labour power.[28] Overall control over the working class also increased under AKP rule, especially through a meltdown of trade union rights.[29] In the absence of a transition to increased surplus value production, the weakening of trade unions made it possible for Turkish capital to increase its global competitiveness on the basis of lower labour costs.[30] This was explicitly stated in a report prepared by the Presidency of the Republic of Turkey Investment Office as a competitive advantage. As of 2015, labour costs in Turkey were almost one-seventh of those in Germany, but they were also lowest among countries such as the Czech Republic, Slovakia, Poland, Hungary, Romania and Bulgaria, at US$4.7 per hour.[31]

The low costs of labour also formed the basis of the so-called 'construction-based' postponement mechanisms, and the major regulations used for this purpose were the amendments in the PPL. The PPL played a central role in providing the AKP with the contingent forms through which contradictions of accumulation were managed. It formed the AKP's first encounter with the clash between the requirements of the global accumulation process and the contingency of domestic class dynamics. When the law was first enacted in January 2002, it was dominated by the interests of global capital, to which it opened up the national procurement market. When the AKP came to power in November 2002, however, it tried to change the law in line with the needs of SMEs.[32] To this end, the AKP government narrowed the scope of the law through many exceptions. Between 2003 and 2013, there were 29 changes to the PPL, while the context and specific articles changed more than 100 times. In 2011, the autonomy of the Public Procurement Agency was also removed. The proportion of open and transparent bidding processes in the total number of contracts fell from 71 per cent in 2005 to 52.5 per cent in 2014, while the other tender procedures and the ones covered by exceptions rose from 29 per cent to 47.5 per cent.[33] As Gürakar notes, through these changes, the AKP not only created new resources for itself but also formed new capital groups supporting its rule.[34] Among these new capital groups that grew between 2002 and 2014, the most notable were ten large private firms – namely, Çalık Holding, IC Holding, Cengiz Group, Ethem Sancak, Fettah Tamince, Kiler Group, Kalyon Group, Kuzu Family, Cihan Kamer and Akın İpek – that were involved in energy production and distribution projects as well as in other sectors.[35]

In sum, the amendments to the PPL were shaped by the intersecting requirements for cheap labour and the creation of new revenues for the state. The growth of the construction sector through these amendments[36] not only fostered the development of a new group of capitalists allied with the AKP and increased the state's manoeuvrability in managing the unequal relationships within capital, but also paved the way for the commodification of nature and public services.[37] The most important mechanism used by the AKP for this purpose were governmental decree laws, which served to bypass parliament in regulations facilitating the rapid subordination of nature first to the legal sphere and then to the valorization of capital. An important step in this direction was the establishment of the Ministry of Development by governmental decree in 2011. The ministry had the duty 'to determine natural, human, economic and other resources' and guide the public and private sector on how to utilize them. The establishment of the Ministry of Forestry and Water Affairs and the Ministry of Environment and Urban Planning in 2011 was part of the same process. The latter was formed by a merger of the 'environment' division of the former Ministry of Environment and Forestry and the former Ministry of Public Works and Housing, which meant the subordination of environmental affairs to the logic of valorization of capital in the construction sector. There were three key components of the construction boom. First was the investment in housing managed by the Turkish Mass Housing Administration (*Toplu Konut İdaresi Başkanlığı* or TOKİ), which itself became a massive capitalist land and property developer.[38] The second key component was investment in the energy sector following its liberalization, especially through micro-dams and hydroelectric power plants built in the valleys and rivers of Anatolia. Although these projects were justified on the grounds of the growing energy deficit, they were part of the construction industry rather than a long-term investment in energy. And the final component was infrastructure investment on a massive scale – such as building a third bridge to span the Bosporus and a third airport in Istanbul's northern forests.[39]

Another important mechanism was the UE Procedure (Law No. 6830), which had its origins in the 1940s. UE was a wartime procedure used to provide the state with power to confiscate private land and property in the case of foreign invasion. The aim was to bypass confiscation procedures that took a long time, and it was used very rarely until the early 2000s. The AKP rediscovered it to appropriate private lands, often from small-scale rural owners, and lease them to energy infrastructure firms for extended periods of time. While there had been only six UE cases in the 1980s and four in the 1990s, the decade between 2004 and 2014 witnessed a total of 1,785 UE decisions; some 1,500 of them were directly related to energy production.[40] As Erensü notes, the law was applied to energy-related projects (particularly small hydropower plants), water management, disaster preparedness, the allocation of land for tourism investments, urban renewal projects and to suppress Kurdish insurgency and redesign Kurdish cities.[41]

However, all these attempts to create revenue did not form a large portion of the general production of value. For instance, the construction sector contributes only 6 per cent of GDP. In the absence of increased relative surplus value production, none of the measures above were enough to meet the need for capital in the form of foreign exchange. At this point, the most important postponement mechanism used by the AKP was international borrowing via high interest rates and the overvalued Turkish lira. This led to an increase in GNP as well as exports over the years. The use of international finance to postpone crisis dynamics depended on the international dynamics of the valorization of money capital, which was managed by the US Federal Reserve System's (FED's) interest rate policies. Throughout the 2010s, fluctuations in the FED's interest rate policies, which in turn reflected the contradictions of the US's role in managing both domestic and international conditions of accumulation,[42] created new problems rather than solutions for late capitalist countries.[43] Due to the favourable international conditions for the internalization of money capital made possible by the FED's policy of low interest rates, the AKP was able to secure the support of both sections of capital during 2001–12. It was also able to postpone the negative effects of wage suppression on labour through the provision of consumption and mortgage credits to poor households.[44] As these favourable conditions transformed after 2013 following the FED's decision to increase interest rates, however, the AKP rapidly started to lose its room for manoeuvre.[45] Therefore, particularly from 2013 onwards, the AKP governments started to pursue other policies involving an increased sub-imperial role in Syria as well as the use of extra-economic coercion mechanisms for the redistribution of capital ownership at home.

Under these conditions, the failed coup in July 2016 provided the AKP with a new opportunity. It used the powers granted to the executive branch via state of emergency decrees[46] to seize hundreds of Gülen-linked companies and transfer their assets to the Savings Deposit Insurance Fund.[47] It also created the Turkish Sovereign Wealth Fund, with functions parallel to those of the central government budget. Other than its name, this had little in common with conventional funds, for Turkey is not a country with current account surpluses. The Fund was created as a company financed by the Privatization Administration, and stakes in major public companies were handed over to it in a privatization programme worth billions of dollars. Led by Erdoğan's senior adviser, and then by Erdoğan himself, the Fund enjoyed tax exemptions and was audit-free, as well as being used for financing giant construction projects carried out by pro-AKP companies and increasing the financial resources in the hands of the state by making external borrowing easier.[48] The extra-economic coercion mechanism provided by emergency decrees was also used for the restructuring of the labour market. The AKP governments effectively used these decrees to deepen the precarization of labour by dismissing 130,000 people from their public-sector jobs on the basis of alleged links to terrorist organizations.[49] Following the end of the state of emergency in 2018, presidential decrees replaced emergency decrees to serve the same purposes.

Conclusion

When the AKP came to power, it was expected to defend the common interests of different sections of capital and resolve the structural problems of capital accumulation. Although it attempted to make some interventions in line with this necessity, it failed to complete them as each of its interventions unleashed contingent forms of tensions among various sections of capital, most notably between big internationalized capital groups and SMEs. In particular, those policies aiming to improve technological infrastructure and meet the need for capital in the form of foreign exchange and a deeper integration with the global accumulation process were reflected in interest rate and exchange rate policies, becoming the major source of these tensions. Therefore, the reorganization of production in line with the need to increase relative surplus value was not achieved. This not only affected state–capital relationships; it also led to deadlock in capital–capital and capital–labour relationships. As the AKP increased its capacity to manoeuvre, it allowed these tensions to grow, but then resorted to a series of postponement mechanisms in order to soothe them. Each of the postponement mechanisms used to secure the support of the electorate, however, worsened the conditions for resolving the structural problems of capital accumulation mentioned above. As the conditions of reproduction of capitalist society deteriorated, the AKP increasingly tried to create new spheres of commodification in order to secure its financial resources and maintain its legitimacy. The creation of these new spheres of commodification in turn created new political conflicts and resistance movements such as the Gezi protests. As a response, the AKP started to transform the state apparatus not only for the reproduction of state and capital accumulation but for the reproduction of its own political power through a stronger mobilization of the ideological and repressive apparatuses of the state, triggering its own process of collapse. Whether this process will lead to the end of AKP rule, however, is dependent not only on the contingent struggles at home but also on worldwide struggles against rising authoritarianism in response to the deepening contradictions of global capitalism.

Notes

1. We would like to thank Leo Panitch and Greg Albo for their comments and suggestions.

2. The contradictions of capital accumulation do not, of course, form the sole source of the recent move towards authoritarianism in Turkey. This chapter rather focuses on these dynamics in a non-exhaustive way.

3. On the historical question initially posed by Murray (1971) as to what institutions assume responsibility for the public functions necessary for the reproduction of international capital accumulation, this chapter follows the tradition starting with Poulantzas, who argued that these functions have to be *internalized* by nation states themselves. For a more detailed discussion, see Oğuz 2015.

4. Althusser 2014 [1968].

5. Poulantzas 1978: 204.

6. Hirschman 1968.

7. Kojin Karatani's concept of 'repetition compulsion' is quite helpful at this point. According to Karatani (2012), Marx focused on the 'repetition compulsion' inherent in capital accumulation in *Capital* and *The Eighteenth Brumaire*. This continually differentiating and repeating nature of capital accumulation not only leads to new patterns of class formation but also requires the regulation and coordination of differences created in this process. If the regulation of these differences is not successful, the state and the ruling party intervene in the process more intensely as a repetition compulsion and the functioning of the state changes accordingly. Thus, it is not only capital accumulation but also the state and ruling party that are differentiated in this process.

8. Celasun 2002.

9. Figures from the Turkish Statistical Institute.

10. Barro's Misery Index (BMI) is calculated as follows: BMI = (annual inflation rate + total unemployment rate) – (growth rate + long-term interest rate). For a detailed analysis, see Ewa 2009.

11. See 'Liranin değer kaybı: Kur kaç kez ve ne zaman rekor kırdı?', BBC Türkçe, 11 August 2018.

12. See Altvater 1973; Hirsch 1978.

13. On the concept of 'premature deindustrialization', see Rodrik 2016.

14. Another reason for the failure of the AKP to increase surplus value production has been its destructive interventions in the education system based on 'creating a pious generation', especially after the general elections of 2011, which made the training of qualified labour power impossible. See Ercan 2015; Lüküslü 2016.

15. Yükseler 2016.

16. Poulantzas used the concept of 'authoritarian statism' to refer to the new state form that emerged to contain the specific contradictions of capitalism in Europe in the 1970s. The core tendencies associated with this new form were the decline of the political scene and the concentration of power in the executive branch (see Poulantzas 1978). The concept gained a renewed currency among Marxist scholars in the context of understanding the increasing role assumed by executive branches of states in managing the contradictions of neoliberal policies. For a detailed analysis of the rise of neoliberal authoritarian statism in Turkey, see Oğuz 2008.

17. As of 2013, 99.5 per cent of all enterprises were small and medium-sized. They form 67.9 per cent of total employment but their share in production value is 44.8 per cent.

The number of large-scale enterprises (employing more than 250 workers) is only 0.49 per cent. See Yükseler 2016.

18. See Kutun (Chapter 7); Dönmez 2019.

19. In Poulantzas's terms, there was a decline in the relative autonomy of ideological apparatuses such as the media and universities, an increase in relative autonomy of repressive apparatuses, a change in the hierarchy of each apparatus (for instance, the predominance of the police over the army), and modifications in the principal aspect of each branch, most importantly the executive assuming the functions of the judiciary. See Oğuz 2016.

20. It is important to note here that there is an intrinsic relationship between the restructuring of economic apparatuses and the restructuring of repressive and ideological apparatuses, because 'the economic functions of the state are in fact expressions of its overall political role in exploitation and class domination; they are by their nature articulated with its repressive and ideological roles in the field of class struggle of a social formation' (Poulantzas 1974: 81).

21. Oğuz 2016.

22. For an analysis of how this process increases the contradictions of articulation with the global accumulation process, see Salama 1986.

23. See, for instance, Adaman et al. 2014.

24. David Harvey's following remarks are worth noting at this point: 'It was not only China that sought to emulate this history of existing crises by construction projects and filling them with things. Turkey, for example, went through the same kind of expansion in its urbanization: a new airport for Istanbul, a third bridge over the Bosporus, the urbanization of the northern part of the city to create a city of some 45 million

people. Every city in Turkey witnessed a building boom. As a result, Turkey was hardly affected by the crash of 2008 (although it too saw its export industries suffer). Turkey had the second highest growth rate after China in the post-2008 period' (Harvey 2019: 188).

25. There is a wide literature covering these programmes under the concept of 'neoliberal populism'. For a comprehensive analysis of neoliberal populism in Turkey, see Akçay 2018.

26. Salama 1986.

27. The case of labour relations in Soma mines, where 301 workers were killed in 2014 in the largest work-related massacre in Turkish labour history, is an important example in this regard. Many of the unskilled workers in Soma were previously tobacco farmers from neighbouring villages who had to give up agriculture after the privatization of TEKEL, the former state-owned alcohol, cigarette and tobacco monopoly; others were farmers from all over Turkey who had left their lands due to dispossessions created by the capitalist transformation of agriculture in recent years. See Ercan and Oğuz 2015: 114.

28. For a more detailed analysis, see Saraçoğlu and Bélanger 2019.

29. For more comprehensive discussions, see Bozkurt-Güngen 2018; Çelik 2013.

30. An interesting example in this regard can be found in Erdoğan's words at a commemoration ceremony for the first anniversary of the 15 July coup attempt: 'We are enforcing emergency laws in order for our business to function more easily. So, let me ask: have you got any problems in the business world? Any delays? When we took power, there was again a state of emergency enforced in Turkey, but all factories were under the risk of strikes. Remember those days! But now, by making use of the state of emergency, we immediately

intervene in workplaces that pose a threat of strike. Because, you can't shake our business world. We use state of emergency for this.' See G. Çamur (2017) 'AKP'li Cumhurbaşkanı Erdoğan'dan OHAL itirafı: Grevlere anında müdahale ediyoruz', *Birgün*, 15 July.

31. T. Tören (2019) 'Volkswagen neden Türkiye'yi seçti?', *Gazete Duvar*, 3 October.

32. In his first public speech, Erdoğan spoke of the reactions of these groups as follows: 'The current version of the public procurement law serves the interests of 50–60 firms only. I will not leave 15 thousand kilometres of construction work to 60 contractors' (quoted in *Sabah*, 28 December 2002).

33. Gürakar 2016: 6.

34. Ibid.: 108.

35. İpek 2017: 190.

36. Between 2004 and 2011, the share of construction projects in the total value of procurements rose from 39 per cent to 57 per cent. See Gürakar 2016: 74.

37. De Soto (2000) had foreseen these developments in his book *The Mystery of Capital*, where he argued that the problem of developing countries is not the insufficiency of capital but the failure to turn assets, especially nature, into capital. This argument was well accepted, and this new type of capital – 'natural capital' – was activated through the strengthened executive branches of the state in many countries, including Turkey.

38. See Doğru 2016 for a comprehensive analysis. See also Çelik (Chapter 8).

39. Erol and Ünal 2015.

40. Erensü 2017: 127.

41. Ibid.

42. See Panitch and Gindin 2005.

43. See Bedirhanoğlu (forthcoming) for a comprehensive analysis.

44. The concept of 'financial inclusion' used to describe this process can also

be considered as a postponement mechanism for the purposes of this chapter. See Güngen 2018 for the specifics of financial inclusion in Turkey.

45. For the details of this process, see Güngen (Chapter 6); Bedirhanoğlu (forthcoming); Akçay and Güngen 2019.

46. See Akça et al. 2017 on the impact of these decrees on the legal-institutional transformation of the state.

47. As of January 2019, the Fund ran 955 companies and had total assets of US$10.24 billion with 27 per cent growth. Muhiddin Gülal, the head of the Fund, said: 'We regard the TMSF companies as a national wealth. We do not want these companies to lose altitude. They need to continue to generate added value' ('Value of 955 trustee-run firms reaches TL 56.5 billion', *Daily Sabah*, 14 January 2019).

48. See İpek 2019 for a more detailed comparative analysis.

49. Amnesty International 2018.

References

Adaman, F., B. Akbulut, Y. Madra and Ş. Pamuk (2014) 'Hitting the wall: Erdoğan's construction-based, finance-led growth regime', *The Middle East in London* 10 (3): 7–8.

Akça, İ., S. Algül, H. Dinçer, E. Keleşoğlu and B. A. Özden (2017) *When State of Emergency Becomes the Norm: The Impact of Executive Decrees on Turkish Legislation*. Cologne: Heinrich Böll Stiftung.

Akçay, Ü. (2018) 'Neoliberal populism in Turkey and its crisis'. Working Paper 100/2018. Berlin: Institute for International Political Economy.

Akçay, Ü. and A. R. Güngen (2019) 'The making of Turkey's 2018–2019 economic crisis'. Working Paper 120/2019. Berlin: Institute for International Political Economy.

Althusser, L. (2014 [1968]) *On the Reproduction of Capitalism: Ideology and Ideological State Apparatuses*. London: Verso.

Altvater, E. (1973) 'Notes on some problems of state interventionism', *Kapitalistate* 1: 96–108; 2: 76–83.

Amnesty International (2018) *Purged Beyond No Return?* London: Amnesty International.

Bedirhanoğlu, P. (forthcoming) 'Financialization, household indebtedness and state transformation in the global South' in E. Babacan, M. Kutun, E. Pınar and Z. Yılmaz (eds), *Authoritarianism and Resistance in Turkey: Contestations, Setbacks and Possibilities*. Abingdon: Routledge.

Bozkurt-Güngen, S. (2018) 'Labor and authoritarian neoliberalism: changes and continuities under the AKP governments in Turkey', *South European Society and Politics* 23 (2): 219–38.

Celasun, M. (2002) '2001 Krizi, Öncesi ve Sonrası: Makroekonomik ve Mali Bir Değerlendirme' in A. Dikmen (ed.), *Küreselleşme, Emek Süreçleri ve Yapısal Uyum*. Ankara: İmge Yayınları.

Çelik, A. (2013) 'Trade unions and deunionization during ten years of AKP rule', *Perspectives* 3: 44–8.

De Soto, H. (2000) *The Mystery of Capital: Why Capitalism Triumphs in the West and Fail Everywhere Else*. London: Bantam Press.

Doğru, E. (2016) 'The "benevolent hand" of the Turkish state: mass housing administration, state restructuring and capital accumulation in Turkey'. PhD thesis, York University.

Dönmez, P. (2019) 'Politicisation as governing strategy versus resistance: demystifying capitalist social relations and the state in Turkey' in J. Buller, P. Dönmez, A. Standring and M. Wood (eds), *Comparing Strategies of (De)Politicisation in Europe: Governance, Resistance and Anti-politics*. Cham, Switzerland: Palgrave Macmillan, pp. 155–88.

Ercan, F. (2011) 'Kanun Hükmünde Kararnamelerin İşaret Ettikleri: Kamu Girişimciliği ve Yeni Değerlenme Alanlarının Açılması', Politeknik.org.

Ercan, F. (2015) 'Yeni Türkiye Pragmatik Neslini Yaratırken' in K. İnal, U. B. Gezgin and N. Sancar (eds), *Marka, Takva, Tuğra AKP Döneminde Kültür ve Politika*. İstanbul: Evrensel Kültür, pp. 423–57.

Ercan, F. and Ş. Oğuz (2015) 'From Gezi resistance to Soma massacre: capital accumulation and class struggle in Turkey', *Socialist Register 51*: 114–35.

Erensü, S. (2017) 'Turkey's hydropower renaissance: nature, neoliberalism and development in the cracks of infrastructure' in F. Adaman et al. (eds), *Neoliberal Turkey and its Discontents: Economic Policy and the Environment Under Erdoğan*. London: I. B. Tauris.

Erol, İ. and U. Ünal (2015) 'Role of construction sector in economic growth: new evidence from Turkey'. MPRA Paper 68263. Munich: University Library of Munich.

Ewa, L. (2009) 'Okun's and Barro's Misery Index as an alternative poverty assessment tool: recent estimations for European countries'. MPRA Paper 37493. Munich: University Library of Munich.

Güngen, A. R. (2018) 'Financial inclusion and policy-making: strategy, campaigns and microcredit *a la Turca*', *New Political Economy 23* (3): 331–47.

Gürakar, E. Ç. (2016) *Politics of Favoritism in Public Procurement in Turkey*. New York, NY: Palgrave Macmillan.

Harvey, D. (2019) *Marx, Capital, and the Madness of Economic Reason*. Oxford: Oxford University Press.

Hirsch, J. (1978) 'The state apparatus and social reproduction: elements of a theory of the bourgeois state' in J. Holloway and S. Picciotto (eds), *State and Capital: A Marxist Debate*. London: Edward Arnold, pp. 57–107.

Hirschman, A. O. (1968) 'The political economy of import-substituting industrialization in Latin America', *Quarterly Journal of Economics 82* (1): 1–32.

İpek, A. M. (2019) 'Sovereign wealth funds in the context of subordinate financialisation: the Turkey Wealth Fund in a comparative perspective'. Master's thesis, Middle East Technical University.

İpek, P. (2017) 'The role of energy security in Turkish foreign policy (2004–2016)' in P. Gözen Ercan (ed.), *Turkish Foreign Policy: International Relations, Legality and Global Reach*. Cham, Switzerland: Palgrave Macmillan, pp. 173–94.

Karatani, K. (2012) *History and Repetition*. New York, NY: Columbia University Press.

Lüküslü, D. (2016) 'Creating a pious generation: youth and education policies of the AKP in Turkey', *Southeast European and Black Sea Studies 16* (4): 637–49.

Murray, R. (1971) 'The internationalization of capital and the nation-state', *New Left Review 67*: 84–109.

Oğuz, Ş. (2008) 'Globalization and the contradictions of state restructuring in Turkey'. PhD thesis, York University.

Oğuz, Ş. (2015) 'Rethinking globalization as internationalization of capital:

implications for understanding state restructuring', *Science and Society 79* (3): 336–62.

Oğuz, Ş. (2016) 'Yeni Türkiye'nin siyasal rejimi' in T. Tören and M. Kutun (eds), *Yeni Türkiye? Kapitalizm, Devlet, Sınıflar*. Istanbul: SAV, pp. 81–127.

Panitch, L. and S. Gindin (2005) 'Finance and American empire', *Socialist Register 41*: 46–81.

Poulantzas, N. (1974) *Classes in Contemporary Capitalism*. London: New Left Books.

Poulantzas, N. (1978) *State, Power, Socialism*. London: New Left Books.

Rodrik, D. (2016) 'Premature deindustrialization', *Journal of Economic Growth 21* (1): 1–33.

Salama, P. (1986) *Azgelişmenin İktisadı*. Istanbul: Belge Yayınları.

Saraçoğlu, C. and D. Bélanger (2019) 'The Syrian refugees and temporary protection regime in Turkey: a spatial fix for Turkish capital' in G. Yılmaz, İ. D. Karatepe and T. Tören (eds), *Integration through Exploitation: Syrians in Turkey. Labor and Globalization* Volume *17*. Munich: Rainer Hampp Verlag, pp. 95–108.

Yükseler, Z. (2016) 'Turkish manufacturing sector'. *Technical Report*, https://www.academia.edu/20101752/T%C3%9CRK%C4%B0YE_%C4%B0MALAT_SANAY%C4%B0_SEKT%C3%96R%C3%9C_K%C4%B1sa_Vadeli_i%C5%9F_%C4%Bostatistikleri_Sekt%C3%B6rel_Geli%C5%9Fmeler_ve_Teknoloji_D%C3%BCzeyi_.

6 | TURKEY'S FINANCIAL SLIDE: DISCIPLINE BY CREDIT IN THE LAST DECADE OF THE AKP'S RULE

Ali Rıza Güngen

Introduction

Under neoliberalism, Turkish economic growth depends on persistent capital inflows and access to cheap sources of finance. The period under the AKP governments is no exception to the rule. The neoliberal authoritarianism of the AKP is intricately related to the credit expansion and financial deepening in Turkey.

The main response of the AKP governments to the economic slump of 2008–09 was to stimulate domestic demand. The renewed economic boom of 2010–11, caused by huge capital inflows and cheap credit, came to an end by 2012–13. After that point, policy-makers not only reframed the global credit squeeze and financial volatility as a conspiracy against the emergent 'New Turkey' but also aimed to spread further the modes of financial calculation. Following the failed coup attempt in July 2016, state-sponsored credit expansion enabled the postponement of economic problems for approximately a year. It provided a venue for re-disciplining small and medium-sized enterprises (SMEs) as well as households. Nevertheless, the same process condensed the tensions within the state as a field of struggle. Global financial tightening in 2018 proved costly for the AKP as a political-economic coalition and heightened tensions within the tangled structure of the party.

The AKP supported financial deepening, employed strategies of 'debtfarism'[1] and achieved the consolidation of its rule through financial discipline imposed on both households and SMEs as organic elements of the support base of the party. Renewing debtfarism in the aftermath of the 2016 coup attempt, however, increased the vulnerability of the Turkish economy against a backdrop of lower levels of capital inflows. By early 2018, it was clear that Turkey could not sustain the same levels of credit expansion. The new discourse was of 'rebalancing the economy', implying lower rates of growth and lower levels of current account deficit. Yet the main response amidst the recurrent currency crises of 2018–19 was once again a resort to state-sponsored credit expansion and discipline by credit. Apparent contradictions in policy choices stemmed from the structure of the AKP as a ruling coalition and reflected the urgent demands of various sector representatives and social segments.

The main argument of this chapter is based on a critical analysis of the AKP's attempts to steer the economy in these turbulent times: renewing debtfarism in Turkey along similar lines to the post-2009 milieu has necessitated capital inflows and cheap sources of credit. Global financial tightening made its mark on Turkey's 2018–19 crisis, yet unsurprisingly the response has been to employ the same strategies that paved the way for the crisis in the first place.

This chapter analyses the financial discipline imposed on households and SMEs in the last decade of AKP rule under five sections. The term 'financial discipline' is not used in a generic sense in this chapter – that is, avoiding a mismatch between saving and spending plans – but in terms of credit dependency and reliance on state support and campaigns to roll over debt. The official data and reports are referred to in order to open up both Turkey's financial slide in the latest phase of its dependent financialization and the renewed cycles of debtfarism via state interventions in the aftermath of the international financial crisis of 2007–09. The second part of the chapter clarifies the concepts of debtfarism and financialization. The third part evaluates the policymaking environment between 2009 and 2019, and the fourth explains the state-sponsored credit expansion of 2016–17 and the ensuing 2018–19 Turkish crisis, focusing on household and SME debt. The conclusion underlines the main arguments.

Discipline by credit and debtfarism

The AKP benefited from debtfarism in consolidating its power and reproducing authoritarian statecraft. It can even be suggested that it was only by being able to repeat credit expansion cycles that the AKP was able to incorporate large sectors of the population while suppressing their organizational capacity at the same time.[2] At the peak of the crisis, challenges affecting the implementation of this strategy resulted in probably the biggest electoral defeat of the AKP in 2019 and will eventually lead to the party's political disintegration.

Debtfarism is basically a reliance on credit and debt to overcome tensions specific to neoliberal states. It refers essentially to spreading financial discipline among the working class and the surplus population to promote marketized forms of social reproduction; capitalists seeking to benefit from formalized financial abstractions (such as interest rates as service fees, or late fees as a penalty for ignoring financial rules) in order to submit larger segments of society to financial discipline; and normalizing the tensions of credit-led accumulation.[3] Since credit has to 'return to its place of origin for redemption',[4] the credit relation carries political characteristics from the start. Credit is a social construct, and 'social inclusion into the community of money' through the credit relation is based on and benefits from the institutionalized practices of debtfarism.[5]

The strategy of policymaking according to financial standards in order to make policy immune to social pressures encourages the internalization of financial discipline within the state, a long-sought target during transitions to neoliberalism in various countries of the global South. Since the narrowing of the policy space restricts economic management to implementing formulae on various economic trade-offs, policy responses are reduced to choosing viable options that support financial deepening.[6] State authorities not only institutionalize international financial reforms, they also attempt to increase the prospects for securitization and spread the financial logic further. Hence, 'the financialization of the state' is another way of expressing how states, institutional configurations and political projects subject large segments of the population to financial discipline.

Such a transformation has been evident in the attempt to promote discipline through credit expansion in the last decade of AKP rule. Through the strategy of discipline by credit, state managers submerged any policy discussion amidst the financialization of the state, which eventually helped them survive financial volatility, but at the expense of persistently increasing economic and political risk. Turkey's financial transformation has been riven by internal struggles and contradictions, and the strategies used to ensure financial discipline have not been composed of fixed, unchanging responses. Access to international markets and gradually deepening financial markets in Turkey provided further opportunities for Turkish industrial conglomerates to hedge their risk. It is debatable to what extent Turkish capital groups succeeded in their attempted technological jump during financialization,[7] but they benefited from the financial transformation of the twenty-first century, by diversifying their portfolios, extending their international markets and finding new outlets at home as households consumed more and more thanks to their increased borrowing capacity. It is also viable to suggest that both the establishment and the perpetuation of the ruling bloc relied on expanding credit to SMEs, the backbone of Turkish employment, despite their persistent problems in financing.

Amidst economic crises, the success of financial discipline brought about by debtfarism depends on the extent of the collapse, the duration of financial volatility, and, in addition, the capacity of social classes to envision a different regime of accumulation or set of socio-economic relations. When faced with a credit crunch, it becomes more probable that the community of money, which has created a sense of equality via exchange, is dispersed. Contraction of the economy, even for a brief period of time, heightens tensions, and, with increasing default rates, the idea shatters that everyone is an equal member of the community of money and will succeed by subjugating themselves to financial discipline. In short, the strategies of debtfarism may give way to other mechanisms in due course. Still, the responses to Turkey's 2018–19 crisis confirm that the AKP cadres insist on maintaining credit-led accumulation, consolidated in the aftermath of the international financial crisis of 2007–09.

More of the same

The financialization of the state in the Turkish case has implied the constant intervention of policymakers, re-treading the path of dependent/peripheral financialization; despite setbacks and tensions, the state managed to keep this model in place until the 2018–19 crisis.[8] This can be grasped by explaining the accumulation model in the post-2001 period and the particular interventions by the Turkish state after 2013, against a backdrop of approaching tighter global financial conditions.

Turkish capital groups and the AKP benefited tremendously from the lower interest rates and the dollar glut between 2002–07 and 2010–13. Despite the crash in GDP in late 2008 due to the international financial crisis, the policy response in the core countries made it unnecessary to seek a new orientation. Corporations borrowed heavily in US dollars as the AKP paved the way through legal changes in 2009 to allow those who lacked foreign exchange (FX) revenues to borrow in FX terms.[9] Data published by the Central Bank of Turkey reveal that FX liabilities of non-financial corporations (NFCs) increased rapidly from US$146.8 billion in 2009 to US$265 billion in 2013. The pace of the increase slowed down in the following years. During the dollar glut, however, NFCs did not borrow directly from international financial markets; the stock of loans borrowed by NFCs from abroad remained almost the same in this period. Loans taken out by the banking sector from abroad increased rapidly, from US$33.8 billion in 2009 to US$91 billion in 2013. Therefore, it is viable to claim that the banking sector borrowed from international financial markets in order to lend to NFCs in Turkey.

Under AKP rule, the Turkish economy faced economic ups and downs, but a downward trend in economic activity can be noted even before the Turkish economy's recent 2018–19 crisis. There is a significant parallel between foreign inflows and economic growth rates under AKP rule. Figure 6.1 shows the strong correlation between

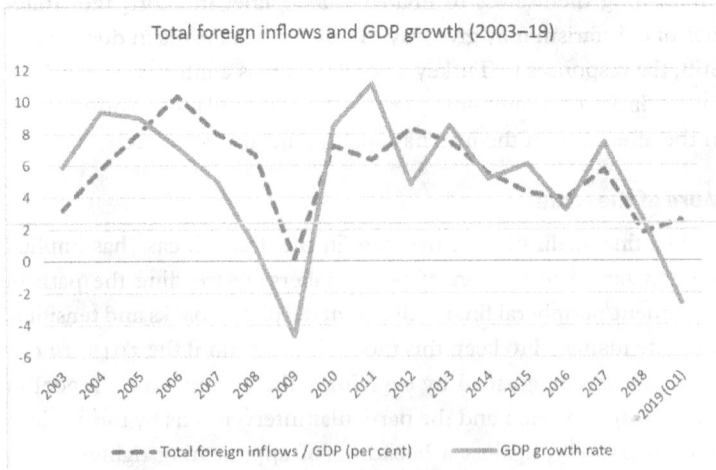

Total foreign inflows and GDP growth (2003–19)

● ● ● Total foreign inflows / GDP (per cent)   GDP growth rate

FIGURE 6.1 Total foreign inflows and GDP growth (2003–19)

Note: 2019 Q1 data shows annualized GDP growth and total foreign inflows.

Source: TURKSTAT and balance of payments data from the Central Bank of Turkey as of July 2019.

total foreign inflows (foreign direct investment (FDI), portfolio inflows and other investments, including foreign deposits and commercial credits to the GDP) and annual economic growth. The graph shows that the level of foreign inflows deteriorated after the 2010–11 boom and had an impact on the economic growth rate.

Table 6.1 indicates that the added value of the construction sector in Turkey grew rapidly in the aftermath of the global financial crisis. While the foreign debt stock increased substantially, it was mainly the construction sector that benefited from inflows and the economic boom of 2010–11.[10] During this period, however, the increase in total debt stock outpaced GDP growth, leading to a surge in the debt stock to GDP ratio, particularly in the post-2013 period. The credit-led and construction-based model of accumulation provided handsome returns for many circles close to the ruling party as well as for the established capital groups, with octopus-like business models. Yet at the same time it deepened the dependency on capital inflows.

Turkey became one of the fastest growing countries in 2010–11, but with a tremendously high current account deficit due to the capital inflows and domestic credit boom after 2009.[11] Although household debt as a percentage of GDP remained low when compared with advanced capitalist markets, the debt to disposable income ratio increased rapidly in 2010–13, reaching a historical high

TABLE 6.1 The share of the construction sector in GDP

	Total debt stock (US$ billion)	GDP (US$ billion)	Share of construction sector in total GDP (per cent)
2009	268.9	646.9	5.6
2010	291.8	772.4	6.1
2011	305.4	831.7	6.8
2012	342.2	871.1	7.0
2013	392.7	950.4	7.4
2014	405.7	934.9	7.4
2015	400.3	861.9	7.3
2016	409.3	862.7	7.5
2017	455.0	851.7	7.6
2018	444.6	787.1	7.2
2019 Q1	452.3	747.6	7.1

Source: TURKSTAT and Ministry of Finance and Treasury. Repeated revisions in 2018–19 decreased the share of the construction sector in GDP and cast doubt on the data.

of 53 per cent in 2013.[12] The hike in household debt rang alarm bells
for policymakers in 2010–11, forcing them to impose measures to
control and limit household borrowing initially.[13] The development
of a new model to displace the existing debtfarism, however, was
eventually left off the AKP agenda because of its possible political
costs. 'Debtfarism' was proved to be more functional in associating
political and financial stability with one-party rule.

The model of accumulation based on cheap credit and the 'stability' discourse also drowned the debate on industrial policy. This is not
to suggest that developmentalist concerns and incentives vanished.
On the contrary, both policy circles and the Islamic think tanks suggested heavy incentives to move up the ladder of technology use and
to narrow the current account deficit. These suggestions, however,
did not take the form of an official development strategy, in contrast to the previous action plans and official documents. Against the
backdrop of plummeting liquidity from 2013 and onwards, Turkish
policymakers remained reluctant to implement a new developmentalist strategy, which was already becoming overdue.[14]

There was a significant change in policymaking and economic
management in the post-2009 period. The AKP distanced itself from
the depoliticization of the 2002–07 period[15] while renewing financial
discipline with a search for Islamic financial deepening.[16] The credit
expansion seen in 2010–11 recalled that of 2003–07, even though
the signs of an end to the dollar glut after 2013 redefined global
financial conditions and decelerated domestic credit expansion. The
heavily indebted Turkish conglomerates kept borrowing, however,
as the government was able to slow down the collapse of the Turkish
currency for some time to come.

Data regarding the rising indebtedness of households and SMEs
make it obvious that the AKP tried to persist with debtfarism, the
root cause of its electoral successes, through new credit campaigns
and strategies. Hence, by supporting new cycles of credit expansion,
the government attempted once again to normalize the very tensions
arising from credit-led accumulation. First, the financial inclusion
agenda was adopted. Even though the official financial inclusion
strategy was launched in 2014, the preparations and explicit support
to NGOs for increased financial literacy dates back to the post-crisis
context, in which household indebtedness started rising rapidly.
Raising financially conscious citizens[17] and spreading the financial

modes of calculation further were justified by the need to increase the country's savings, which would eventually be channelled by financial markets to corporations in debt as new funds. The financial inclusion strategy itself was questionable from the beginning, since the ratio of gross savings to GDP stagnated for most of the period of Turkish neoliberalism, the gist of which resided in wage suppression. Despite stagnant real wages, the push for increased savings in the 2010s emerged as part of the long-desired project of financial deepening.[18]

In this period, SMEs were supported by new credit opportunities, which makes the second point. This support was in addition to the already existing incentives and export assistance provided by the Small and Medium Enterprises Development Organization (*Küçük ve Orta Ölçekli İşletmeleri Geliştirme ve Destekleme Daire Başkanlığı* or KOSGEB). The new cheap loans were given by development agencies, as well as by the state-owned investment and development banks with new credit facilities. The attempts to provide support to the backbone of the Turkish manufacturing industry increased the proportion of loans to SMEs of total bank loans from 21.2 per cent in 2009 to 26.8 per cent in 2014.[19] The share of long-term bank loans as a source of funds more than doubled (from 9 per cent in 2009 to 19.7 per cent in 2014) for small-scale manufacturing enterprises and increased dramatically for the medium-scale manufacturing enterprises (from 10.2 per cent in 2009 to 15.6 per cent in 2014).[20] While SMEs' approaches to the growing corporate bond markets and the nascent Islamic bond markets were almost non-existent before, the use of state-owned investment and development banks alongside state-owned commercial banks strengthened the ties of SMEs to the banking sector, as SMEs' profitability, particularly in the industrial sector, started to diminish. The consolidated integration of SMEs compounded their dependence on state support for cheap credit and the partial socialization of their financial risks.

State-sponsored credit expansion and the 2018 currency crisis

The AKP succeeded in disciplining its electoral base and SMEs through credit expansion throughout its rule. This was more visible in the aftermath of the 2008–09 Turkish economic crisis and has become more notable in recent years. The 2016 coup attempt led the way for a small currency shock and an interest rate hike in late

2016. To postpone economic stagnation, policymakers initiated a new state-sponsored credit expansion, which started in late 2016 and went on for almost a year.

The expansion of the credit card industry in the post-2001 period brought many people into the financial sector who were previously excluded from it. The constant surveillance of household debt by the financial arm of the state became clearer in the post-2009 period. The Banking Regulation and Supervision Agency (*Bankacılık Düzenleme ve Denetleme Kurumu* or BDDK) and the Central Bank, although they cooperated to limit credit expansion to over-indebted households in 2010–11,[21] then took steps to support credit expansion in autumn 2016. Those measures included restructuring credit card debt and consumer credit debt with a renewed maturity of 72 months as well as increasing the maximum limit for new consumer debt from 36 to 48 months. The aim was to stimulate the domestic market in order to prevent the post-coup collapse to turn into a recession. The results of the new measures on the household debt market were not completely satisfactory for the policymakers since the average funding cost of the banking sector increased from 8.28 per cent to 12.75 per cent in 2017, and rising interest rates further squeezed household borrowing.

Pushing households towards more consumption was accompanied not only by a breach of the public borrowing limit and increased state expenditure, but also by extraordinary support to SMEs throughout 2017. The government postponed the social security premium payments to be made by firms, provided cheap sources of finance to export-oriented firms, and designed credit campaigns targeting SMEs in particular. Moreover, guarantees to the banking sector were provided in order to make the commercial banks offer cheaper and more advantageous loans to SMEs via the *Kredi Garanti Fonu* or KGF. This included a no payment facility in the first year of three-year loans, for which the KGF was used as a facilitator.

The KGF is a mechanism through which part of the counterparty risk in extending loans to SMEs are socialized. In case of default, part of the loss was to be absorbed by the Turkish state, while the banks converted non-liquid collateral for their own use. By pledging 25 billion Turkish lira (TRY) (roughly US$6.8 billion) in 2017 to support the KGF mechanism, the Turkish Treasury attempted to create loans for SMEs with a value of 250 billion TRY (US$68 billion). Although the figure might have been exaggerated, according to official announcements, 350,000 firms benefited from the credit campaign during the state-sponsored credit expansion. Briefly, the campaign succeeded in containing bankruptcy numbers and helped troubled SMEs to stay afloat. More importantly, and combined with the renewal of capital inflows in 2017, the intervention created a brief boom, helping the AKP government win a dubious victory in the 2017 referendum. The cost of the stimulus was reflected in a dramatic increase in the current account deficit, whereas the share of portfolio investment in financing the current account increased rapidly. Therefore, the credit expansion of 2016–17 intensified further the dependency of the economy on capital inflows, right before the tightening of global financial conditions in the spring of 2018.[22]

The problem in August 2018 was that, as an economy with a current account deficit to GDP ratio of 6.5 per cent, double digit inflation, a double digit unemployment rate and an increased need to roll over private debt and refinance loans, Turkey was among the most vulnerable countries in the global South. The currency crisis that hit Turkey at that time was a direct extension of the intensified dependency on capital inflows combined with higher interest rates in the advanced capitalist countries and lower levels of capital inflows to the periphery. This was the final episode in the slow drift of the country towards crisis since 2013. As already noted, policymakers had had to increase interest rates significantly in early 2014 and in the autumn of 2016 to avoid further depreciation of the TRY, while repeatedly sponsoring credit expansion to stimulate the domestic market and keep the economy running. In a nutshell, Turkey's credit-led accumulation regime needed continuous access to cheap sources of finance and continued credit expansion. Against the backdrop of global tightening, this simply meant increased vulnerability to capital flows and sudden reversals.

The sudden stop of capital inflows in the spring of 2018 was exacerbated by increased portfolio outflows by residents. The lira lost 41 per cent of its value in the first eight months of 2018 and the depreciation could be stopped only by a dramatic rise in the policy interest rate, which led the country into a severe recession in the second half of the year.[23] Adopting a countercyclical policy and benefiting from public expenditure would have avoided the acuteness of the economic collapse, and it seems that the Turkish public debt to GDP ratio, which hovered around 30 per cent, allowed a great deal of room for manoeuvre. Nevertheless, since the cost of borrowing by the state increased dramatically in mid-2018 and any attempt to bail out the real sector and financial sector would be too expensive, a comprehensive savings programme to strengthen the state's rescue capacity was demanded by international financial circles in early September. The economic bottleneck reaffirmed the monetary and financial limits of deriving support via credit expansion in a peripheral economy against a backdrop of global financial tightening.

The AKP's New Economic Programme (NEP) (Medium-Term Programme, 2019–21), announced in September 2018, resorted to a classical austerity plan to consolidate the capacity of the state to intervene during the forthcoming recession. According to data from the Turkish Statistical Institute (TURKSTAT), however, the state's consumption expenditure increased in the final quarter of 2018 and in the first quarter of 2019 compared with the third quarter of 2018. Therefore, to what extent the Erdoğan administration remained loyal to the NEP before the local elections in 2019 is open to debate. Yet it is certain that the state's response to a currency crisis that was turning rapidly into a credit crunch and economic recession recalled previous responses to the drift of the economy in the aftermath of autumn 2016. Policy discussion was sidelined, while, yet again, policymakers attempted to continue subjecting large segments of the population to financial discipline. To do this, the state-owned banks were used as a tool.[24]

State-owned banks played a crucial role in the persistence of financial discipline through the restructuring of household credit card debt and the extension of new loans. First, the biggest state-owned bank in Turkey, Ziraat Bank, joined later by another state-owned bank, VakıfBank, launched a campaign to restructure household debt with interest rates below average. At the time of writing there is no data regarding the size of the Ziraat-Vakıf operation, but the 'income losses' of these banks, due to cheap credit during the campaign as well as retail sales in early 2019, indicate that it was not a success. Second, the state-owned banks were used to end the credit crunch in late 2018 and early 2019. While private commercial banks hesitated in extending new loans, decreasing their TRY credit volume by almost 10.9 per cent in nominal terms between August 2018 and March 2019, the state-owned banks increased their loan volume by 5.4 per cent, trying to compensate for most of the credit squeeze. The ratio of SME loans to total loans given by state-owned banks increased marginally during this period, yet the volume of SME loans provided by state-owned banks increased 12.5 per cent between August 2018 and March 2019, while the volume of SME loans from private banks declined by 15.1 per cent.[25] Despite new rounds of KGF use in the first half of 2019 to create new credit to the value of more than 70 billion TRY, it seems that using the state-owned banks not only to end the credit crunch but also to support SMEs has been the preferred option during the 2018–19 crisis (see Figure 6.2).

There were other responses, such as reducing tax rates in numerous sectors to stimulate the domestic market and revising the debt restructuring framework to push for corporate debt restructuring. The new securitizations helped state-owned banks to postpone liquidity problems and hence continue lending, precipitating household and SME debt dependency still further. However, it is questionable whether resorting to state-owned banks would be enough this time. Renewing debtfarism in 2019–20 depends on renewing capital inflows at levels much higher than in the previous cycles, as the ratio

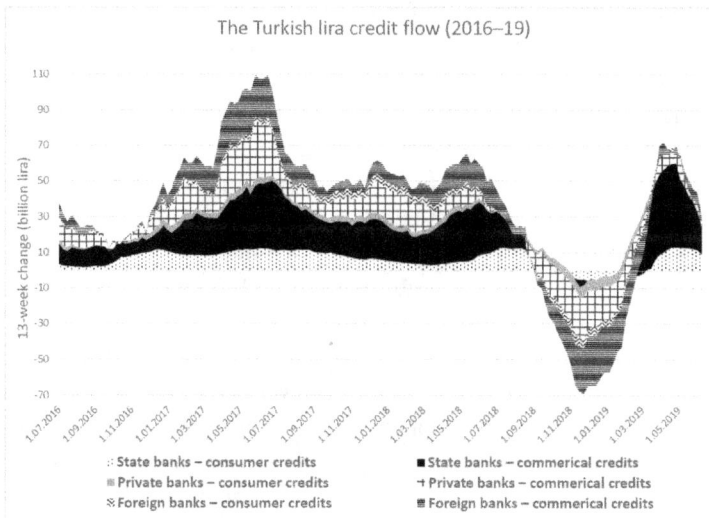

FIGURE 6.2 The Turkish lira credit flow (2016–19)

Source: Weekly bulletins from the Banks Association of Turkey.

of total foreign debt to GDP increased from 39.3 per cent in the first quarter of 2013 to 60.6 per cent in the first quarter of 2019.

All in all, the state's responses during the 2018–19 Turkish crisis formed a continuum with the previous attempts at credit expansion and the reinforcing of financial discipline on both households and SMEs. The problems of such a crisis-management perspective reside in the inconsistencies stemming from higher unemployment rates and a contracting economy. Households spend less on consumer durables and lose the capacity to borrow more, whereas SMEs face an uphill battle to stay in the market, facing a radical decline in sales.

Conclusion

The long-term burden of neoliberal authoritarianism in Turkey has been combined in recent years with the practical but short-sighted solutions of the government and conservative policy cadres. Discipline by credit and boost by credit expansion succeeded as a strategy in making the new neoliberal Turkish state but resulted in the increased accumulation of financial risks and renewed economic instability.

In the aftermath of the 2016 abortive coup attempt, the further loss in competitiveness due to zombie firms dominating the economy and the socialized financial risks of SMEs accelerated the financial slide of the AKP. Demand stimulation and the breach of the public borrowing limit in 2017 pushed interest rates higher in Turkey, but the country did not have the financial muscle needed to cope with the withdrawal of financial capital from emerging markets during 2018. The Erdoğan administration succeeded in channelling discontent along nationalist lines, but it could not make households spend more or make SMEs maintain the same level of production. By early 2019, while waiting for a shift in global financial conditions to the advantage of Turkey and the emerging markets, the state's economic managers started to try a variety of approaches to access new sources of finance. An IMF bailout was deemed to be out of the question by conservative policymakers because of the tremendous political cost, but the financing needs of the real sector pushed the state into taking significant measures, something that had not been experienced before.

The success of the ongoing bailouts of the real sector and debt restructuring means that the same movie, the one that has been playing in the Turkish economic theatre since 2009, is being screened once again. As the discontent of the masses hits the AKP, financial discipline and renewed invitations for inclusion in the community of money have been introduced, paving the way for a renewed debt-farism. During the 2018–19 crisis, a narrative emerged underlining the need to narrow the current account deficit and boost the export capacity of the Turkish industrial sector, with 'reforms' meaning austerity policies to maintain the state's bailout capacity. The AKP policymakers, however, mainly stuck to debtfarist strategies and the credit-led accumulation model. This left them with no option but to help the banks restructure more than US$20 billion of commercial credit in 2018, using state banks to open up credit channels for both SMEs and households in late 2018 and 2019, and ultimately expecting a relaxation in global financial conditions so that international financial capital can flood the veins of the Turkish economy.

Notes

1. 'Debtfarism' bolsters the reliance of large segments of society on expensive consumer loans to meet basic needs. It is a facet of credit-led accumulation and signifies the search of capitalists to benefit from formalized financial abstractions, imposing financial discipline further on society. Susanne Soederberg (2014) introduced the concept of 'debtfare' to elaborate the disciplinary power of money and credit, and the disciplining of debtors by the state, as one of the main features of neoliberal governance.

2. Bozkurt Güngen 2018.

3. Soederberg 2014.

4. Harvey 1999: 245–6.

5. Soederberg 2014: 61–5.

6. Having acknowledged Soederberg's critique of the heterodox financialization literature, this chapter suggests that we can also refer to financialization to understand the impact of new forms of fictitious capital and fictitious capital speculation on corporate and household behaviour. 'The financialization of the state' is used to denote the 'internalization of financial imperatives by the state and the neoliberal restructuring of the state with reference to financial norms, reflecting itself not only in fiscal policy and debt management, but also monetary policy and financial regulation'. In more concrete terms, the financialization of the state refers to a more comprehensive restructuring, imposed by state managers and the state, and in which labour–capital–state relations are embedded more and more in interest-paying financial transactions and fictitious capital accumulation. See Güngen 2019: 163; cf. McNally 2009: 56; see also Güngen 2014.

7. For a critical analysis on this question, see Ercan and Oğuz (Chapter 5).

8. Elaborating on the argument, this study benefits from not only the burgeoning literature on peripheral/dependent/subordinate financialization but also a recent analysis of the Turkish crisis along these lines. For the aforementioned financialization

literature, see Becker et al. 2010;
Kaltenbrunner and Painceira 2018. For
a recent analysis of Turkey's crisis, see
Akçay and Güngen 2019.

9. This decision means that
policymakers decided to liberalize
regulations on borrowing in foreign
exchange-denominated loans, especially
for non-financial corporations. For the
official text of the Decree of the Council
of Ministers, see T. C. Başbakanlık (2009),
'Türk parası kıymetini koruma hakkında
32 sayılı kararda değişiklik yapılmasına
dair karar', *Resmi Gazete*, 16 April.

10. Yeldan 2018. Almost one in
every three dollars of the GDP increase
between 2010 and 2017 was related to
added value in the construction sector.
After revision by TURKSTAT in 2018–19,
this share in the added value declined
considerably.

11. Güngen 2019: 174; see also
Cömert and Yeldan 2019.

12. Güngen 2018a: 340.

13. Ibid.; Eren Vural 2019: 272.
14. Güngen and Akçay 2016.
15. For a detailed analysis of this
process, see Kutun (Chapter 7).
16. Ibid.
17. Ayhan 2019.
18. Güngen 2018a: 339.
19. Topal 2019: 234.
20. Ibid.
21. Güngen 2018a.
22. Güngen 2018b.
23. For a summary of the initial
weeks of the currency crisis, see Ü.
Akçay and A. R. Güngen (2018) 'Lira's
downfall is a symptom: the political
economy of Turkey's crisis', Critical
Macro Finance blog, 18 August.
24. For a brief history and on the
functions of the public banks in Turkey,
see Marois and Güngen 2016.
25. Data for banking sector
loans, from 2014 onwards, can be
accessed at https://www.bddk.org.tr/
BultenHaftalik/.

References

Akçay, Ü. and A. R. Güngen (2019) 'The making of Turkey's 2018–2019 economic crisis'. Working Paper 120/2019. Berlin: Institute for International Political Economy.

Ayhan, B. (2019) 'Constituting financialized subjectivities: cultural political economy of financial literacy in Turkey', *Turkish Studies* 20 (5): 680–707.

Becker, J. et al. (2010) 'Peripheral financialization and vulnerability to crisis: a regulationist perspective', *Competition and Change* 14: 225–47.

Bozkurt Güngen, S. (2018) 'Labour and authoritarian neoliberalism: changes and continuities under the AKP governments in Turkey', *South European Society and Politics 23* (2): 219–38.

Cömert, H. and E. Yeldan (2019) 'A tale of three crises in Turkey: 1994, 2001 and 2008–09' in G. Yalman, T. Marois and A. R. Güngen (eds), *The Political Economy of Financial Transformation in Turkey*. London: Routledge, pp. 88–107.

Eren Vural, İ. (2019) 'Restricted but significant: financialization of households and retail banking activities in Turkey' in G. Yalman, T. Marois and A. R. Güngen (eds), *The Political Economy of Financial Transformation in Turkey*. London: Routledge, pp. 269–93.

Güngen, A. R. (2014) 'Hazine Müsteşarlığı ve Borç Yönetimi: Finansallaşma Sürecinde Bir Kurumun Dönüşümü', *Amme İdaresi Dergisi 47* (1): 1–21.

Güngen, A. R. (2018a) 'Financial
inclusion and policy making:
strategy, campaigns and microcredit
a la Turca,' New Political Economy
23 (3): 331–47.
Güngen, A. R. (2018b) 'Aus der
Pfanne herausspringen? Die
wirtschaftspolitischen Präferenzen
der AKP und ihre Auswirkungen seit
dem Putschversuch 2016' in İ. Ataç
et al. (eds), Anthologie: Nach dem
Putsch. 16 Bemerkungen zur 'neuen'
Türkei. Vienna: Vienna Institute
for International Dialogue and
Cooperation, pp. 124–38.
Güngen, A. R. (2019) 'The neoliberal
emergence of market finance in
Turkey' in G. Yalman, T. Marois
and A. R. Güngen (eds), The
Political Economy of Financial
Transformation in Turkey. London:
Routledge, pp. 162–84.
Güngen, A. R. and Ü. Akçay (2016)
'Türkiye'de Ekonomi Politikasında
Arayışlar, Çıkmazlar ve Alternatifler'
in T. Tören and M. Kutun (eds), Yeni
Türkiye'de Kapitalizm, Devlet ve
Sınıflar. Istanbul: SAV, pp. 246–80.
Harvey, D. (1999) The Limits to Capital.
London: Verso.
Kaltenbrunner, A. and J. P. Painceira
(2018) 'Subordinated financial
integration and financialisation in
emerging capitalist economies: the
Brazilian experience', New Political
Economy 23 (3): 290–313.
Marois, T. and A. R. Güngen (2016)
'Credibility and class in the
evolution of public banks: the
case of Turkey,' Journal of Peasant
Studies 43 (6): 1285–309.
McNally, D. (2009) 'From financial crisis
to world slump: accumulation,
financialization and the global
slowdown', Historical Materialism
17: 35–83.
Soederberg, S. (2014) Debtfare States
and Poverty Industry: Money,
Discipline and Surplus Population.
London and New York, NY:
Routledge.
Topal, A. (2019) 'The state, crisis and
transformation of small and
medium-sized enterprise finance
in Turkey' in G. Yalman, T. Marois
and A. R. Güngen (eds), The
Political Economy of Financial
Transformation in Turkey. London:
Routledge, pp. 221–43.
Yeldan, E. (2018) 'Küresel Krizin
Onuncu Yılında Türkiye ve Dünya
Ekonomisi için Dersler', Türkiye'nin
Krizini Anlamak Sempozyumu,
Mülkiyeliler Birliği ve Türk Sosyal
Bilimler Derneği, Ankara, 6
October.

7 | THE AKP'S MOVE FROM DEPOLITICIZATION TO REPOLITICIZATION IN ECONOMIC MANAGEMENT

Melehat Kutun

Introduction: beyond a binary exposition

Neoliberalism, as a class project of the reorganization of social relations in favour of capital,[1] forced states towards pro-capital policy changes in response to the crisis of the 1970s that manifested itself with high inflation and rising budget deficits. With regard to money management, this meant institutionalization of price stability, fiscal discipline and anti-inflationist economic policies, as well as monetarism. From the perspective of labour, monetarism referred to a decrease in pro-labour public support, rise of unemployment, imposition of precarious working conditions, decrease of wages and longer work hours to increase both the absolute and relative surplus value.[2]

The management of this process that caused labour to gradually lose its achievements against capital was implemented by the political strategy defined by Burnham as 'depoliticization in economic management'.[3] This strategy, having been applied with success in many countries until the 2008 global capitalist crisis, aimed at breaking resistance against anti-inflationist policies based on low wages in societies in which labour was politically powerful, and blocking labour from decision-making processes in the economy. On the other hand, in the mainstream liberal discourse, depoliticization in economic management has been presented as technocratization, stability, accountability, transparency, and the end of arbitrary or populist government policies.

According to Burnham, depoliticization in economic management is a strategy that aims to hide the political character of decision-making processes in monetary policies and to relieve governments of the political responsibility of anti-labour economic policies.[4] Huge bailout operations of states in the financial markets following the 2008 crisis have proven that, contrary to neoliberal arguments, it is not really possible to free economic management from politics.[5] In other words, states that used to be invisible in economic management in the name of depoliticization until 2008 took to the stage again with all their instruments during the global crisis to socialize the effects of the crisis, provide new profit opportunities to capital and manage class conflicts. This process has also revealed that economic policies are being shaped not only through struggles between labour and capital but also among different capital groups, other elements of the capitalist class, and different constituents of the state.[6] Setting off from these arguments and observations, this chapter argues that the move from depoliticization to repoliticization in economic management signifies not a rupture from but an insistence on the neoliberal class project.

I focus here on the depoliticization of the institutional structure and policy instruments of economic management in Turkey, which follows a path parallel to global developments to a great extent. Two key periods in this regard are the Motherland Party (*Anavatan Partisi* or ANAP) rule that started after the 1980 military coup, and the long AKP period after the 2001 crisis, both being single-party governments. Repoliticization has been experienced after 2008 under the AKP governments, and was institutionalized from 2014 onwards. The chapter problematizes depoliticization and repoliticization practices under the AKP governments since 2001 in order to contribute to our understanding of the authoritarian transformation taking place in the state in the 2010s. Within this frame, first, the period of depoliticization from 2001 to 2008[7] will be discussed, followed by the 2008–14 period during which repoliticization practices started due to depoliticization policies reaching their limits. Then, it will evaluate the post-2014 period, during which the economic, political and social effects of the global capitalist crisis deepened, economic management became totally repoliticized, and this process finally culminated in regime change. Mapping this process as depoliticization–tensions–repoliticization will enable us to understand both the institutional transitions in economic management and the centralization and personification dynamics emerging with the new regime.

Depoliticization in economic management and its limits

The AKP, coming to power after the 2001 crisis in Turkey, immediately took over the austerity programme that former coalition governments had not been able to apply and made an agreement with the IMF for a macro-economic stability and structural adjustment programme that would be in effect until 2008. Arrangements granting 'independence' to the Central Bank of the Republic of Turkey (*Türkiye Cumhuriyeti Merkez Bankası* or TCMB), the institute responsible for relations with global money markets, and to other regulatory boards were among the priorities of this programme. One of the most significant premises of a depoliticized economic management strategy supported by the IMF was the need of the TCMB to be independent from any 'populist' interventions by the political power. This premise was based on the assumption that price stability was dependent on long-term, stable and determined policy implementation, something that should not be affected by short-term, variable, arbitrary policies of political power. With the independence of the TCMB, the intention was to avoid the use of the bank as a source of public finance expenses and the rise of public debt with political, 'populist' objectives. In the first AKP period, this neoliberal concern was guaranteed by granting power to the TCMB to determine money policy and the instruments to be used to this end.[8]

Another tool was the regulatory boards structured in accordance with the TCMB's money policy and instruments, boards that were meant to work in coordination with the bank. These boards were established based on the argument that the state should be forced to adhere to tight fiscal and money discipline in order to sustain a well-functioning, highly competitive market economy, and they were granted broad authority in areas including norm setting, regulation and auditing.[9] This institutionalization was coupled with various regulations,[10] arguably aiming at the rational management of public debts, the construction of a stable market economy, and the solution of administrative problems faced by national and international investors.[11]

According to Burnham, these policies have aimed at attaining financial stability and fiscal discipline, and securing a 'free market' against society.[12] With the apparent 'independence' of the TCMB and the regulatory boards, the state could resist both the demands for inflationist money policy and political pressures. In this way, the state could also enjoy the opportunity to 'hide behind a monetary authority' and be relieved of the responsibility of decreasing wages due to anti-inflationist money policies.

The reason why Turkey became an attractive option for financial investments during the 2001–08 period[13] is that these regulations favoured technocratic, rule-based, predictable, accountable and depoliticized economic management. The monetary glut that prevailed in international markets during this period was reflected in households and capital circuits as cheap credit, a trend that enhanced the AKP's positive image in money management.[14] However, these regulations did not prevent big resource transfers to pro-AKP capital groups via public contracts and privatizations. This should be noted as a point that questions the effectiveness of depoliticization policies.[15]

Due to increasing concerns about the unsustainability of indebtedness following the 2008 global crisis, depoliticized economic management in Turkey approached its limits. This meant a new period until 2013 during which repoliticization efforts were observed, but without changes in the basic depoliticized institutional structure of the economy. In this period, the transformation of the crisis into a general crisis of the state and society was partially prevented to the extent that the political character of economic decision-making processes could be hidden thanks to some depoliticization strategies. On the other hand, the deepening crisis paved the way for the state to move away from the depoliticization strategy in critical areas by developing tools for direct state intervention in the economy.

During this transitional period, bureaucrats and politicians responsible for monetary issues in economic management, as well as representatives of financial markets, insisted on a depoliticization strategy, whereas, beginning with Erdoğan – the Prime Minister at the time – the politicians responsible for industrial policies and SMEs that could only survive with public money transfers started to push for policies in favour of repoliticization. Financial interests favoured a new standby agreement with the IMF for the continuation of the macro-economic stability programme and depoliticized institutionalization, as they did not want price stability and fiscal discipline to deteriorate before election periods. For small-sized capital groups, however, fiscal discipline and a new standby agreement with the IMF meant additional taxes and fewer public transfers. The Minister of Finance, Mehmet Şimşek, requested a more flexible programme from the IMF in order to reconcile these contradictory concerns.[16] When the talks remained fruitless, Ali Babacan, the Deputy Prime Minister, responsible for the economy at the time, announced that they were working on a fiscal-rule law that would undertake the function of the IMF. The aim was to reassure the financial markets that public deficits and debts would be re-regulated and that this would not be done arbitrarily.[17] However, according to Erdoğan, the country had only recently been relieved of the IMF's tutelage and there was no need to 'create our own IMF'[18] with this fiscal-rule law. As a result, under crisis conditions and with the approaching 2011 elections, the government chose not to proceed with the austerity programme and cut back on public expenses.

The fact that the repoliticization tendency continued despite the AKP's re-consolidation of power in the 2011 elections indicated that the crisis could only be managed now through the direct intervention of the state. Hence, it was stated in the Tenth Development Plan that the 2008 crisis necessitated stronger regulations in financial markets in the international arena. Moreover, it was emphasized that the dependency of developing countries on the multifaceted rules and regulations of the international economy could be provided only by powerful governments with high administrative capacity.[19]

Economic re-regulation and policies in the post-2011 period strengthened the tendency for centralization and direct interventions in economic management, while leading to an increase in tensions within political power. During these years, while the government tried to sustain its depoliticized money policy with an independent TCMB, it also loosened the fiscal discipline and debt policy.[20] The government called for a decrease in interest rates on the grounds that high interest rates prevented 'growth',[21] and it correspondingly bent the law, stating that the money policy should not bother itself with supporting growth and employment policies – that is, public debt. The borrowing limit of the Treasury was doubled at the discretion of the Cabinet of Ministers; it was emphasized that this was not an intervention in the institutional independence of the TCMB, but a response to external shocks.[22] The capital flight resulting from the decreasing credibility of the monetary policy due to the government's pressure for low interest rates under crisis conditions[23] and debates on whether this policy supported the government's goals for 'growth' further increased tensions around the TCMB.[24] As a result, although the institutional structure, organization and status of the TCMB were not altered during this period, the government had clearly started to intervene in the bank's indebtedness and other policy areas by increasing the borrowing limits of the Treasury.[25]

Meanwhile, the major critical intervention was seen in the working of the regulatory boards. Following Erdoğan's statement after the elections that '[s]ome independent boards are not useful; in the near future we may need to re-reform those boards',[26] Babacan said: 'Limits are overstepped; it is necessary to revise some authorizations of these boards and some have to be handed over to the government.'[27] That statement was the first sign of the repoliticization of these boards. Then, they were repoliticized by being transferred to the jurisdiction of related ministries on the grounds that they had hindered political decision-making processes.[28] In this way, the government acquired the authorization for auditing all fiscal or administrative activities and transactions of these boards. This move paved the way for the start of direct state intervention in the markets, with instruments such as tax exemptions and consumer and housing credit.[29]

Depoliticization was a strategy applied in Turkey to handle the management of the 2001 crisis; by the same token, policy changes made in the period of institutional repoliticization should be understood as a reaction to the crises of the post-2008 period. At that time, depoliticization, which can be compared with automatization in economic management, became an inappropriate tool to manage the problems of the post-2008 period. The new atmosphere needed manual and repoliticized decision-making mechanisms, and policies determined just in time according to monthly, daily and even hourly developments.[30]

The repoliticization of economic management since 2014

The worsening macro-economic conditions since 2013 and the AKP's concern to seek remedies for growth in the domestic market have been two factors that have further boosted the repoliticization tendency in economic management.[31] This tendency has increased conflicts among capital groups struggling for domination and profits in the domestic market. Moreover, spontaneous, temporary, flexible interventions that the state used to resort to in order to manage such conflicts have become too frequent. The persistent erosion of the depoliticized appearance of economic management as a result of state interventions and the AKP's political concern with acting quickly[32] paved the way for centralized, personalized, authoritarian/ autocratic economic management.

The AKP's Tenth Development Plan, issued in 2013, is illuminating regarding the party's agenda in relation to crisis management, and a prologue to important transformations in economic management in the shadow of the risks and uncertainties of the global economy.[33] The plan, while repeating the proposals of earlier plans, with its emphasis on money and price stability, pro-capital fiscal policies, incentives for technological upgrading and institutional and financial support to business in response to the demands of international and domestic capital groups, also underlined the need for powerful direct state intervention in the economy in response to the risks in the global markets. It hence underlined that global risks after the 2008 crisis required stronger regulations and rules to enhance the capacity of the state in the field of international finance, while increasing the level of institutionalization was needed to respond effectively to global, regional and national developments. The plan's vision was realized through the institutional and political changes put into effect de facto after 2014 and legalized after July 2018.

In fact, the transformations in Turkey's economic management since 2014 have parallels with the changes in the political regime after that date. The process of regime change that started with the President being elected – and hence strengthened – by a direct vote was to a great extent completed by the state of emergency decrees after the 2016 military coup attempt and by the presidential system of government (*Cumhurbaşkanlığı Hükümet Sistemi* or CHS) after the 2018 elections. With the transition to the CHS, presidential decrees have replaced KHKs (*Kanun Hükmünde Kararname* or decrees with the force of law),[34] which were issued by bypassing the parliamentary process during the state of emergency, and within this new context, economic management has been put under the authority of the presidency and all its institutions. Hence, since 2018, the institutional content and operation of the whole state structure have been continuously redefined by the current President, Erdoğan, who has the capacity to assign as well as remove all deputies, ministers, high-level public administrators and officers.[35]

This change should be considered together with the economic crisis becoming a political crisis and the increasing threat of rising social unrest on political power. A new process started from 2013 with the narrowing of credit opportunities, which interrupted the reproduction of big holdings and households. As will be discussed in detail in following sections, in this period major changes towards repoliticization were realized in the institutional structure of the economic management. The TCMB and the regulatory boards working in the field of monetary policy have been reorganized in a repoliticized way, and a series of new offices, boards, presidencies and ministries have been founded with the aim of consolidating all control and information flow functions within the economy under the authority of the President; the management of financial resources, debts, expenses and budgets of all public institutions has been centralized in one person. The following overview of these changes, which have been put into effect by the CHS, reveal the instruments, goals and class content of this new institutional design.

Reorganization of the TCMB

The repoliticization tendency in monetary policy has continued since 2013, with increasing pressure on the TCMB and the reorganization of its institutional structure. In short, pressures on the TCMB to keep interest rates low have become more and more intense to protect the AKP's indebted political base from the costs of expensive credit, especially in the housing sector. The recycling of SMEs' debts through cheap credit has been another concern in this regard.[36] It should also be noted that, in order not to shoulder the responsibility of the ongoing crisis and rising interest rates, President Erdoğan has put the burden on the 'interest rate lobby' and has continuously applied pressure on the TCMB to end official interest rate practices.[37] These pressures resulted in the lifting of market control on monetary policy decisions in January 2017; to a great extent, this authority has passed to the government.[38] Under the new regime, the TCMB has been put under the jurisdiction of the Ministry of Treasury and Finance – a ministry formed using another presidential decree – and has lost all its independence.[39] With its loss of independence, audit and control of the bank's institutional organization and operations have become centralized and personalized.[40] The President has been authorized to select and appoint the TCMB president and his or her deputies, as well as the monetary policy board members; the latter's four-year term in office has been limited to the length of the President's, a provision directly linking the fates of the political and monetary authorities.[41] The President, having used this power on 6 July 2019, appointed a new president to the TCMB, stating that, in contrast to the 'unbearable' independence of the old president, the new TCMB president would work in harmony with the government.[42] Following this appointment, the bank declared a substantial decrease in interest rates on 25 July – a decrease that would continue throughout the year – arguing that the decision was taken after consideration of global financial dynamics.[43]

Reorganization of regulatory boards

During and after the state of emergency, additional regulations were made for the administration of regulatory boards, which were already under the control of the political power. For instance, with the amendments made to the Banking Law,[44] embezzlement charges in credit allocations and restructuring operations were hampered; the application of a concordato preventivo was expanded in place of the suspension of bankruptcy; and the Banking Regulation and Supervision Agency (*Bankacılık Düzenleme ve Denetleme Kurumu* or BDDK) was authorized to restructure the financial debts of companies in favour of debtors through administrative decrees.[45] During the BDDK's use of this new authority,[46] many highly indebted holding companies known to be pro-government applied to this scheme and were bailed out by the state.[47] Another important monetary institution, the Competition Board, was also reorganized, arguably to effectively apply 'market surveillance and audit', while the public statement regarding this change claimed that the aim was to create a more dynamic and efficient market by reconciling the concerns of various actors determining market conditions with those of political power.[48]

Other legal modifications

Besides the repoliticization of existing economic institutions under the control of political power, a series of offices, boards, presidencies and new ministries were established under the new administrative structure, with the President placed at the centre. All public resources, and their use and management, were put under the authority of the President. The goal was to coordinate the country's production, finance and trade from a single centre via Finance and Investment Offices working under the presidency. In order to produce applicable strategies and policy recommendations from the reports prepared by these offices, boards such as the Board of Economic Policies and the Board of Science, Technology and Innovation were established. Moreover, the overview of the management of state debts was given to the Directorate of Strategy and Budget, which was also directly accountable to the President.

The Turkey Wealth Fund[49]

The objective of the Turkey Wealth Fund (*Türkiye Varlık Fonu* or TVF), which has shares in public companies such as Turkish Airlines, Halkbank, Ziraat Bank, BOTAŞ, Türksat and Borsa-İstanbul, is defined in its stated purpose as finding cheap credit via the privatization of big-budget public assets, land or collateral.[50] The fund, having been established during the state of emergency, however, could not start functioning due to administrative problems,[51] was put under the authority of the President under the new regime, and the President's son-in-law, Berat Albayrak (who was also appointed Minister of Treasury and Finance), was assigned to manage it as the acting president. The President, as the head of its executive board, still holds the authority to make all fund decisions, including those on the management and use of all public resources.[52] The TVF, which is not answerable to the Turkish Court of Accounts and enjoys wide tax exemption opportunities, is assumed to manage public assets more 'efficiently and effectively'. As a joint stock company subject to private legal provisions, it is a unique institution within the presidential organization.[53]

The Savings Deposit Insurance Fund

The Savings Deposit Insurance Fund (*Tasarruf Mevduatı Sigorta Fonu* or TMSF) was established in 2003 as the second largest Turkish company with autonomous status. It was reorganized during the state of emergency as the trustee[54] for companies belonging to the Fethullahist Terrorist Organization (*Fethullahçı Terör Örgütü*)/ Parallel State Organization (*Paralel Devlet Yapılanması*).[55] In 2018, it was placed under the authority of the President together with the 937 companies under its trusteeship. This meant that almost all state-owned companies were put under the authority of the President via the fund, making the President the final decision maker in the management of all of them.[56]

The merger of ministries

Ministries, which are lower in the hierarchy of the CHS's internal organization in terms of position and power compared with offices and boards, are designed as executive organs of the policies identified by government.[57] Six ministries relating to economic management were merged in order arguably to provide resource diversity for public debts and effectiveness, efficiency and speed in the decision-making processes.[58] However, the Ministry of Treasury and Finance headed by the President's son-in-law, despite the limited role attributed to the ministries, has become de facto the second most important institution in economic management following the President. As well as working in coordination with the new economy boards, the ministry has acquired power over many important economic institutions such as the TCMB, BDDK and the Development Bank. Moreover, all public finance accounts, except that of the Unemployment Insurance Fund, were combined under the name of the Single Treasury Account for Institutions and given over to the control and management of this ministry.[59] This shows that, despite the initial design, the working of the new state structure has been subject to change due to internal power struggles within the state.[60] Lastly, the position of deputy minister was created in the ministries with the flexibility that they would be appointed by the President from the private sector if required. The periods in office of the deputy ministers would also be limited by that of the President.

The centralization of all public assets under the authority of the presidency and the Ministry of Treasury and Finance reflects the politicized, personalized and arbitrary character of the new economic management in Turkey. It is clear that behind this approach there lies a concern for managing inter- and intra-class conflicts and possible political crises that would arise in relation to these conflicts. On the other hand, it should not be overlooked that these arrangements have been promoted with pro-capital public statements in order to assuage the anxiety of domestic and foreign capital over the trend towards politicization. As a matter of fact, the President himself clearly announced that the political power was market-friendly; domestic and foreign markets and finance circles should feel secure; the liquidity required by the banks would be provided to them without limit; and even the state of emergency itself had been declared to benefit the markets themselves.[61] Although the Turkish Industry and Business Association (*Türk Sanayicileri ve İşadamları Derneği* or TÜSİAD), which represents internationalized capital in Turkey, frequently stated in its annual reports that it was hesitant about the repoliticization process and emphasized the need for structural regulation, financial discipline, financial stability and a gradual rise of interest rates, the TÜSİAD finally got the President's message and declared its support to the government in its new economic programme.[62] For SMEs, which are most vulnerable to high interest rates and currency fluctuations in the Turkish economy, the government relieved their concerns by announcing that it was preparing a joint action plan with the banks. This promise was realized with tax reductions and low interest rate credits under a state guarantee, and direct transfers from the Treasury within the framework of the 'new bailout' agreement. Moreover, the application of 25 per cent capital blockage and the suspension of bankruptcy in limited companies were lifted while the Credit Guarantee Fund and Export Promotion Bank were converted to institutions functioning as means of money transfer from the state to SMEs. Emlak Bank was restructured with the good news that the construction sector – a sector with high priority for political power – would be expanded further. Representative institutions in all these sectors soon declared that they would always stand by the President against attacks targeting 'the national economic model', whatever the cost, with the partisan motto 'We won't lose this economic war'.[63] This common stance between political power and capital circles proves that the centralization of economic management aims to serve the reproduction of both capital and state in conditions in which the 'self-operating market' cannot overcome prevailing accumulation problems. Therefore, the repoliticization process that marked the post-2013 period in economic management is a precursor to an understanding of intervention that does not go against capital; on the contrary, it aims to reshape social relations on behalf of capital.

Eventually, all these legal-institutional arrangements in economic management, from taxation policies to public debt management, should be understood as an expression or consequence of class struggles fought within the contradictory development of the capital accumulation process in Turkey.[64] As Erol[65] argues, with President Erdoğan at the very top of the institutional hierarchy of the new economic management and people within his closest circle and from various constituents of capital among the mid-management cadres, Turkey is now managed by a 'cabinet of capital'.[66] The fact that the majority of these cabinet members are representatives of a variety of capital sectors such as housing, energy, transportation, agriculture, tourism, health and education affirms this argument. For capital circles, this means that the demands and policy preferences of different sectors of capital in the crisis environment can be represented quickly within government.[67] These are basic class dynamics behind the repoliticization strategy that started to be crystallized from 2014 onwards and institutionalized with the move to the CHS in 2018. This is a situation that shows that discretion in economic management in Turkey means institutionalization in favour of capital. Similar discretionary processes can be identified in the workings of offices, boards and ministries, with overlapping duties and unclear job descriptions.[68]

Conclusion: state-centred neoliberalism

Do all these changes in economic management mean a rupture from the neoliberal discourse and/or policy set-ups that have prevailed in the field since the beginning of the 1980s? Or should we understand that authoritarian-autocratic governments coming to power not only in Turkey but also in Hungary, Austria, the Philippines and India, among other places, are in fact the results of neoliberalism, or even its success, despite its earlier claims to 'democracy' and 'rule of law'?

Bank bailout operations of states and the accompanying political measures marking the post-2008 crisis period once more negated the liberal assumption that the markets reach an equilibrium when left alone. The Tenth Development Plan of the AKP government in Turkey states that the stability of financial markets and financial discipline can be achieved only by continuous surveillance, control, audit and action by the state, a statement which indicates that the AKP has learned the right lessons from this process.[69] On the other hand, as Bedirhanoğlu[70] asserts, in today's financial capitalism, where public expenses and national economies have become highly dependent on hard cash flows and foreign debt cycles, political control over and audit of economic management do not necessarily mean moving away from the 'market rationale'. Therefore, repoliticization, considered in the context of money and labour management, does not mean moving away from neoliberalism; on the contrary, it refers to a political intention to insist on neoliberalism. It is an effort to sustain the monetarist policies institutionalized during the period of depoliticized economic management through repoliticized discretionary state strategies under conditions of new financial dependency; it is therefore the institutionalization of irregularity rather than re-regulation, the latter being the lost promise of the post-Washington Consensus in Turkey.

Both strategies are technocratic in the sense that economic decision-making processes are attempted in order to be close to labour interventions. In the recent arrangements, the State Supervisory Council was given a wide remit in the audit of labour unions, a development that represented the final step in the suppression and debilitation of labour since 2001.[71] In Turkey's new political regime, in which the coordination of economic institutions such as the TCMB, regulatory boards, new offices and presidencies is handled by 'the cabinet of capital', the political interventions of labour and other social sectors are not desired – more than that, they are seen as a threat to market rationality. In conclusion, the move from depoliticization to repoliticization in the economic management of Turkey is a manifestation of a new period in which pro-capital state interventions in the market are visible. As Bedirhanoğlu[72] argues, this change of strategy is not only against labour but is also the result of the weakening of its organized power by the divisive and repressive labour policies of neoliberalism, as well as the fact that labour has been subordinated by finance capital since 1980. This change of strategy, reflecting the passage to a state-centred neoliberalism in Turkey,[73] implies a deepening of the distinction between democracy and liberalism, and transforms the apparently weak and 'neutral' form of the neoliberal state into a powerfully discretionary one 'in favour of capital'.

Notes

1. Harvey 2006.
2. See Bonefeld 2003; Clarke 2005.
3. Burnham 2001.
4. Ibid.: 128, 137.
5. Ibid.: 362–4.
6. Burnham 2017: 361; Clarke 1991.
7. Also see Kutun Gürgen 2013; Erol 2016; Dönmez and Zemandl 2018.

8. *Resmi Gazete*, no. 4651, 25 April 2001. See also TCMB 2015: 21; 2012: 13–14.
9. Öniş 2009: 414.
10. For example, the Law of Public Finance and Debt Management, Board of Coordination of Improvement of Investment Environment.

11. DPT 2006: 27.

12. Burnham 2001: 128.

13. See Güngen (Chapter 6).

14. See Bedirhanoğlu (Chapter 1).

15. Kutun Gürgen 2013; Erol 2016.

16. 'IMF ile anlaşma yapıldı mı?', *Habertürk*, 13 April 2009.

17. Boratav 2016.

18. 'Kendi IMF'mizi yaratmaya gerek yok', *Radikal*, 9 October 2010.

19. DPT 2013.

20. Dönmez and Zemandl 2018; Erol 2016.

21. 'Politika faizleri hala sabit tutuluyor', *Habertürk*, 11 January 2012.

22. TCMB 2008.

23. Bedirhanoğlu 2015.

24. Şener 2016: 144.

25. Dönmez and Zemandl 2018.

26. 'Özerk kurullara bakan denetimi', *Dünya*, 24 August 2011.

27. 'Bağımsız kurulların yetkilerinde düzenleme şart', Bloomberg, 5 May 2011.

28. *Resmi Gazete*, no. 2808, 17 August 2011; Legislative Decree no. 649 having the force of law.

29. In addition to those regulations expanding the room for direct intervention and manoeuvre, the Economic Coordination Board undertook critical functions. *Resmi Gazete*, no. 5838, 18 February 2009.

30. 'Çok senaryolu bir ekonomimiz var', *Hürriyet*, 12 October 2011.

31. See Güngen (Chapter 6).

32. See Bedirhanoğlu (Chapter 1).

33. DPT 2013.

34. For these detailed arrangements, see State of Emergency Report 2016.

35. Bedirhanoğlu 2019; Güzelsarı 2019.

36. Şener 2016: 147–8.

37. 'Erdoğan'dan Merkez Bankası'na: Söylediklerinizin hiçbiri tutmuyor, tutmaz', CNN Türk, 17 November 2017.

38. Ü. Akçay (2017) 'Kalkınmacı' Merkez Bankası I', *Gazete Duvar*, 13 November.

39. *Resmi Gazete*, no. 30474, 10 July 2018; Presidential Decree no. 3.

40. *Resmi Gazete*, no. 30473, 10 July 2018.

41. *Resmi Gazete*, no. 30653, 12 January 2019.

42. 'Dava arkadaşlığı terkedilmez', CNN Türk, 10 July 2019.

43. 'Para politikasi kurulu karari', https://www.tcmb.gov.tr/wps/wcm/connect/tr/tcmb+tr/main+menu/duyurular/basin/2019/duy2019-29.

44. *Resmi Gazete*, no. 29974, 9 February 2017; KHK no. 687.

45. *Resmi Gazete*, no. 30510, 15 August 2018; *Resmi Gazete*, no. 30602, 21 November 2018.

46. 'BDDK kredi borcu yapılandırması için yönetmelik hazırladı', NTV, 4 August 2018.

47. 'Hangi şirketler borcunu yeniden yapılandırma sürecine girdi?', BBC Türkçe, 29 November 2018.

48. '100 günlük eylem planı', Presidency of the Republic of Turkey, 3 August 2018, pp. 8–9.

49. *Resmi Gazete*, no. 30533, 12 July 2018.

50. Akça et al., 2017: 81–65.

51. *Resmi Gazete*, no. 29813, 26 September 2016.

52. *Resmi Gazete*, no. 30474, 10 July 2018; Presidential Decree no. 1.

53. 'Varlık Fonu'nun başına kendi geçti, damadını yardımcılığına getirdi', *Birgün*, 3 September 2018.

54. *Resmi Gazete*, no. 6758, 1 September 2016; KHK no. 674.

55. The parting of ways with the Gülenists took place on 17–25 December 2013, the week that marked the major corruption of the state.

56. *Resmi Gazete*, no. 30479, 15 July 2018; Presidential Decree no. 4. See also 'Dev Şirketler Erdoğan'a bağlandı!', *Cumhuriyet*, 18 July 2018.

57. *Resmi Gazete*, no. 30474, 10 July 2018; Presidential Decree no. 1.

58. 'Yeni Ekonomik Model', CNN Türk, 10 August 2018. See also *Resmi Gazete*, no. 30473, 9 July 2018; Legislative Decree no. 703. The under-secretariat of the Treasury under the Deputy Prime Minister was merged with the Ministry of Finance and given the new name Ministry of Treasury and Finance. The Ministries of Science, Industry, Technology and Development were merged under the name of the Ministry of Industry and Technology. The Ministries of Customs and Trade and Economy were merged under the name of the Ministry of Trade.

59. 'Devletin tüm parası Albayrak'ta toplanacak: İşte hesaba dâhil olacak kurumlar', *Cumhuriyet*, 10 August 2018.

60. Bedirhanoğlu 2019.

61. Ü. Akçay (2018) 'Yeni yönetim ve ekonomik gidişat', *Gazete Duvar*, 26 June; Bedirhanoğlu 2019; see also 'Erdoğan'dan itiraf: OHAL'den istifade ederek grevlere anında müdahale ediyoruz', *Cumhuriyet*, 12 July 2017.

62. '8 maddeli seçim sonrası reform talebi', *BusinessHT*, 25 June 2018.

63. 'Yeni ekonomik model hususunda MÜSİAD basın duyurusu', 10 August 2018.

64. Depoliticization, meaning the closure of the political arena to the masses, refers to precluding class politicization and controlling it via labour. For a study assessing this institutional move regarding class relations, see Ercan and Oğuz (Chapter 5).

65. E. Erol (2018) 'Yeni ekonomi yönetimi devlet, sermaye ve emek', *Birgün*, 22 June.

66. The President's son-in-law, Albayrak, was assigned as Minister of the Treasury and Finance, and Ruhsar Pekcan, the former executive of the Union of Chambers and Commodity Exchanges of Turkey, to the Ministry of Trade. Fuat Oktay, the Deputy President, Minister of Industry and Technology and TÜRKSAT executive board member, is still an executive board member of Turkish Airlines Technic. See 'Özel sektörden kabineye atanan beş bakan', *Bianet*, 16 November 2018

67. O. Oyan (2018) 'Rejimin niteliği', *SoL*, 25 December; Güzelsarı 2019.

68. Bedirhanoğlu 2019.

69. DPT 2013: 1–5.

70. Ibid.

71. Presidential Decree no. 5.

72. Bedirhanoğlu 2019.

73. See also Bonefeld 2012.

References

Akça, İ., S. Algül, H. Dinçer, E. Keleşoğlu and B. A. Özden (2017) *When State of Emergency Becomes the Norm: The Impact of Executive Decrees on Turkish Legislation*. Cologne: Heinrich Böll Stiftung.

Bedirhanoğlu, P. (2015) 'Corruption and state under the AKP rule in Turkey: retreat from the modern bourgeois state?', *Centre for Policy Analysis and Research on Turkey 4* (5): 35–44.

Bedirhanoğlu, P. (2019) 'Cumhurbaşkanlığı Hükümet Sistemi ve Türkiye'de

Ekonomi Yönetiminin Dönüşümü: Neoliberalizmin Sonu mu?' in E. Karaçimen, M. Yaman, N. Özkaplan, Ö. Akduran and Ş. Oğuz (eds), *Nuray Ergüneş için Yazılar: Finansallaşma, Kadın Emeği ve Devlet*. Istanbul: SAV, pp. 211–32.

Bedirhanoğlu, P. (forthcoming) 'Financialization, household indebtedness and state transformation in the global South' in E. Pınar, Z. Yılmaz, M. Kutun and E. Babacan (eds), *Regime Change in Turkey: Neoliberal*

Authoritarianism, Islamism, and Populism. Abingdon: Routledge.

Bonefeld, W. (2003) 'The capitalist state: illusion and critique' in W. Bonefeld (ed.). *Revolutionary Writing.* New York, NY: Autonomedia, pp. 200–26.

Bonefeld, W. (2012) 'Freedom and the strong state: on German ordoliberalism', *New Political Economy 17* (5): 633–56.

Boratav, K. (2016) 'The Turkish bourgeoisie under neoliberalism', *Research and Policy on Turkey 1* (1): 1–10.

Burnham, P. (2001) 'New Labour and the politics of depoliticisation', *British Journal of Politics and International Relations 3* (2): 127–49.

Burnham, P. (2017) 'Neo-liberalism, crisis and the contradictions of depoliticisation', *Open Journal of Sociopolitical Studies 10* (2): 357–80.

Clarke, S. (1991) 'State, class struggle and the reproduction of capital' in S. Clarke (ed.), *The State Debate.* London: Palgrave Macmillan, pp. 183–203.

Clarke, S. (2005) 'The neoliberal theory of society' in A. Saad-Filho and D. Johnston (eds), *Neoliberalism: A Critical Reader.* London: Pluto Press, pp. 50–9.

Dönmez P. and E. Zemandl (2018) 'Crisis of capitalism and (de-)politicisation of monetary policymaking: reflections from Hungary and Turkey', *New Political Economy 24* (11): 123–45.

DPT (2006) 9. *Kalkınma Planı (2007–2013)* [Ninth Development Plan (2007–2013)]. Ankara: Prime Minister's State and Planning Organization.

DPT (2013) 10. *Kalkınma Planı (2014–2018)* [Tenth Development Plan (2014–2018)]. Ankara: Prime Minister's State and Planning Organization.

Erol, M. E. (2016) 'AKP Döneminde İktisadi Politika Yapımının Siyaseti: Süreklilik ve Kopuş Bağlamında Bir Tartışma' in T. Tören and M. Kutun (eds), *'Yeni' Türkiye? Kapitalizm, Devlet, Sınıflar.* Istanbul: SAV, pp. 280–326.

Güzelsarı, S. (2019) 'Neoliberal Otoriterleşme, Devletin Şirketleşmesi ya da Şirket-Devlet: Cumhurbaşkanlığı Hükümet Sistemi', *Ayrıntı Dergi 29*: 39–50.

Harvey, D. (2006) 'Neo-liberalism as creative destruction', *Geografiska Annaler: Series B, Human Geography 88* (2): 145–58.

Kutun Gürgen, M. (2013) 'Türkiye'de Neoliberal Ekonomi Politikalarının Uygulanması Sürecinde Bir Yönetim Stratejisi Olarak Apolitizasyon ve Depolitizasyon', *Praksis 30–31*: 43–76.

Öniş, Z. (2009) 'Beyond the 2001 financial crisis: the political economy of the new phase of neo-liberal restructuring in Turkey', *Review of International Political Economy 16* (3): 409–32.

Şener, U. (2016) 'Central banking and monetary policy under the AKP government in Turkey: the politics of national conservatism', *Austrian Journal of Development Studies 32* (1/2): 135–60.

TCMB (2008) *Finansal İstikrar Raporu.* No. 7. Ankara: Türkiye Cumhuriyeti Merkez Bankası (TCMB).

TCMB (2012) *Yıllık Rapor.* Ankara: Türkiye Cumhuriyeti Merkez Bankası (TCMB).

TCMB (2015) *Finansal İstikrar Raporu.* No. 21. Ankara: Türkiye Cumhuriyeti Merkez Bankası (TCMB).

8 | THE AKP'S INCOME-DIFFERENTIATED HOUSING STRATEGIES UNDER THE PRESSURE OF RESISTANCE AND DEBT

Özlem Çelik

Introduction

This chapter examines the income-differentiated housing provision strategies of the state under AKP rule after the 2001 economic crisis, which prepared the ground for historical changes in housing policy in Turkey. In the existing literature, the growth of the housing sector in the economy is portrayed as one of the main targets of the AKP's economic programme, based on the bourgeoning construction sector. While this is definitely an important issue in understanding the current conditions of capital accumulation in the country, this chapter pays attention to the central political role attributed by the AKP to the housing sector in the creation of consent to its rule. Due to this focus, the chapter prioritizes developments on the demand side of the housing provision process while providing a relatively limited analysis of the suppliers, except for the big public players in the sector. Based on the findings of two field research projects conducted in Istanbul in 2016 and 2017–18,[1] it argues that the state has played a deliberate mediator role in creating a new and lucrative housing market on public lands and *gecekondu*[2] areas within the context of financializing the Turkish economy since 2002. Furthermore, due to economic and political opportunities, as well as the risks this process comprises, the state has followed carefully designed housing strategies, differentiated on the basis of income and continually redefined according to changing market conditions and resistances. The mediator role of the state has thus been shaped by the initial conditions of the AKP government's economic programme, as well as by the contingent interaction between global financial flows into the built environment and the social and economic tensions and risks accumulating in the housing field.

The period after the 2001 crisis witnessed significant changes in housing policy in Turkey. This meant a series of new legislations in urban governance and housing provision in the early years of the AKP's rule, leading to cycles of centralization and decentralization in urban planning powers. Changing power relations between different scales were shaped by the EU membership process, the new economic measures imposed by the IMF–World Bank programme of 2001,[3] and the 2003 McKinsey report targeting growth in the construction sector as a remedy for the crisis.[4] The AKP's new economic programme included measures that aimed to attract global capital to invest in the built environment in Turkey. This was a strategy that was designed to fulfil the interests of investors on the one hand, and to provide the government with political room to manoeuvre in the housing sector. One of the main effects of this new economic programme was a change in housing policy, which envisaged the provision of housing to different groups in society via the promotion of homeownership and the redefinition of the housing market on an ownership-based model. The state has played the leading role in the expansion, regulation and promotion of this new housing agenda for both attracting investors into the housing market and involving consumers in the homeownership model.

The newly developing housing sector has been defined by differing demands and conflicting interests. Large-scale developers and upper- and middle-income households have been in favour of the state's new housing strategies, including the lowering of interest rates on loans and the promotion of new financial tools. The poor, however, have powerfully resisted being indebted due to the forced regeneration process in their neighbourhoods in the big cities. Small- and medium-scale contractors have also put pressure on the state to be active in the expanding house-building sector rather than serving only as subcontractors to large companies. The state responded to the demands of contractors by enacting regulations for the small-scale renewal of middle-income housing units without any displacement. The state's involvement in creating this new housing market – one that would bring together middle-income households and small- and medium-scale contractors – has comprised a strategy to expand the construction sector's capacity in the economy. The state has played a more critical role in the housing processes affecting lower- and upper-income groups as this area has been defined by the powerful resistance of poor *gecekondu*-holders and by the expectation of high profits on the part of large-scale developers and the well-off. The various state strategies in housing thus reflect the class character of housing policy, particularly during the last decade in Turkey. The involvement of lower-income households in home-ownership carries a specific importance in understanding how the constituency of the AKP has also resisted regeneration projects and how the party has responded to this resistance in order not to lose consent to its rule.

An analysis of the state's income-based housing strategies can be made on the basis of very limited statistical data available on mortgage and loan use in Turkey. To overcome this limitation, 24 semi-structured interviews were conducted with a variety of actors in the housing sector, including state personnel at local and central levels, financiers, property developers, representatives of real-estate investment trusts (REITs), members of professional bodies, neigh-bourhood residents, and activists who have taken part in the resistance against state-led gentrification processes. In addition to these pri-mary sources, secondary sources including interviews, reports, city plans and available statistics on housing production and on mortgage loan use were utilized. The field research included three important neighbourhoods in Istanbul – Sarıyer, Maltepe and Güngören – that have been targeted by the state for new and lucrative property development. Both the importance and the varied character of the neighbourhoods selected have provided data for generalization.

This chapter first examines the historical background of housing in Turkey. As will be discussed, increased levels of global capital flows have led to a significant change in the housing policies of AKP governments since 2002. Second, the income-differentiated housing strategies of the state will be analysed to understand how the state has economically and politically recomposed the poor in particular, a group that has been the AKP's main constituency so far despite the inequality-generating implications of neoliberalism.

Tracing the changes in the housing agenda in Turkey

Historically, there used to be various housing provision methods for lower-income households in Turkey, such as cooperatives, lodge-ments (rented accommodation for some state personnel at below market rate) and *gecekondu* housing, alongside a private housing market for middle- and upper-income households. The new housing agenda has aimed to redefine the conditions of housing by introducing new financial tools to the market, providing long-term housing loans for middle- and upper-income households, enabling non-Turkish citizens to own land and real estate,[5] and putting an end to the production of *gecekondu* housing by forcing low-income households to buy new housing units from regeneration projects.

The national strategy to start a new housing programme across the country was initiated by the AKP's 2003 Emergency Action Plan. This targeted: (1) the prevention of new *gecekondu* production and the regeneration[6] of existing schemes; and (2) debt-based housing provision via financial tools. As part of the action plan, the Mass Housing Administration (*Toplu Konut İdaresi Başkanlığı* or TOKİ), which used to be a finance institution for housing, was empowered as the central institution under the Prime Minister's Office to plan and implement housing provision policies for the various income groups, including by awarding contracts to the private sector. Consequently, TOKİ gained the authority for planning housing at all scales, opening up tenders for new housing projects, running urban regeneration (UR) projects in *gecekondu* neighbourhoods, as well as in 'risky zones' defined under the Disaster Law No. 6306, administering large-scale projects including shopping malls, schools and hospitals, and implementing a revenue-sharing model for profit and non-profit housing production with private developers. While the public land stocks under the authority of a variety of state institutions were transferred to the control of TOKİ, the administration was also exempted from the Procurement Law[7] for its construction practices in 2011. TOKİ was also freed from budgetary controls and auditing by the High Court of Accounts in 2005.[8] Following the empowerment of TOKİ, the state-owned Emlak Konut REIT[9] was established to regulate the housing market for upper-income housing production, to initiate large-scale projects and to facilitate the bureaucracy for investors in the luxury housing market.[10]

In order to boost the economy via the construction sector and to sustain a conflict-free planning process by the empowerment of TOKİ and the establishment of Emlak Konut REIT, the state worked to respond to the interests of global investors and domestic firms by providing them with large areas of land in city centres, together with new development rights and high revenues. The provision of large-scale land was enabled by the privatization of public lands,[11] including ports, forests and green areas,[12] and also via UR projects in *gecekondu* neighbourhoods. These projects targeted the whole of the neighbourhood, turning the area into vacant land by displacing existing residents to the peripheries of the cities.[13]

State housing strategies for middle- and upper-income households

Middle- and upper-income households used to be the main components of Turkey's formal housing sector as actual or potential owners up to the 2000s. The AKP's main housing strategies for these groups have thus aimed to increase demand by creating the conditions for a booming and profitable sector.

The first strategy of the state to increase demand and supply in the existing housing sector and sustain capital accumulation was to expand the volume of buyers via the Mortgage Law No. 5582, enacted in 2007, the promotion of UR mortgages, and the amendment of the Real Estate Reciprocity Law in 2012. By the enactment of the new mortgage law, middle-income households started to become involved in the housing market, accounting for 34 per cent of residential sales by 2016.[14] The dominance of middle-income groups in mortgage lending was also because regulations limited the involvement of lower-income groups in the mortgage market in order to prevent the risks of a financial crisis.[15] As Aslan shows in his research on Istanbul between 2010 and 2014, the users of mortgage loans have an income that is approximately six times the minimum wage in Turkey.[16] The same research also showed a high education level among mortgage holders, whereas the education level was quite low among lower-income households. Thus, accessing the mortgage system[17] has had a class character in Turkey.

The involvement of middle-income households in the housing market was also supported by UR mortgages provided by the Risky Zones Law, which offered mortgages to a variety of consumers, including residents in 'risky' buildings (either buildings in a disaster zone or buildings that are unlikely to survive a disaster), tenants who lived in a risky building for at least one year, and residents living in a risky building and therefore needing to buy another flat.[18] UR mortgages have been made available with no payment required for a resource utilization support fund and no banking or

insurance transaction taxes. The second target of the UR policy
was middle-income housing units, mainly apartment blocks on a
single plot rather than the whole neighbourhood,[19] that required
rebuilding without any displacement. As mentioned before, this was
a response to the demands of small- and middle-scale companies
and contractors in housing production[20] as part of a construction economy. This strategy aimed not only to include small- and
middle-scale housing companies in housing production but also to
involve a wider segment of society in the financialized housing market by providing them with UR mortgages on specific terms. The
regeneration projects under this new law were also subsidized by the
state through rent support to the homeowners for 18 months during
the regeneration and reduced taxes for the companies. In this way,
middle-income households, and small- and middle-scale building
companies, started to be a part of the redistribution of capital in the
growing housing sector.

While middle- and upper-income households cooperated with
the state in the UR policy due to the gains of both getting new flats
and the rising rent gap, as will be discussed in the next section, low-
income households responded to this new housing policy through
organized resistance, since it would lead to their ultimate removal
from their *gecekondu* neighbourhoods.

Housing strategies for low-income households

The housing of the poor had not been systematically regulated
in Turkey before the 2000s. During the massive migration of rural
populations to the big cities in the 1950s, the state had remained
largely silent on their housing needs, and 'self-help' housing,[21]
mostly on state-owned land, was promoted as a solution by the new-
comers. The inclusion of self-help housing in the capitalist housing
market by giving such housing legal or semi-legal status became a
question of negotiation between the new residents and politicians at
the time of elections, leading to 16 amnesty legislations and laws as
part of improvement and development plans up to the early 1990s.[22]
Those plans aimed to provide titles or title deeds to the people living
in these houses in exchange for certain payments. However, having a title deed for the land still meant that the houses were not
legally recognized. This process also involved tensions and conflicts
between the residents and the state authorities. In the 1970s, in

some neighbourhoods, the attempts of local authorities to knock down those housing units turned into a clash between residents and the police.[23] In the 1980s, under a populist and clientelist system, the state took some limited measures to include *gecekondu* units in the housing market by giving subsidies for the construction of mass housing elsewhere or in the neighbourhood for *gecekondu* dwellers through the Mass Housing Fund. However, housing production stagnated due to the effects of the economic crisis of the 1990s,[24] while the subsidies helped encourage middle-income housing production rather than housing the poor.[25]

UR projects targeting the transformation of *gecekondu* neighbourhoods as a whole meant a new era for *gecekondu* housing. Following the AKP's 2003 Emergency Action Plan, new UR policies displaced urban planning procedures, bypassing different levels of the decision-making process. Since 2005, when the first UR law was enacted, UR schemes have varied for *gecekondu* neighbourhoods, dilapidated housing areas in historical parts of cities, and neighbourhoods with households of different income levels. In the initial phase of the UR projects, the first target was the demolition of whole *gecekondu* neighbourhoods and the displacement of existing residents to the peripheries of the cities, where mass housing units were constructed by TOKİ, although only for the 'rightful owners' of the demolished units, not tenants. The main consequences of this zero-tolerance scheme were displacement due to forced eviction and homelessness, and the dispossession of residents with no income or insufficient income to afford the units,[26] as well as indebtedness. Rather than offering deeds or title deeds to residents, the new scheme aimed to transfer the centrally located valuable *gecekondu* and dilapidated historical neighbourhood land to TOKİ to use it for luxury housing under market conditions.

This housing strategy led to opposition in the designated neighbourhoods, gaining the attention and solidarity of professional bodies of urban planners and architects, civil society organizations, political groups and parties against the UR projects. Residents demanded a decentralized decision-making process with the right to participate, to not be forced into debt, and to not be displaced; instead, they wanted regeneration in situ, so they could stay where they used to live. The resistance of the *gecekondu* dwellers expanded across cities, and particularly in Istanbul, where the majority of

gecekondu neighbourhoods were located. The residents created
district- and city-wide platforms and established associations that
acted together[27] and also mobilized activists, professional bodies
and political groups.[28] Neighbourhood resistance took a different
form in each locality, including marches, neighbourhood meetings,
solidarity campaigns against police violence, legal cases to cancel
the projects, and stopping construction companies from entering
the neighbourhoods.

In the targeted areas, 11,543 units were rapidly demolished
between 2004 and 2008; this is a very high number historically.[29]
The new Municipality Law enabled the demolition and rebuilding
of the houses for their rightful owners through a partnership with
TOKİ. Following the new regulations between 2002 and 2008,
TOKİ became the only institution with responsibility for UR projects to construct housing for profit on state-owned land or through
the expropriation of land in UR areas.[30] The housing strategies of
the state had to be revisited after the 2008 crisis – and particularly
after a number of poll defeats at the district level in the 2009 local
elections.[31] The political defeats of the AKP were mostly in districts
where there was coercive pressure on residents for regeneration purposes. The AKP's response to this has been the promotion of some
cooperative measures to get the consent of residents in those neighbourhoods as well as some new redistributive mechanisms to include
small- and middle-scale contractors in the housing market again.
The state started offering protocols at the local level in cooperation
with TOKİ and the greater and district municipalities to dissolve
resistance or overcome obstacles in order to start UR projects anew,
or to continue those announced since 2004.

Making protocols at the local level based on the situation of the
particular neighbourhood has been defined as a strategy during
the negotiation process between residents and district municipality
representatives.[32] While this method started in *gecekondu* neighbourhoods, the main aim of making protocols has been to get the consent
of all residents in order to launch the projects. The process of getting
consent has included negotiations on the right to housing, including
in situ regeneration. With the help of this method, residents started
to agree to the loan terms of the municipality and TOKİ, while the
state has ensured the availability of negotiation channels to continue
regeneration in central *gecekondu* neighbourhoods in the big cities.[33]

However, as residents said in the interviews – both those who gave their consent willingly[34] and those who did not[35] – it is clear that they considered the process unavoidable.

The second 100 Day Action Plan of the President, announced on 13 December 2018 in response to the ongoing economic crisis, also supported the local protocol approach by emphasizing the social dimension of UR projects at the decision-making and implementation stages. This meant the issuing of local protocols, tailored to each locality, to continue with housing production plans and ensure legitimacy for the whole process. The first strategy to this end has been to depoliticize organized resistance by responding to some demands of the residents. The main tool used to depoliticize resistance has been TOKİ's acceptance of in situ UR projects rather than eviction-based ones. In addition to the in situ UR strategy, another approach has been to make agreements with residents individually, but this has created conflicts among them in relation to the agreed value of their assets in the neighbourhood. Individual negotiations have brought varying payments or subsidies to residents. This was part of a 'divide and rule' strategy to depoliticize the residents.[36]

The second strategy has been to create vacant land for investors to provide economic prosperity in a time of recession in the housing sector in Turkey. After the shift of UR projects from eviction-based to in situ, the existing residents of the neighbourhoods have been directed to move to high-density apartment blocks in the same district to create vacant land for luxury housing projects. The existing parks and green areas in the neighbourhoods have also been transformed into 'vacant land' through the devastation of nature.[37] Another strategy to expand homeownership among the poor is to promote campaigns[38] offering a variety of payment models for consumers, including reductions when the house loan is repaid in full.

TOKİ produced 500,000 new housing units from 2007 to 2011 in total,[39] while housing produced for the poor remained very limited.[40] Recent data on the affordability of housing in Turkey show that the increase in housing production by the state has not resulted in sufficient affordable housing for low-income households.[41] While the private sector no longer produces housing for low-income households, the number of housing units produced by TOKİ is still very low. The limited affordability of housing for lower-income groups has been due to high regular expenses, such as management fees, in new housing units, as well as expensive housing loans, higher rents, long- or short-term unemployment, and the low number of people working in each household.[42] The new strategies to involve low-income households in homeownership have hence remained inadequate so far.

Conclusion

This chapter has discussed the changing role of the state in housing production by analysing housing policy changes and strategies since 2001. It has argued that the state plays a significant role in the inclusion of different income groups in homeownership through its designs for the construction sector and financial institutions. However, the strategies and tactics of the state have varied from repressive to more cooperative ones due to growth expectations based on the construction sector and the AKP's political expectations to stay in power by meeting the demands of different classes. This process has been a rather conflictual one.

Conflicts between residents and the state have been more evident since 2005, after the economic crisis and strong resistance in UR neighbourhoods, where whole populations were forced to move to the peripheries of the cities as a part of the state's revenue-sharing model of housing production. This top-down UR policy led to coercive measures to relocate poor inhabitants of *gecekondu* settlements out of the centres of the cities, and therefore it was met with organized resistance by residents against the UR. This resistance has created barriers for the accumulation of capital in the housing sector. To overcome this obstacle, the state has started to implement new cooperative measures to continue urban regeneration, the most important of which has been opening up negotiation process between residents and state institutions. However, the two sides do not have the same power in the negotiation process, and negotiations have created uneven consequences for residents depending on their specific characteristics, such as land ownership, political affiliation to the AKP, having a legal document relating to housing rights, and their capacity to take on debt in order to get a new flat that is equivalent to what they used to have. This strategy has substantially weakened struggles in these neighbourhoods, in addition to the dissipating effects of being in debt.

Notes

1. This chapter is based partially on research undertaken as part of the project titled 'Financialization, Economy, Society and Sustainable Development (FESSUD) 2011–16', which received funding from the EU Seventh Framework Programme (FP-7/2007-2013) under grant agreement no. 266800, and follow-up research to understand the latest housing strategies of the state in 2018, funded by the Swedish Institute under grant agreement no. 23997/2017. While the first half of the research was conducted in 2016, a second phase was conducted in 2018 to grasp the current stage of changing state strategies.

2. Self-help housing is called *gecekondu* in Turkish, which literally means 'built-overnight'.

3. Kuyucu 2017.

4. Karaçimen and Çelik 2017.

5. Following an amendment of the Real Estate Reciprocity Law in 2012, the citizens of Saudi Arabia, Qatar, Kuwait, England and Germany were allowed to buy real estate in Turkey. See Karaçimen and Çelik 2017. Homeownership by non-Turkish citizens almost doubled from 2013 to 2015, and after a decrease in 2016 it almost doubled again in 2018 (in the first ten months) to 30,500 units sold. See TURKSTAT, 2018, http://www.tuik.gov.tr/UstMenu. do?metod=temelist.

6. In the new legislation, the process of transforming neighbourhoods by demolition and rebuilding and by displacing existing residents is called 'urban regeneration'. However, it carries a different meaning from the one in the literature on urban regeneration. While some scholars call it 'urban transformation', others call it 'state-led gentrification'. Both of these conceptualizations have important aspects for grasping the implementation of 'regeneration projects', aspects that I share. The 'regeneration' concept used in this chapter therefore takes account of the critical aspects in the literature.

7. The law had been changed 35 times by 2013 to include exceptional measures. See Kuyucu 2017: 63.

8. Atiyas 2012.

9. The development of REITs and their effect on the expansion of housing and the real-estate sector sped up after the establishment of Emlak Konut, which has the highest market value among REITs, at almost €1 billion by the first quarter of 2018. See SPK 2018.

10. Interviews 1, 2, 6 and 7.

11. Demiralp et al. 2016.

12. Çarıkçı 2017.

13. Kuyucu and Ünsal 2010; Karaman 2014; Lovering and Türkmen 2011; Türkün 2011.

14. Aslan and Dinçer 2018: 148.

15. Interview 9.

16. Aslan 2019: 185.

17. It is important to mention that the 2018–19 economic crisis in Turkey had a significant impact on the housing sector, where there was an important rise in housing loans to consumers and investors. To reduce the risk of having a twin crisis in the housing sector, the state started some new campaigns to ease the mortgage payments of consumers and loan payments of investors. See Çelik 2018.

18. See https://www.vakifbank. com.tr/kentsel-donusum-kredisi. aspx?pageID=871 (accessed 14 May 2019).

19. Interview 7.

20. Interviews 4 and 5.

21. *Gecekondu* is a self-help housing model in Turkey where houses are built by the residents without any support from the state or private companys.

22. Özer et al. 2007.

23. Aslan 2004.
24. Öktem-Ünsal 2015.
25. Gülöksüz 2009.
26. Lovering and Türkmen 2011.
27. Interviews 13, 14, 15, 16 and 17.
28. Interviews 10, 11, 12, 13, 14, 15, 16 and 17.
29. Kuyucu and Ünsal 2010: 1484.
30. Ibid.
31. Sakarya 2011; Kuyucu 2014, 2017.
32. Interviews 19 and 20.
33. Interview 18.
34. Interviews 23 and 24.
35. Interviews 21 and 22.
36. Interviews 21, 22, 23 and 24.
37. Interviews 11, 14, 15 and 18.
38. A striking example is 'Time for Turkey to prosper' (*Türkiye için kazanç vakti*) at http://www.turkiyeicinkazancvakti.com/.
39. Özdemir Sarı and Aksoy Khurami 2016.
40. The figure was 11,408 new housing units produced for low-income households by 2009. See Özdemir Sarı and Aksoy Khurami 2018.
41. Ibid.
42. Ibid.

References

Aslan, A. S. (2019) 'Barınma Problemine Çözüm Olarak Sunulan İpotekli Konut Kredilerine Erişilebilirliğin Değerlendirilmesi', *Megaron 14*: 177–91.

Aslan, A. S. and I. Dinçer (2018) 'The impact of mortgage loans on the financialization process in Turkey', *Planlama Dergisi 28* (2): 143–53.

Aslan, Ş. (2004) *1 Mayıs Mahallesi*. Istanbul: İletisim Yayinlari.

Atiyas, İ. (2012) 'Economic institutions and institutional change in Turkey during the neoliberal era', *New Perspectives on Turkey*, *47*: 57–81.

Çarıkçı, Ç. (2017) '2001 krizi sonrası Türkiye'de büyük ölçekli kentsel yatirim projeleri: İstanbul örneği' in P. Bedirhanoğlu, Ö. Çelik and H. Mıhçı (eds), *Finansallaşma Kıskacında Türkiye'de Devlet, Sermaye Birikimi ve Emek*. Istanbul: Notabene, pp. 103–28.

Çelik, Ö. (2018) 'Yeni Konut Kampanyaları ile Tanışın: Fedakâr Borçluluk', *Ayrinti Dergisi*, 15 November, http://ayrintidergi.com.tr/yeni-konut-kampanyalari-ile-tanisin-fedakar-borcluluk/.

Demiralp, S., S. Demiralp and I. Gümüş (2016) 'The state of property development in Turkey: facts and comparisons', *New Perspectives on Turkey 55*: 85–106.

Gülöksüz, E. (2009) 'İnşaat Sanayinde Uluslararasılaşma ve Sermayeler Arası İlişkiler', *Praksis 19*: 157–89.

Karaçimen, E. and Ö. Çelik (2017) 'Türkiye'de Gayrimenkul ve Finansın Derinleşen ve Yeniden Yapılanan İlişkisi' in P. Bedirhanoğlu, H. Mıhçı and Ö. Çelik (eds), *Finansallaşma Kıskacında Türkiye'de Devlet, Sermaye Birikimi ve Emek*. Istanbul: Notabene, pp. 83–102.

Karaman, O. (2014) 'Resisting urban renewal in Istanbul', *Urban Geography*, *35* (2): 290–310.

Kuyucu, T. (2014) 'Law, property and ambiguity: the uses and abuses of legal ambiguity in remaking Istanbul's informal settlements', *International Journal of Urban and Regional Research 38* (2): 609–27.

Kuyucu, T. (2017) 'Two crisis, two trajectories: the impact of the 2001 and 2008 economic crises on urban governance in Turkey' in F. Adaman, B. Akbulut and M. Arsel (eds), *Neoliberal Turkey and Its Discontents*. London: I. B. Taurus, pp. 44–74.

Kuyucu, T. and Ö. Ünsal (2010) '"Urban transformation" as state-led property transfer: an analysis of two cases of urban renewal in Istanbul', *Urban Studies 47* (7): 1479–99.

Lovering, J. and H. Türkmen (2011) 'Bulldozer neo-liberalism in Istanbul: the state-led construction of property markets, and the displacement of the urban poor', *International Planning Studies 16* (1): 73–96.

Öktem-Ünsal, B. (2015) 'State-led urban regeneration in Istanbul: power struggles between interest groups and poor communities', *Housing Studies 30* (8): 1299–316.

Özdemir Sarı, Ö. B. and E. Aksoy Khurami (2016) 'Excess production, rising prices and declining affordability: Turkish housing experience' in I. Wroot (ed.), *Government and Housing in a Time of Crisis: Policy, Planning, Design and Delivery*. AMPS Conference Publication Series 8. Liverpool: Liverpool John Moores University, pp. 162–70.

Özdemir Sarı, Ö. B. and E. Aksoy Khurami (2018) 'Housing

affordability trends and challenges in the Turkish case', *Journal of Housing and the Built Environment*, DOI: 10.1007/s10901-018-9617-2.

Özer, G., A. Vardar and M. Nazım (2007) 'Unplanned settlements within the context of urbanization process of Turkey', FIG Commission 3 workshop, Athens, 28–31 March.

Öztürk, Ö. (2011) *Türkiye'de Büyük Sermaye Grupları*. 2nd edition. Istanbul: SAV.

Sakarya, İ. (2011) 'The role of the local municipalities in the urban regeneration projects of Istanbul'. Conference proceeding from New Housing Researcher's Colloquium.

SPK (2018) 'Sermaye Piyasası Kurulu Aylık Raporları', https://www.spk.gov.tr/SiteApps/Yayin/AylikIstatistikBultenleri (accessed 30 November 2018).

Topal, A., G. L. Yalman and Ö. Çelik (2019) 'Changing modalities of urban redevelopment and housing finance in Turkey: three mass housing projects in Ankara', *Journal of Urban Affairs 41* (5): 630–53.

Türkün, A. (2011) 'Urban regeneration and hegemonic power relationships', *International Planning Studies 16* (1): 61–72.

Interviews conducted in 2016

Interview 1: High-ranking civil servant 1, TOKİ Ankara

Interview 2: High-ranking civil servant 2, TOKİ Ankara

Interview 3: Head of an REIT

Interview 4: Middle-scale housing company owner based in Istanbul

Interview 5: The Turkish Employers Association of Construction Industries (INTES)

Interview 6: High-ranking civil servant, Emlak Konut REIT

Interview 7: Real-estate developer, Ankara

Interview 8: Previous head of the REIT Association

Interview 9: Manager of a well-known commercial bank

Interview 10: Chamber of urban planners

Interview 11: Interviewee 1, chamber of architects

Interview 12: Interviewee 2, chamber of architects

Interview 13: Dayanışmacı Atölye
Interview 14: İmece
Interview 15: Toplum İçin Şehircilik
 Hareketi

Interview 16: Müştereklerimiz
Interview 17: Kuzey Ormanları
 Savunması

Interviews conducted in 2018

Interview 18: Manager, TOKİ Istanbul
Interview 19: District municipality
 representative 1
Interview 20: District municipality
 representative 2
Interview 21: Neighbourhood dweller 1
 (living in *gecekondu* regeneration
 area)

Interview 22: Neighbourhood dweller 2
 (living in *gecekondu* regeneration area)
Interview 23: Neighbourhood dweller 3
 (living in *gecekondu* regeneration
 area)
Interview 24: Neighbourhood dweller 4
 (living in *gecekondu* regeneration
 area)

PART III

POLITICS OF DOMINATION

PART II
POLITICS OF DOMINANCE

9 | THE TRANSFORMATION OF THE STATE–RELIGION RELATIONSHIP UNDER THE AKP: THE CASE OF THE DIYANET

Zana Çitak

Introduction

The question of state–religion relations can rightly be seen as one of the central issues in relation to the broader transformation of the state in Turkey in the last decade. Interestingly, though not unexpectedly, many observers who have been greatly influenced by the academic debates and concepts that have emerged since the early 1990s, such as de-secularization, post-Islamism and post-secularism, quickly seized the opportunity – from 2002, when the AKP came to power, to 2010 – to claim that, as the de-secularization[1] paradigm dictated, there was a return of religion. This was already to be expected in a society with deep Islamic roots, a country that was forcibly modernized with the establishment of the Republic in 1923. Accordingly, the AKP was a post-Islamist[2] party – that is, a political party with clear awareness of the failure of the Islamist project of an Islamic state, and thus now seeking the Islamization of society within the framework of universal values of freedom, equality and rights.[3] At the same time, Turkish society was increasingly described as a post-secular[4] society,[5] a term coined by Habermas to define Western liberal democratic societies with a new form of consciousness about the continuing salience of religion, in the context of the growing public visibility and demands of people of Muslim immigrant origin. Thus, the recognition of religious voices in the public spheres of Western societies would lead to greater pluralism and democracy. Ahmet Kuru[6] defined this change in Turkey as a shift from assertive secularism to passive secularism, with a growing visibility of religion in the public sphere and the state's equal distance from all faiths, both of which expanded the space for freedom of religion, which was previously suppressed under the assertively secular Kemalist regime. Thus, according to various scholars and observers of Turkish politics, the AKP was at the intersection of these concepts, clearly pointing towards a more democratic, open and pluralist society: a post-Islamist party as a carrier of a passive secularist vision in a post-secular society. The process of the so-called Alevi opening (2009–10) – together with the (limited) transfer of non-Muslim foundations, which had been under the control of the General Directorate of Foundations since 1974, back to their communities after 2002[7] – has contributed to reinforce this conception, thereby postponing for its proponents the need to come to terms with the underlying and already existing problems, contradictions and limitations of this portrayal of AKP rule.

This perspective, however, began to give way to growing concerns about the Islamization of Turkish society, with the dead end reached in the Alevi workshops[8] and in recognition of equality and freedom of religion for non-Muslim minorities, two initiatives that had both aimed to impose a Sunni understanding of the regulation of the religious field.[9] The replacement of the eight years of uninterrupted education with the 4+4+4 system made the *İmam Hatip* schools, vocational secondary-level schools for religious education, the backbone of the AKP's educational policy, in line with Erdoğan's emphasis on 'raising pious generations'.[10] Religious orders have expanded and have been enriched; the Gülen movement in particular became the main ally and collaborator of the AKP government, until their eventual falling-out, which began with the 17–25 December 2013 corruption charges and ended with the 15 July 2016 coup attempt. This chapter argues that focusing on the transformation of the Directorate of Religious Affairs (*Diyanet İşleri Başkanlığı* or Diyanet) in the 2010s gives a clearer idea of the Islamization of the state in Turkey under AKP rule, in contrast to the expectations for and/or narratives of a post-Islamist political regime and post-secular society. The Diyanet, which is a constitutional institution and a bureaucratic branch of the state, has been the main pillar of state–religion relations in Turkey since 1924. Even though its centrality in religious affairs has persisted, significant ruptures in the role, duties and functions of the Diyanet were observed in the 2010s; these resulted in its legal and social expansion, the redefinition of its role, and its dissociation from the secular character of the state.

The Diyanet: a biography

The Diyanet has been considered one of the peculiarities of the Turkish state–religion relationship. In fact, for many observers, it is the main source of what is frequently seen as the *sui generis* Turkish secularism, which separated religion from the state but not the state from religion. The Diyanet has also become a very controversial institution, especially since the mid-1960s, for two main reasons. First, there has been an increasing emphasis on the Sunni doctrine at the expense of other branches of thought in Islam. Second, since the 1950s, the Diyanet has evolved into a giant organization with a considerable budget, a large number of employees and organizational capacity, and a wide range of missions and activities that go beyond its original responsibility for religion as a public service, confined mainly to the mosque.

The Diyanet was established on 3 March 1924, within the framework of a series of foundational secularizing reforms of modern Turkey. On that day, the caliphate was abrogated and the Law on the Unification of Education (*Tevhid-i Tedrisat*) was passed, abolishing the traditional educational institutions, the *medreses* (centres of Islamic learning). At the same time, the Ministry of Sharia and Pious Endowments (*Şeriye ve Evkaf Vekâleti*) and all religious courts were abrogated and the *Diyanet İşleri Reisliği*, as it was named then, was founded by Act no. 429, which stated that the institution was responsible for implementing 'all provisions concerning faith and worship aspects of the religion of Islam and the administration of religious institutions'.[11] Crucially, this placed the new institution under the authority of the Prime Minister and defined it as an administrative bureau rather than a ministry in its own right.[12] It was also deprived of responsibility in the area of religious education, which was now assigned to the Ministry of Education. In other words, the Diyanet did not have any say in training its own personnel.

Together, these attitudes reflected the republican founders' attitude towards the place of Islam in the new polity. In that sense, as İsmail Kara argues, analyses that see a continuity from the Ministry of Sharia and Pious Endowments to the Diyanet miss the crucial rupture between the Diyanet and its predecessor.[13] With no 'sacred significance attached to it',[14] and withdrawn from some crucial prerogatives such as education and the judiciary, the Diyanet was now an institution with little prestige.[15] Responsible only for the administration of mosques and the appointment of religious personnel, the Diyanet was a product of the deep distrust of Islam on the part of the regime, which also engaged in other radical secularizing reforms ranging from the political and legal to the symbolic realm.[16] The Diyanet thus epitomized the republican founders' conception of secularism as one of control over religion, while at the same time they acknowledged the important place of Islam in Turkish society by recognizing religion as a public service under the responsibility of the Diyanet.[17] It also reflected the perception of religion as limited to the private realm.[18] The new regime's expectation was to shape Islam as an individualized set of beliefs. With state funding and control, this 'enlightened Islam' would be compatible with science and modernity.

A major reversal of this original design of the Diyanet began with the transition to a multiparty democracy in 1946. This date proved to be a turning point in the evolution of the place of Islam in Turkish society and politics. Finding that it was a source of electoral support and popularity, political parties, especially on the right, promoted a greater role and visibility for Islam. Given the context of the Cold War, religion became a popular tool in the fight against communism. Thus, religious brotherhoods, which had been banned and had gone underground under the single-party regime, established various links with political parties.[19] Religion courses were reintroduced in school curricula in 1949 and *İmam Hatip* schools made a comeback in 1951, spreading rapidly in the 1960s and 1970s.[20] Not coincidentally, political parties with explicit Islamist agendas emerged from the early 1970s onwards and became an unchanging component of Turkish politics despite closures and name changes.

Among these many manifestations of the greater role of Islam in Turkish society, one could also see the evolution of the Diyanet from a demoted institution to a giant organization. The first change came in 1950 when the management of mosques and prayer rooms, which had been transferred to the Directorate for Foundations in 1931, was reassigned to the Diyanet.[21] This first boost to the power of the Diyanet followed in 1965 in the form of considerable expansion and a redefinition of the Diyanet's mission, as well as an increase in its budget.[22] Under Law No. 633, the Diyanet was now also given responsibility 'to carry out affairs related to the beliefs, prayers and *moral foundations* of Islam, *to enlighten society about religion* and to manage places of prayer'.[23] Thus, as Gözaydın observes, the Diyanet became an 'ideological tool' of government,[24] a practice that the 1982 Constitution further reinforced by expanding its duties, adding 'promoting and consolidating national solidarity and unity' in Article 136.[25] This was a reflection of the military junta's adoption of the 'Turkish–Islamic synthesis'[26] as the semi-official ideology of the state, which was pursued by all post-1983 right-wing governments in Turkey. This has led to the introduction of religion as a compulsory subject on the school curriculum through Article 24 of the 1982 Constitution, and also to the Diyanet's embrace of the Turkish–Islamic synthesis. Thus, Islam was instrumentalized as cementing national unity, based on the conception of the close relation between Islam and national identity. The 1982 Constitution also constituted the basis on which the Diyanet developed its de-territorialized activities abroad, particularly in Europe, therefore transforming itself into a transnational actor.

The use of the Diyanet as an ideological tool by politicians, which began in 1965, was also paralleled by an increasing emphasis on the Sunni doctrine. An attempt failed to redefine the Diyanet as a 'Presidency of Religious Sects' in a draft law in 1963[27] and the Diyanet effectively emerged as the representative and promoter of Sunni Islam. The Diyanet claims that it provides religious services 'without any discrimination by sect, interpretation or practice of Islam, on the pure basis of "citizenship"'.[28] For the Diyanet's officials and employees, its 'equal distance to all in society and its unifying role'[29] are its principal strengths. Yet this self-perception, which is based on the argument that there is only one Islam, ignores the diversity within the Muslim population and alienates non-Sunni Muslims such as the Alevis and Caferis. It also overlooks the plurality within the Sunni majority, not to mention those who do not adhere to any religion. Its ever-expanding mission, which now also includes 'outside mosque' activities since the new Law No. 6002 of 2010,[30] only reinforces its Sunni character by giving the Diyanet more room to propagate Sunni orthodoxy in belief and practice as well as morality. Afraid of sectarian chaos, the Diyanet takes seriously its mission of 'consolidating national unity and solidarity'.

The Diyanet under the AKP

Those who try to make sense of the changing role of Islam in Turkish society under the AKP point to the increase in the Diyanet budget and the number of personnel, particularly since 2010. Gözaydın[31] has demonstrated that, after a sharp drop in 1930, the Diyanet saw its budget gradually decreasing throughout the single-party period. A major upward dynamic emerged in 1952 and stayed more or less stable at less than 1 per cent of the total state budget; until 2003, it went above 1 per cent on only six occasions – in 1965, 1966, 1967, 1990, 1991 and 1994. With the coming to power of the AKP, the Diyanet entered a period of increasing prosperity, with a gradual budget increase from 2003 onwards, reaching 1.27 per cent of the total state budget in 2014.[32] The 2016 budget was four times larger than the 2006 budget.[33] As for the increase from 2003 (the first year when the ruling AKP determined the budget) to 2017, one can see an eightfold increase.[34]

As well as the budget, the increase in the number of personnel and of mosques has added to the perception that the Diyanet has transformed into a giant organization. From 74,114 personnel in 2003,[35] it reached 112,724 in 2018.[36] It is also important to note that, while the numbers of mosques and of personnel had been more or less the same until 2003, with the latter lower (though still significant) than the former at times, there was a tremendous increase in personnel after that year which was not matched by a corresponding increase in the number of mosques. As Watters has pointed out, while there were 74,374 staff and 75,941 mosques in 2002, the figures were 117,378 and 86,762 respectively in 2015 (increases of 57.8 per cent and 14.2 per cent). This difference can be explained, as Mustafa Şen argues,[37] by the increase in the number of con-tractual employees rather than religious functionaries in mosques. Perhaps, however, the largest increase in staff number has been in Qur'anic course teachers and female preachers in the new Family and Religious Counselling Bureaus (*Aile ve Dini Rehberlik Bürosu*), established in 2003.[38]

While the expansion of financial and human resources as well as organizational capacity under AKP rule are of great significance both in themselves and in their implications, it is more important to examine the underlying reasons for this quantitative change. This chapter argues that it is possible to talk about three major changes leading to the overall quantitative growth of the Diyanet, signifying simultaneously a qualitative change in its role and mission. These are problematized below by focusing on: (1) legal and social expansion;

(2) a transformation in the understanding of its role; and (3) its increasing dissociation from the principle of secularism.

Legal and social expansion

Two factors have been decisive in the legal and social expansion of the Diyanet under the AKP. The first is Law No. 6002 of 2010,[39] which amended Law No. 633 of 1965. The second is one of the governmental decrees that have been characteristic of the state of emergency put in place after the 15 July 2016 coup attempt: namely, KHK (*Kanun Hükmünde Kararname* or decree with the force of law) no. 703[40] of 9 July 2018. Together, they formed the basis of the change in the nature of the Diyanet as an institution and its legal and social presence in Turkish society.

The significance of the 2010 law has been mentioned in almost every official report published by the Diyanet.[41] Besides limiting the term of the president to five years and the number of terms to two, and restructuring the internal organizational structure of the institution, the 2010 law introduced fundamental changes in three principal areas. First and foremost, the law changed the status of the Diyanet in the public administration by elevating it from a general directorate to an under-secretariat.[42] At the same time, KHK no. 703 also attached the Diyanet directly to the presidency (previously, the Office of the Prime Minister), following the shift to a presidential system with the 24 June 2018 referendum. This promotion in the state hierarchy constituted a major departure from its original status as defined at its establishment in 1924. As İsmail Kara pointed out, despite many interpretations of the Diyanet as a successor to its Ottoman counterpart, the *Şeyhulislamlık*, it had no sacred credentials and few prerogatives under its authority. While the Diyanet, as previously explained, has grown in size and resources with the shift to multiparty politics, its status within the public administration had remained the same. At the same time, as an institution with little prestige or power, the Diyanet, in its early years, benefited from the appointment of presidents who were known for both their support of the newly established republic and their scholarship in Islam; these presidents included Rıfat Börekçi (1924–41), Mehmet Şerafeddin Yaltkaya (1942–47) and Ahmet Hamdi Akseki (1951–60).[43] In other words, there was an effort to appropriate prestige in the institution through the president. However, this was not the case after 1960, when there were frequent changes in presidencies, with some presidents staying in office for as little as nine months. With the 2010 law, one could argue that there was an effort to invest prestige in the institution itself. Unfortunately, this came paradoxically through a succession of controversial individuals, with little prestige, if any, as Diyanet presidents, primarily Mehmet Görmez (2010–17) and the current incumbent, Ali Erbaş (from 2017).

The 2010 law has also given the Diyanet a new mission, expanding its area of responsibility. What have been called the 'outside mosque' activities of the Diyanet were not invented by the 2010 law. In fact, the Diyanet President Ali Bardakoğlu (2003–10) was a keen supporter of 'outside mosque services', which he mentioned as a concept as far back as 2008.[44] Accordingly, 'religion is not just about daily prayers or fasting; it encompasses the totality of social life ... and religious functionaries should be opinion leaders who can interfere in the whole social life of a society'. He also argued that the Diyanet is more a civil than a bureaucratic entity.[45] The 2010 law defined these activities in a concrete way, determined additional activities, and gave them a legal basis. Hence, the institution was given the task, among others, of 'enlightening people in religious matters, via radio and TV', 'developing educational programmes, planning and implementation through cooperation with relevant government agencies and institutions, organizing and monitoring activities', and 'enlightening and guiding various sections of society, such as family, women, youth and others, in religious matters'.[46] In other words, in the Diyanet's own account, it was 'assigned to take advantage of all means and opportunities to enlighten the society about religion'.[47] The Diyanet took this assignment to heart and established its own radio and television channels, namely Diyanet Radyo and DiyanetTV, in 2013, and Diyanet Kur'an Radyo in 2015.[48] As for cooperation with the relevant government agencies and institutions, it has established many protocols with various government agencies as well as with municipalities, civil society institutions and the media.[49] This has allowed the Diyanet to extend its reach into areas and among people who had previously not been within its scope. It has also led to the exposure of the whole of society to Diyanet officials, religious functionaries and teaching. Also, KHK no. 703 of July 2018 further extended the Diyanet's reach to different social units and groups by assigning it the task of 'spiritual counselling' (*manevî danışmanlık*) in student dormitories, educational institutions, youth centres and camps, prisons, hospitals and social service institutions, as well as with immigrants, disabled people and addicts.

The most significant assignment provided to the Diyanet by the 2010 law seems to be the enlightenment and guidance in religious matters for family, women and youth. Significantly, the Diyanet defines its ultimate mission as 'keeping alive the religious, spiritual and moral values of society',[50] and its 'outside mosque' activities must be understood from the perspective of this ultimate mission, which places women and family at its centre. While this emphasis on morality could be considered continuous with Law No. 633 of 1965, which had included morality as another area of consideration for the Diyanet, it has really been with the 2010 law that the Diyanet has turned this into a major area of teaching and activity. In fact, a quick glance at the books published by the Diyanet would reveal how family, women, youth and morality have become its main preoccupations.[51] Taken together, a widespread campaign to invite women to mosques, including by accommodating mosques to women's needs,[52] the increasing inclusion of women employees in the Diyanet bureaucracy,[53] and the establishment of Family and Religious Counselling Bureaus in 2003 constitute, in Serpil Sancar's words, the 'womanization'[54] of the Diyanet. However, as Sancar argues, the process of womanization has emphasized less women's rights than women's duties and their mission in the 'protection of family values', a tendency, she argues, that has been more visible since 2012.[55] Again, Maritato observes that 'docility, obedience to authority and patience are among the recurring [themes]' of the Diyanet's women preachers who have been sent abroad.[56]

The 2010 law has also been instrumental in empowering the Diyanet through providing a firm legal basis for its cooperation with the Turkish Diyanet Foundation (*Türkiye Diyanet Vakfı* or TDV), established in 1975.[57] It is a giant foundation with branches in all 81 provinces and 919 sub-provinces (*ilçe*) of the country, and is also active in 143 countries worldwide. It has a university (29 Mayıs University in Istanbul) and a high school (Private Bornova College in İzmir), as well as a preschool (Private Reyyan Preschool in Ankara on the Diyanet campus) and dormitories for undergraduate and graduate students called 'benevolence houses' (*iyilik evleri*). It offers scholarships to students in Turkey and abroad and funding to selected educational institutions in foreign countries; it builds mosques in Turkey and abroad; it has its own publishing house and its own company (KOMAŞ A.Ş.), with business mainly in construction but also in tourism (GİNTAŞ Turizm ve Seyahat Acentası), agriculture, and luggage and other goods for pilgrims.[58] It has also signed protocols with a number of government agencies, such as the Migration Agency (*Göç İdaresi Genel Müdürlüğü*) and the national postal service (PTT). Together with some other foundations and associations, it was granted tax exemption in 1977 and in 2007.[59] It also has the right, along with two other associations,[60] to collect donations without official permission.[61]

The TDV is organically linked to the Diyanet, with the latter's president the president of the TDV's board, and financially supports all of the Diyanet's activities, including the International Theology Programme (*Uluslararası İlahiyat Programı*), financing the salaries of a number of religious functionaries sent abroad and giving financial support to them, and financing and constructing buildings of the *muftilik* (the Diyanet's provincial branch) and of the Diyanet's representation in some Asian countries. This organic relationship between the two institutions has gained a legal basis through the 2010 law, which, in Article 17, introduced an exemption to the Law on Associations of 2004, which banned associations and foundations from using the names of public agencies and institutions, and civil servants from taking positions in associations and foundations. Thus, the use of the name Diyanet in the name of the TDV and the fact that the president of the Diyanet is automatically the president of the TDV were both legalized. Article 17 stated that the Diyanet, when necessary, cooperates with the TDV and that the articles of the 2004 Law on Associations do not apply to the TDV.[62] With the legalization of its link to the Diyanet and its activities, we have to consider the TDV and the Diyanet not as two separate institutions but as one, and the Diyanet budget has to be re-evaluated by taking into account that of the TDV and the latter's financial capacity.

Transformation from a national to a transnational to a global actor

Having started to provide religious services abroad in 1971, the Diyanet has become a transnational actor, first in Europe, followed by Australia, and then in other parts of the world, particularly since the early 1980s. Starting with sending first, imams, and then religious attachés with diplomatic status,[63] it proceeded to establish a network of mosque associations called the Turkish–Islamic Union of Religious Affairs (*Diyanet İşleri Türk-İslam Birliği* or DİTİB) or the Diyanet Foundation, depending on the legal framework of the host country. The realization of the permanency of the Turkish migrant population in Europe led to a realization of their religious needs on the part of both the Turkish state and European host states. There was also the added motivation, for both the junta regime in Turkey (1980–83) and its civil successors, to use the Diyanet as a way to 'consolidate national unity and solidarity' on the basis of a fusion of Turkish and Muslim identities. This combined with a willingness to counterbalance the Turkish dissident movements of both the right and the left, and the Diyanet soon became the most significant actor in the European religious field,[64] even in countries where Muslims of Turkish origin make up only a small minority, as in France.[65] Along with many other countries that are pursuing a similar strategy of reaching out to their diaspora through a wider range of means and using them as a source of remittances, as well as for lobbying to promote political and economic interests, the Turkish state has established tighter links with its migrants in Europe and Australia.[66] The size, the organizational capacity and the identity of the Diyanet as a representative of the secular Turkish state, promoting a moderate Islam, have made it one of the most important interlocutors of European governments in their relations with their Muslim communities. Thus, the Diyanet has evolved from a domestic tool for regulating and controlling the religious field to a foreign policy instrument, more or less replicating its domestic missions and activities after the 1980s. The end of the Cold War opened up a wider space of activism for Turkish foreign policy, leading the Diyanet to become a transnational actor in the Balkans[67] and Central Asia as well.[68] In the 2000s, under AKP rule, the USA and Africa[69] have become new sites of the Diyanet's activism, with international conferences and students coming to Turkey.

Under AKP rule, there has been an important shift in the Diyanet's transnational activism. The 2010 law provided a legal foundation for the Diyanet's transnationalism, which had been in a legal vacuum for a long time.[70] Again, it was the 2010 law that 'rendered possible the hiring of non-Turkish citizens in foreign countries on a contractual basis', enabling graduates of the Diyanet's International Theology Programme to be hired as religious personnel abroad.[71] It formulated clearly the organizational structure of the Diyanet's mission abroad. This is important as the Diyanet has increasingly begun to see its domestic and foreign mission and activities as complementary, and it takes pride in this external role, seeing it as strengthening the competence of its staff and the prestige of the institution. It also finds in 'Turkey's increasing global influence' another reason for wanting to extend its role beyond Turkey's borders.[72] The Diyanet's self-confidence was apparent as early as in 2008, when Mehmet Aydın, the then state minister responsible for the Diyanet, stated that the Diyanet should be recognized as a global institution.[73] Therefore, as the Diyanet's 2012–16 strategic plan explicitly states, its main long-term vision is 'to become the main reference and the most influential and respected institution in Turkey and in the world on every matter related to Islam'.[74] For the Diyanet, there is also room for it to play an active and global role, since religion has a 'rising value' worldwide. At the same time, the tendency to associate Islam with terrorism and Islamophobia in the West requires a more engaged presence on the part of the institution. Since 2016, there has also been greater emphasis on the 'abuse of religion' (*din istismarı*), as it is commonly referred to in the Diyanet's discourse. According to the Diyanet, FETÖ (the Fethullahist Terrorist Organization) and ISIS are thus epitomizing a misinterpretation of Islam and its abuse. In such a context, the Diyanet is seen as needed even more to 'enlighten people about true religion'. The TDV's mosque-building programme is active and geographically wide, from Tirana to Maryland to Bishkek, with plans to build mosques in Cuba, Romania and Venezuela;[75] students from many countries are coming to Turkey to study theology on TDV scholarships; and the Qur'an is being translated into 16 languages and distributed in 47 countries in the 'Let My Gift be the Qur'an' project (*Hediyem Kur'an Olsun Projesi*).[76] All of this signals how the Diyanet's interest is not just in the promotion of national solidarity and unity but in the promotion of its own understanding of Islam on a global scale and in its own self-promotion as a global religious authority, in line with Erdoğan's ambition to become the protector of Muslims everywhere.

Dissociation from secularism

Perhaps the most striking transformation of the Diyanet under the AKP is its evolution towards a self-proclaimed religious authority. Established originally as a bureaucratic branch of the government, with no religious credentials and in charge of only the maintenance and management of mosques and religious personnel (not their training), the Diyanet has seen its role and responsibility expand since 1950. But several developments since the AKP came to power indicate how the Diyanet has increasingly been conceived not as a secular bureaucratic body but as a religious authority, with little effort, if any, to respect the principle of secularism.

One important manifestation of this transformation is the establishment of *Alo Fetva 190* (Hello Fatwa 190), a phone service to answer personal religious questions, by the Diyanet in 2012. While the Diyanet has long conducted the answering of religious questions through the offices of local muftis, it has not considered itself a fatwa agency. In fact, its former president, Ali Bardakoğlu (2003–10) was particularly careful about not portraying the Diyanet as a fatwa authority, underlining that 'the Diyanet's statements [on its website] can not be seen as fatwa'.[77] As Samil Öcal argues, Bardakoğlu's choice of the expression 'answering religious questions', thus using the traditional meaning of fatwa, instead of the term 'fatwa' was deliberate as he might have wanted to 'emphasize that the Diyanet is an institution of the secular state in which there is no room for fatwas'.[78] However, the establishment of the *Alo Fetva 190* service signals a major shift in the Diyanet's public discourse and policy. The recent publication by the Diyanet of a book, *Fetvalar*, which includes an exhaustive list of religious questions and answers (a total of 1,029), testifies to the new assertiveness of the Diyanet on this issue.[79]

Another striking manifestation of the Diyanet's distancing itself from the principle of secularism can be seen in its unequivocal support for and promotion of Erdoğan's and the AKP's discourse and policy since 2010. In that respect, we can talk about the Diyanet having become both the instrument and a loyal ally of the AKP regime. While Ali Bardakoğlu and previous presidents had followed what could be seen as a semi-autonomous discourse and policy, since 2010, under Mehmet Görmez's and Ali Erbaş's presidencies, we see a complete loss of autonomy on the part of the institution. Hence, the Diyanet's supportive statements about abortion following Erdoğan's statements on caesarean birth and abortion in 2012,[80] its plea for all mosque imams to call for prayers in support of Erdoğan following the 15 July 2016 coup attempt, its orders to all mosque imams for prayers on the anniversaries of 15 July,[81] its active engagement against FETÖ,[82] and its penetration into every aspect of society through protocols with government agencies have all rendered the Diyanet the principal domestic instrument of Islamization under Erdoğan regime. Externally, the Diyanet has also served as a useful tool for Erdoğan's foreign policy. The building of mosques through the TDV and the attempt to place people close to the AKP as DİTİB representatives in Muslim institutions such as the French Council for Muslim Religion (*Conseil Français du Culte Musulman*)[83] could be seen as the Diyanet supporting Erdoğan's foreign policy. Significantly, we even see what had previously been a moderate and conciliatory institution in its relations with European governments becoming increasingly confrontational in its dealings with European host states in the pursuit of its activities abroad; hence, the Diyanet is not just supporting but also adopting Erdoğan's foreign policy style and mood.[84] The Diyanet has also established ties with the Muslim Brotherhood, and, since 2006, has even hosted several conferences of the Dublin-based European Council for Fatwa and Research (ECFR), headed by Qatar-based Sheikh Yusuf al-Qaradawi.[85] A senior official of the Diyanet, Ekrem Keleş,[86] has even become a member of the ECFR,[87] and the Diyanet-affiliated DİTİB held a meeting in Cologne with a considerable number of attendees from the ECFR.[88] This cooperation with the ECFR reveals an increasing self-confidence on the part of the Diyanet in openly displaying its support for and promotion of Erdoğan's foreign policy of solidarity with the Muslim Brotherhood worldwide. It also epitomizes how the Diyanet has been claiming a global role – one that is not just confined to the Muslim communities of Turkish origin but encompasses all Muslims, and not just as a representative of the secular Turkish state but as an extension of Erdoğan's regime and its Islamist sensitivities.

Most importantly, any mention of the secular character of the Turkish state seems to have completely disappeared from the statements and main reports of the Diyanet, which is an institution of that state. While Ali Bardakoğlu referred to the principle of secularism as the 'basis of living together',[89] as the 'foremost principle of the Diyanet',[90] and as the 'fundamental ground for freedom of religion',[91] his successors, Mehmet Görmez and Ali Erbaş, have openly attacked the concept on several occasions, seeing it as responsible for wars[92] and the problems humanity is facing in our times.[93] Secularism has also been absent in the annual performance reports of the Diyanet, including in a section on the 'fundamental values' of the Diyanet; here, one can find such values as genuineness, religiosity, morality, merit, universalism, accountability and respect for fundamental human rights and liberties, but not secularism.[94] Again, its 2015 report on ISIS failed to mention secularism as the principle of living together as Bardakoğlu had formulated in 2008, and challenged ISIS's exclusionary understanding of Islam with the argument of pluralism, which, the report argues, is inherent in Islam.[95] Thus, the report does not even bother to pay lip service to the principle of secularism.

Conclusion

The Diyanet under AKP rule, particularly since 2010, has been transformed from an agency that regulates and controls the religious field to one that not only regulates and controls but also promotes religion in complete subordination to the whims of Erdoğan's regime. The main steps to this end have been the legal and social expansion of the institution and its claim to a global role as well as an emergent ease and self-confidence in asserting itself as a religious authority, and thus in dissociating itself from secularism. Together, these transformations indicate not a political party or a regime that can be described as post-Islamist, or a society that can be defined as post-secular, but rather a regime that follows an Islamization of society, politics and foreign policy, and a society where the visibility of religion in the public sphere and the expansion of freedom of religion are seen as the rights and prerogatives of the majority Sunni orthodox adherents. The Diyanet, in this framework, has been the main tool of Islamization as it has itself been transformed while transforming society. It seems that the only limit to the Diyanet's further assertiveness is secular civil society, in the face of tremendous pressure from political power but also displaying unprecedented democratic resistance, and the limits of the AKP's authoritarian reach in a society with almost a hundred years of experience of the separation of religion and state.

Notes

1. Berger 2000; Stark 1999.
2. Bayat 2007.
3. Dağı 2004; Robins 2007; Grigoriadis 2009.
4. Habermas 2006.
5. Bilgili 2011; Göle 2012.
6. Kuru 2009.
7. Soner 2010.
8. Boravali and Boyraz 2015; Zengin Arslan 2015.
9. Beylunioğlu 2015.
10. Lüküslü 2016.
11. *Diyanet İşleri Başkanlığı Stratejik Planı 2012–16* (DSP 2012–16): 16, https://www.diyanet.gov.tr. See also Gözaydın 2008.
12. Gözaydın 2008: 218.
13. Kara 2008. See also Bein 2011. For an example of the argument of continuity by the Diyanet officials themselves, see DSP 2012–16: 15–16.
14. Gözaydın 2008: 218.
15. Kara 2008: 62–3.
16. For an excellent review of these reforms, see Berkes 1998.
17. Gözaydın 2006.
18. Ibid.
19. Kaplan 2006.
20. On the *Imam Hatip* schools, see especially Gökaçtı 2005; Çakır et al. 2004; Çakmak 2009.
21. Gözaydın 2006: 3. Between 1931 and 1950, the Diyanet's role was minimized with the administration of mosques and religious personnel. See Onay 2009: 53–4.
22. Gözaydın 2009.
23. Gözaydın 2006: 4, emphasis added.
24. Gözaydın 2009: 164–6.
25. Gözaydın 2008: 223.
26. For the 'Turkish-Islamic synthesis', see Çetinsaya 1999.
27. Gözaydın 2008: 223.
28. *Diyanet İşleri Başkanlığı 2011 Yılı Performans Programı*: 50, https://www.diyanet.gov.tr.
29. DSP 2012–16: 25.
30. Diyanet İşleri Başkanlığı Kuruluş ve Görevleri Hakkında Kanun ile Bazı Kanunlarda Değişiklik Yapılmasına Dair Kanun, Kanun no. 6002, 13 July 2010 (2010 law), https://resmigazete.gov.tr/eskiler/2010/07/20100713-2.htm.
31. Gözaydın 2009: 220–5.
32. Şen 2019: 45.
33. Watters 2018: 362. For the 2015 numbers, see also *Diyanet İşleri Başkanlığı Stratejik Plan 2017–21* (DSP 2017–21), https://www.diyanet.gov.tr.
34. Şen 2019: 48.
35. Gözaydın 2009: 191.
36. *Diyanet İşleri Başkanlığı 2018 Yılı Performans Programı*: 31, https://www.diyanet.gov.tr. Of 112,724 personnel, 1,122 are in the central organization in Ankara; 110,465 work in the *müftülükler* (provincial branches); 1,084 are employees of the education centre; and 53 are sent abroad.
37. Şen 2019: 44, 48.
38. The number of Qur'an course instructors rose from 3,810 in 2006 to 19,416 in 2017. The number of preachers climbed drastically from 1,210 to 2,487. Şen 2019: 48.
39. 2010 law.
40. See https://resmigazete.gov.tr/eskiler/2018/07/20180709M3-1.pdf.
41. In the statement on the institution's website, 'Institutional and historical development', it says that the 2010 law has brought 'very important achievements' for the Diyanet. See dib.gov.tr/tr-TR/Kurumsal/Detay/1 (accessed 31 August 2019); DSP 2017–21.
42. There are references to the 2010 law and the elevation of the Diyanet in the state hierarchy in every report of the Diyanet since 2012 (2011 is the only exception). For a few examples, see *Diyanet İşleri Başkanlığı 2012 Yılı Performans Programı; Diyanet İşleri Başkanlığı 2015 Yılı Performans*

Programı; DSP 2017–21; all available at
https://www.diyanet.gov.tr.

43. Kara 2008: 81–4.

44. 'Diyanet İşleri Başkanı
Bardakoğlu: Din Hizmeti Cami İçinde
Olduğu Kadar Dışında da Önemli',
Haberler.com, 10 October 2008.

45. 'Bardakoğlu: Din Görevlisi
Kanaat Lideri Olmalı', NTV, 3 October
2010. For the reactions against this
project by the opposition, see 'CHP'li
Öztürk'ten Başbakan'a: Sosyal hayat
din kurallarına göre mi düzenlenecek',
Milliyet, 7 October 2010.

46. See 2010 law.

47. DSP 2017–21: 16.

48. Ibid.: 15.

49. Among the various agencies
and institutions were the Ministry of
National Education, Ministry of Family
and Social Policies, Ministry of Health,
Ministry of Foreign Affairs, Ministry of
Justice, Ministry of Interior, Ministry
of Youth and Sports, Turkish Radio and
Television (TRT), faith-based NGOs,
media agencies and municipalities. See
DSP 2017–21: 19.

50. DSP 2017–21: 34.

51. Among the Diyanet's
publications, there are many books on
family, women, youth and morality.
In Lütfi Doğan's book on the major
social problems, the first chapter is
on family and the second on youth.
See Doğan 2012. See also two volumes
on 'education in values' designed
for children aged from 7 to 15 years:
Etkinliklerle Değerler Eğitimi I and II
(Ankara: DİB Yayınları, 2019); *İntihar
ve Töre Cinayetleri Bağlamında Sosyal
Sorunlar ve İslam* (Ankara: DİB Yayınları,
2018); *Diyanet İşleri Başkanlığının
Ailenin Korunması ve Kadına Yönelik
Şiddetin Önlenmesi Konusunda Görüş
ve Uygulamaları* (Ankara: DİB Yayınları,
2019); *Ailem* (Ankara: DİB Yayınları,
2018); Çubukçu 2016. There are also
several books published by the Turkish

Diyanet Foundation. See, for example,
Kılıç 2010; Karagöz 2018; Bice 2008. The
latter is written by a paediatrician and is
meant to help parents from their child's
birth onwards with medical issues.
The book begins with verses from
the Qur'an and some hadith are also
mentioned. There are also other books
on similar themes, published by various
publication houses, that are being sold
at the Diyanet Foundation's bookstore
in Ankara.

52. D. James (2011) 'Turkey: making
mosques a place for women', *Eurasianet*,
9 December.

53. The number of Qur'anic
teachers, women preachers and vice-
muftis increased from 2,696 in 2004
to 17,738 in 2017, and a woman, Huriye
Martı, currently holds one of the vice-
presidencies. See Maritato 2018.

54. Sancar 2015.

55. Ibid.: 204.

56. Maritato 2018: 6. Fatma Tütüncü
arrives at a similar conclusion in her
own research. See Tütüncü 2010.

57. On the TDV, see Turan 2008.

58. For a more exhaustive list of
operational areas and activities, see
*Türkiye Diyanet Vakfı Faaliyet Raporu
2017* at https://tdv.org.tr.

59. *Resmi Gazete*, 13 January 1978,
No. 16168, 20 December 1977, Decree of
the Council of Ministers; 2 April 2007,
Ministry of Finance.

60. The other two are *Omurilik
Felçlileri Derneği* and *Deniz Feneri
Yardımlaşma ve Dayanışma Derneği*.

61. *Resmi Gazete*, 5 August 2005,
No. 25897, Decree of the Council of
Ministers, No. 2005/9171.

62. 2010 law.

63. At the end of 2015, there were
19 counsellors and vice-counsellors,
33 attachés and vice-attachés, 3
coordinators of religious affairs and
1,975 religious functionaries abroad. See
DSP 2017–21: 22.

64. Çitak 2018.

65. Çitak 2018; El Karoui 2018: 355.

66. Şenay 2012.

67. Öktem 2012.

68. Korkut 2009; Gümüş 2010.

69. 'Diyanet'ten Afrika açılımı', *Yeni Şafak*, 1 May 2015. See also Özkan and Akgün 2010.

70. Gözaydın 2009: 136.

71. Bruce 2020.

72. DSP 2012–16: 50.

73. Aydın 2008: 164.

74. *Diyanet İşleri Başkanlığı 2011 Performans Programı*. 54, https://www.diyanet.gov.tr.

75. 'Turkey's bid for religious leadership: how the AKP uses Islamic soft power', *Foreign Affairs*, 10 January 2019.

76. Among these 16 languages are Amharic and Tamil. *TDV Faaliyet Raporu 2017*. 31; https://tdv.org.tr.

77. 'Diyanet'ten 'flört zina değil' fetvası', Haber7.com, 31 May 2008. For a criticism of Bardakoğlu's attitude, see M. Bardakçı (2010) 'Din adamı konuşmazmış!', *Habertürk*, 15 October.

78. Öcal 2008.

79. Din İşleri Yüksek Kurulu (2019) *Fetvalar*. Istanbul: Diyanet İşleri Başkanlığı.

80. 'Diyanet'ten Kürtaj Açıklaması', *Sabah*, 4 June 2012.

81. '90 bin camide sela', *Yeni Şafak*, 11 July 2019.

82. 'Abuse of religion' is the principal theme of the Diyanet's FETÖ reports. See *Kendi Dilinden FETÖ: Örgütlü Bir Din İstismarı* (Ankara: DİB Yayınları, 2017). For examples of Diyanet publications on the same topic, see *Din İstismarı* (Ankara: DİB Yayınları, 2017); *FETÖ: Din İstismarının Arkasına Gizlenen Terör Örgütü* (Ankara: DİB Yayınları, 2018); *DEAŞ: Dehşete Dayalı Bir Din İstismarı* (Ankara: DİB Yayınları, 2018). See also the special issue on 'concepts that are taken out of context'

('*bağlamından koparılan kavramlar*'), *Diyanet Aylık Dergi* 343 (July 2019).

83. 'Macron ve değişmeye hazırlanan laiklik yasası', *Euronews*, 8 January 2019.

84. Çitak 2018: 392.

85. The sixteenth opening conference of the ECFR was hosted in Istanbul, with an enthusiastic speech praising Istanbul given by Qaradawi. See 'Uyanın Ey Müslümanlar', *MilliGazete*, 5 July 2006. The current president of the Diyanet, Ali Erbaş, spoke at the twenty-eighth ordinary session of the ECFR, held in Istanbul in November 2018, and 'extended his congratulations to the ECFR for its contributions to Islamic jurisprudence [*fiqh*]'. See 'The most important cooperation is to eliminate Islamophobia' at https://www.diyanet.gov.tr/en-US/Content/PrintDetail/12122.

86. Ekrem Keleş was a member of the High Religious Council of the Diyanet for many years, and became one of the Diyanet's vice-presidents. He has recently been appointed as head of the Helal Accreditation Agency by Erdoğan. See 'Ekrem Keleş Kimdir?', *MilliGazete*, 30 March 2019.

87. 'New Turkish members of the European Fatwa Council show growing relationship of global Muslim Brotherhood and Turkey', *The Global Muslim Brotherhood Watch*, 10 July 2017.

88. 'Turkey seeking to expand influence among Europe's Muslims – analyst', *Ahvalnews*, 21 January 2019; T. Seibert (2019) 'Turkey moves to widen influence among Muslims in Europe', *The Arab Weekly*, 20 January.

89. 'Ali Bardakoğlu'ndan laiklik tarifi', Memurlar.net, 16 April 2008. For a more comprehensive expression of Bardakoğlu's views on religion and state relations, see Bardakoğlu 2006, 2010.

90. 'Bardakoğlu: Laiklik, Diyanet'in öncelikli ilkesi', Memurlar.net, 2 September 2005.

91. 'Bardakoğlu: Laiklik Din Özgürlüğünün Temeli', *Hürriyet*, 12 September 2008. For a more comprehensive account of Bardakoğlu's understanding of state–religion relations, see Bardakoğlu 2006, 2010.

92. 'Diyanet İşleri Başkanı Görmez: "Laiklik dünyayı savaşa soktu"', *İstanbul Gerçeği*, 15 December 2015.

93. 'Yeni Diyanet İşleri Başkanı ilk mesajında laikliği hedef aldı: İnsanlık sekülerizm kıskacında!', *BirGün*, 18 September 2017. Ali Erbaş has also stated that the public reaction against the Diyanet's fatwas stem from the duality of religion and state. See 'Diyanet laikliği tartışmaya açtı: Sorun din-devlet ikilemi', *Evrensel*, 16 December 2017.

94. See *Diyanet İşleri Başkanlığı Performans Raporları* for 2010, 2011, 2012, 2013, 2014, 2015, 2016, 2017 and 2018, https://www.diyanet.gov.tr.

95. What is even more striking in this argument is the Diyanet's language of legal pluralism to make a case for pluralism, rather than the principles of secularism and equal citizenship in liberal democratic societies. The report also sees the Muslim identity as an identity transcending political, social and sectarian sub-identities and one above all others. See *DEAŞ: Dehşete Dayalı Bir Din İstismarı* (Ankara: DİB Yayınları, 2018). Interestingly, the report's bibliography does not mention any international academic works written on ISIS.

References

Aydın, M. (2008) 'Diyanet's global vision', *The Muslim World 98* (2–3): 164–72.

Bardakoğlu, A. (2006) *Religion and Society: New Perspectives from Turkey*. Ankara: Publications of Presidency of Religious Affairs.

Bardakoğlu, A. (2010) *21. Yüzyıl Türkiye'sinde Din ve Diyanet*. Ankara: DİB Yayınları.

Bayat, A. (2007) *Making Islam Democratic: Social Movements and the Post-Islamist Turn*. Stanford, CA: Stanford University Press.

Bein, A. (2011) *Ottoman Ulema Turkish Republic: Agents of Change and Guardians of Tradition*. Stanford, CA: Stanford University Press.

Berger, P. (2000) 'Secularism in retreat' in A. Tamimi and J. Esposito (eds), *Islam and Secularism in the Middle East*. New York, NY: New York University Press, pp. 38–51.

Berkes, N. (1998) *The Development of Secularism in Turkey*. 2nd edition. London: Routledge.

Beylunioğlu, A. M. (2015) 'Freedom of religion and non-Muslim minorities in Turkey', *Turkish Policy Quarterly 13* (4): 139–47.

Bice, H. (2008) *Annenin Rehberi*. 8th edition. Ankara: TDV.

Bilgili, A. (2011) 'Post-secular society and the multi-vocal religious sphere in Turkey', *Journal of European Perspectives of the Western Balkans 3* (2): 131–46.

Boravalı, M. and C. Boyraz (2015) 'The Alevi workshops: an opening without an outcome?', *Turkish Studies 16* (2): 145–60.

Bruce, B. (2020) 'Imams for the diaspora: the Turkish state's International Theology Programme', *Journal of Ethnic and Migration Studies 46* (6): 1166–83.

Çakır, R., I. Bozan and B. Talu (eds) (2004) *İmam Hatip Liseleri: Efsaneler ve Gerçekler*. Istanbul: TESEV Yayınları.

Çakmak, D. (2009) 'Pro-Islamic public education in Turkey: the Imam-Hatip schools', *Middle Eastern Studies 45* (5): 825–46.

Çetinsaya, G (1999) 'Rethinking nationalism and Islam: some preliminary notes on the roots of "Turkish–Islamic synthesis" in modern Turkish political thought', *The Muslim World 89* (2–3): 350–76.

Çitak, Z (2018) 'National conceptions, transnational solidarities: Turkey, Islam, and Europe', *Global Networks: A Journal of Transnational Studies 18* (3): 377–98.

Çubukçu, A. (2016) *İslâm'da Ahlâk ve Manevî Vazifeler*. 12th edition. Ankara: Diyanet İşleri Başkanlığı.

Dağı, I. D. (2004) 'Rethinking human rights, democracy, and the West: post-Islamist intellectuals in Turkey', *Critique: Critical Middle Eastern Studies 13* (2): 135–51.

Doğan, L. (2012) *Toplumun Temeli Sarsan Belli Başlı Problemler*. Ankara: Diyanet İşleri Başkanlığı.

El Karoui, H. (2018) *The Islamist Factory*. Paris: Institut Montaigne, https://www.institutmontaigne.org/en/publications/islamist-factory.

Gökaçtı, M. A. (2005) *Türkiye'de Din Eğitimi ve İmam-Hatipler*. Istanbul: İletişim Yayınları.

Göle, N. (2012) 'Post-secular Turkey', *New Perspectives Quarterly 29* (1): 7–11.

Gözaydın, İ. (2006) 'A religious administration to secure secularism: the Presidency of Religious Affairs of the Republic of Turkey', *Marburg Journal of Religion 11* (1): 1–8.

Gözaydın, İ. (2008) 'Diyanet and politics', *The Muslim World 98* (2–3): 216–27.

Gözaydın, İ. (2009) *Diyanet: Türkiye Cumhuriyeti'nde Dinin Tanzimi*. Istanbul: İletişim Yayınları.

Grigoriadis, I. N. (2009) 'Islam and democratization in Turkey: secularism and trust in a divided society', *Democratization 16* (6): 1194–213.

Gümüş, B. (2010) 'Diyanet İşleri Başkanlığı'nın Orta Asya Faaliyetleri', *Sosyal ve Beşeri Bilimler Dergisi 2* (1): 1–8.

Habermas, J. (2006) 'Religion in the public sphere', *European Journal of Philosophy 14* (1): 1–25.

Kaplan, S. (2006) *The Pedagogical State: Education and Politics of National Culture in Post-1980 Turkey*. Stanford, CA: Stanford University Press.

Kara, I. (2008) *Cumhuriyet Türkiyesi'nde Bir Mesele Olarak İslam*. Istanbul: Dergâh Yayınları.

Karagöz, I. (2018) *Aile ve Gençlik*. 14th edition. Ankara: TDV.

Kılıç, R. (2010) *Âyet ve Hadislerin Işığında İnsan ve Ahlâk*. 6th edition. Ankara: TDV.

Korkut, Ş. (2009) 'The Diyanet of Turkey and its activities in Eurasia after the Cold War', *Acta Slavic Iaponica 28*: 117–39.

Kuru, A. T. (2009) *Secularism and State Policies toward Religion: The United States, France, and Turkey*. New York, NY: Cambridge University Press.

Lüküslü, D. (2016) 'Creating a pious generation: youth and education policies of the AKP in Turkey', *Southeast European and Black Sea Studies 16* (4): 637–49.

Maritato, C. (2018) 'Addressing the blurred edges of Turkey's diaspora and religious policy: Diyanet women preachers sent to Europe', *European Journal of Turkish Studies 27*: 1–17.

Öcal, S. (2008) 'From "the fetwa" to "the religious questions": main characteristics of *fetwas* of the Diyanet', *The Muslim World 98*: 324–34.

Öktem, K. (2012) 'Global Diyanet and multiple networks: Turkey's new presence in the Balkans', *Journal of Muslims in Europe* 1: 27–58.

Onay, A. (2009) 'Osmanlı'dan Cumhuriyet'e Camilerin Finansmanı', *Değerler Eğitimi Dergisi 7* (18): 43–80.

Özkan, M. and B. Akgün (2010) 'Turkey's opening to Africa', *Journal of Modern African Studies 48* (4): 525–46.

Robins, P. (2007) 'Turkish foreign policy since 2002: between a "post-Islamist" government and a Kemalist state', *International Affairs 83* (1): 289–304.

Sancar, S. (2015) 'Diyanet'in "Kadınlaşması": Diyanet İşleri Başkanlığı'nın Yeni Kadın ve Aile Politikası' in Ç. Kağıtçıbaşı et al. (eds), *Kadın Odaklı*. Istanbul: Koç Üniversitesi Yayınları, pp. 203–39.

Soner, B. A. (2010) 'The Justice and Development Party's policies towards non-Muslim minorities in Turkey', *Journal of Balkan and Near Eastern Studies 12* (1): 23–40.

Stark, R. (1999) 'Secularization, RIP', *Sociology of Religion 60* (3): 249–73.

Şen, M. (2019) 'The AKP rule and the Directorate of Religious Affairs' in N. Christofis (ed.), *Erdoğan's 'New' Turkey: Attempted Coup d'État and the Acceleration of Political Crisis*. New York, NY: Routledge, pp. 40–57.

Şenay, B. (2012) 'Trans-Kemalism: the politics of the Turkish state in the diaspora', *Ethnic and Racial Studies 35* (9): 1615–33.

Turan, O. (2008) 'The Turkish *Diyanet* Foundation', *The Muslim World 98*: 370–84.

Tütüncü, F. (2010) 'The women preachers of the secular state: the politics of preaching at the intersection of gender, ethnicity and sovereignty in Turkey', *Middle Eastern Studies 46* (4): 595–614.

Watters, S. W. (2018) 'Developments in AKP policy toward religion and homogeneity', *German Law Journal 9* (2): 351–74.

Zengin Arslan, B. (2015) 'Aleviliği Tanımlamak: Türkiye'de Dinin Yönetimi, Sekülerlik ve Diyanet', *Mülkiye Dergisi 39* (1): 135–58.

10 | FROM MILITARY TUTELAGE TO NOWHERE: ON THE LIMITATIONS OF CIVIL–MILITARY DUALISM IN MAKING SENSE OF THE RISE OF AUTHORITARIANISM IN TURKEY IN THE 2010s

Ahmet Akkaya

Introduction

The debate on the political role of the military in Turkish politics has been dominated by a liberal conceptual framework that is known as the military tutelage regime analysis. This framework has defined the crux of Turkish politics as the privileged position of the Kemalist military elites at the centre vis-à-vis the peripheral masses, as well as civilian actors and institutions, including the elected governments. The argument is that this privileged position has allowed the military to define itself as the guardian of modernization, secularism and territorial unity in Turkey. The central role thus attached to the military in Turkish politics has been redefined over time, shifting from a relatively positive one of modernization up to the 1960s to a negative view of the military as the main obstacle to Turkey's democratization.

The primary strategy for democratization derived from this analysis has been defined as the search for a correction to the imbalance in power sharing between the military and civilian institutions. In other words, the strategy has associated democratization with the civilianization of state institutions, popularized with the slogan of 'dismantling the military tutelage regime'. This understanding of democratization as civilianization characterized most political analyses up until the late 2010s, which saw the rise of authoritarianism under the civilian rule of the AKP. Ironically, the AKP was defined as a democratic actor in the early 2000s and then celebrated by ending the military tutelage regime in the country in 2011.

This chapter highlights how this perspective, popularized by liberal perspectives on both the right and the left, contributed to the

rise of authoritarianism in Turkey by promoting justifications of
the AKP's policies that have been designed for this purpose since
2002. It argues that this was largely due to the obsession of liberals
with the Kemalists, which they have turned into the sole explanatory
dynamic for all the evils in Turkish politics. By problematizing the
liberals' arguments on some recent crucial developments that have
redefined the position of the military in politics, the chapter also
provides a historical overview of the so-called military reformation
under AKP rule in Turkey. Finally, it underlines the deficiencies
of this liberal construct to make sense of the 'civilian' AKP's move
towards authoritarianism in Turkey due to its methodological inability to understand the social constitution of political regimes.

The liberal dream: the AKP as the democratic actor ending the military tutelage regime

Those who promoted the AKP as an agent of democratization in
the early 2000s relied on a liberal reading of Turkish political history
that made sense of the republican political regime as one of 'military
tutelage'. As a term underlining the domination of the Turkish armed
forces over politics beyond the period of military rule, 'military tutelage' has been based on two conventional arguments on the historical
characteristics of the experience of modernization in Turkey. First,
the principal contradiction of Turkish politics since the imperial era
has been one between the central and the traditional forces, where
the former holds bureaucratic positions, dominating peripheral religious groups and ethnic minorities in order to protect their narrow
interests.[1] Second, it has been argued that the efforts of the Ottoman
state elites to respond to their disadvantaged military position by
modernizing the armed forces resulted in the recruitment of a new
elite group of modernist soldiers, who, after the proclamation of the
republic, successfully placed themselves at the centre of the state, but
without a strong relationship to the society.[2] The guardianship mission attached to the army with reference to the founding principles
resulted in the development of the military both as an autonomous
institution with asymmetrical powers vis-à-vis other state institutions
and society[3] and as a conscious actor protecting its own interests.[4]

During the early years of the Cold War, military tutelage used to
be problematized with reference to the military's progressive role in
the advancement of modern democratic institutions in opposition to

traditional society;[5] however, military interventions in Turkey, starting with the one in 1960, reversed this formulation. The so-called
'Second Republican' liberal democratization strategy promoted
after the 1980s therefore required the military's privileged and
autonomous position to be challenged through the empowerment of
peripheral forces.[6] It was this reversal that shaped the EU's democratization package for Turkey after 1999[7] and helped the AKP come
to power, as well as to reproduce legitimacy for its rule for almost
17 years from a very useful 'dissident but hegemonic' position, as
Yalman describes it.[8] The liberal intellectuals' rapid endorsement
of this strategy as a new modernizing opportunity for Turkey put
them on the side of the ruling party throughout the 2000s, providing
the latter with strategic intellectual support whenever they needed.
Hence, even though the AKP enjoyed broad executive authority as
a single-party government with a parliamentary majority, the AKP
government was defined as powerless vis-à-vis the state status quo,
which was identified with the judiciary and the military. This formulation effectively helped the AKP establish hegemony over different
segments of the society with an *anti-militarist* tone.[9]

The AKP, thanks to the domestic and international support it
thus ensured, started implementing a military 'reform' through
legislative changes that were also supported by the opposition in
parliament. Overall, these changes aimed to reduce the institutional
autonomy of the military vis-à-vis the executive and the judiciary.
Specifically, the National Security Council (*Milli Güvenlik Konseyi*
or MGK) was transformed from a *shadow cabinet* into an advisory
body by redefining its decisions as recommendations rather than
primary considerations by the cabinet; the number of civilian members of the MGK was increased and new civilian security bodies
were introduced to break the military's monopoly on the security
agenda; judicial review was introduced in relation to decisions made
by the Supreme Military Council (*Yüksek Askeri Şura* or YAŞ), the
body responsible for appointments and promotions within the army,
as well as to decisions made by military courts; the military courts'
authority to review civilian cases that were not directly related to military affairs was abolished, while a timetable was established to abolish
military courts altogether; military roles in the higher civilian non-
elected bodies such as the Radio and Television Supreme Council
and Higher Education Board were abolished; specific articles in

laws including the Turkish Armed Forces Internal Service Law that provide the legal basis for the military to intervene in domestic affairs were abolished; and the Court of Auditing was authorized to audit specific military spending.[10] Criticisms continued, however, as parliament still lacked oversight over military spending.[11]

The vital importance of liberal support for the AKP surfaced in 2007 when tension between the AKP and the so-called status quo powers reached its peak due to the army's e-memorandum, expressing concerns about the anti-secular activities of the government. The government responded to this challenge with a series of arguably anti-coup trials, known as *Ergenekon* and *Balyoz*, that resulted in a large-scale purge within the army, using claims that putschist criminal groups were being organized. With the *Ergenekon* case, Turkey experienced for the first time the arrest and trial of active or retired military officers, including the former Chief of General Staff, İlker Başbuğ, by order of a civilian court. In August 2013, the court determined the existence of such a criminal organization after hearing 275 suspects, including active military officers, retired generals, politicians and journalists. The second major case, *Balyoz*, was initiated in 2010 after a journalist close to the Gülen network noted an alleged coup plan prepared back in 2004. The court found 325 out of 365 suspects guilty in 2012. The cases were justified as moves to eliminate the so-called 'deep state' in Turkey, changing the power balance in Turkish politics substantially in favour of civilian authority.[12]

Despite suspicions raised regarding irregularities in due process, which were later related to the agency of the Gülen network, the AKP and the liberals presented these cases as being equivalent to truth commissions for revealing state crimes conducted over the last century.[13] Ironically, without any concern for reality – a perfect example of post-truth politics – any opponents were met with the accusation that they wanted to topple a legitimate government through illegal means. Similarly, the AKP and its liberal supporters displayed little hesitation in picturing the Gezi protests of 2013 as a measure to prepare the ground for a military coup by claiming similarities with the street events that preceded the 1960 takeover.[14]

Even though the trials created outrage, as expressed publicly by active generals, such objections were limited to individual cases and failed to transform the feeling of discomfort into institutional military action. Hence, the end of the military tutelage regime was celebrated with the resignation of the Chief of the General Staff together with three force commanders in 2011 in protest at the attitude of the government in the anti-coup trials.[15] Following all these developments, Metin Heper, one of the key scholars of the military tutelage regime analysis, with his stress on the dominance of the state elites in Turkish politics,[16] attempted to reformulate his earlier arguments with a return to the first-generation problematic of civil–military relations on military professionalism. Heper[17] commented that the soldiers, who traditionally had followed professionalism, encouraging political activism as depicted by Samuel E. Finer,[18] started to internalize the professional ethics of respecting democratic values and civilian supremacy, as Janowitz predicted,[19] and became the foremost actors of the visible transformation. Somehow, it was arguably the soldiers themselves who put an end to military tutelage in Turkish politics. Others, such as Ersel Aydınlı, however, recognized the military as an institution with internal divisions, and argued that the failure of the 2004 coup attempt, the ineffectiveness of the 2007 memorandum and the appeasement of the military during the *Ergenekon* and *Balyoz* trials showed the reformists getting the upper hand within the army, and that this transformation could be a good example of a transition to democracy in the Middle East in the context of the Arab Spring.[20] Based on such interpretations of the reform, the democratization literature started suggesting that Turkey had experienced a democratic transition in the first decade of the 2000s, that this had ended the military tutelage regime, and that democratic consolidation would be tested in the 2010s.[21]

The rise of authoritarianism and the liberals' hopeless search for the 'Kemalist agent'

This liberal story of the end of military tutelage over civilian politics in the 2000s, thanks to the AKP's role as a democratic actor, was too good to be true; it had to be substantially revisited in the 2010s due to the rapid move of the government towards authoritarianism, with many important historical turning points along the way. Among these, two episodes need to be specifically noted in terms of their crucial implications not only for civil–military relations but also for liberal 'military tutelage' theorizations.

The first is the development of a confrontation between the Gülenist and the AKP state cadres after the 17–25 December 2013 corruption inquiry, in which three ministers, together with their sons, and high-level bureaucrats and businessmen were detained on allegations of bribery, money laundering and gold smuggling.[22] This confrontation had a direct impact on the anti-coup trials discussed above, as the Constitutional Court, acknowledging the irregularities in due process, granted the right to a retrial following an application by the convicts in 2014. Given the politicized working of the judiciary, this decision in favour of a retrial was interpreted as a partial pardon granted by Erdoğan to the non-Gülenists. It was argued that, in his search for a new ally to respond to the Gülenist challenge, Erdoğan was seeking the support of 'the old owners of the state', which would bring the Kemalists back to power.[23] This argument became more popular with the re-militarization of the Kurdish question following the 7 June 2015 elections. The cost of this new elite alliance for democracy in Turkey was seen as a backsliding from the civilianization process and the return of military tutelage, which indeed became more threatening due to the provision of new legal protections for the military in their fight against the Kurdish militia.[24] Because of this specific interpretation, Erdoğan's re-empowerment of the military was seen as the re-empowerment of Kemalist cadres, paving the way for another possible Kemalist coup as history repeated itself.[25]

The second episode – namely, the coup attempt on 15 July 2016 – came as a shock due to the dominance of such concerns among liberal circles. In contrast to the core explanation of the military tutelage regime analysis, which centred on the reactionary Kemalist cadres, however, this attempt was distinguished as a clash of two factions of political Islam in Turkey, in which the arguably Kemalist cadres played, if anything, a secondary role. Moreover, the event revealed the ability of the Gülenist movement to get organized at the top levels of the military, an institution considered to be the bastion of Turkish secularism.

It is interesting to see that some liberals simply ignored the loss of their core explanatory agent. Ömer Laçiner, a prominent left-liberal intellectual with a military background who has made a significant contribution to the popularization of the military tutelage narrative, argued that it was not convincing to claim that the Gülen movement had the power to initiate a coup; rather, he noted the need to question the agency of Kemalism.[26] Similarly, Ümit Cizre, who had made valuable contributions to the study of the autonomy of the military, stressed that there was a possibility that Kemalist officers – the usual suspects in Turkish coups – had been involved in presenting the 15 July coup attempt as a Gülenist act.[27] Showing that old habits die hard, Tim Jacoby[28] claimed that the coup attempt was yet more proof of the interventionist attitude of the military in Turkey, an attitude that could be traced back to the political agency of the Janissaries in the Ottoman Empire. He also contributed to a UK Foreign Office report on the coup attempt that included Kemalist officers in the list of plotters.[29]

On the other hand, whatever their involvement in the coup attempt, the old military cadres definitely reacted to the AKP-led post-15 July reformation of the military. The leading figures of the nationalist clique, such as General İlker Başbuğ and the former commander of the Turkish Military Academy General Ahmet Yavuz, argued that the reformation of the General Staff, the abolition of military schools, the transfer of military hospitals to the Ministry of Health, and the civilianization of the YAŞ disrupted the institutional integrity of the army, which had been protected since the imperial era.[30] The exclusion of the Kemalist clique's criticisms from the parliamentary report prepared on the 15 July coup attempt was also revealing as far as the arguable rise of Kemalists within the state was concerned. The report found the cause of the coup attempt to be the deviant belief system developed by Fethullah Gülen, as well as the weakness of the intelligence services to detect the Gülenists' growing influence within the army.[31] A similar exclusion can also be detected in the appointments made to the YAŞ, which reflect a continuation in the purge of Kemalists from the military rather than their re-inclusion. It was also claimed that, in general, the principal criterion for appointment after 15 July was loyalty rather than merit.[32] In this context, the retirement of General Nerim Bitlislioğlu in 2019, the head of the committee that had prepared the military's official report on the coup attempt,[33] attracted particular attention.[34]

The 15 July trauma as the AKP's founding myth of the 'New Turkey'

The 15 July 2016 coup attempt differs from Turkey's earlier coups and/or coup attempts because of the plotters' excessive use of violence, causing around 250 civilian deaths and over 2,000 serious injuries. It was also remarkable because parliament became a target for the first time in its history. Some claim that the putschist jets' bombing of parliament twice (five and six hours into the attempt) was a response to the fact that political parties had not aligned with them; in fact, all the parties represented in parliament declared their stance against the ongoing attempt.[35] In the extraordinary sitting on the following day, the parties also prepared a joint declaration underlining that their delivery of their duty to protect the national will in a heroic and determined manner was an opportunity for the consolidation of democracy in Turkey.[36] This anti-coup attitude of parliament was also shared by the people on the streets, who condemned the attempt.

On the other hand, concrete popular and parliamentary demands regarding the return to democratization were also concerned with the clashes between the plotters and people on the streets that night and with the protection of the rule of law in the plotters' trials. The clashes between protestors and plotters led to yet another trauma that night. The scenes of anti-coup protestors lynching soldiers and the publication of photographs of captured plotters showing signs of torture were the main topics of concern. During parliamentary sittings held after 15 July, opposition members turned these demands into concrete proposals. The naivety of such initiatives became clear when Erdoğan, in his 'address to the nation', criminalized such concerns as acts supporting the coup, and claimed that there was no grey zone between the terrorists and the nation, protecting the democracy and independence of Turkey. It was clear that he was trying to use the anti-coup social response as a base to realize his own political agenda by reframing this reaction as a second War of Independence, led by himself.[37]

Hence, any hope for democracy disappeared quickly as the AKP started reconstructing the coup attempt and the resistance on the streets as the founding myth of Erdoğan's 'New Turkey', which he had been advocating since 2013. According to this new myth, the attempt had been planned by FETÖ, and Erdoğan reaching out to the nation via a FaceTime call broadcast on television while the plotters surrounded him was the decisive moment of the coup attempt's failure. As FETÖ was a mere instrument of imperialist Western powers – primarily the US – its action should in fact be considered an act of foreign invasion. Following the call of its leader, the nation, which had heroically resisted imperialist powers during the War of Independence, took the initiative without hesitation in these extraordinary conditions and confronted the enemy to save the motherland. Erdoğan also called on people to establish Democracy Watches[38] on the streets in the aftermath of the coup attempt, to transform the spontaneous popular reactions against the coup into an organized mass promotion of his own leadership.

The Democracy Watches were justified as a protective measure against the threat of another attempt and celebrated as the victory of the nation and its commander-in-chief in their resistance to the invasion attempt.[39] Despite the masculine language that promoted Erdoğan as the glorious and powerful commander leading the nation, Çelik and Balta point to the fact that the most remarkable aspect of the 15 July myth has been its display of Erdoğan as a human being with vulnerabilities, helping people identify with their leader.[40] Hence, Erdoğan was portrayed as a helpless president surrounded by FETÖ members who had proven skills in concealing their true identity, until Erdoğan's brother-in-law – not the National Intelligence Organization (*Millî İstihbarat Teşkilatı* or MİT) or the General Staff – notified him about the ongoing extraordinary developments.

Another important characteristic of the 15 July myth is its anti-Western tone. The 15 July myth suggested that the Gülenist putsch should be considered as an invasion attempt by Western powers. Official reports stressed that the power of the Gülenist network was rooted in its connections to the imperialist powers, since it lacked any social bonds in Turkey.[41] Accordingly, the birth of the Gülenist movement was found in NATO's anti-communist activities during the Cold War era, during which covert networks had been established by the West to this end. Fostered and protected by the CIA and figures such as Graham Fuller, the Gülenists had found an opportunity to infiltrate the bureaucracy and establish a broad network in Turkey and abroad. Their ideology of moderate Islam was designed in accordance with US interests in the Middle East. By portraying the Gülenist project in this way, the myth suggested that the threat they posed moved beyond Turkey, covering the broader area of the Middle East and Central Asia, and the 15 July coup attempt reflected the Western powers' aim to eliminate Erdoğan, who resisted such imperialist designs. In this way, the myth was used to explain the wider conflict experienced in the Middle East. This connection was also voiced by Erdoğan himself when he addressed a gathering by saying that their heroic resistance would be followed by resistance in Syria, Iraq and Libya.[42]

The proof of the Western connection to the 15 July attempt was found in the West's delayed reaction to the Gülenist action, in Western media coverage on 15 July, and in the US's refusal to hand Gülen over to Turkey. It was claimed that the West's delayed reaction to the coup attempt showed clearly that if the coup had succeeded, the West would have recognized the new regime imposed by the plotters in undemocratic ways, just like they had done before in Egypt when el-Sisi toppled a legitimate government in 2013.[43] A SETA[44] report argued that Western media analyses of the event proved the Western desire for the success of the coup attempt, as they misleadingly portrayed Erdoğan as an authoritarian leader while promoting Gülen, the leader of a terrorist organization, as a pious religious figure.[45] The US rejection of Turkey's demand for the expedition of Gülen on the grounds that there was not enough evidence for his involvement consolidated the belief that the US had played a part in the 15 July coup attempt.

This nationalist anti-imperialist narrative on 15 July, besides its mobilizing impact on the masses, also aimed to shadow the AKP's agency in the empowerment of the Gülenists in the previous decade. The AKP's partnership with the Gülenists in the first decade of its rule was not in the distant past, as exemplified best in their collaboration in the *Ergenekon* and *Balyoz* trials. Ironically, the dismissal of one-third of the generals from the army was itself proof of the AKP's responsibility in empowering the Gülen movement in the army's ranks.

The absurdities of the myth and the draconian measures taken after 15 July led the last remaining liberals to leave the side of the AKP. Ali Bayramoğlu,[46] one of the few liberal intellectuals who insisted on supporting the AKP after the Gezi events, expressed his concern about the drift away from the rule of law in anti-coup measures, which resembled the practices of the Kemalist single-party rule; in this, he was criticizing the large-scale purges of dissidents and the arrests of intellectuals, including Ahmet Altan, Ali Bulaç and Nazlı Ilıcak, for their association with the Gülen movement. Indicating the total collapse of the AKP's cooperation with liberals, this statement cost him his job at *Yeni Şafak*, an Islamist newspaper that hosted liberal columnists but became the major actor in pro-Erdoğan disinformation after the Gezi movement. He later joined *Karar*, another Islamist newspaper, established by former Prime Minister Davutoğlu, who was known for his criticism of the AKP. His first article at *Karar* expressed his confusion about the Gülen movement acting in militarist Kemalist ways.[47]

Post-coup measures and the new context of civil–military relations in Turkey

The 15 July myth was used by the AKP to justify the declaration of emergency rule in Turkey on 20 July 2016. In the name of taking measures to eliminate threats to the existence of the state, emergency rule was extended seven times and lasted for two years. The state of emergency provided the AKP with legislative powers to substantially transform the Turkish state structure in general, and the military in particular. During these two years, 36 decrees were introduced with over 1,000 articles, as well as purges that dismissed over 130,000 state employees for their alleged connections to terrorist organizations.[48] Of these dismissals, 15,242 were from the armed forces, including 150 generals and 7,602 officers.[49]

The state of emergency decrees led to a wholesale change in the military bureaucracy as well as its institutional structure. The presidential decrees issued in July 2018, which introduced the presidential system of government as the new political regime, ensured direct control of the military by the President. Moreover, the decision-making capabilities of the Chief of the General Staff on military issues were transferred to civilian bodies, turning the military into an advisory and executive body. Deprived of his authority over force commanders, the Chief of the General Staff was made accountable to the Ministry of National Defence, which emerged as the main body controlling the armed forces. The military schools were closed down, and the National Defence University was established as an institution under the Ministry. The gendarmerie and coast-guard were put within the institutional framework of the Ministry of the Interior, which became the central security institution in the state's security apparatus. Military hospitals were transferred to the Ministry of Health, and the military courts were abolished. The President's authority over the YAŞ was increased. Overall, while the President's authority over the military increased, parliament's capacity to oversee military activities declined.[50]

The question of whether all these measures led to the establishment of civilian rule in Turkey – something that had long been expected by liberals – can be problematized best by focusing on the critical role the former Chief of the General Staff and the present Defence Minister Hulusi Akar played in the establishment of the new presidential regime. The most notable moment in this regard was his – and other generals' – support for Erdoğan during the presidential elections in June 2018. In April 2018, while opposition parties were trying to identify a powerful presidential candidate to run against Erdoğan, General Akar and İbrahim Kalın, the presidential spokesperson, visited former president Abdullah Gül to discourage him from standing as a rival to Erdoğan in the upcoming elections.[51] This controversial visit was the first in the history of the Turkish military, not only because a sitting Chief of the General Staff participated in the election process by clearly favouring a political party, but also because the high-ranking guests landed in Gül's garden by helicopter.[52] This alignment was solidified by Akar's active involvement in Erdoğan's election campaign, which Erdoğan's rival Muharrem İnce harshly criticized by stating that he would rip off the General's epaulet,[53] and fulfilled by Akar's appointment as the first Minister of National Defence in the newly formed regime in July 2018.

Akar's dedicated support to Erdoğan during the presidential elections attracts attention because his position during the attempted coup is still obscure. Akar's own narration of the night of 15 July, which was accepted later as the official story, asserts that the plotters had broken into his office to force him to have a meeting with Gülen and to discuss his leadership in the operation. His refusal led to him being held hostage at Akıncılar airbase, the headquarters of the attempt. His resistance as the Chief of the General Staff played a significant role in preventing the plotters from capturing the General Staff and hence resulted in the low level of participation by military ranks in the attempt. After his rescue, he had attended Prime Minister Yıldırım's press briefing with signs of torture on his neck, proving his heroic resistance. Nonetheless, the gaps in his narration created suspicions over his role in the attempt and led to him being labelled the 'black box' of the event. Questions were raised over the reasons why he had not taken the necessary precautions and had not informed the presidency, despite having a meeting on the day of the coup attempt with the MİT Undersecretary Hakan Fidan, who had been informed about the preparations by a lieutenant who had confessed.[54] These questions were voiced not only by the opposition but also by pro-government columnists,[55] while Akar tried to prove his loyalty to Erdoğan through his heroic participation in the Democracy Watches. In the last Democracy Watch, the Yenikapı gathering, he openly expressed his gratitude to Erdoğan and announced the unification of the army and the nation under his leadership.[56]

After his appointment as the Minister of National Defence, Akar has become a key foreign policy figure. He was the person who negotiated with US representatives on most of the recent conflictual topics, such as the extradition of Gülen, the Syrian problem, and the purchase of the S-400 air defence system from the Russian Federation.[57] Within such a context, General Akar was also the first official who publicly assured Turkey's commitment to the NATO alliance. He informed the members of parliament about the purchase of the Russian S-400 air defence system in a budget committee meeting with a warning that Turkey's purchase should not be considered a drift away from the Western alliance.[58]

Conclusion

This chapter has argued that political developments in Turkey in the 2010s in general and in the post-15 July period in particular have shown the inadequacy of a military tutelage regime analysis in making sense of military politics and the rise of authoritarianism.

First, the concepts employed by the military tutelage analysis are inadequate in this endeavour. The 15 July coup attempt – if not the earlier experiences – has constituted a significant challenge to the conceptual stance of this analysis, which sees the military as an autonomous and uniform actor. The 15 July event has revealed that the military is an institution harbouring various political groups that conflict and/or cooperate. Related to this, the event has proven the ability of a religious cult to take root within the military, and so the identification of the army with the Kemalists – the core argument of the military tutelage perspective – has lost its explanatory power. Another categorization that was shown to be useless by the 15 July event is the civilian–military duality that has continued to define liberal democratization strategies until very recently. The position of the former Chief of the General Staff and the current National Defence Minister Hulusi Akar is telling in this sense, as his political activities and preferences have effectively blurred the line between the civilian and the military in Turkish politics. It is now clear that the study of military politics requires conceptualizations that can move beyond dualities such as civilian versus military, centre versus periphery, and/or Kemalist versus Islamist in Turkey.

Second, Turkish developments in military politics in the 2010s have also shown the deficiencies of the democratization strategy proposed by the military tutelage analysis. Its argument that the rectification of the power imbalance between civilian and military institutions would enable democratization in the country has simply collapsed due to the AKP ensuring almost full civilian control over the Turkish military, while simultaneously establishing an authoritarian regime that has had no equivalent in Turkish political history. This has meant that the empowerment of non-military offices in the security sector vis-à-vis the military does not ensure democratization.

Third, the inadequacy of the military tutelage analysis in making sense of the role of international and global dynamics in military politics needs to be underlined. This is mainly because of the normative stand attributed to these dynamics, without reference to the underlying power relations. Reducing Turkey's EU accession process to the transfer of democratic norms to Turkey can be given as one example of this. This silence has become particularly strange as the coup attempt has been widely discussed with reference to international dynamics, such as Turkey's membership of NATO, the US's moderate Islam project in the Middle East and the Arab Spring. The lack of a proper analytical framework to make sense of these dynamics has left the field to normative readings of international relations or to conspiracy theories.

These three weaknesses imply the need for a major revision or reconsideration of the conceptual framework of the military tutelage regime analysis. Similar calls for the need to reconsider the limitations of the civil–military approach in Latin American, post-Soviet and Asian studies imply that this is not a problem limited to the analysis of Turkish politics.[59] It is clear that making sense of the recent rise of authoritarianism – not only in Turkey but also elsewhere – requires consideration of some common global dynamics at play in the constitution of states and militaries.

202 | AHMET AKKAYA

Notes

1. Mardin 1973; Heper 1985; Aydın and Taşkın 2014.
2. Demirel 2004.
3. Sakallıoğlu 1997.
4. İnsel and Bayramoğlu 2004.
5. Frey 1965: 406–19; Huntington 1968: 256–8.
6. Erdoğan and Üstüner 2002: 198–200.
7. Following Turkey's recognition as a candidate for membership in 1999, the EU started demanding reforms in civil–military relations for the fulfilment of political criteria. The first progress report, issued in 2000 by the Commission, listed the political influence of the military employed through the MGK and the military courts as the main problems. The report also called for the reformation of the military bureaucracy in line with the EU, NATO and OSCE (Organization for Security and Co-operation in Europe) standards, based on the empowerment of civilians in the security sector. '2000 regular report from the Commission on Turkey's progress towards accession', European Commission 8 November 2000, https://www.ab.gov.tr/files/AB_Iliskileri/Tur_En_Realitons/Progress/Turkey_Progress_Report_2000.pdf.
8. Yalman 2002.
9. Saraçoğlu and Yeşilbağ 2015: 894–900; Çalışkan 2017: 104–7.
10. Güler and Bölücek 2016.
11. Gürsoy 2011: 303; Güler and Bölücek 2016: 259–62.
12. Kuru 2012.
13. Polat 2011; Söyler 2013; Karakaya-Polat and Kayhan-Pusane 2016.
14. A. Bayramoğlu (2013) 'Büyüyen çığ ve Taksim'in neresindeyiz?', Yeni Şafak, 4 June.
15. Gürsoy 2012: 205–6.
16. Heper 1985.
17. Heper 2011: 247–8.
18. Finer 1962.
19. Janowitz 1960.
20. Aydınlı 2009, 2011, 2013.
21. Keyman and Gümüşçü 2014: 44–69.
22. '10 soruda: 17–25 Aralık operasyonları', BBC Türkçe, 16 December 2014.
23. 'Sabancı suikastından bu yana DHKP-C ile ilgili çok karanlık şeyler var', T24, 6 April 2015.
24. A. Bayramoğlu (2016) 'Askeri vesayet ışıkları ...', Yeni Şafak, 11 June.
25. D. Nissenbaum (2016) 'Turkish military's influence rises again', Wall Street Journal, 15 May; Gönül Tol (2016) 'Turkey's next military coup', Foreign Affairs, 30 May.
26. Ö. Laçiner (2016) '15 Temmuz'dan Sonra?', Birikim, 18 July.
27. Ü. Cizre (2016) 'Turkey in a tailspin: the foiled coup attempt of July 15', Middle East Research and Information Project, 8 November.
28. Jacoby 2016.
29. 'The UK's relations with Turkey', FCO, 25 March 2017, https://publications.parliament.uk/pa/cm201617/cmselect/cmfaff/615/615.pdf.
30. Başbuğ 2017; Yavuz 2017.
31. 'Fethullahçı Terör Örgütünün (FETÖ/PDY) 15 Temmuz 2016 Tarihli Darbe Girişimi ile Bu Terör Örgütünün Faaliyetlerinin Tüm Yönleriyle Araştırılarak Alınması Gereken Önlemlerin Belirlenmesi Amacıyla Kurulan Meclis Araştırması Komisyonu Raporu', May (Ankara: Grand National Assembly of Turkey (Türkiye Büyük Millet Meclisi), May 2017).
32. F. Taştekin (2019) 'Turkish army brass at odds over military operation in Syria', Al-Monitor, 4 January; D. Zeyrek (2019) 'Org. Temel'in alınması, 3 Aralık 1990'ın tekrarı mı?', Sözcü, 2 January; A. Yavuz (2019) 'YAŞ Kararları:

Turbun Büyüğü Heybede', *Cumhuriyet*, 5 August.

33. 'Fetullahçı Terör Örgütü Paralel Devlet Yapılanması (FETÖ/PYD) ve Türk Silahlı Kuvvetleri', GKB, 2 February 2017.

34. 'Yeni Dizayn', *Cumhuriyet*, 2 August 2019.

35. Altınordu 2017: 148.

36. 'Darbe Girişimine Karşı TBMM Ortak Bildirisi' (Ankara: Grand National Assembly of Turkey (*Türkiye Büyük Millet Meclisi*), 16 July 2016), https://www.tbmm.gov.tr/docs/ortak_bildiri.pdf.

37. Somay 2019: 159–63.

38. Democracy Watches took place in all of Turkey's provinces and some centres abroad. The goal of the organization was to keep the city squares crowded for 24 hours a day to intimidate a possible second coup attempt. The Watches, which are marked with a call for the re-legalization of the death sentence, were organized for 28 days as a response to the Gezi movement. The most crowded gathering was held in Yenikapı Square in Istanbul on 7 August 2016; opposition parties except the pro-Kurdish HDP were also invited.

39. Küçük and Türkmen 2020: 254–7.

40. Çelik and Balta 2018: 7–10.

41. Uzun et al. 2017.

42. 'Beştepe Millet Kongre ve Kültür Merkezi Açılışı ile Şehitleri Anma Programında Yaptıkları Konuşma', TCCB, 29 July 2016, https://www.tccb.gov.tr/konusmalar/353/49832/bestepe-millet-kongre-ve-kultur-merkezi-acilisi-ile-sehitleri-anma-programinda-yaptiklari-konusma.

43. Ataman and Shkurti 2017.

44. For a detailed analysis on SETA, see Özkan (Chapter 12).

45. '15 Temmuz Darbe Girişimi ve Batı Medyası', SETA, 12 July 2017, https://setav.org/assets/uploads/2017/07/Rapor86.pdf.

46. A. Bayramoğlu (2016) 'İkaz', *Yeni Şafak*, 15 September.

47. A. Bayramoğlu (2018) '15 Temmuz'da ve sonrasında ordu', *Karar*, 10 January.

48. 'OHAL sona erdi: İki yıllık sürecin bilançosu', BBC News Türkçe, 19 July 2018.

49. 'TSK'dan 15 bin FETÖ'cü ihraç edildi,' *Yeni Şafak*, 5 August 2018.

50. 'Olağanlaşan OHAL – KHK'ların Yasal Mevzuat Üzerindeki Etkisi', HBSD, 10 January 2018, https://olaganlasanohal.com/files/olaganlasan_ohal.pdf; '15 Temmuz'dan On Beş Ay Sonra: Ordunun Reformu, Devletin Dönüşümü', IPC, November 2017, https://ipc.sabanciuniv.edu/wp-content/uploads/2017/11/15-Temmuzdan-15-Ay-Sonra_Keyman_Gurcan.pdf.

51. 'Erdoğan Türkiye'yi paşalarla yönetecek', *Gerçek Gazetesi*, 10 July 2018.

52. 'Kalın ve Akar'ın Abdullah Gül'ü ziyaretinin perde arkasını CHP'li vekil açıkladı', *Cumhuriyet*, 27 April 2018.

53. 'Muharrem İnce'den İsmail Metin Temel'e tepki: Apoletlerini sökeceğim', *Habertürk*, 2 June 2018.

54. A. Nesin (2017) 'Hulusi Akar ve MİT darbe gecesi Erdoğan'a ...', *Artı Gerçek*, 6 December 2017; '15 Temmuz: Yanıtsız kalan sorular', *Deutsche Welle Türkçe*, 15 July 2018.

55. K. Öztürk (2017) 'Darbeyi ne tarafa çekelim?', *Yeni Şafak*, 2 June 2017.

56. 'Hulusi Akar, Yenikapı'daki 'Demokrasi ve Şehitler Mitingi'nde konuştu', CNN Türk, 7 August 2016.

57. For a detailed analysis on the political economic context of this decision, see Kurç (Chapter 4).

58. 'Bütçe görüşmelerinde S-400 tartışması', *Aydınlık*, 2 November 2018.

59. Diamint 2015; Pion-Berlin and Martinez 2017; Sebastian et al. 2018; Pion-Berlin et al. 2019.

References

Altınordu, A. (2017) 'A midsummer night's coup: performance and power in Turkey's July 15 coup attempt', *Qualitative Sociology 40* (2): 139–64.

Ataman, M. and G. Shkurti (2017) 'Coup d'état record of the West and the Western reaction to the July 15 coup attempt' in M. Ataman (ed.), *July 15 Coup Attempt in Turkey: Context, Causes and Consequences.* Istanbul: SETA Publications, pp. 219–49.

Aydın, S. and Y. Taşkın (2014) *1960'tan Günümüze Türkiye Tarihi.* Istanbul: İletişim.

Aydınlı, E. (2009) 'A paradigmatic shift for the Turkish generals and an end to the coup era in Turkey', *The Middle East Journal 63* (4): 581–96.

Aydınlı, E. (2011) 'Ergenekon, new pacts, and the decline of the Turkish "inner state"', *Turkish Studies 12* (2): 227–39.

Aydınlı, E. (2013) 'The reform–security dilemma in democratic transitions: the Turkish experience as model?', *Democratization 20* (6): 1144–64.

Başbuğ, İ. (2017) *Sorunlarla Yüzleşmek.* Istanbul: Kırmızı Kedi Yayınevi.

Çalışkan, K. (2017) 'Explaining the end of military tutelary regime and the July 15 coup attempt in Turkey', *Journal of Cultural Economy 10* (1): 97–111.

Çelik, A. B. and E. Balta (2018) 'Explaining the micro dynamics of the populist cleavage in the "New Turkey"', *Mediterranean Politics*, pp. 1–22.

Demirel, T. (2004) 'Soldiers and civilians: the dilemma of Turkish democracy', *Middle Eastern Studies 40* (1): 127–50.

Diamint, R. (2015) 'A new militarism in Latin America', *Journal of Democracy 26* (4): 155–68.

Erdoğan N. and F. Üstüner (2002) 'Quest for hegemony: discourses on democracy in Turkey in the 1990s' in N. Balkan and S. Savran (eds), *The Politics of Permanent Crisis: Class, Ideology and State in Turkey.* New York, NY: Nova Science Publishers, pp. 195–213.

Finer, S. E. (1962) *The Man on Horseback: The Role of the Military in Politics.* London: Pall Mall Press.

Frey, F. W. (1965) *The Turkish Political Elite.* Cambridge, MA: MIT Press.

Güler, A. and C. A. Bölücek (2016) 'Motives for reforms on civil–military relations in Turkey', *Turkish Studies 17* (2): 251–71.

Gürsoy, Y. (2011) 'The impact of EU-driven reforms on the political autonomy of the Turkish military', *South European Society and Politics 16* (2): 293–308.

Gürsoy, Y. (2012) 'The final curtain for the Turkish armed forces? Civil–military relations in view of the 2011 general elections', *Turkish Studies 13* (2): 191–211.

Heper, M. (1985) *The State Tradition in Turkey.* Beverley, UK: Eothen Press.

Heper, M. (2011) 'Civil-military relations in Turkey: toward a liberal model?', *Turkish Studies 12* (2): 241–52.

Huntington, S. P. (1968) *Political Order in Changing Societies.* New Haven, CT: Yale University Press.

İnsel, A. and A. Bayramoğlu (2004) *Bir Zümre, Bir parti: Türkiye'de Ordu.* Istanbul: Birikim Kitapları.

Jacoby, T. (2016) 'A historical perspective on the July 2016 coup attempt in Turkey', *Insight Turkey 18* (3): 119–38.

Janowitz, M. (1960) *The Professional Soldier: A Social and Political Portrait.* Glencoe, IL: Free Press.

Karakaya Polat, R. and Ö. Kayhan Pusane (2016) 'Technology and politics: have the ICTs turned into a domain for civil-military relations in Turkey?', *South European Society and Politics 21* (3): 301–18.

Keyman, E. F. and Ş. Gümüşçü (2014) *Democracy, Identity, and Foreign Policy in Turkey*. London: Palgrave Macmillan.

Küçük, B. and B. Türkmen (2020) 'Remaking the public through the square: invention of the new national cosmology in Turkey', *British Journal of Middle Eastern Studies 47* (2): 247–63.

Kuru, A. T. (2012) 'The rise and fall of military tutelage in Turkey: fears of Islamism, Kurdism, and communism', *Insight Turkey 14* (2): 37–57.

Mardin, Ş. (1973) 'Center–periphery relations: a key to Turkish politics?', *102* (1): 169–90.

Pion-Berlin, D. and R. Martinez (2017) *Soldiers, Politicians, and Civilians: Reforming Civil–Military Relations in Democratic Latin America*. Cambridge: Cambridge University Press.

Pion-Berlin, D., I. Acácio and A. Ivey (2019) 'Democratically consolidated, externally threatened, and NATO aligned: finding unexpected deficiencies in civilian control', *Democratization 26* (6): 1070–87.

Polat, N. (2011) 'The anti-coup trials in Turkey: what exactly is going on?', *Mediterranean Politics 16* (1): 213–19.

Sakallıoğlu, Ü. C. (1997) 'The anatomy of the Turkish military's political autonomy', *Comparative Politics 29* (2): 151–66.

Saraçoğlu, C. and M. Yeşilbağ (2015) 'Minare ile İnşaat Gölgesinde' in G. Atılgan, C. Saraçoğlu and A. Uslu (eds), *Osmanlı'dan Günümüze Türkiye'de Siyasal Hayat*. Istanbul: Yordam.

Sebastian, L. C., E. A. Syailendra and K. I. Marzuki (2018) 'Civil–military relations in Indonesia after the reform period', *Asia Policy 25* (3): 49–78.

Somay, B. (2019) 'The undead father: the "epic" of 15 July as a gothic tale' in *The Dubious Case of a Failed Coup*. Singapore: Springer Singapore, pp. 141–67.

Söyler, M. (2013) 'Informal institutions, forms of state and democracy: the Turkish deep state', *Democratization 20* (2): 310–34.

Uzun, C. D., M. H. Akgün and H. Yücel (2017) *İddianamelerde 15 Temmuz Darbe Girişimi ve FETÖ*. Ankara: Political, Economic and Social Research (SETA), https://setav. org/assets/uploads/2017/07/ Rapor87.pdf.

Yalman, G. (2002) 'The Turkish state and the bourgeoisie in a historical perspective: a relativist paradigm or a panoply of hegemonic strategies?' in N. Balkan and S. Savran (eds), *The Politics of Permanent Crisis: Class, Ideology and State in Turkey*. New York, NY: Nova Science Publishers, pp. 21–54.

Yavuz, A. (2017) *Vesayet Savaşları*. Istanbul: Kırmızı Kedi Yayınevi.

11 | COURTROOMS AS SOLIDARITY SPACES AND TRIALS AS SENTENCES: DEFENDING YOUR RIGHTS AND ASKING FOR ACCOUNTABILITY IN TURKEY

Zeynep Alemdar

Introduction

In 2019, the judicial year started with a dispute and an unprecedented confrontation in Ankara. The Bar Associations of the main cities of Izmir, Istanbul and Ankara, whose membership represents 81 per cent of the lawyers in Turkey, did not participate in the traditional opening ceremony of the judicial year as it took place at the Presidential Palace. The Bar Associations protested against the ceremony on the grounds that the space where the ceremony was held is symbolic and represents the power of the executive over the judiciary. While this was not the first rift between the President and the Bar Associations,[1] the head of the Istanbul Bar Association, Mehmet Durakoğlu, declared that the Supreme Court, by approving the decision to hold the ceremony in the Presidential Palace, had made a choice in support of the President and the presidential system.[2]

The wholesale politicization of the judiciary in Turkey began in the 2010s. This politicization, acquiring its first impetus with the 2010 constitutional amendments, consolidated itself powerfully after 2015 through various controversial trials against journalists, academics and civil society activists, as well as the persistent legal harassment imposed on those taking a critical stand against the governments' policies towards the Kurdish people. The 2010 constitutional amendments had changed the composition and election procedure of the High Committee of Judges and Prosecutors, effectively increasing control of the executive over the judiciary.[3] Even though these amendments enhanced the Gülenists' already existing power in the judiciary at that time, the clash of interests between the AKP and the Gülenists after the 17–25 December 2013 corruption probes redefined the content of power struggles within the judiciary. Paving the way for the AKP's alliance with the once disfavoured nationalists, the subsequent interventions of the government in the judiciary have led to the latter turning into a disciplinary arm of the AKP against not only the Gülenists but also leftist opposition in the country.[4] This chapter critically problematizes the trials against the *Cumhuriyet* newspaper, the Gezi 'suspects', and the Academics for Peace, which have all been conducted within such a politico-institutional context.

The AKP's use of the judiciary as a disciplinary agent against its opponents on its trajectory towards authoritarianism is not limited to these groups. As early as 2008, the *Ergenekon* and *Balyoz* trials[5] had targeted some leading figures in the military, including the former Chief of Staff, with accusations of attempting to overthrow the government. Kurdish activists and politicians have always been criminalized through judiciary processes in Turkey, except for a short period during the 'Kurdish Opening', which the AKP itself launched in 2004. Without underestimating the importance of such other cases, this chapter focuses on trials against journalists, academics and intellectual civil society activists, as these attract attention to some other political and ideological processes at work during the authoritarian drive in Turkey beyond the politicization of the judiciary.

The three selected cases also help us understand Turkey's situation in the current international climate of anti-intellectualism. The rise of authoritarianism in Turkey has not occurred in isolation from the post-truth, fake news world that we live in, where it has become harder for intellectuals to battle against falsehood and where the right to dissent is frowned upon.[6] As in other countries, the left-wing, well-educated and intellectual sections of society are targeted in Turkey, yet, as these cases show, the amount of repression they have faced through the judiciary has transformed the whole domestic political scene in Turkey, especially since 2013. The journalists, academics and civic actors who are targets of the lawsuits in these three cases are also the activists who take, or are likely to take, an active stand on a variety of topics including the Kurdish problem, women's emancipation and LGBT struggles, with a potential to affect public opinion. This potential possibly seemed very threatening for the government in a period in which its hegemonic influence over its wide constituency entered into a decline after the June 2015 general elections. Hence, as will be problematized below, the *Cumhuriyet*, Gezi and Academics for Peace trials have been used to criminalize, degrade and paralyze the intellectual capacity of these circles through a bold anti-intellectualism.

Through these trials, other journalists, academics and civil activists have been 'educated' about the new limits of their freedom of expression and criticism, and thereby disciplined towards self-censorship. This has proved to be a rather hard balance to strike, however, as what these people have been accused of are the fundamentals of their professions or activities. So, in practical terms, accepting the new boundaries drawn by the government, particularly for academia and the media, would have meant invalidating the very meaning of their professional existence.

Most importantly, the *Cumhuriyet*, Gezi and Academics for Peace trials have also shown the level of politicization in the Turkish judiciary, which has produced 'lawsuits' with no consistency or legitimacy. It can be argued that laws and courtrooms have always been used by the state to circumvent or oppress opposition forces in Turkey. Hence, Articles 141 and 142 of the Penal Code used to be utilized widely from the 1950s to the 1990s to punish any expression of communist or socialist ideas. Even after the changes in the Penal Code and the constitution during the EU membership process, Articles 216 (against Islamic extremism), 299 (insult against the President) and 301 (degrading the Turkish nation and the state) continued to 'protect' the so-called unity of the state.[7] The Anti-Terror Law has become another legal safeguard that judges did not refrain from using previously. However, what possibly differentiated the current state of the judiciary from these old practices is its wholesale unlawful character. Earlier, it was primarily the exceptional State Security Courts (*Devlet Güvenlik Mahkemeleri* or DGMs) or emergency rule courts that made decisions by order rather than principle, while the rest of the civilian courts used to be overseen by some principled and even democratic judges who enjoyed professional autonomy. Yet, the possibility of such decisions in the current Turkish courts has declined substantially, particularly in politically 'sensitive' cases. This level of politicization is also reflected in the courts' almost total disregard for established judicial procedures. This is a defining feature of the compilation of evidence, interrogations, custody and courtroom processes.

The chapter does not aim to evaluate the cases on a legal basis – this would be far beyond a political scientist's expertise – nor does it attempt to provide complete details of how each of the cases evolved, some of which are still going through due process. It intends to present the overlapping similarities and contrasts, according to the available data, to set out how the logic of state apparatuses works. The word 'logic' here does not imply a coherent, consistent framework that prosecutors and judges use or can use during these cases. Rather the chapter attempts to show the waves of behaviour that are constantly challenged by the tumultuous political environment in Turkey. Data consist of indictments, observations, monographs and news pieces on the cases, from lawyers, journalists and academics who follow the events and/or are being judged, as well as scholarly work. Hence, the anti-intellectualism of the Turkish state will be identified in the complex social and political processes at work in the selected legal cases.

The *Cumhuriyet* trials

Cumhuriyet (meaning 'Republic') is the oldest newspaper in Turkey, practically founded by Atatürk. Journalists from *Cumhuriyet* have always been the target of trials and even political murders.[8] As Coşkun suggests, it is possible to identify three different trial cases against the newspaper in the 2000s. The first one is when *Cumhuriyet* journalists and columnists were taken to court during the *Ergenekon* cases, mostly for reporting that was critical of Fethullah Gülen. The second set of trials took place after the corruption probe in 17–25 December 2013, when journalists and editors were taken to court for unearthing and publishing news about it. The probe implied a severing of relations between the AKP and the Gülenists. Once it was brought under the control of the government through the allocation of a new prosecutor to the case, the investigation was dropped in October 2014,[9] although this also meant that the state increased its revengeful pressure on *Cumhuriyet*. The third trial period took place after the attempted coup in July 2016 and saw accusations against the journalists of supporting the FETÖ as well as the PKK/KCK.[10] Hence, while the government tried to criminalize *Cumhuriyet* because of its critical anti-Gülenist stand at the beginning, after 2013 the newspaper was targeted for its alleged support for the Gülenists and other terrorist organizations.

This section will take a closer look at the trials against *Cumhuriyet* after the dissolution of the AKP–Gülen partnership after 2013. The first incident is related to the publication of a four-page selection from the latest issue of the French satirical magazine *Charlie Hebdo*, in an act of solidarity. *Charlie Hebdo* was attacked on 7 January 2015, and 12 employees of the magazine were killed in a terrorist attack. Following the incident, *Cumhuriyet* decided to act in solidarity with the magazine by publishing the cover of *Charlie Hebdo*'s special edition following the event. The next day, prosecutors launched an investigation against two *Cumhuriyet* writers, Hikmet Çetinkaya and Ceyda Karan, on suspicion of 'inciting public hatred and insulting religious values'.[11] Canan Coşkun sees this investigation as revenge for the effective journalism that *Cumhuriyet* pursued during the 17–25 December graft investigation.[12] Trials were conducted in July 2015, March 2016 and April 2016. At the final decision, two writers were sentenced to two years in prison for 'insulting religious values of a portion of society'.[13]

Another case that proved to be more crucial for *Cumhuriyet* during the same period was the trial of its chief editor Can Dündar and its Ankara representative Erdem Gül on political and military espionage charges following a news story related to MİT trucks published on 29 May 2015. Trucks that belonged to the National Intelligence Organization (*Milli İstihbarat Teşkilatı* or MİT) were stopped and investigated by the Turkish gendarmerie on 1 January 2014 in Hatay, and on 19 January 2014 in Adana, two provinces close to the Syrian border.[14] The news that these trucks were reportedly carrying guns and ammunition only made it into a small paper, *Aydınlık*, at the time.[15] However, on 29 May 2015, right before the June elections, when Can Dündar, the chief editor of *Cumhuriyet* at the time, published the images in the newspaper and shared the videos on the website under the headline 'Here are the weapons Erdoğan claims not to exist', media–state relations took a new turn in Turkey.[16] The next day, prosecutor İrfan Fidan launched an investigation into Dündar on suspicion of 'political and military espionage', 'revealing confidential information' and 'propagandizing for a terror organization'. Two days later, President Erdoğan said on a live programme:

'This is espionage and the journalist who made the news will pay a heavy price for it.'[17] On 12 June 2015, Erdem Gül, the Ankara representative of *Cumhuriyet*, published another news piece on the MİT trucks headlined 'The gendarmerie said there are [guns]'.[18] On the same day, a court order was issued, prohibiting access to the internet page and blocking the news.

Dündar and Gül were taken into custody when they were called to the Istanbul courthouse at the request of the Istanbul Chief Public Prosecutor's Office, and they were arrested on 26 November 2015.[19] The prosecutor's indictment was completed on 27 January 2016, two months after the arrests. In February 2016, Turkey's Constitutional Court (*Anayasa Mahkemesi* or AYM), ruling that the journalists' rights had been violated, ordered their release; this was executed on 26 February 2016.[20] Two days later, President Erdoğan criticized the AYM decision, saying that he was not of the same opinion and he did not respect the decision.[21]

The trials of the MİT trucks continued, and in May 2016 Dündar was sentenced to five years and ten days in prison, and Gül to five years. During the break before the court was going to declare its verdict, Dündar was shot at and was saved only by the efforts of his wife and a CHP parliamentarian.[22] The court stated in its verdict:

> [t]here was no final judgment that confirmed the existence of the FETÖ/PDY organization, and judgment should not be passed based on charges of helping such an organization, the existence of which could not be confirmed.

The court announced that the investigations into the FETÖ/PDY organization would continue and thus ordered the files be separated and attached later when the investigation was complete.[23]

In November 2016, Barış Pehlivan, another journalist working for an opposition TV station, *Oda TV*, broke the news that the prosecutor in the *Cumhuriyet* case, Murat İnam, was actually a defendant in a FETÖ case.[24] The Justice Minister of the time, Bekir Bozdağ, declared that it was 'unlucky' that the case had been assigned to a prosecutor who was on trial himself.[25]

In the meantime, Can Dündar fled the country, and in March 2018, the Supreme Court of Appeal ruled that, in Dündar's case, a judgment should be made on the basis of Turkish Penal Code Article 328, foreseeing a 15- to 20-year prison sentence for Dündar on the charge of 'obtaining confidential information for purposes of espionage'.

As for Erdem Gül, the Supreme Court of Appeal ruled that there was no sufficient, conclusive or convincing evidence to penalize Gül on the charge that he had personally tried to obtain confidential information classified as a state secret, and his file was separated from that of Dündar.[26] While Gül was acquitted of these charges on 16 July 2018,[27] he was also tried with Enis Berberoğlu (a journalist and parliamentarian from the opposition party CHP, who was the first elected parliamentarian from the CHP to be arrested[28]) in the MİT trucks case on the charge of 'aiding a terrorist organization without being a member and violating the confidentiality of an investigation'. Yet, as the prosecution was apparently late in changing the type of offence in Gül's case, the four-month statute of limitations for pressing charges as per Article 26/1 of Turkey's Press Law expired and the court ruled to dismiss the case.[29] As for Dündar, the court decided to wait for a response from German judicial authorities concerning Turkey's extradition request for Dündar and set 31 October 2019 as the date for the next hearing.[30]

While the MİT trucks case was still ongoing, after the attempted coup of 15 July, *Cumhuriyet* was the target of another legal investigation. On 31 October 2016, the Istanbul Chief Prosecutor's Office stated: 'An investigation was launched into certain suspects on the grounds of claims and discoveries made that some executives of the *Cumhuriyet* Foundation had been sponsoring the PKK/KCK, FETÖ/PDY and they had been producing articles justifying the coup shortly before the coup attempt on 15 July.'[31]

Police raided the houses of several *Cumhuriyet* employees, including the editor-in-chief Murat Sabuncu, president of the executive board Akın Atalay, and *Cumhuriyet* Foundation executive board member and writer Güray Öz. In total, 13 people from *Cumhuriyet* were taken into custody that day; nine were arrested on the charge of sponsoring the PKK/KCK terrorist organization and FETÖ on 5 November 2016.[32]

The prosecutor prepared the indictment on 4 April 2017, five months after the arrests. As Bertil Emrah Oder stated, 'Regular news and columns, including direct political criticism published before the coup attempt in 2016, have been treated as evidence of the support of terrorism.'[33] The first trial was on 24 July 2017, and, after several trials, on 25 April 2018 the court sentenced 15 journalists in total to 81 years and 45 days in prison while three journalists were acquitted.[34] The court's decisions relating to *Cumhuriyet* employees ranged from 'malpractice' to 'aiding an illegal organization', from 'aiding a terrorist organization' to 'aiding and propagandizing for a terrorist organization'.[35] After the defendants went to appeal, first on 18 February 2019 through the Court of Appeals (for the local court)[36] and then through the Supreme Court of Appeals,[37] journalists in prison were released. The former financial officer of the newspaper, Emre İper, who was kept in jail for another eight months, was ultimately released on 25 October 2019.

It is true that freedom of the press and freedom of expression have never been fully achieved in Turkey. Judges and attorneys have always adopted their own visions of what freedom of speech should be in cases where those critical of the state are tried, and they have interpreted criminal law, the Anti-Terror Law and the Press Law in ways to keep the state's well-being intact.[38] There have always been problematic indictments, journalists have often had various fines imposed for their reporting, and investigative journalists have even been murdered. Yet the *Cumhuriyet* trials still constitute a turning point in the history of media–state relations in Turkey, as a well-respected daily paper's employees, from both administrative and journalism departments, were either arrested and put in jail without indictment or kept under the continuous threat of being tried or going to jail. This was a systematic and severe curtailing of freedom of speech and freedom of the press, and a punishment of journalists who were basically doing their jobs. Moreover, the fact that the prosecutors who were pressing the charges were themselves being tried in other 'terrorism' cases was also new for the Turkish justice system.

The Gezi trial

Gezi Park is the only green space in Taksim Square, Istanbul's social and cultural centre. During the construction craze of the 2000s, Gezi was to be turned into a shopping mall, with a reconstruction of the Ottoman-era artillery barracks that had once occupied the site.[39] When the Istanbul Metropolitan Municipality granted permission for the demolition of Gezi Park, a group of environmental activists began to organize a campaign and the Union of Chambers of Turkish Engineers and Architects (*Türk Mühendis ve Mimar Odaları Birliği* or TMMOB) applied for a court order to stop the work. Yet, on 27 May 2013, when bulldozers started demolishing the park and tearing down trees, activists on the ground managed to stop further demolition work. When opposition members of the Turkish parliament and activists who had gathered in the park to oppose the demolition were attacked in the early hours of 29 May, far greater numbers joined them. When Erdoğan, the Prime Minister at the time, declared that the government would press ahead with the shopping mall, no matter what its opponents said, the movement snowballed and the numbers taking part rose from tens to hundreds and then thousands between 27 and 30 May, finally reaching hundreds of thousands on the night of 31 May, when thousands walked across the Bosporus Bridge, normally closed to pedestrians, to reach Taksim.[40] During a night of clashes, over a thousand demonstrators were injured. The central point of the Istanbul clashes was outside the Prime Minister's Office in Beşiktaş, and confrontations in virtually every street in the district were showered with teargas.[41]

In Ankara and İzmir there were fiery clashes as well, and the Interior Minister Muammer Güler said that 1,730 people had been detained in 235 protests held in 67 cities.[42] The police withdrew from the park the next day and a liberated zone in Gezi Park – the Taksim commune – was created. In the meantime, Erdoğan dismissed the protests and defended the police efforts in a press conference before leaving on a four-day trip to Morocco, Tunisia and Algeria, while President Abdullah Gül met with CHP members and released a statement that 'the message of the protesters has been received', urging people to remain calm.[43] The police did not intervene again until 11 June, by which time around 1.5 million people had joined the protests.[44] However, although Gezi Park was calm – and a place where money didn't circulate – clashes in other districts of Istanbul and throughout Turkey continued. On 2 June, 20-year-old Mehmet Ayvalıtaş in Istanbul and 22-year-old Abdullah Cömert, a CHP youth branch member, in Antakya lost their lives in the protests. The Turkish Medical Association (*Türk Tabipler Birliği* or TTB) reported that

4,177 people were injured during the protests.[45] After the events were over, people's assemblies and neighbourhood forums were formed.

Taksim Solidarity, which first convened in February 2012 and brought together 128 organizations against the pedestrianization of Gezi Park, became the voice and 'common mind' of the resistance during the Gezi events.[46] On 6 June, a group of six representatives from Taksim Solidarity met with Turkey's Deputy Prime Minister Bülent Arınç, yet when Erdoğan announced from Tunisia, during his visit, that the artillery barracks would be built no matter what, it became clear that no reconciliation was possible. Erdoğan's severe intervention also caused a severe drop in Turkey's stock exchange.[47] Despite other meetings and a belated court decision to suspend the demolition of the park, protests around Turkey did not end. Furthermore, society was further polarized by Erdoğan and his supporters' harsh reaction and interesting accusations blaming activists, Jews, 'Western financiers', the 'interest rate lobby', and even 'telekinetic' events for the Gezi protests, and actions such as arresting pianos.[48] There were also direct attacks on groups who were involved in the events. For instance, the Ministry of Health investigated the Istanbul Chambers of Medicine for organizing a temporary health centre in Gezi Park, a draft law was prepared to curtail TMMOB's power, and selected activists in the Gezi events and members of Taksim Solidarity were tried on charges of founding a criminal syndicate, violating public order and organizing illegal protests through social media.[49] Although all the defendants were acquitted in 2015, the trial was a clear indication of how the judiciary could be used as a scare tactic to silence the opposition in Turkey. As human rights associations underlined, the politically motivated case aimed at wiping out dissident voices in Turkey.[50] In fact, Mücella Yapıcı, who was among the acquitted defendants in the case, made the same defence at court during the Gezi trial in June 2019, not only demonstrating the absurdity of the claims in the latest indictment but also pointing out that the last trial was in fact against the law since a person could not be tried for the same crime twice.

The 2019 Gezi trial is a 'fantastic fiction', as Osman Kavala, who has been held behind bars since 1 November 2017 and without charge for more than two years, says in his defence. A human rights advocate and businessman, Kavala was taken into custody on 18 October 2017 at Istanbul's Atatürk Airport upon his return from a meeting relating to a project planned in cooperation with the Goethe Institute in Gaziantep. As chair of the Anadolu Kültür executive board, Kavala is a well-known and well-respected philanthropist among Turkish civil society not only because of his endless efforts and support to bring non-violent solutions to Turkey's long-standing conundrums such as the Armenian conflict, but also because of his kind and humble personality. Kavala was personally attacked by Erdoğan, who called him the 'Soros of Turkey' when speaking at the weekly group meeting of his party right after his detention, and Kavala's arrest followed.[51]

The EU delegation to Turkey and the Council of Europe raised their concerns about the justice system in Turkey and supported Kavala, and the European Court of Human Rights (ECHR) decided to hear Kavala's appeal case in an accelerated procedure. Yet, as the judiciary was determined to punish Kavala – and, through him, wider civil society – further arrests of civil society activists followed. In November 2018, 13 academics and rights defenders were taken into custody for having 'acted in a hierarchical order' with Kavala, who was presumably responsible for organizing and financing the Gezi Park protests in 2013.[52] In February 2018, an indictment appeared – 657 pages long, legally incorrect and ungrammatical – that made outrageous claims against 16 citizens, including Kavala, for 'setting up and planning the Gezi Park protests, playing the role of "influence agency" by posting provocative messages and directing acts of violence'.[53] The prosecutor, Yakup Ali Kahveci, was well-known for the earlier indictments he had prepared in the RedHack case filed against journalists for reporting on the emails of the Minister of Energy and Natural Resources Berat Albayrak, Erdoğan's son-in-law, the FETÖ prison organization case and the FETÖ courthouse organization case.[54] The prosecutor who had started the first investigations into the Gezi events, Muammer Akkaş, was dismissed from his job because he was suspected of being a member of the FETÖ, and he has been a fugitive as of November 2019.

The indictment also demanded that the 16 defendants be charged with 'attempting to overthrow the government of the Republic of Turkey or preventing it from performing its duties', according to Turkish Penal Code (*Türk Ceza Kanunu* or TCK) Article 312/2, which required a life sentence for the defendants. Additional charges included damage to property, holding or handing over dangerous material, damage to places of worship and cemeteries, violation of Law No. 6136 on firearms and knives, qualified looting (TCK Article 149), qualified bodily injury (TCK Article 86), violation of Law No. 2836 on the conservation of cultural and natural property. Even if the defendants could avoid life sentences, these charges would still have resulted in them spending many years in jail.[55]

The hearings of the Gezi trial took place in the newly built Silivri courthouse, which is a Kafkaesque space in which the distance between the defendants and the public is about 70 metres.[56] During the hearings, the public were surrounded by police officers dressed like robocops. As of October 2019, the Gezi trials are still ongoing, and the only somewhat encouraging news came on 28 June 2019, when the dissenting opinion of the president of the AYM, Judge Arslan, on the justified ruling on Kavala's application to the AYM made it into the media. As one of the five dissenting opinions, Arslan said that it is not the AYM's duty to approve any of the different views on the Gezi protests.[57] Yet, despite this opinion, Kavala was not acquitted in the first or the second Gezi trial and was still in jail as of November 2019.

Like journalists, civic opposition and rights defenders in Turkey have never been comfortable. Yet, during the EU-led reform years, especially before Turkey–EU relations were transformed into an immoral bargain over refugees by both sides, it was still possible for domestic actors in Turkey to operate within a civic space. From the late 1990s to 2013, various civic groups, affiliated with non-governmental or civil society organizations, could go into the streets and demand their rights through their civic activities. There were occasional clashes with the police during May Day celebrations, for instance, yet the response shown by the police to the Gezi events was unprecedented, with deaths and innumerable injuries.[58] The Gezi trials took a further toll on civil activism, not only due to the absurdity of the indictment, but also because of the way in which Kavala – and, later, Aksakoğlu – was arrested and the representatives of TMMOB who had formerly been acquitted were taken to court for the same offences. In terms of the judicial system, as in the *Cumhuriyet* trials, the prosecutors were those involved in FETÖ cases or even fugitives; the indictments were prepared by these prosecutors in a way that completely disregarded basic judicial procedures; and, in fact, the charges went against the constitutional rights of citizens, such as freedom of assembly, freedom of thought and freedom of expression.

The Academics for Peace trials

Academics for Peace (*Barış için Akademisyenler* or BAK) is an informal group including academics and researchers who released the public petition 'We will not be a party to this crime!' on 11 January 2016, following at least 58 open-ended and round-the-clock curfews in seven south-eastern cities in Turkey from August 2015 to January 2016 that affected a total of 1,377,000 civilians.[59]

The petition was originally signed by 1,128 academics from Turkey; in the end, the internationally known 'Peace Petition' was submitted to parliament with a total of 2,212 signatures on 21 January 2016,[60] resulting in a vast operation against the signatories by the state and higher education authorities. Following the petition's publication, the pro-government daily *Yeni Şafak* ran 'PKK's accomplices' as the headline the next day, naming the academics; President Erdoğan called the academics 'vile and ignorant, and accomplices to terrorists', while the Justice Minister of the time, Bekir Bozdağ, said that they 'did not have eyes to see nor the intelligence to comprehend'.[61] Yet the most dramatic declaration came from a mafia leader in jail at the time. Sedat Peker said: 'We would shed blood and take showers under their blood' – meaning that they would sacrifice the academics.[62] Not surprisingly, criminal and administrative investigations were launched against the signatories, who were accused of 'propagandizing for a terrorist organization'.

Most of the signatories faced criminal investigations and prosecutions, as well as professional retaliation, for endorsing the petition. Nearly 200 petition signatories were sentenced either to a standardized 15-month suspended prison sentence or to anything up to 36 months of imprisonment.[63] Four academics – Meral Camcı, Esra Mungan, Muzaffer Kaya and Kıvanç Ersoy – who reiterated their continuing support for the petition in March 2016 were taken into custody, thrown in jail, and then released on bail after one month.[64]

After the failed coup on 15 July 2016, as well as being subject to criminal proceedings relating to links to Fethullah Gülen, hundreds of signatories lost their jobs at Turkish universities. The process dramatically accelerated when the BAK signatories and other opponents in higher education were fired. The civil servants dismissed by the emergency decrees not only lost their jobs; they also saw their passports revoked and received a lifetime ban on public service. This process has been described as 'civil death' by some signatories and continues to have dramatic moral and material consequences.[65] This 'civil death' caused an actual death as well: Mehmet Fatih Traş, a young academic at Çukurova University, committed suicide on 25 February 2017 because of the despair he fell into.[66] Furthermore, academics who went to his funeral were even put on blacklists.

The trials of academics started on 5 December 2017, with a dozen academics brought in front of a judge at ten-minute intervals.[67] Journalist Coşkun, who was watching the trial, likened the courtroom to a factory assembly line, with the academic next in line getting into the defendant's seat, the lawyer making a plea and the judge rejecting it.[68] Most of the academics who faced prosecution were sentenced to one year and three months in prison. In April 2018, Galatasaray University professor Füsun Üstel was the first academic to refuse the suspension of the announcement of the verdict and was sentenced to 15 months' imprisonment, a sentence that she appealed. On 1 March 2019, her appeal was denied and she became the first academic who was sentenced to imprisonment for signing the petition.[69]

During this period, calls for solidarity had grown within both domestic and international academic circles in support of BAK in Turkey who had been dismissed by executive decrees without due process or legal recourse. A solidarity network was developed by university academics, their students and civil society organizations. Academic conferences, workshops and seminars were organized to which the excluded academics were invited to be the main speakers; there were also lecture boycotts. Other academics were sent to prison not only for signing the Peace Petition but also for other freedom of expression charges; these included Tuna Altınel, Onur Hamzaoğlu, Serdar Başçetin and Hanifi Barış.[70]

The targeting and sentencing of academics have wider consequences. As Aslı Odman, herself an Academic for Peace and a rights defender, indicated, what was going on was more than punishment of those who signed the petition; it had a qualitative effect on all academics working for public services rather than the government.[71] The whole process revealed that there were police files on academics, both within the universities by administrators and by the police, and those who resisted the system and/or criticized the state were thrown out. As another member of BAK says: 'The targeting of Academics for Peace is a sign that says [the Turkish government] will not keep any academics who make statements critical of the state or the government, or allow them to survive in academia.'[72] As noted by the Scholars at Risk (SAR) network in their declaration:

> The ongoing prosecution and recent imprisonment of these scholars remains a grave violation of Turkey's obligations under the International Covenant on Civil and Political Rights, the European Convention on Human Rights, and related instruments and standards. Not only do these actions strip individuals of their rights to academic freedom, freedom of expression, and freedom of association; they also threaten to do irreparable harm to Turkey's higher education sector, and to its democracy.[73]

In the case of Üstel, a significant turning point occurred in the trials of BAK that affected all trials. The AYM examined the applications of ten Academics for Peace, including Üstel, on 26 July 2019, and ruled that their convictions on charges of 'making propaganda for a terrorist organization' had violated their right to freedom of expression, with the verdict accepted eight to eight.[74] With this verdict, it became possible to hold retrials of those who had been convicted, to reverse the verdicts in cases to be heard by the Court of Appeal, and to issue acquittals in ongoing cases.[75] Following the first acquittal in İzmir on 8 August 2019, similar joint and separate verdicts followed.[76]

Assembly-line trials of academics, the unprecedented defamation of scientists and open threats made to intellectuals by the mafia were all firsts in Turkey. The opening of individual appeals for academics who had signed the same petition, rather than combining the cases, even on appeal; the dismissal of academics from their jobs, stripping them of their rights if they were public employers; and the AYM's decision that opened the way for the acquittals before the EU demanded a judicial reform package – these all demonstrated the arbitrariness and the unlawfulness of the process. In the meantime, BAK developed unprecedented solidarity among academics that was especially visible during the trials. Therefore, the solidarity of the Academics for Peace and their victorious stand against a despicable process by not becoming victims are what will be remembered in the history of Turkish academia.

Conclusion

Delving into the absurd and tragic trials against journalists, civic activists and academics in Turkey through these three cases illustrates how courtrooms became places of solidarity and resistance, and trials with interminable, copy-and-paste, false indictments became punishments in themselves. In all three cases, the people who were sentenced were not only those who were subject to the trials but the wider society that they represented. In all the cases, the defendants were doing what they were supposed to do as members of a profession, and as citizens reporting the news, working for the public good, defending their rights, asking for accountability. The state officials and the judicial system enabled the illegal processes of these trials by adopting unprecedented practices, such as prosecutors who were themselves on trial, incorrectly written indictments, and second trials for the same charge.

As stated above, the *Cumhuriyet* trials and the punishment of journalists for doing their jobs, with false indictments from prosecutors who were themselves under suspicion, have created a new atmosphere where self-censorship becomes inherent. The Gezi trials, again dotted with erroneous indictments and procedures, dissuaded ordinary citizens from taking part in demonstrations, asking for their rights and even using social media. The cases against the Academics for Peace, accompanied by irreparable damage to their social rights and by their defamation, impoverished the universities and the university atmosphere, demotivating scholars and future social scientists. The real effects of these processes on wider society are yet to be observed.

While the state in Turkey has never been a space for reconciliation on an equal basis for the media, civic activism or academia, the past two decades have been especially hard on these pillars of democracy. The AKP's unprecedented debasing of the state, capturing all governmental power, stripping dissident citizens of their rights through the courtrooms and discretionary judicial processes, will continue to have an effect on the future of civic life in Turkey.

Notes

1. Traditionally, the Supreme Court hosts the opening meeting of the judicial year. The opening speeches by the President of the Turkish Bar Association (*Türkiye Barolar Birliği* or TBB) and the head of the Supreme Court are always considered important. In 2014, Tayyip Erdoğan protested against TBB president Metin Feyzioğlu's talk and a change in the procedure followed, such as not letting the TBB president talk during these meetings. In 2018, it was organized at the Presidential Congress Centre for the first time and the Istanbul Bar Association was not invited. See M. Durakoğlu (2019) 'Sosyal Hukuk interview', Medyascope, https://www.pscp.tv/Medyascopetv/1yNGaprrwLVKj.

2. Ibid.

3. Kaygusuz 2018: 10.

4. See Uzgel (Chapter 3) for a detailed analysis of the reasons for and implications of the AKP's political alliance with the nationalists in the 2010s.

5. In June 2007, the Turkish police found a cache of hand grenades on the roof of an apartment in a low-income Istanbul neighbourhood. The weapons belonged to retired members of the military, and it was claimed that grenades with adjacent serial numbers had been used in an attack on the offices of the newspaper *Cumhuriyet*, a staunchly secular establishment. Alparslan Arslan, the young lawyer who launched the attack, also killed a senior judge because of a headscarf case, which resulted in protests by secularists who accused the ruling AKP of inciting violence. The *Ergenekon* case broke in the press over the apparent controversy of this incident. *Ergenekon* was argued to be a clandestine organization with strong ties to the military, which acted as a 'deep state' trying to govern the country as it pleased. By 2010, a total of 270 people, including 116 military officers and six journalists, had been charged with attempting to overthrow the government and to instigate armed riots. The trial took an odd turn, however, with the arrests of journalists Nedim Şener and Ahmet Şık in March 2011. They were arrested on claims that they were members of the *Ergenekon* organization. These arguments casted doubt on the soundness of the *Ergenekon* case, since the type of reporting that they engaged in made it highly unlikely that they really were members of the organization. Nedim Şener had investigated the assassination of Hrant Dink, arguing that there were links between the suspects of the Dink and *Ergenekon* cases, and Ahmet Şık's unpublished book manuscript explored the intricate connections within the deep state. See Alemdar 2014: 581.

6. Waters and Dionne 2019.

7. Venice Commission 2016.

8. The most notable case was the assassination of Uğur Mumcu, who investigated Islamic extremists and especially Hezbollah cases in the 1990s. See 'Car bomb kills Turkish foe of extremists', *Los Angeles Times*, 25 January 1993.

9. 'Turkey's massive corruption case dropped by prosecutor', *Hürriyet Daily News*, 17 October 2014.

10. Coşkun 2019: 26.

11. 'Turkish prosecutors launch probe into 2 journalists for publishing Charlie Hebdo cover', *New Europe*, 15 January 2015.

12. Coşkun 2019: 39.

13. 'Cumhuriyet columnists sentenced to 2-year jail term over Charlie Hebdo cover', *Bianet*, 26 April 2016.

14. 'Cumhuriyet, MİT TIR'ları Operasyonundan Fotoğrafları Yayımladı: Devletin Bittiği An!', T24, 4 June 2015.

15. See 'İşte Tırdaki Cephane', Aydınlık, 21 January 2014.

16. 'Journalists Can Dündar, Erdem Gül arrested', Bianet, 26 November 2015.

17. 'Erdoğan threatens to sue Can Dündar', Bianet, 1 June 2015.

18. See Erdem Gül (2015) 'Jandarma Var Dedi', Cumhuriyet, 12 June.

19. 'Journalists Can Dündar, Erdem Gül arrested', Bianet, 26 November 2015.

20. 'Can Dündar ve Erdem Gül Serbest Bırakıldı', Voice of America, 26 February 2016.

21. Coşkun 2019: 53.

22. Ibid.: 57. The gunman was acquitted after five months of imprisonment.

23. 'Court sentences Can Dündar, Erdem Gül to 10 years, 10 months total', Bianet, 7 May 2016.

24. Coşkun 2019: 62.

25. Ibid.

26. 'Supreme Court: penalty increase for Dündar, acquittal for Gül', Bianet, 12 March 2018.

27. 'Son Dakika: Erdem Gül Beraat Etti', CNN Türk, 16 July 2018.

28. Coşkun 2019: 55.

29. 'Acquittal for Erdem Gül, no penalty for Enis Berberoğlu', Bianet, 15 May 2019.

30. 'Can Dündar', Expression Interrupted, https://express024interrupted.com/can-dundar/.

31. 'Operation on Cumhuriyet daily, 16 taken into custody', Bianet, 31 October 2016.

32. The nine arrested Cumhuriyet workers were Murat Sabuncu, Kadri Gürsel, Musa Kart, Önder Çelik, Bülent Utku, Mustafa Kemal Güngör, Güray Öz, Hakan Kara and Turhan Günay. See 'Cumhuriyet'ten 9 Yazar ve Yönetici Tutuklandı', Bianet, 5 November 2016.

33. B. E. Oder (2019) 'Independent journalism v. political courts: the Cumhuriyet trial in Turkey and Strasbourg', Verfassungsblog, 4 May.

34. 'Sentence of 81 years in prison in Cumhuriyet trial, Akın Atalaya released', Bianet, 26 April 2018.

35. 'Court of Appeals upholds verdict on Cumhuriyet case, journalists say "goodbye"', Bianet, 19 February 2019.

36. Ibid.

37. 'Verdict on Cumhuriyet newspaper case taken to Supreme Court of Appeals', Bianet, 27 February 2019.

38. Alemdar 2014.

39. Yörük and Yüksel 2014.

40. Ibid.

41. 'Timeline of Gezi Park protests', Hürriyet Daily News, 3 June 2013.

42. Ibid.

43. Ibid.

44. Yörük and Yüksel 2014.

45. 'Timeline of Gezi Park protests', Hürriyet Daily News, 3 June 2013.

46. Akınhay 2013.

47. 'Timeline of Gezi Park protests', Hürriyet Daily News, 3 June 2013.

48. For the unrealistic accusations and conspiracy theories, see F. Gibbons (2013) 'Erdoğan's chief adviser knows what's behind Turkey's protests – telekinesis', The Guardian, 13 July; P. Zalewski (2013) 'Protocols of the interest rate lobby', Foreign Policy, 27 June.

49. 'Turkey stages "show trial" of Taksim solidarity platform members for "organizing" Gezi protests', Hürriyet Daily News, 11 June 2014.

50. Ibid.

51. 'Observations on "Osman Kavala": Gezi cannot have been organized by single person', Bianet, 16 January 2019.

52. 'Statement by Security Directorate about detention of academics and civil society', Bianet, 16 November 2018.

53. 'Charges in Gezi indictment: "influence agency", "using method of civil insurrection"', *Bianet*, 5 March 2019.

54. Ibid.

55. 'Can Atalay'ın Savunması', *Bianet*, 25 June 2019.

56. 'First hearing of Gezi protests case on June 24', *Bianet*, 5 March 2019.

57. See 'Constitutional Court president: Kavala's attendance in Gezi not sign of an offense', *Bianet*, 26 June 2019.

58. '1 Mayıs 2013: Künye ve Bilanço', *Bianet*, 2 May 2013.

59. 'Fact sheet on declared curfews between 16 August 2015 – 21 January 2016 and violations of right to life against civilians', Human Rights Foundation of Turkey, 23 January 2016, http://en.tihv.org.tr/fact-sheet-on-declared-curfews-between-16-august-2015-21-january-2016-and-violations-of-right-to-life-against-civilians/.

60. HRFT Academy (2016) *Academics for Peace: A Brief History*. Ankara: Human Rights Foundation of Turkey, http://www.tihvakademi.org/wp-content/uploads/2019/03/AcademicsforPeace-ABriefHistory.pdf.

61. Coşkun 2019: 132.

62. 'Notorious criminal threatens academics calling for peace in Turkey's southeast', *Hürriyet Daily News*, 13 January 2016.

63. E. Redden (2019) 'Peace petition signatories face continued prosecutions', *Inside Higher Ed*, 1 July.

64. 'Chronology: the case against four academics', OpenEdition, https://afp.hypotheses.org/documentation/the-case-against-four-academics.

65. S. Paley (2019) 'Cases against Academics for Peace have become emblematic of the attacks on freedom of expression in Turkey', OpenEdition, 30 August, https://afp.hypotheses.org/1467.

66. 'Mehmet Fatih Traş "Akademik Gelecek Öngöremiyorum" Demişti', *Bianet*, 27 February 2018.

67. Coşkun 2019: 135.

68. Ibid.

69. 'Turkey's Academics for Peace punished for anti-war protest', Deutsche Welle, 29 April 2019.

70. 'Aslı Odman ve Nazım Dikbaş Anlatıyor: "Barış Talebimiz Devam Ediyor ve Eskisi Kadar Güçlü"', *Sendika63*, 10 October 2019.

71. Ibid.

72. E. Redden (2019) 'Peace petition signatories face continued prosecutions', *Inside Higher Ed*, 1 July.

73. 'Peace Petition scholars, Turkey', Scholars at Risk, https://www.scholarsatrisk.org/actions/academics-for-peace-turkey/.

74. 'Constitutional Court: freedom of expression of Academics for Peace violated', *Bianet*, 26 July 2019.

75. Ibid.

76. The AYM's ruling that the freedom of expression of Academics for Peace has been violated was also criticized, with 1,071 academics signing a manifesto condemning the AYM's verdict. The '1071' declaration shows their political loyalty to the government by accusing the top court of 'disrespecting the memories of the martyrs and veteran soldiers' and 'hurting consciences'.

References

Akınhay, O. (2013) *Gezi Ruhu: Bir İsyanın Halesi*. Istanbul: Agora Kitaplığı.

Alemdar, Z. (2014) '"Modelling" for democracy? Turkey's historical issues with freedom of speech', *Middle Eastern Studies* 50 (4): 568–88.

Coşkun, C. (2019) *'Burası Mahkeme': Yeni Türkiye'de Yargı Rejimi*. Istanbul: İletişim Yayınları.

Kaygusuz, Ö. (2018) 'Authoritarian neoliberalism and regime security in Turkey: moving to an "exceptional state" under AKP', *South European Society and Politics 23* (2): 281–302.

Venice Commission (European Commission for Democracy Through Law) (2016) 'Opinion on articles 216, 299, 301 and 314 of the Penal Code of Turkey, 15 March'. Strasbourg: Council of Europe, https://www.venice.coe. int/webforms/documents/default. aspx?pdffile=CDL-AD(2016)002-e (accessed 8 October 2019).

Waters, A. and E. J. Dionne Jr (2019) 'Is anti-intellectualism ever good for democracy?' *Dissent,* https://www.dissentmagazine.org/article/is-anti-intellectualism-ever-good-for-democracy.

Yörük, E. and M. Yüksel (2014) 'Class and politics in Turkey's Gezi protests', *New Left Review 89*: 103–23.

12 | SETA: FROM THE AKP'S ORGANIC INTELLECTUALS TO AK-PARATCHIKS

Behlül Özkan

Introduction

Under the AKP, which has ruled Turkey single-handedly since 2002, Islamist intellectuals and think tanks have obtained considerable financial resources and media exposure and have become more visible in universities. Until 2013, Islamist intellectuals and think tanks, including the Gülen movement, played a key role (along with the centre-right, liberals and a portion of the Turkish left) in helping to shore up the AKP's hegemony. This hegemony was founded on the claim that Turkey's secular, authoritarian political establishment, made up mostly of the army and the judiciary, constituted the biggest obstacle to the flourishing of democracy in Turkey, EU membership, and the smooth functioning of a free-market economy. The AKP and the Islamists, so the argument ran, were democratic actors representing much of the social periphery; they were opposing a system of military tutelage and a secular, authoritarian elite whose Western values had led to its own cultural alienation. In the pre-2013 period, Islamist think tanks helped garner public support for the suppression and silencing of anti-AKP voices in academia, the media and the bureaucracy, all in the name of ending Turkey's system of military tutelage and creating a more democratic society.[1] Yet the AKP and the Islamist think tanks heralding the arrival of a *Yeni Türkiye* (New Turkey) failed dramatically in delivering on that promise.

This chapter seeks to examine the transformation undergone by Turkey's Foundation for Political, Economic and Social Research (*Siyasi, Ekonomi ve Toplum Araştırmaları Vakfı* or SETA) – the country's largest Islamist think tank in terms of employees and budget – from its founding in 2005 until the present day. While SETA may describe itself on its website as 'a platform for dialogue, bringing together different views in an entirely non-partisan manner', it nonetheless meets the textbook definition of a partisan institution and a GONGO (government-organized non-governmental organization) when it comes to its publications, political stance, ideology and financial resources. In the 15 years since its founding, SETA has provided an ideal vantage point for observing the transformation in the nature of the ruling party. Diverse voices could be found in SETA's publications until 2013, while they still served the goals of the AKP. During this period, SETA maintained that the only way for Turkey to democratize was for the AKP to enjoy sole, unchallenged power, and SETA, bringing together the AKP's cadre of 'organic intellectuals',[2] helped sway public opinion by creating a like-minded coalition of considerable size.

This chapter will show how SETA, since its founding, has served the interests of AKP politics, Islamist ideology and Islamist capital, as a cadre of organic intellectuals. During the establishment of a one-party state in Turkey in 2013–15 and of a one-man regime centred on the presidential palace from 2015 onwards, however, SETA has gradually ceased to function as organic intellectuals fulfilling the traditional tasks of persuasion and knowledge production. Having first helped the AKP enjoy unfettered power by popularizing the party's political discourses in dialogue with opposition voices, it then transformed itself into an organization of party apparatchiks entirely devoted to defending the post-2015 AKP regime. Now that the ranks have closed within the AKP, every sort of opposition has been painted as a threat and Turkey's national interests have become synonymous with those of the AKP and Erdoğan, SETA's publications no longer feel compelled to appeal to anyone other than AKP voters. They have instead resorted to a vulgar discourse in which the ruling party is defended at all costs.

The founding of SETA and its place in a system of quid pro quo relationships

The first think tanks were founded in Turkey following the 1960 coup; their influence and numbers began to grow in the 1990s, after the end of the Cold War, in an atmosphere of 'debate, even rivalry, in which different intellectual and ideological preferences were expressed'.[3] Starting in the 2000s, there was a boom in the number

of think tanks; by 2018, there were 48 in all.[4] The first Islamist
think tank, founded in 1969 by *Milli Görüş* (National Vision) cadres
under the leadership of Necmettin Erbakan, was the Economic and
Social Research Centre (*Ekonomik ve Sosyal Araştırmalar Merkezi*
or ESAM). Two important AKP partisan think tanks were founded
in the 2000s: SETA in 2005 and the Institute of Strategic Thinking
(*Stratejik Düşünce Enstitüsü*) in 2009. With nearly 100 part-time
and full-time employees, SETA has become one of the largest think
tanks in Turkey in terms of its activities, budget and facilities.

While SETA makes a point of emphasizing its non-partisan
nature, its own directors seem to be confused on this issue. In a
December 2015 interview, SETA's General Coordinator Muhittin
Ataman described the organization as taking the 'AKP line'; by contrast, in April 2017, İsmail Çağlar, SETA's Director of Social and
Media Research, made the following remarks: 'There are no ties
between SETA and the AKP ... if you are asking if we are part of a
larger entity known as the AKP, we certainly are not ... [SETA] is
not a part [of the AKP] either formally or organically.'[5] Behind this
denial of any ties, even organic ties, to the AKP is a wish to boost
SETA's reputation, both in Turkey and abroad, by staking a claim
to scientific objectivity. On nearly every issue, SETA's publications
have defended the AKP's policies, and claims that these publications are scientific and objective have resulted in a serious credibility
problem for the organization. Hence, despite these conflicting statements by SETA's directors, SETA was ranked number 34 in the
world on *Global Go To Think Tank Index Report*'s list of 'Best think
tanks with a political party affiliation'.[6]

Many current or former AKP officials played a role in the establishment of SETA, including former Foreign and Prime Minister
Ahmet Davutoğlu and his entourage, as well as businessmen with
close ties to the AKP. SETA's founding director, İbrahim Kalın,
headed the organization until 2009; upon Davutoğlu's appointment
as Foreign Minister, Kalın became Chief Foreign Policy Adviser
to the Prime Minister, and later – in December 2014 – a presidential spokesperson. Kalın acquired his MA from the International
Islamic University of Malaysia, where Davutoğlu was a professor;
from 1996 onwards, the two collaborated on articles for *Divan*, the
journal of the Islamist think tank the Foundation for Sciences and
Arts (*Bilim ve Sanat Vakfı* or BSV). BSV was founded by Islamist

intellectuals and businessmen including Davutoğlu and Murat
Ülker in 1986, making it possible to trace SETA's historical roots all
the way back to the second half of the 1980s.[7] In his book *Stratejik
Derinlik* (*The Strategic Depth*), published before the AKP had come
to power, Davutoğlu identified a 'deficit of strategic theory and
analysis' as one of the main shortcomings in Turkey's foreign policy. According to Davutoğlu, the solution was for 'universities and
independent research institutions to contribute to the building of
strategy', for which they ought to be provided with 'the necessary
financial support'.[8] Four years after their publication, these musings
by Davutoğlu would inspire the founding of SETA.

Islamist businessmen and holding companies also played a crucial role in SETA's founding and in the financial support it received.
Of the five individuals listed as 'founders' in the posting in Turkey's
Official Gazette (*Resmi Gazete*) that announced the establishment of
SETA, two – Yusuf Aksu and Barbaros Ceylan – were among the
shareholders of the Tivnikli family's Eksim Holding.[9] During the AKP
era, Eksim Holding experienced a boom in construction and energy
tenders and investments, with Fahreddin Tivnikli, the son-in-law of
Osman Nuri Topbaş (the leader of the Erenköy *cemaat*, a branch of
the Nakşibendi religious order), on its board of directors. Abdullah
Tivnikli, the chair of the board of directors of Eksim Holding, who
had close ties to Saudi capital, was on SETA's board of trustees at the
time of his death in November 2018.[10] Another founder of SETA,
Ruşen Ahmet Albayrak, has had a high-level managerial position at
Kuveyt Türk Bank since 2002. Strikingly, aside from the posting in
Resmi Gazete and related news stories, SETA's own official website
contains no information whatsoever about the makeup of its board
of trustees or about its financial resources and budget. One plausible
explanation might be a wish to hide SETA's close financial ties and
quid pro quo relationships with Islamist *cemaats* and holding companies from the public. In the words of SETA director Çağlar:

> I only know the chairman of our board of trustees. As far as
> who else is on our board of trustees, who donates how much
> money, what each person does – I don't know any of this. I am
> not informed about our financiers … but as I have already said,
> we meet with those financiers at the highest level, at the level of
> conservative politics and the conservative community.[11]

The term 'conservative' is undoubtedly Çağlar's preferred euphemism for 'political Islam', whose preservation of power is a matter of shared interest for SETA as a foundation and for its employees and financiers. Businessmen who have enjoyed success in the AKP era have donated to SETA, while SETA's directors have been rewarded for their efforts by climbing the career ladder.

Following Kalın, SETA was headed until 2014 by Taha Özhan, who then served as chief adviser to Prime Minister Davutoğlu before becoming an AKP deputy in the 2015 elections. Burhanettin Duran, an individual with close ties to the AKP, stepped into Özhan's shoes as SETA director, a position he still holds. Burhanettin Duran, the nephew of former Sakarya Metropolitan Municipality mayor Aziz Duran, currently serves on the Presidential Security and Foreign Policy Council. Beyond those at the level of director, there are others as well, such as Talip Küçükcan, who served first as Director of Foreign Policy Research at SETA and then was elected to parliament as an AKP deputy in 2015. Nuh Yılmaz, formerly the coordinator for SETA's Washington DC bureau, became the director of foreign news for the pro-AKP newspaper *Star*, before becoming the press adviser for Turkey's National Intelligence Organization (*Milli İstihbarat Teşkilatı* or MİT) in 2013. Fahrettin Altun, in charge of SETA's Istanbul office, became communications director for the Turkish presidency in 2018, thus attaining a position of great influence over the local and foreign press corps in Turkey and managing Erdoğan's relations with the media. In short, since its founding in 2005, many academics and researchers who have served in high-level positions in SETA have gone on to fill critical positions in politics and public institutions under the AKP.

The 2005–13 era: SETA as the home/sanctuary/heaven of AKP's organic intellectuals

After its founding in Ankara in 2005, SETA immediately began to make a name for itself through its panels and events, as well as newspaper columns written by its founder and general coordinator İbrahim Kalın. In 2007, SETA took over publication of the English-language journal *Insight Turkey* – formerly published by the Ankara Center for Turkish Policy Studies (*Ankara Dış Siyaset Araştırmaları Merkezi*) – thus coming into possession of what is even today its most important propaganda tool. The 2007 elections in Turkey resulted in two important victories for the Islamists: an even wider margin of victory for the AKP in the general elections, and Abdullah Gül's ascension to the presidency. The following year, when the AKP faced a closure trial on charges of anti-secular activities, the Islamists began a wholesale campaign to suppress and eradicate all their opponents in the media, bureaucracy, army and academia. It was precisely during this period that SETA began publishing in English via *Insight Turkey*, aiming to win international sympathy – especially from the US and the EU – for the Islamists' power struggle within the Turkish state. At the same time, high-ranking SETA directors began to be featured in programmes on the Turkish Radio and Television Corporation (*Türkiye Radyo ve Televizyon Kurumu* or TRT) and elsewhere in the Turkish media, seeking public support for the AKP.

Between 2008 and 2013, SETA's propaganda focused on the claim that the AKP led a democratic front made up of both conservatives and liberals fighting against a system of military tutelage; the AKP, in short, represented civil society against an authoritarian, secular political establishment. This point was constantly reiterated in SETA's publications. Notably, the AKP and the Gülen movement were allies in this struggle until 2013, working side by side in the pages of *Insight Turkey* and at SETA events. In SETA's propaganda efforts, the Islamists took great pains to portray this struggle not as an attempt on the part of political Islam to suppress its opponents and seize power, but rather as a fight for democracy. To this end, prominent liberal and leftist intellectuals and academics – both in Turkey and the West – featured in the pages of SETA's publications. Such individuals played a crucial role in Islamism's legitimation, which facilitated the subsequent consolidation of its own hegemony; by becoming associated with SETA's publications, they were unwittingly supporting the AKP in its struggle for power – a remarkably successful propaganda coup on the part of the Islamists.

Until 2013, when the fight broke out between the AKP and the Gülen movement, the journal's publishing policy reflected its aforementioned strategy of co-opting liberal and leftist voices. Its editor-in-chief was İhsan Dağı, a liberal academic who was also a columnist for the Gülenist newspaper *Zaman* between 2007 and 2014. Prior to 2013, *Insight Turkey* published numerous articles by journalists, academics and intellectuals who were either

Gülenists themselves or had close ties to the Gülen movement; these included İhsan Yılmaz, Emrullah Uslu, Mücahit Bilici, Ali Bulaç and Mümtazer Türköne.[12] The close relationship between the Gülen movement and SETA could also be seen in the analytical and opinion pieces by SETA directors and academics published in *Zaman*.[13] Thus, from 2007 to 2013, SETA played an essential role in knowledge production on behalf of the AKP–Gülen partnership.

The basic assertion made in most of these pre-2013 articles in *Insight Turkey* – that the AKP represented a wide swath of the population (Islamists, liberals, Kurds and the poor) who were seeking democracy in Turkey – was driven home by editor-in-chief Dağı in the immediate aftermath of the AKP's 2011 electoral victories:

> People who vote for the AK Party ... demand services and wish to have better living conditions, but they also want greater democracy, civilian control of the military and the non-interference of the state in their private affairs, including what they believe in. For these people, the AK Party has meant the taming of the Jacobin–Kemalist state and keeping its institutions and ideology under control ... More importantly, in the 'new Turkey' people are increasingly celebrating their differences, be they ethnic, religious or ideological, as opposed to the homogenized vision of the nation defined by Kemalism.[14]

Insight Turkey constantly reiterated the need for EU and US support for the AKP against its authoritarian, illiberal, Kemalist opponents in the army, judiciary, academia and media, all of whom it described as resisting a process of democratic change. With cover stories such as 'Juristocracy, AK Party and the West', 'Turkey's illiberal judiciary' and 'Towards a post-Kemalist Turkey?', SETA's media outlet sought to provide academic legitimacy to the AKP–Gülen partnership's attempt to suppress opposition through the *Ergenekon* and *Balyoz* show trials.[15] SETA did not merely portray the AKP's opponents as democratically illegitimate; it also sought to criminalize them. Writing in *Insight Turkey*, Emrullah Uslu, one of the Gülen movement's media henchmen, described the AKP's opponents as 'a neo-nationalist criminal network, involving military and police officers, politicians, media members, labor union leaders, and academics', stating that the purpose of the *Ergenekon* trials was to eliminate 'a clandestine criminal organization embedded deep within the state and charged with plotting to topple the democratic government'.[16]

SETA argued that Turkey had a Kemalist, secular, centralized state that had held onto power in an authoritarian fashion since 1923. Yet this constantly reiterated claim has not taken into account the nature of the Cold War-era Turkish state (whose very *raison d'être* was fighting against communism and the left) or the influence from the late 1960s onwards of the Turkish–Islamic synthesis, which would become the fundamental state ideology following the 1980 coup. Moreover, such an approach has ignored the way in which political Islam was used by the Cold War-era Turkish state as an antidote to the rising power of the left, the working class and student activism.[17] SETA's founding director, İbrahim Kalın, sought to legitimize rule by the AKP and political Islam by means of this same historical distortion:

> Kemalist modernization attempted to create a nation by proposing a civilizational pan-Turkism as a secular religion; however, it did not succeed in doing so ... Jacobin-style leftism in Turkey has generally been on the side of putschist, military-dominated, top-down state structures and has been unable to develop a culture of democracy. Leftist internationalism has resulted in the Turkish left becoming alienated from Turkey's history, religion and culture.[18]

Here, Kalın employs concepts such as 'Kemalism', 'Jacobin', 'putschist' and 'top-down' as stand-ins for all political tendencies and ideologies other than Islamism, using them as stock epithets free of any context and feeling no need to rely on data or citations. The same point is emphasized over and over again: that only the AKP could bring about democratic change as the national, authentic representative of Turkish society against authoritarian, secular elites who were in 'an eternal conflict with the nation'.

In the wake of the 2011 elections, in which the party further increased its share of the vote following the opposition being curbed by means of show trials, *Insight Turkey* editor-in-chief Dağı remarked: 'Unless Kemalism is abandoned as an ideology protected by the constitution and the law, there can be no full-fledged liberal democracy in Turkey.' He added: 'A post-Kemalist republic is needed in order to consolidate democracy, establish civilian control over the military, redefine secularism, and resolve the long-standing Kurdish question.'[19] Again, SETA has put every movement and individual opposed to political Islam into the same Kemalist pigeon-hole, branding them as illiberal, authoritarian and even, at times, criminal, while pleading for Western support on behalf of the AKP. Such support would allow Turkey to achieve true democracy and would help resolve the Kurdish question; the AKP would also be a model for the authoritarian regimes of the Middle East in their transition to democracy and a free-market economy. Significantly, such attempts to promote the AKP to the West as a democratic model made no mention of the party's pan-Islamist foreign policy in the post-Arab uprising, which aimed to use the Muslim Brotherhood to establish its own hegemony in a region stretching from Tunisia to Syria. Thus, SETA and its English-language publications were instrumental in ensuring US and EU support for the suppression of the AKP's opponents in Turkey as well as the AKP's pan-Islamist foreign policy in the Middle East. Hence, well-known journalist Cengiz Çandar, for instance, supported the AKP's Kurdish initiative; Stephen Larrabee, a specialist at the RAND Corporation (a prominent US think tank), describing Turkey as a 'rising regional power', argued that the Obama administration needed to lend its support to the AKP's 'New Turkey'.[20] The international scholarly prestige of *Insight Turkey* and SETA was likewise boosted by its publication of articles by respected academics such as Marina Ottoway, Ali Çarkoğlu and Ziya Öniş; almost none of these articles featured criticism of the AKP or its policies.

The collapse of the AKP hegemony and SETA's transformation into party apparatchiks

Three crucial developments in 2013 marked the collapse of the Islamist hegemony that had been in place since 2002 and that had painted the AKP as the sole actor striving for democracy in Turkey. These were the Gezi Uprising, the failure of the AKP's Muslim Brotherhood-based Middle Eastern policy following the coup in Egypt, and the beginning of the rift between the AKP and the Gülen movement, which turned into a fully fledged power struggle with the corruption allegations of 17–25 December.

Of these three events, it was the Gezi Uprising that undoubtedly did the most to shatter the myth which the Islamists had promulgated both in Turkey and abroad since 2002: namely, that the AKP had emerged from the periphery as the spokesperson of democracy and civil society against a Kemalist, secular, authoritarian and centralized state. The Gezi Uprising saw millions of non-violent protesters demand democratic rights and freedoms from an increasingly authoritarian AKP regime. SETA's writings on Gezi are a perfect illustration of what discourse theory would term 'dislocation', which Torfing describes as 'a destabilization of a discourse that results from the emergence of events which cannot be domesticated, symbolized or integrated within the discourse in question'.[21] SETA initially took an even-handed approach to the uprising, publishing a report on its fieldwork conducted with the Gezi protesters.[22] However, once the AKP government had branded the protesters as 'terrorists', SETA's academic discourse gave way to a more and more vulgar tone. In an article published in *Insight Turkey*, the pro-AKP academic Atilla Yayla called attention to the 'Leftist-Kemalist aura of the protests', stating that the 'Gezi Park protests marked the bureaucratic-authoritarian establishment's most recent move against the democratically elected government'.[23]

No longer attempting to persuade anyone but AKP voters, SETA staff and administrators had now become the AKP's de facto apparatchiks. Their main tasks were now to legitimize the government's day-to-day political decisions and thereby constantly reaffirm their loyalty to the ruling party; to increase party discipline; to make the AKP's continued existence synonymous with the national good; and to portray the AKP's opponents as a threat to the nation, or even, at times, as working in partnership with 'terrorists'. Some comments made by İsmail Çağlar, SETA's Director of Social and Media Research, on Gezi are indicative of this tendency: in Çağlar's words, the 'violent Gezi Park demonstrations' saw 'the masses terrorize the city'.[24] In another piece, Çağlar writes: 'What are the images we remember from the violent Gezi Park demonstrations? Terrorists attacking the police.'[25] According to a report by the Ministry of the Interior, 2.5 million people in 79 provinces took part in the Gezi Uprising.[26] Based on the information that four out of these 2.5 million people died fighting for the PYD against ISIS, SETA analyst

Yusuf Özkır concludes that 'Gezi Park protesters joined the ranks of the PKK, a terror organization which Turkey has fought for 30 years'. In Özkır's words, the Gezi Uprising was a 'global project' that 'directly targeted the national will'.[27]

Another traumatic event in 2013, from SETA's standpoint, was the coup in Egypt that overthrew the Muslim Brotherhood, which the AKP viewed as its ally. Following the 2012 election of Muslim Brotherhood candidate Morsi to the presidency, SETA was brimming with confidence, opening an office in Cairo; Taha Özhan, the director of SETA at the time, claimed that the partnership between the Egyptian Muslim Brotherhood and the AKP would create a new order in the Middle East.[28] In line with Davutoğlu's pan-Islamist world view, SETA predicted that the Muslim Brotherhood would rise to power throughout the Middle East and that the AKP, which had assisted them in the process, would become the regional hegemon. However, even as late as June 2013, when there were signs that a coup was imminent in Egypt, Can Acun, a SETA analyst based in Cairo, wrote: 'The balance of power in Egypt continues to tilt towards Morsi and the Brotherhood.'[29] At the time, giving interviews to TRT, the Anatolian Agency (*Anadolu Ajansı* or AA) and other pro-AKP media outlets, Acun frequently expressed his view that Morsi would remain in power; when Morsi was ousted, Acun predicted that the Sisi regime would soon be overthrown. Such opinions on the part of Acun, who was stationed in Cairo, were clearly not based on his observations in the field. Rather, they were attempts by a party apparatchik to bend the truth in line with the AKP's interests. In June 2014, when ISIS was growing more powerful, Acun wrote in a striking report for SETA entitled 'The Sunni revolt in Iraq' that 'it would be insufficient and mistaken to understand the events in Iraq merely through the lens of ISIS and "terror"' as they could better be seen as a 'Sunni revolt'.[30] Without a doubt, the sole aim of Acun's report – and other SETA reports on the subject – was to legitimize the AKP's foreign policy as directed by Davutoğlu. Around the same time, Davutoğlu stated that the threat of ISIS had arisen as the result of popular anger, arguing that 'if the Sunni Arabs had not been excluded, this anger would not have accumulated'.[31] Even as Davutoğlu's Middle East policy was collapsing – and as Turkey's big cities were experiencing the largest terrorist attacks in history, carried out by groups from Syria – SETA refused to admit that Davutoğlu might have been in error. A series of articles by SETA analysts published in a 2014 book entitled *Stratejik Zihniyet* (*The Strategic Mentality*) – whose editors included present-day SETA director Burhanettin Duran – contained not even a single criticism of Davutoğlu's foreign policy. Quite the contrary, as good apparatchiks, SETA's analysts heaped praise upon Davutoğlu.[32] In the end, it was the then Deputy Prime Minister Numan Kurtulmuş who, following Davutoğlu's resignation as Prime Minister, admitted what SETA could not: according to Kurtulmuş, many of the problems from which Turkey was suffering were the result of Turkey's 'Syria policy'.[33]

Finally, the feud between the AKP and the Gülen movement that began following 17–25 December 2013 was an existential crisis for SETA, which had previously featured the Gülenists in the pages of its journal, had invited them to its panels, and for years had seen its directors write op-eds in newspapers owned by the movement. While publishing dozens of 'analytical' pieces on the Fethullahist Terrorist Organization (*Fethullahçı Terör Örgütü* or FETÖ), now seen as the mastermind of the 15 July 2016 coup attempt, SETA never made reference to the AKP–Gülen partnership, which had lasted until 2013. SETA never even took a cue from President Erdoğan, who eventually criticized his own previous stance towards the Gülen movement, stating: 'I apologize: I made a mistake.' On the contrary, SETA director Duran claimed that the Gülenists had been inspired by Kemalism in trying to overthrow the Turkish state; Enes Bayraklı, SETA's Director of European Studies, wrote an article entitled 'A Frankenstein's monster created by Kemalism: FETÖ'.[34]

Conclusion

SETA was founded with the aim of knowledge production – specifically, knowledge required to purge all of the AKP's opponents from the levers of power in order for the AKP to enjoy complete supremacy. Thus, SETA's ideology and financial resources, the careers and positions of its employees – in short, the very reasons for its existence – have depended on the AKP remaining in power. Until 2013, SETA helped the AKP silence its opponents by forming alliances with left-liberals, liberals and, above all, the Gülen movement, claiming that this bloc, under the leadership of the Islamists, would lead to a freer, more democratic Turkey. A look at the individuals and topics featured on the talk show *Enine Boyuna* (broadcast on the state television channel TRT-1) between 2007 and 2008 – at which time it was hosted by SETA director İbrahim Kalın – is instructive. On topics such as the Kurdish question, rights and freedoms, the media, and the rule of law, the programme's guests included opposition politicians such as Selahattin Demirtaş (currently serving a prison sentence); academics and journalists now in prison who had close ties to the Gülenists, such as Sedat Laçiner, Mümtazer Türköne and Nazlı Ilıcak; and anti-AKP leftist intellectuals such as Ali Sirmen and Ragıp Duran.[35] In the period leading up to 2013, regardless of SETA's ultimate goals, it proceeded towards these goals by means of knowledge production, by working together with members of different social strata, and by explaining current events to whatever third parties it was seeking to convince.

After 2013, as the AKP took an increasingly harsh stance on matters including the Gezi Uprising (which it labelled as 'terrorism'), the Kurdish question, freedom of the press and academic freedom, SETA's basic mission became defending and legitimizing every political position taken by the AKP, no matter how contradictory it might be. Since 2013, there has been a marked decline in the number of articles in *Insight Turkey* offering support for the AKP's policies by academics from diverse political backgrounds. Instead, publishing the views of such individuals as Foreign Minister Mevlüt Çavuşoğlu, Chief Adviser to the Turkish Presidency Mehmet Uçum, and Mesut Özcan, an academic working for the Foreign Ministry, *Insight Turkey* has effectively become a megaphone for the AKP.[36] The aforementioned TRT-1 programme *Enine Boyuna* is also quite different from what it was ten years ago, having become a show in which three members of SETA – Burhanettin Duran, Nebi Miş and Hasan Basri Yalçın – along with pro-AKP journalist İsmet Berkan give no room to any opposing or critical voices. In newspapers and on television shows, SETA representatives no longer defend the AKP's domestic and foreign policy on technical and scientific grounds; rather, all of the AKP's political positions are portrayed as highly moral, as beneficial to Turkey's 'national interest', and as the sole way to prevent the break-up of the nation. Conversely, those who oppose the AKP's policies are written off as immoral, as enemies of the national interest, and as the accomplices of 'terrorists' seeking to divide Turkey; SETA members now refuse even to meet with such individuals, let alone debate with them.

The most striking example of SETA's targeting of opposition voices in Turkey occurred with its 202-page report, published in 2019, entitled *Uluslararası Medya Kuruluşlarının Türkiye Uzantıları (International Media Organizations' Extensions in Turkey)*.[37] Presenting highly selective excerpts from the CVs and social media accounts of dozens of journalists working for international media organizations such as the BBC, Deutsche Welle, Sputnik and Voice of America, the report accused them of displaying an anti-AKP bias in their journalism. Characterized as an attempt to restrict freedom of the press, the report drew widespread condemnation from professional journalism organizations and journalists' unions, which denounced SETA for targeting and blacklisting journalists.[38] Instead of a comprehensive analysis of the journalists' published news pieces, the report cherry-picked excerpts from their social media accounts and CVs in order to single them out and accuse them of anti-AKP activities.

Thus, the transformation of SETA cadres from AKP's organic intellectuals to AK-paratchiks has been accompanied by a change in the party's political discourse from democracy and freedom to morality, national interest and nationalism. At present, SETA members talk only to each other and refer only to each other's writings, losing all their claims – if they ever really had any – to reach out to people. They are now entirely at the service of the government, which is itself in the process of forming Turkey's new authoritarian state.

Notes

1. For a critical evaluation of this discourse with regard to its use in the transformation of the military in Turkey, see Akkaya (Chapter 10).

2. This conception is borrowed from Gramsci to refer to the SETA researchers' conservative social background and their hegemonic aspirations to popularize the AKP's political discourses from 2005 to 2013 only. A detailed investigation on the class identity of the SETA cadres is not intended here. See Gramsci 1971: 15–20.

3. Güvenç 2007: 142.

4. McGann 2019.

5. Bedir 2017: 235; Eyigün 2017: 105.

6. McGann 2019: 198.

7. For more information on BSV, see 'Bilim ve Sanat Vakfı Hakkında', https://www.bisav.org.tr/Kurumsal/Hakkimizda.

8. Davutoğlu 2001: 49–51.

9. *Resmi Gazete*, 8 February 2006, http://www.resmigazete.gov.tr/ilanlar/eskiilanlar/2006/02/20060208-4.htm; 'İş Adamı Tivnikli Hayatını Kaybetti', *Posta*, 4 December 2014.

10. S. Yılmaz (2008) 'Türkiye'nin Düşünce İklimi Değişiyor', *Milliyet*, 20 November; 'Tivnikli Hayatını Kaybetti', *Yeni Şafak*, 6 November 2018.

11. Eyigün 2017: 105–6.

12. Yılmaz 2009; Uslu 2010; Bilici 2009; Bulaç 2012; Türköne 2012.

13. İ. Kalın (2007) 'CHP Milletle Uzlaşabilir mi?', *Zaman*, 17 August; İ. Kalın (2009) 'Yeni Bir Coğrafi Tasavvura Doğru', *Zaman*, 21 February; İ. Kalın (2013) 'Türkiye ve Afrika: Yeni Bir Stratejik Ufka Doğru', *Zaman*, 14 January; F. Altun (2009) 'Değişim ve Statüko Kıskacında AK Parti', *Zaman*, 23 March; T. Özhan (2009) 'Bugün Gelinen Noktada Kürt Meselesi', *Zaman*, 3 September; T. Özhan (2011) 'Cumhuriyet Mitinglerinden Sivil İtaatsizliğe', *Zaman*, 30 March; H. Ete (2009) 'Şimdi Somut Adımlar Zamanı', *Zaman*, 15 November.

14. Dağı 2011: iv.

15. These headlines appeared on the cover of issues of *Insight Turkey* in the years 2008, 2010 and 2012.

16. Uslu 2010: 16.

17. Özkan 2017.

18. Kalın 2013: 19.

19. Dağı 2012.

20. Çandar 2009; Larrabee 2011.

21. Torfing 1999.

22. Ete and Taştan 2013.

23. Yayla 2013.

24. İ. Çağlar (2015) 'Gezi'nin ve 17-25 Aralık'ın Yarattığı Değer Erozyonu', *Sabah*, 17 October.

25. İ. Çağlar (2017) 'Gezi'nin Şedit ve Vandal Gençleri', *Takvim*, 1 June.

26. T. Şardan (2013) '2.5 Milyon İnsan 79 İlde Sokağa İndi', *Milliyet*, 23 June.

27. Y. Özkır (2017) 'Bir Akıl Tutulması Olarak Gezi', *Star*, 4 June.

28. T. Özhan (2012) 'Mısır-Türkiye Ekseni', *Sabah*, 17 November.

29. C. Acun (2013) 'Mısır'da Karşı Devrim', *Sabah*, 29 June.

30. Acun 2014.

31. 'Davutoğlu'ndan IŞİD Açıklaması', *Cumhuriyet*, 8 August 2014.

32. Köse et al. 2014.

33. M. Yetkin (2016) 'Numan Kurtulmuş, Başımıza Gelen Birçok Şey Suriye Politikası Sonucu', *Hürriyet*, 18 August.

34. E. Bayraklı (2017) 'Kemalizmin Yarattığı Bir Frankeştayn: FETÖ', *Fikriyat*, 15 June; B. Duran (2016) 'FETÖ'nün Günahı Kimin', *Sabah*, 5 August.

35. Kalın 2009.

36. See *Insight Turkey* volumes 19 (1) and 19 (2) of 2017.

37. Çağlar et al. 2019.

38. 'SETA'nın Raporuna Fişleme Tepkisi', Deutsche Welle Türkçe, 7 July 2019.

References

Acun, C. (2014) 'Irak'ta Sünni İsyanı', *SETA Perspektif 55* (June).

Bedir, U. (2017) 'Türkiye'de Muhafazakâr Düşünce Kuruluşlarının Kamuoyu Oluşturma Faaliyetleri'. PhD thesis, Galatasaray University, Istanbul.

Bilici, M. (2009) 'Black Turks, white Turks; on the three requirements of Turkish citizenship', *Insight Turkey* 11 (3): 23–35.

Bulaç, A. (2012) 'On Islamism: its roots, development and future', *Insight Turkey* 14 (4): 67–85.

Çağlar, I., H. K. Akdemir and S. Toker (2019) *Uluslararası Medya Kuruluşlarının Türkiye Uzantıları*. Istanbul: SETA.

Çandar, C. (2009) 'The Kurdish question: the reasons and fortunes of the "opening"', *Insight Turkey* 11 (4): 13–19.

Dağı, I. (2011) 'Editor's note', *Insight Turkey* 13 (3): iv.

Dağı, I. (2012) 'Why Turkey needs a post-Kemalist order', *Insight Turkey* 14 (1): 29–36.

Davutoğlu, A. (2001) *Stratejik Derinlik.* Istanbul: Küre.

Ete, H. and C. Taştan (2013) *Gezi Eylemleri.* Ankara: SETA.

Eyigün, C. (2017) 'Kamu Diplomasisi Aktörü Olarak Düşünce ve Strateji Kuruluşlarının Medya ile İlişkisi: SETA Örneği'. Master's thesis, Marmara University, Istanbul.

Gramsci, A. (1971) *Selections from the Prison Notebooks.* Translated by Q. Hoare and G. N. Smith. New York: International Publishers.

Güvenç, S. (2007) 'Türkiye'de Düşünce Kuruluşları ve Uluslararası İlişkiler Disiplini', *Uluslararası İlişkiler Dergisi 4* (13): 137–44.

Kalın, İ. (2009) *Enine Boyuna Türkiye: Siyaset, Toplum, Kültür.* Ankara: SETA.

Kalın, İ. (2013) *Akıl ve Erdem.* Istanbul: Küre.

Köse, T., A. Okumuş and B. Duran (2014) *Stratejik Zihniyet.* Istanbul: Küre.

Larrabee, F. S. (2011) 'The "New Turkey" and American–Turkish relations', *Insight Turkey 13* (1): 1–9.

McGann, J. G. (2019) *2018 Global Go To Think Tank Index Report.* Philadelphia, PA: Think Tanks and Civil Societies Program, University of Pennsylvania, https://repository. upenn.edu/cgi/viewcontent.cgi? article=1017&context=think_tanks.

Özkan, B. (2017) 'The Cold War-era origins of Islamism in Turkey and its rise to power', *Current Trends in Islamist Ideology 22*: 41–57.

Torfing, J. (1999) *The New Theories of Discourse.* Malden, MA: Blackwell.

Türköne, M. (2012) 'The birth and death of Islamism', *Insight Turkey 14* (4): 87–100.

Uslu, E. (2010) 'Turkish domestic politics in 2009: towards normalization', *Insight Turkey 12* (1): 11–21.

Yayla, A. (2013) 'Gezi Park revolts: for or against democracy?', *Insight Turkey 15* (4): 7–18.

Yılmaz, İ. (2009) 'Muslim democrats in Turkey and Egypt: participatory politics as a catalyst', *Insight Turkey 11* (2): 93–112.

PART IV

POLITICS OF COERCION

13 | DOMESTICATING POLITICS, DE-GENDERING WOMEN: STATE VIOLENCE AGAINST POLITICALLY ACTIVE WOMEN IN TURKEY

Funda Hülagü

Introduction

The state in Turkey has been violent towards politically active women throughout its whole history. This state violence has reached record levels during military interventions including counter-guerrilla operations in Kurdish-populated regions of Turkey in the 1990s and, more recently, in the post-2013 era. During violent and top-down political transformations, women and especially the politically active women who position themselves against political power become special targets of incumbent ruling powers and their proponents. Still, the historically specific forms of this violence display significant differences. Identifying the actual form of physical violence operationalized against politically active women during the AKP era is important to understand the nature of the new neoliberal state in Turkey, as gendered violence is not just symptomatic but also constitutive of it.[1] In short, it is not a surplus violence that can easily be annulled to restore 'human security'.[2] This chapter argues that Islamist political power perceives oppositional women as destabilizing forces by virtue of their culture rather than their nature, and tailors two state strategies to deal with them: de-gendering and victimization.

The republican state in Turkey had established a political sphere in the image of modern bourgeois politics and introduced political rights for women at a very early stage. However, this came at a price, as politically active republican women were simultaneously disempowered. The first political party of the young republic, Nezihe Muhiddin's Women's People Party, was officially closed in 1923 and the feminist agenda of young republican women was depoliticized.

Participation in the political sphere required many women to masculinize and/or to de-gender themselves and repress their femininity.[3] This was in tune with the quasi-universal patriarchal argument that women are destabilizing forces 'by virtue of their nature'.[4] Parallel to this tacit understanding, during acute political crises politically active women were re-gendered by the state. The introduction of strip searches for left-wing female political prisoners following the 1980 coup d'état is one of the ways in which the female body became a specific state target. In the post-2011 AKP era, there has been a twist to this *raison d'état*: women who participate in politics are now expected to be feminine (even as feminine as possible). Simultaneously, the political regime has redefined the meaning of political participation. Accordingly, the 'woman in politics' should principally be involved in affective labour and should domesticate politics. Women are not expected to stay at home and/or participate in public life only when wearing a masculinized mask or be exemplary, virtuous citizens, as was mostly the case with the republican imaginary; rather, they are asked to bring 'home' to the public sphere. Thus, in contrast to secular bourgeois modernity, political Islamism in Turkey brings femininity back to politics, albeit without any reference to gender equality. This constitutes the making of a new encounter between the state and politically active women. The state wants to foster acceptable forms of femininity, but also, whenever it is faced with feminine consciousness on the part of opposition women, its reflex is to de-gender those women. De-gendering – that is, the act of denying the femininity of women political agents – has become a key state strategy through which the Islamist political regime consolidates itself; however, this scheme does not function as smoothly as the incumbent powerholders would hope it to.

This chapter aims to understand and explain the nature of state-induced violence against politically active or violent women with the help of a historical materialist-feminist methodology. What I mean by this is twofold. First, studies on political domination generally tend to ignore the selective deployment of state coercion.[5] Rather than focusing on the 'who' and 'why' questions, priority is given to describing the governmental rationality of political power as a whole. Second, those who focus on the 'who' questions sometimes have a tendency to romanticize the subject of violence by absolutizing its counter-political power characteristics.[6] Therefore, this chapter invites the reader to first adopt an intersectional analysis of the state violence displayed against politically active women. Neither the state nor the patriarchy is a monolithic bloc with consistent governing strategies or political rationalities towards dissimilar women. Second, I aim to reintroduce the concept of contradiction to studies of political power. Political power is itself imbued with contradictions. It is not just a subjectifying structure, but rather a dialectical relation. Hence, this chapter focuses on state violence against politically active women by keeping these two theoretical reminders in mind: selectivity and relationality.

The imaginary of the 'woman in politics'

In order to understand the ideological content that state-led violence against politically active women has acquired under AKP rule, it is important to focus on the transformative impact of the 2013 Gezi Uprising on Turkish politics. This is not because just political activism has become more difficult and more personally risky since then, but because the ruling bloc in Turkey, which includes different shades of nationalists and Islamists, has disambiguated its imaginary about the nature of politics. Inevitably, this imaginary has direct implications for the political participation and representation of women in politics because it leans on the counter-gender narrative of the ruling bloc, based on *gender complementarity*. Gender equality is argued to be a Western construct specifically tailored to the female-unfriendly nature of Western modernity. Gender complementarity, however, assumes that women and men are born into their natural destinies; their worldly missions differ according to their biological sex – this is not inequality but rather some divine act (*fitrat*). One of the Islamist commentators on gender complementarity, Nazife Şişman, argues that the feminist notion of gender equality inevitably relies on a never-ending conflict between the sexes, whereas the Islamist conception of gender is based on the idea that humans are created as pairs, woman and man, whose unity is a divine manifestation.[7] It is obvious that even if it denies the conflictual character of the sexes, this conception still relies on a dichotomy between genders. What is more, the assumed 'unity' does not exclude a social hierarchy among the sexes, although this notion differs to some extent from the classical division of social roles attributed to the sexes in early industrial societies. In the AKP-style Islamist neoliberalism, women are neither exempt from politics nor from working life – in theory. They are not secluded in a private sphere. Nor, however, is politics confined to the public sphere. The modern patriarchal distinction between private and public does not apply.

In this new imaginary, politics itself is conceived as homemaking in a big household. It is imagined as being not very different from domestic labour, which includes caregiving, emotional support and housework. Serving and giving service to the people (*millet*) are themes that are frequently used and usurped by political power. In that sense, political power is conceived by the ruling party as performing a kind of patriarchal power, reflecting the image of the head of the household who is responsible for both the welfare and the security of his subjects. Of course, this kind of political imaginary has its roots in the concrete experience of political Islamists in municipal politics in Turkey, and especially of Recep Tayyip Erdoğan as the mayor of Istanbul during the 1990s. On the other hand, it is directly related to the tendency to subsume politics under morality, whose teleological rationality has been re-empowered through neoliberalism as an ideology that consumes nearly all modern politics under the rubric of corruption and inefficiency.

A direct result of this imaginary for politically active women is that they are asked to get involved in a specific type of affective labour. This new imaginary asks them to manage the country like they would – and like they do – manage their own households. For example, just before the 2019 municipal elections, the women who are affiliated to the AKP's women's branches conceptualized this as 'bringing the female touch to cities'. They are asked to assist the poor, the disabled and the old. They are required to be the bearers of the authentic morality of Anatolian Islamic civilization, and its main representatives. That means, according to them, to be 'ladylike' (*hanımefendi* is the word used, which literally means gentlewoman) and 'industrious', among many other things. But most importantly, their mission is to empower the political vocation of the family, which is seen as the most authentic and strongest institution of that civilization.

Therefore, an important marker of positive femininity is motherhood. Mothering and motherly affection are perceived as pillars of and for state capacity. However, while they do all this missionary work, 'home' emerges as the primary site of and for mobilization; women are not asked to retreat to the private sphere but rather are asked to domesticate the public sphere. In that regard, in addition to possessing some of the general traits of Middle Eastern nationalism – where, for example, women's reproductive role (child-rearing and care work for the whole community) is conceived as a political act against the colonizer – the 'woman in politics' imaginary of Islamist political power in Turkey selects affective labour as the central political activity. As Minister of the Interior Süleyman Soylu, the recent instigator of fierce anti-feminist policing practices under Erdoğan's rule, argued during his visit to a north-eastern town on the occasion of Mother's Day celebrations: 'We [all men] all need our mothers' good prayers.'[8] Women's active emotional support to the political regime and the transmutation of their personal emotional labour to the public-cum-political arena therefore strengthens the initial proposition of gender complementarity in all fields of life. Motherly love becomes the new invisible labour, without which the regime would find it difficult to generate a new gender order.

Every other form of ideological call to women to support political power faces serious obstacles: a significant proportion of women in Turkey are already outside 'the home', either in productive life or in higher education; many Muslim women choose visibility rather than invisibility; and, last but not least, the urbanization of women has made it impossible to sustain high levels of biological reproduction, especially as women claim personal control over their own bodies and are protective of their personal choice to give birth or not.[9] Thus, affective labour emerges as the only seemingly non-contradictory political vocation through which consent to and participation in the Islamist political regime can be secured. In fact, the adoption of intensive mothering as a way of life by middle-class women in Turkey unquestionably does support the concrete basis of and for such an ideological call made by Islamist political power. Not only pro-government women but also secular women have recently turned to 'natural mothering' – propaganda for which is publicized by a cohort of mediatized human development professionals including mother-bloggers and psychologists – which portrays motherly love as 'the new gold'.[10] On the one hand, consumption of motherhood by middle-class women as an alternative way of life has provided the neoliberal market with new commodification possibilities. On the other, this new raw resource has further helped neoliberal Islamists to privatize the public in Turkey through motherly affection.

However, sustaining a smooth link between motherly affection and micro-activism in favour of the incumbent regime is not without its contenders. This is mainly because there are competing nationalisms, such as Kurdish nationalism, and competing Islamisms, whose imaginary of motherhood as a political activity is not very different from the one adopted by those in power politically. Therefore, not only are women asked by political power to engage in affective labour as a form of political activity, they are required to be 'loyal'. Loyal women are thought of as those who actively support the political regime, and, as such, their femininity becomes an asset to underline.

The struggles within the inner ruling bloc of political power comprise one of the factors that have further shaped this loyalty criterion. These struggles caused a period of uncertainty as the rift between the different factions of political Islamists in Turkey led Erdoğan and his political entourage to engage in new political engineering, not only to find new forces with which to coalesce but also to create cadres to build up and consolidate the new regime. Women, who have always been crucial in the makeup of the political constituency that supports the AKP governments, appeared to gain a new importance as a social force during these times. They have certainly been needed to fill the legitimacy and governance void emanating from the discharged ranks of public bureaucracy. Moreover, it was probably believed that they were non-threatening compared with their old male compatriots who had recently been turned into 'traitors'. Affective labour for the sake of political power has been framed as the dominant measure of patriotism, civic responsibility and political activity. It has become a tool of discrimination against other women.[11] Women's difference from men turned into a privilege that they can benefit from – indeed, a patriarchal privilege – but only if they are loyal.

De-gendering to monopolize 'femininity'

When one looks at recent numbers of political detainees, about half are women, most of whom are politically active in the ranks of the HDP. Although to some extent the imprisonment of opposition women can be explained by the rise of autocratic power in Turkey and the accompanying criminalization of the parliamentary opposition of the HDP, whose members are frequently accused of supporting terrorism, there are still questions to be answered. This is because those women who are detained, criminalized and/or imprisoned strongly argue that political power in Turkey specifically targets the liberated stance of women associated with the Kurdish political opposition. In other words, the women feel that they are deliberate targets of authoritarian political power. Second, the agency of these women constitutes a potential and actual theoretical and practical challenge to the 'woman in politics' imaginary of political power.

One of the ways in which women's agency creates a challenge for the political imaginary of those in power is the 'feminine consciousness' of the political opposition.[12] What is meant here by 'feminine consciousness' is the act of adopting femininity in its more essentialist forms (such as peacefulness and mothering as essential features of women) from an outspoken personal and political standpoint. Feminine consciousness leans on *gender difference* both to explain the sources of political oppression and to plant the seeds of resistance. A practical and theoretical example of resistance that relies on gender difference would be the idea that women's perspective fosters peace, unlike that of men. This is not necessarily based on a biological foundation but assumes that, due to their position in the web of social relations of reproduction (i.e. care work), women tend to oppose militarization. As this stance is adopted by many of the women activists and/or women politicians who oppose the coercive policies of the Turkish state, when it encounters the incumbent political regime there is inevitably a confrontation between two gender perspectives: gender complementarity versus gender difference. However, as these two world views on gender are not very different from each other ontologically, and, even though they are in competition, they make use of a similar symbolic/semantic gender discourse, the political regime pursues various strategies to monopolize 'feminine consciousness' so as to make it its own exclusive project. The violence of the state towards the Saturday Mothers in Turkey since August 2018 is a good example to illustrate this.

After many years of positive rapprochement with the state, the return of the police to the Saturday meetings of the mothers of the lost can be considered a return of state violence in Turkey. However, unlike the state violence of the late 1990s against the Saturday Mothers, this time the aim is not to 'disrupt the meaning of the silent resistance of women and to show that their claim of missing people was only an illusion',[13] but to de-gender them.

In August 2018, the Saturday vigil, a peaceful gathering of the relatives of people disappeared by the state, took place for the seven hundredth time. Yet, after years of non-intervention in the protests by the state, riot police broke up this gathering of the Saturday Mothers, the name given by the public to the vigils in Taksim, Istanbul. When public reaction was triggered by the detention of one of the oldest participants in the protest group, Emine Ocak, the mother of Hasan Ocak, whose political murder is still to be investigated, Minister of the Interior Süleyman Soylu said, 'It's true we didn't let them [Saturday Mothers] demonstrate because we wanted to end this abuse and trickery,' adding that 'motherhood' had become a cover for terrorist groups.[14]

This case exemplifies the fact that the de-gendering of politically active women who oppose the government has become one recent state strategy to delegitimize anti-government political protests. Through the de-gendering of the femininity of women protestors, the patriarchal state of the AKP tries to degrade the positive link between femininity (as an identity) and opposition to the security state in Turkey. This is not because femininity as an identity is unwanted in politics as such, but because political power wants to possess exclusive control over this concept. The attempt on the part of political power to establish a monopoly over femininity constitutes a part of its broader strategy of building up a cultural hegemony on behalf of the Islamist ruling bloc in Turkey.

The women in opposition reflect on political power's recourse to violence against the Saturday Mothers by focusing on the biological sex of the police officers who took the Saturday Mothers into custody. The fact that the police officers who dragged the mothers to the police cars were female has stimulated the following question: 'What did these female police officers think about this encounter?'[15] This focus on the encounters stem, I would argue, from a reified perception of the AKP's patriarchal state in Turkey. Critiques of state violence think of the patriarchal state as an entity acting on another entity: 'woman'. However, it appears that the aim of the patriarchal state is to govern women selectively. 'Femininity' as such is not a threat to the new Islamist patriarchal political power in Turkey; as the following words of the Minister of the Interior testify, only some women's femininity is a threat: 'How could we let the terrorist organizations to abuse motherhood for their own sake? ... They do create a kind of vulnerability by using the notion of motherhood and thus provide terrorism with a cover of vulnerability.'

Interestingly, in contrast to the political opposition in Turkey, which tries to highlight the inconsistencies of political power on the issue of motherhood, those in power deny any such inconsistency. Ömer Çelik, the spokesman of the AKP at the time of the police attack, says: 'There is no inconsistency between receiving Saturday Mothers [by Erdoğan, to listen to their demands] and the latest police intervention.'[16] The opposition condemns the state's violent treatment of the Saturday Mothers and argues that the exaltation of motherhood by political power is a lie because it also attacks aged mothers who are looking for their disappeared and/or suffering children.[17] The message of political power is simply that this exaltation is not a lie but is conditional. In a recent court verdict concerning a man who was denied employment in a public post due to 'security reasons', it was stated that the mother of the person in question was someone who was not loyal to the state (since she participated in protests against state violence in one of the Kurdish-populated cities of Turkey) and that there were serious doubts about whether she had passed on to her son any concept of loyalty to the state.[18] Hence, the state, for example, by de-gendering and categorizing motherhood on the basis of loyalty, tries to forge a new social contract to secure its internal sovereignty, which was severely damaged during and after the Gezi events. The first signal flare of this state strategy could be considered the crowd booing Gülsüm Elvan, the mother of 15-year-old Berkin, who was shot and killed by the police during the Gezi events in Istanbul, during one of Erdoğan's post-Gezi rallies. Gülsüm was presented at the rally as the disloyal mother of a 'terrorist' child. She was most probably expected to feel ashamed of her mourning and stay silent rather than openly asking for justice.

The ambition of political power to monopolize all affective features of 'femininity', however, is also related to the regime's need for credit and appreciation by the international community. One of the moments when external sovereignty and the political regime's longing for international recognition were thoroughly jeopardized was when the struggle of Kurdish women fighters against ISIS received extensive international coverage. The publication of an article on this issue in *The New York Times*,[19] praising the gender equality of the PYD in Syria, a group that the AKP associates with the PKK, triggered a further governmental backlash in relation to female political agency. The government tried to de-gender this agency as the feminine consciousness of the Kurdish women fighters attracted sympathy for the PKK and other groups that resort to political violence. An article by Meryem Göka, published in the daily newspaper *Star* in response to the *New York Times* piece, underlines this fact. As the Head of the Foreign Relations Department of the Women's Branch of the AKP, she argued that the women promoted by the Western media are not '*female* freedom fighters but terrorists, just as their male counterparts are'.[20] As this shows, the femininity of Kurdish women fighters is targeted by political power due to the concern that the relationship between gender and politics should be established only in accordance with the AKP's model of 'woman in politics', which puts femininity in direct service of the regime's infrastructural needs.

Victimization of politically violent women

De-gendering has not been the only state strategy to challenge the international romanticizing of female warriors. The Turkish Ministry of the Interior published a report in February 2017 with the title *The Abuse of Children and Women by the PKK/KCK Terrorist Organization*. Both the timing and the design of this English–Turkish bilingual document say a lot about the state's strategy of dealing with the agency of women. This report, published just after the *New York Times* article, complains that 'PKK's women are praised in the international media, especially, within the scope of the fight against [ISIS]'. The cover design features a male hand closing the mouth of a child, presumably a girl. In fact, this photograph reflects the key argument of the report – the idea that the participation of children and women in organizations using political violence reveals a process of deceit, and that these children and women are in fact victims of the PKK/KCK, whose male fighters abduct innocent children to turn them into warriors.

It appears that the state prefers to depict women warriors as victims of abusive political groups. This is consistent with the self-perception of the AKP's neoliberal state as a nanny state and its violent treatment of politically active women. Parallel to this attempt at reconciliation, one can watch dozens of state-issued videos of guerrilla women who have allegedly recently surrendered to the state forces to benefit from the amnesty law. In these videos, women guerrillas tell of their experiences in the PKK and most point out the disappointment they felt after joining the armed struggle. This victims' perception of the role of women in political violence tries to convey to an international public the message that 'your heroes are in fact victims'. By way of nullifying the agency of politically violent women, the state in Turkey tries to restore its complementarity discourse on the ontological difference between masculinity and femininity. Once political violence is de-gendered by equating masculine and feminine violence, as in the discourse of 'there are no female terrorists, only terrorists', there emerges the risk that the state will unwillingly admit gender equality. Thus, victimization turns into a complementary strategy for the patriarchal state in Turkey. If this were the other way round, it would be a self-defeating act for the political Islamist government.

In the meantime, a related difficulty for the state has emerged from the fact that, during the anti-15 July protests, the AKP's own women supporters appeared to be very organized and well-equipped to stop the putschists; this meant that gendering war and targeting women fighters by focusing on the female body became counterproductive for the party. In other words, demonizing the implication of femininity in the act of fighting has become a problematic strategy for the regime, which opted for armed public vigilance to stay in power during the coup d'état attempt. Indeed, the 15 July putsch attempt meant a transgression for pro-government women, thereby forcing the AKP to develop a new statist narrative on them. Subsequently, they were described as 'women independence warriors', harking back to Turkey's National War of Independence.

In Turkey, gendered state violence has always been a state tradition used to demoralize and dehumanize opponents. In the 1990s, the Kurdish-populated regions of Turkey saw intensive use of this strategy (through rapes and sexual harassment by security personnel) in relation to the bodies of Kurdish women.[21] The post-2015 war between the state and Kurdish armed groups has demonstrated a need on the part of the state to revise its gendering strategy. This has been needed not only to avoid the sympathizing effects of femininity but also because the strategy was working against one of the main ideological tenets of the AKP on gender complementarity: men are assigned by God as trustees/protectors (*kavvum*) of all women in society.[22] Victimization has therefore been added to the state's strategic repertoire to deal with the challenges of the past and the present.

Nonetheless, the regime's conundrum caused by gender goes deeper when it is the opposition forces in Turkey that are victimizing politically violent women suffering from state violence. This can be seen in President Erdoğan's reaction to opposition media during the Women's Day celebration on 8 March 2016; he accused the media of presenting 'murdered women terrorists' as innocent by running a headline that stated 'Two women murdered by the state'. Erdoğan, angry with the opposition daily *Cumhuriyet*, said: 'Can women not become terrorists?'[23] However, it became not easy for opposition forces to stand against Erdoğan's scolding after 13 March 2016, when a suicide bombing in the middle of Ankara changed the political atmosphere in Turkey. The deadly terrorist attack, which cost 37 people their lives – mostly civilians – was claimed by an armed Kurdish group, TAK, while the Ministry of the Interior identified the assailant as Seher Çağla Demir, a female university student.

This lethal event triggered a new round of media focus on pro-PKK female suicide bombers. Seher Çağla Demir was described by the state- and AKP-associated media using a dual narrative that pointed to her agency as well as her abuse. The first narrative focused on her successful university life and on the rapid and unexpected process of becoming an armed Kurdish militant. In this narrative, Çağla Demir's sudden disappearance from university and then reappearance in Syria to be trained as a recruit of the PKK is underlined. In state-associated media, it is argued that the women armed militants who were involved in the fight against ISIS in Kobane returned to Turkey to escalate the PKK's war against the state in the Sur and Cizre districts.[24] This narrative, although highlighting the sex of the women militants, mainly tried to avoid gendering them using the usual misogynist motives used for female suicide bombers, such as 'demons' and/or 'whores'.[25] But the patriarchal motive comes back in the discourse of victimhood. Accordingly, the female suicide bombers are robotized women who are forced to take sedatives and are strategically sacrificed by the PKK, to escape political and military entrapment.[26] This narrative is easier for the state to sustain, since, unlike many other women suicide bombers, for example in Palestine, who record their voices or videos to communicate their distressing decisions, the public never hears the voices of PKK-affiliated women suicide bombers. Moreover, this void is filled not only by the state but also by male figures in the PKK, who, for example, declared Seher Çağla Demir to be 'the ideal woman to fall in love with'.[27] Not only does the public have no real clue about the motives or convictions of the female suicide bombers, but also such a semantic renders femininity directly and proudly complicit in lethal violence. Such an instrumentalization undeniably helped the political regime cement the shaky basis of its victimization and de-gendering strategies, paving the way for the monopolization of femininity and the promotion of the 'woman in politics' imaginary.

Conclusion

Taken together, the state strategies of de-gendering and victimization point to a restructuring of the patriarchal state in Turkey. First, not all women are conceived as disorderly for the state, and nor is femininity as such. The patriarchal state does not act in a uniform way or as a monolithic bloc. Accordingly, politically active women who are 'at peace with their femininity' are invited to reproduce society; they are indeed required, among others, for their affective labour. Others who resist engaging in such an affective labour but who adopt femininity and feminine consciousness as a positive asset in their political acts are perceived as competitors to this statist femininity. In other words, they are considered not as threats or enemies but rather as competitors. Therefore, unlike the gendered violence of the classical patriarchal state, which equates femininity with demonic powers and thus aims to annihilate it, the new patriarchal state in Turkey aims for the selective governance of femininity and of politically active women.[28]

Finally, political power in Turkey is riven with contradictions. Strategies fail or become counterproductive. But in order to deepen the crisis of these authoritarian state strategies based on the complementarity of gender, it appears that the politics of gender difference should be adopted very cautiously. Politically active women aiming to oppose the new patriarchal state in Turkey should be aware of the limits of strategies that depend on underlining femininity in essentialist and/or traditional bases. The resurgence of AKP-type gendered nationalism might reach wider audiences beyond the traditional circles of the regime. Political power tries to establish a patriarchy that underwrites women with excessively ascribed 'femininity'. This is itself a way of denying equal status to human beings in interaction. This revalorization of the 'feminine' emerges as a political burden rather than as recognition. Hence, there is a need to go beyond binary conceptions of gender and dichotomous modalities of femininity and political activity. Notwithstanding this need to resist the gendering or de-gendering practices of the new patriarchal state, there is no one simple way out of this, as the dilemma of refusing all traditional gender roles and epithets might end up with the wholesale weakening of women's movements.

Notes

1. Kandiyoti 2016.
2. Human security has recently been adopted by civil/feminist activists both abroad and in Turkey to press the state to retreat from its state security understanding. It assumes that once the state, as a rational actor, accepts the priority of a human-centred approach to security, state violence will be curtailed. For a discussion in the context of the Israeli–Palestine conflict, see Kotef 2010.
3. Durakbaşa 2000.
4. Rajan 2010: 166.
5. Weis 2017.
6. Lea and Young 1984.
7. N. Şişman (2019) 'Müslüman Kadın Feminist Olabilir Mi?', İslamiAnaliz, 19 April.
8. 'Anneler Günü', Radikal, 10 May 2015.
9. Altunok 2016.
10. On the conceptualization of care work and love as the new gold to be exploited, see Hochschild 2004.
11. For other cases of discrimination against women who do not fit the criteria of the incumbent regime in Turkey, see Babül 2015; Ayata and Doğangün 2017.
12. On the difference between feminine and feminist consciousness, see Mojab 2001.
13. Ahmetbeyzade 2007: 177.

14. 'Saldırı Emri Veren Soylu'dan Cumartesi Anneleri Açıklaması', Cumhuriyet, 27 August 2018.
15. Ü. Doğanay (2018) 'Cemile Ocak, Hrant Dink, Tahir Elçi, buradayız!', Gazete Duvar, 27 August.
16. 'Ömer Çelik'ten Cumartesi Anneleri Açıklaması', Evrensel, 29 August 2018.
17. T. Torun (2019) 'Anneler ve "teröristleri"', Gazete Duvar, 28 August.
18. 'Mahkemeden devlete sadakatli çocuk kararı', Gazete Duvar, 3 May 2019
19. 'Crackdown in Turkey threatens a haven of gender equality built by Kurds,' The New York Times, 7 December 2016.
20. 'Bati Medyasinin PKK aklayiciligi: Cinsiyet Esitligi', Star, 14 January 2017, italics added.
21. Keskin and Yurtsever 2006.
22. 'Erdoğan: Bu feministler filan var ya ...', Hürriyet, 17 February 2015.
23. 'Cumhurbaşkanı'ndan Cumhuriyet'e DHKP-C tepkisi', Sabah, 8 March 2016.
24. 'PYD'nin keskin nişancıları Türkiye'de eğitim vermis', Sabah, 23 February 2016.
25. Sjoberg and Gentry 2007.
26. F. Ünlü (2016) 'İntihar terörizminin anatomisi', Sabah, 20 March.
27. N. Demirtaş (2016) 'Doğa Zamanı!', Yeni Özgür Politika, 2 May.

28. Another case that is not covered in this chapter due to space limitations but must be closely analysed is the antagonistic approach of the state to politically active women who choose non-feminized forms of struggle.

Indeed, leftist women coming from working-class and/or Alawite origins have recently been faced with violent state strategies other than de-gendering and victimization. See Hülagü forthcoming.

References

Ahmetbeyzade, C. (2007) 'Negotiating silences in the so-called low-intensity war: the making of the Kurdish diaspora in Istanbul', *Signs: Journal of Women in Culture and Society 33* (1): 159–82.

Altunok, G. (2016) 'Neo-conservatism, sovereign power and bio-power: female subjectivity in contemporary Turkey', *Research and Policy on Turkey 1* (2): 132–46.

Ayata, A. and G. Doğangün (2017) 'Gender politics of the AKP: restoration of a religio-conservative gender climate', *Journal of Balkan and Near Eastern Studies 19* (6): 610–27.

Babül, E. M. (2015) 'The paradox of protection: human rights, the masculinist state, and the moral economy of gratitude in Turkey', *American Ethnologist 42* (1): 116–30.

Durakbaşa, A. (2000) *Halide Edib: Türk Modernleşmesi ve Feminizm.* Istanbul: İletişim Yayınları.

Hochschild, A. R. (2004) 'Love and gold' in A. R. Hochschild and B. Ehrenreich (eds), *Global Women: Nannies, Maids, and Sex Workers in the New Economy.* New York, NY: Owl Books.

Hülagü, F. (forthcoming) *Police Reform in Turkey: Human Security, Gender and State Violence under Erdoğan.* London: Bloomsbury and I. B. Tauris.

Kandiyoti, D. (2016) 'Locating the politics of gender: patriarchy, neo-liberal governance and violence in Turkey', *Research and Policy on Turkey 1* (2): 103–18.

Keskin, E. and L. Yurtsever (2006) *Hepsi Gercek: Devlet Kaynakli Cinsel Siddet.* Istanbul: Punto.

Kotef, H. (2010) 'Objects of security: gendered violence and securitized humanitarianism in occupied Gaza', *Comparative Studies of South Asia, Africa and the Middle East 30* (2): 179–91.

Lea, J. and J. Young (1984) *What Is to Be Done about Law and Order?* New York, NY: Penguin Books.

Mojab, S. (2001) 'Theorizing the politics of "Islamic feminism"', *Feminist Review 69* (1): 124–46.

Rajan, R. S. (2010) 'From antagonism to agonism: shifting paradigms of women's opposition to the state', *Comparative Studies of South Asia, Africa and the Middle East 30* (2): 164–78.

Sjoberg, L. and C. E. Gentry (2007) *Mothers, Monsters, Whores: Women's Violence in Global Politics.* London: Zed Books.

Weis, V. V. (2017) *Marxism and Criminology: A History of Criminal Selectivity.* London: Brill.

14 | THE WAR ON DRUGS: A VIEW FROM TURKEY

Zeynep Gönen

Introduction

In February 2018, the AKP government announced its *2018–2023 Five-year Activity Plan and Strategy Document for the Fight against Drugs*, rearticulating its commitment to the ongoing war on drugs. In one of the public messages about the strategy, a government official proclaimed that it would be 'equal to the war on terror'. The issue of drugs and the state responses to drugs are generally seen as criminal questions, thus marginal to contemporary authoritarianism in Turkey. This chapter argues that, contrary to this perspective, the war on drugs is about the expansion of state capacities in the criminalization and penalization of 'problem populations', and, in that, it is constitutive in the consolidation of the authoritarian state. To this end, the chapter excavates the sources available to illustrate the elements and dimensions of the war on drugs in Turkey, delineating the new repertoire of force it produces. Then, it situates the war on drugs within the project of regulating and containing particular 'problem populations' and in the expansion of penal/security formations that are central to contemporary authoritarian states around the world.

As of 2018, there were 264,842 people in Turkish prisons. Compared with 60,000 in 2002, the year when the AKP came to power, this was more than a fourfold increase (see Table 14.1).[1] In turn, there is a corresponding growth in prison facilities. According to the 2017 data, there were 384 prisons in Turkey, out of which 290 were closed facilities (eight of them are women's prisons), 71 open facilities (five women's[2]), 16 high-security facilities (14 type F and two type D maximum security prisons), and seven closed facilities for minors.[3] The AKP government plans to expand prison construction in the coming years, replacing dormitory-style prisons mostly located in cities with mega-prison facilities – or so-called 'penitentiary campuses' – to be located in the countryside.

TABLE 14.1 Prison population (1998–2016)

Year	Total	Male	Female
1998	66,096	63,576	2,520
1999	67,676	65,278	2,398
2000	50,628	48,758	1,870
2001	55,804	53,732	2,072
2002	59,512	57,398	2,114
2003	63,796	61,594	2,202
2004	58,016	56,062	1,954
2005	55,966	54,128	1,838
2006	70,524	68,075	2,449
2007	90,732	87,553	3,179
2008	103,435	99,842	3 593
2009	115,920	111,853	4,067
2010	120,194	116,002	4,192
2011	128,253	123,648	4,605
2012	136,638	131,732	4,906
2013	144,098	138,906	5,192
2014	158,690	152,902	5,788
2015	177,262	170,754	6,508
2016	200,727	192,354	8,373
2017	232,340	222,444	9,896

Source: Turkish Statistical Institute; Directorate of Prisons and Detention Houses.

Prisons have always been an important part of the history of the authoritarian state formation and the containment of political dissidence in Turkey.[4] Yet, as the numbers above show, the contemporary growth of prisons and prison populations during the AKP period is unprecedented. This is partly connected to the use of imprisonment for 'political criminals', especially members of the Kurdish movement and other left-wing dissidents, and more recently members of the Gülen movement. An inquiry into prisons as containment of political dissidence during AKP rule illustrates how courts and prisons are central to the recent rise of authoritarianism. But what if we direct our attention to the use of law, policing and prisons for common crimes? Are common crimes such as murder, theft, rape and robbery outside politics? Does authoritarianism operating through the criminal justice system concern only the treatment and punishment of political dissidence?

Critical criminology argues the contrary. Crime in any form is a question of politics. Common crimes and the state-sanctioned responses to them are integral to creating and maintaining political and economic orders, and to state formation and transformation. Crime is always defined by the state and any form of response to crime is a result of the political processes of law and policymaking. It is about the project of creating a particular ordering of society. As situated in complex socio-political contexts, common crimes, much like political crimes, are fields upon which states engage in creating social order, in controlling populations, and thus are central to state formation processes, including those towards authoritarianism with which this volume is concerned.

In their seminal work, Stuart Hall et al. situate crime in relation to state responses to it:

> If you look at this relation in terms of the social forces and contradictions accumulating within it (rather than simply in terms of the danger to ordinary folks), or in terms of the wider historical context in which it occurs (i.e. in terms of a historical conjuncture, not just a date on the calendar), the whole terrain of the problem changes in character.[5]

Steven Spitzer also suggests that 'deviance cannot be understood apart from the dynamics of control'.[6] Thus, the field of crime is located within the field of politics, which defines the former and produces responses to it with respect to the particular order the state tries to establish and maintain.[7]

Crime in this respect, in its role in constituting a particular order, is integral to political processes. This chapter, in an attempt to show the importance of common crimes as constitutive of authoritarian state formation, focuses on narcotic drug crimes and the state responses to them in Turkey. In particular, it gives attention to the AKP's 'war on drugs' (*uyuşturucu ile mücadele*) and its effects on expanding the penal/security state.[8] As will be shown in the following pages, the AKP governments have been increasingly criminalizing the use and sale of drugs, while expanding their policing and militarized control, and broadening the use of imprisonment as a response to an alleged growth in narcotics crimes. This, in turn, has consequences not only for the people implicated in drug-related crimes but also for the state's expanding ability to control and penalize the social body and buttress its authoritarian repertoire. Put simply, the war on drugs is a means to reinforce the Turkish authoritarian state.

A brief history of narcotic drugs and their criminalization in Turkey

Turkey's war on drugs – in other words, the growing criminalization and penalization of narcotics – is a recent development, even though historically Turkey has been an important actor in the international drug trade. During the early twentieth century, up until the 1970s, Turkey used to be one of the major opium producer countries. In 1932, the Turkish government signed the Hague Convention, which criminalized the production, distribution and export of opium. Following the legislative changes, while there were attempts to control heroin production and trafficking through policing, as well as through international cooperation (especially with the involvement of the US agency the Federal Bureau of Narcotics during the 1950s and 1960s), the flow of heroin from Turkey could not be halted.[9] It was in 1971 that heroin production started to be controlled thanks to the strict curtailment policy imposed by the US, a development with grave implications for local poppy farmers whose subsistence suffered greatly. Since 1971, poppy production in Turkey has been taking place only under strict regulation, especially by the International Narcotics Control Board. In addition to this specific curtailment policy, Turkey also signed the three important US-imposed conventions that shape global drug policies.[10] Thus, Turkey's drug policies have been closely tied to the US, whose war on drugs is fought at both the national and the global level.

Whereas the policy for the curtailment of opium production was successful, Turkey assumed a new role in drug trafficking. Rather than being a producer country, it became a hub in the major routes of trafficking of opium and synthetic drugs, especially from Afghanistan through Iran and onward through the Balkans, the Black Sea and the Eastern Mediterranean region en route to Europe.[11]

The actors involved in narcotics trafficking today are connected to Turkish and Kurdish immigrant groups in European countries. Despite the claims of the Turkish state, which describes the PKK as the central actor in narcotics trafficking, according to scholars in the field the picture is far more complex. Especially during the 1990s, drug trafficking involved 'deep state' actors – namely, the state-sponsored militia in the south-eastern region as well as the security forces.[12] As Robins argues, drug trafficking has indeed been employed by the state in the war against the PKK through the incorporation of ultranationalist militia and organized crime groups and with implications on the livelihoods and security of local Kurdish populations. The ultranationalists have been protected by the state, while engaging in organized crime and violence over the Kurdish populations.[13] Similarly, having investigated the relationship between narcotics and state building in Turkey, Ryan Gingeras also shows how a variety of actors within the deep state have been organizing narcotics trafficking and other forms of organized crime in the country.[14]

While drug trafficking is considerable in Turkey, the use of drugs has not been a great concern until recently. There are no reliable statistics regarding drug use, and those that are available do not date back a long time. Marijuana constitutes the largest share of drug use in Turkey: according to 2012 data, 86 per cent of all drug use is marijuana, followed by 9 per cent heroin. However, despite the lack of evidence, there is a perception that is conveyed by both the media and politicians that drugs are a 'growing threat' in Turkey. As a result of this moral panic, many parliamentary members with different political views have submitted proposals to establish research commissions on drugs. Addiction, as an increasing problem, has repeatedly been cited as a justification for such demands.

Criminalization of and penal responses to narcotic drugs in Turkey

The period from when the Turkish government acceded to the Hague Convention in 1932 to the curtailment of poppy seed production in 1971 can be seen as the initial phase of the criminalization of drugs in Turkey. Later, in 1996, drugs were described as a national security concern by the National Security Council (*Milli Güvenlik Kurulu* or MGK). But it was not until the 2000s that a more widespread and coherent fight against drugs was put in place. According to Robins, the anti-narcotics bureau of the Turkish National Police had only 173 officers in 1997 with a budget of US$30 million a year.[15] Police resources against drug traffickers were quite limited.

Starting from 2006, however, the government started to set out clear strategies and policies on the fight against drugs and action plans for applying these strategies; this then implied a growth in state capacity to engage in anti-narcotics policies.[16]

An important year in the war on drugs was 2014. After launching *The Rapid Action Plan against Drugs* in 2014, the government introduced new police units, called *Narkotims*, that specialized in drug busts, particularly in those neighbourhoods where drug-related criminality was concentrated. Even though the action plan proposed not only the policing of drugs but also rehabilitation and awareness-related policies, most funds were allocated to policing efforts.[17] *Narkotims* conducted 88,096 operations and arrested 159,099 suspects during the years 2015–18.[18] Moreover, as the importance of the war on drugs grew, the Counter-Narcotics Department was made a separate department within the Turkish National Police in 2015. The narcotics police were previously part of the Anti-Smuggling and Organized Crime Department. These institutional changes meant more autonomy and resources for the policing of narcotics crimes, which in turn expanded the state's capacity to control and intervene in the population.

With new policing strategies, police units and reinforcements in the war against drugs, the number of recorded drug-related incidents rose along with the arrest and imprisonment numbers. Between 2009 and 2018, the Turkish police conducted 705,636 operations in all and 1,063,143 suspects were detained. As Figure 14.1 shows, drug-related incidents started an upward trend after 2006, rapidly growing after 2008. This does not necessarily imply a rise in drug-related crimes, but is indicative of the increasing police intervention in drug-related incidents.

One of the ways in which increased police intervention in drug trafficking has been seen is in the aggressive and militarized operations conducted in neighbourhoods associated with the problem. Since the beginning of the war on drugs, the Turkish police have organized drug operations ranging from targeted police busts to 'neighbourhood-wide operations', where whole neighbourhoods are placed under siege by a large number of police officers. In such drug operations, hundreds – and in some cases thousands – of police are employed to search for suspects in the neighbourhoods.[19] Publicized as 'dawn operations' and 'peace operations', the narcotics police along

Drug-related incidents and number of suspects (2006–18)

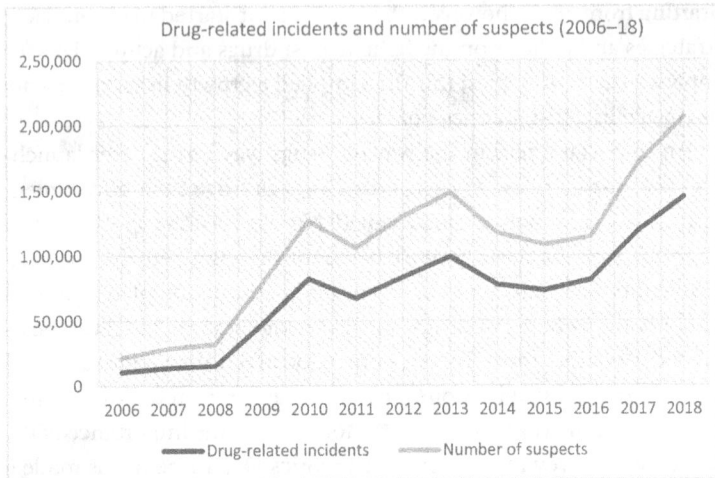

FIGURE 14.1 Drug-related incidents and number of suspects (2006–18)

Source: Compiled from Turkey Narcotic Reports, 2006–19.[22]

with other police units – and in some cases the gendarmerie – engage in a large-scale search as a way to find suspects, drugs and weapons. These operations have effectively criminalized working-class neighbourhoods, and have used militarized tactics and weaponry with little respect for the rights of the residents.

In another spatial policing strategy, the Turkish narcotics police also started an 'Area Control Project'[20] in 2018 in various pilot cities. In this project, the narcotics police make traffic stops and searches at 'the *entrance and exits* of criminal areas, where preventive policing techniques are difficult to apply'.[21] As a result of this project, the police stopped 326,000 cars and apprehended around 6,500 drug-related suspects in 2018. These indiscriminate searches, like the neighbourhood operations, mark and target particular neighbourhoods and spaces as criminal. They also utilize expanded police powers to intervene in the everyday lives of citizens, especially those who live in or have relations to these neighbourhoods.

As part of expanding police powers over the population, one important strategy is to incorporate citizens and other non-governmental sectors into policing, especially via the creation of informant networks. One innovative approach is a project called UYUMA, which started in 2018. UYUMA is an application that allows users to send notifications to the police regarding drug incidents they encounter. The application gives information about the location of the incident, which is then shared with an emergency call centre, allowing the narcotics police to intervene rapidly. Civilians' incorporation in police work, as police sources indicate, is a way to be more effective not only in policing drugs but also in establishing 'societal surveillance',[23] an important element of the AKP's policing schemes in a variety of other areas of life. From university students to media viewers, citizens are encouraged to make anonymous complaints via new call centres regarding 'criminal elements' in their respective contexts. Like UYUMA, another narcotics police project, Open Door,[24] tries to increase communication between citizens and the police via electronic means, as well as newly established bureaus that have been inviting citizens to make drug-related complaints since 2017.[25] Finally, the training and educational activities of the Counter-Narcotics Department can also be understood within this context of creating citizen-police, and of expanding the narcotics police beyond their institutional capacity. Focusing on legal and policing matters regarding narcotics and their policing, education modules reach out, educate and train civilians from different backgrounds, and thus potentially allow them to police drug-related incidents.[26]

In line with the diversified, expanded and more aggressive police interventions in drug-related offences, we also observe a growing use of imprisonment. Figure 14.2 shows the numbers both of imprisoned convicts and of people awaiting trial for drug-related crimes. While the number of people in prison due to drug-related crimes remained steady (at around 5,000) until 2005, the number grew rapidly after that year, reaching 57,674 in 2018.

The rise of imprisonment for drug-related offences reflects the increased policing of drug offences. However, another very important factor in this rise is the changing legal framework. Among the existing legal repertoire[27] for drugs in Turkey, the most important laws are Articles 188, 190 and 191 of the Turkish Penal Code, which relate to the control of trade, purchase, possession and use of drugs, and drug propaganda. In 2014, all penalties regarding drug-related crimes under these articles were substantially increased. The punishment for cultivation of cannabis was raised from 1–7 years of imprisonment to 4–12 years; for production and import/export of drugs from 10–20 years to 20–30 years; for drug trafficking from

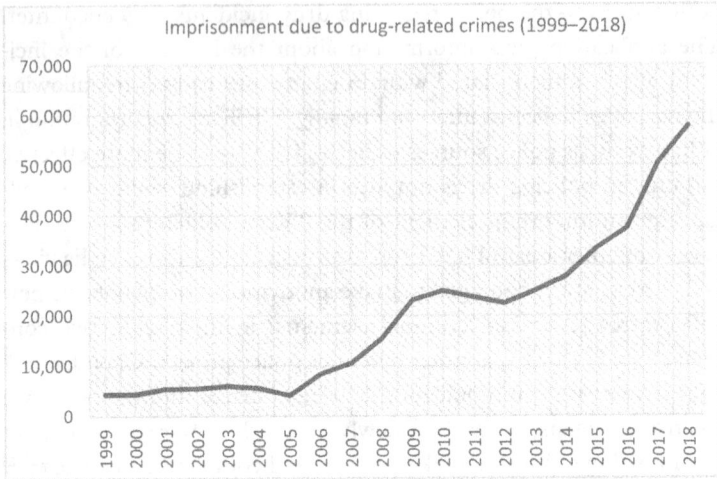

FIGURE 14.2 Imprisonment due to drug-related crimes (1999–2018)

Source: Compiled from Turkey Narcotics Reports, 2006–19.

5–10 years to 10–20 years; for drug propaganda from 2–5 years to 5–10 years; and for drug use from 1–2 years to 2–5 years (with the possibility of probation for a first offence). In turn, the increase in the numbers of people convicted or awaiting trial with regard to drug offences is partially the result of such drastic changes in penalizing drugs.

Authoritarianism and the war on drugs

To problematize the Turkish state's strategy for its war on drugs, one can also look at critical analysis of other areas from which Turkey borrows this particular strategy. The US war on drugs since 1971 – which has employed continual new laws, policing strategies and penal practices – is one of the primary sources for the new regulatory mechanisms launched in Turkey. As argued by many critical scholars, at its inception, the US war on drugs was in fact a response to the growing anti-war left and black movements of the 1960s, even though politicians managed to promote a discourse that pitched drugs as the common enemy for society as a whole. As the war on drugs proceeded, however, it became clear that it mainly targeted the poor and people of colour and their communities, whose very existence was identified as a 'threat' to the established order.[28]

Similarly, since the 1980s, the war on drugs in the US has played a massive role in criminalizing, penalizing and controlling poor communities, marginalized by declining social welfare spending and increasingly insecure labour market. The cities and the neighbourhoods in which this redundant class live have deteriorated economically, socially and politically, as drug sales used to provide a source of livelihood for the poor. The war on drugs has also attempted to control these populations and their everyday lives. It expanded the state's capacity in the policing and penalization of the social body, and constituted one of the main reasons for the unprecedented growth in the prison population in the US. Prisons in the US hold more than 2.2 million people today. Compared with 1970, the prison population has increased tenfold, and much of this growth can be traced to the war on drugs and other policy changes that have arguably had the aim of cracking down on crime.[29]

Other geographical regions, such as Latin America, have also been integrated into this global war. There, the increasing reliance of local communities on the illicit narcotics markets during the neoliberal era and the interventions imposed by the US in these markets have constituted the conditions of this war. In his work on Latin America, Bourgois not only reveals the links between the global neoliberal economy and drugs, but also shows how wars on drugs and the violence they produce in Latin America are part of neoliberal regulatory arrangements. The war on drugs in Latin America, supported and backed by the US and the narco-trafficking cartels, reproduces the forms of violence that were established by the authoritarian regimes in the region. In turn, Bourgois sees the war on drugs, along with narco-trafficking violence, as a continuation of the repressive and authoritarian politics that existed before.[30] Mostly waged with the help of billions in US aid to Latin American governments, wars on drugs fuel the militarization and violent repression that are not only mobilized to fight the drug cartels, but also intervene, control and regulate the everyday lives of citizens, especially the poor and the racialized. In this sense, the war on drugs around the world has been an important element in the expansion of a 'transnational penal apparatus',[31] where the logic, mechanisms and institutions of security and control are tied together towards the authoritarian control of particular populations.

As various critical scholars in Turkey have shown, the expansion of the penal apparatus has been quite dramatic under the

AKP regime.[32] Diversification, militarization and expansion of the police, the formation and expansion of private security, integration of new technologies of surveillance, legal transformations that allow the democratic rights of citizens to be overridden and large-scale prison constructions have been effective in achieving this outcome. As the AKP integrated the country fully into the global neoliberal economic regime, it has also increased the penal and security capacities of the state in an unprecedented way, in parallel to similar developments elsewhere.

As some scarce but important ethnographic studies on Turkey reveal, however, similarities with other parts of the world are not limited to this. Social and political processes at work in the wars on drugs in other geographical areas can also be observed in Turkey.[33] Following the trials of other wars on drugs around the world, poor and marginalized populations and their neighbourhoods in Turkey are subjected to both the hazards of the drug economy and the penal responses of the state. The studies of poor and marginalized urban neighbourhoods show how drugs and drug trafficking have been part of the everyday life of these neighbourhoods, especially for young men. Yonucu explains how, in working-class neighbourhoods, drugs have become a way to destroy the youth and criminalize them since the 2000s. As she observes, one of the main reasons for such a widespread presence of drugs is police neglect of racialized and poor communities. At the same time, drugs infiltrate these neighbourhoods through extra-legal practices of the police, implicating the state itself. While police neglect and extra-legal practices are common knowledge among the residents of these neighbourhoods, with the implementation of the war on drugs, some new dynamics emerge.[34] Gönen's study on İzmir's police and its strategies shows how marginalized young Kurdish men constitute the target populations of policing and penalization through public order crimes and drugs. The police regularly produce new strategies to intervene in this area, since drugs constitute a legitimate field for policing Kurdish populations. Günay's recent work,[35] on the other hand, shows how drugs and religious sects are operating to contain Kurdish youth. He explains how drugs, along with other vices, are commonplace for the young Kurdish men and the religious sects operate as 'spiritual police stations' to control this potentially unruly population.

Lastly, the war on drugs in Turkey converges with the other, more prevalent war against the Kurdish rebels both ideologically and on the ground. The Turkish government continuously links drugs to the PKK, thus transferring the already existing terror discourse to the field of criminality, and in particular to drug-related crimes. Framed through the concept of 'narco-terror', drugs, according to the Turkish state agencies, constitute an important source of finance for the PKK. Connecting drugs to 'terror' justifies a diversified security/penal repertoire and technologies in dealing with these crimes and with 'dangerous populations'.

Conclusion

To sum up, especially since 2005, the AKP has been consolidating a war on drugs that involves restructuring and strengthening the criminal justice institutions with respect to narcotics crimes. The main pillars of this war on drugs have been policy and legal changes to reinforce narcotics policing, and to criminalize and penalize drug-related crimes with a militarized discourse. While the available data suggest that there is a growth in drug use and that Turkey is central to transnational drug routes, the current level of concern and investment in this war needs to be understood beyond the discourse of a 'fight against drugs'. Indeed, if drugs really are the main concern, the 'war on drugs' can be described as a 'failed war', as UN reports suggest.[36] In addition, despite the existing voices that urge for public health-centred policies for solving the drug problem, the Turkish government's approach has mainly involved security/penal mechanisms to deal with it. This strategic choice is in line with the AKP's security-oriented politics of control and offers a new technology to its authoritarian state repertoire. The criminalization and imprisonment of political dissidence, policing and penalization of social movements, increasing and militarized policing of everyday life as well as of social protests, and the expansion of police and prisons are important components of this politics of control. The war on drugs, in turn, should be seen as integral to this larger regulatory mechanism of the Turkish state that rests largely on force, while ignoring and limiting the individual and collective rights of its citizens.

More specifically, the war on drugs in Turkey should be investigated as a means to regulate and contain 'problem populations' such as the poor, marginalized Kurdish youth, who are considered to be likely to pose a 'threat' to the current political and economic regime. It is definitely based on the legitimacy ensured by the moral panic about drugs and the 'narco-terror'. The war on drugs, through its expansion, use of militarized and excessive policing, and strategies, practices and frameworks for criminalization and penalization, reinforces and diversifies the authoritarian state formation in Turkey. Hence, in the populations it targets and the methods it uses, the war on drugs is not a tangential element but an integral part of the new penal/security formations of the authoritarian state in Turkey.

In its latest strategic plan, namely the *2018–2023 Five-year Activity Plan and Strategy Document for the Fight against Drugs*, the Turkish government has announced that its war on drugs is 'equal to the war on terror', and that the government 'treat[s] drug dealers as terrorists'. The plan also signals that the government is getting prepared for 'a fully fledged wartime mobilization [*seferberlik*]' against drugs.[37] Such propositions are hence warning signs of the new conditions of the war on drugs in Turkey, which is now linked directly to the war on terror, which has a long history of human rights abuses and state violence. A war on drugs that adopts such practices promises to be equally violent and destructive.

Notes

1. The information is derived from the website of the Directorate of Prisons and Detention Houses. Also see http://www.prisonstudies.org/country/turkey.

2. The number is seven, according to the Directorate of Prisons and Detention Houses.

3. Türkiye Barolar Birliği İnsan Hakları Merkezi 2017.

4. For a historical account of the imprisonment of leftist politics, see, for instance, Öztürk 2000.

5. Hall et al. 1978: viii.

6. Spitzer 1975: 639. See also Spitzer 1975; Taylor et al. 1973; Cohen and Scull 1983.

7. One of the important scholars who exposes the complexities of crime as an ideological and political question is Eric Hobsbawm. In two of his works, *Bandits* (2000) and *Primitive Rebels* (1965), he poses novel questions about the relationship between crime and political action, between 'criminals' and social resistance. Banditry, he argues, is most common at times of crises and pauperization, and it arises as a reaction against those who constitute the exploiting classes. Moreover, in *Bandits*, he looks at 'criminal' figures who take on some heroic character in public opinion. While the law defined banditry as a criminal act, peasant communities often remained on the side of the social bandit against the common oppressor classes. Robin Hood, the 'noble robber', committed illegal acts, according to the authorities, but he was never seen as a criminal by the commoners.

8. The exact translation for *uyuşturucu ile mücadele* is 'fight against drugs'. The chapter prefers to use 'war on drugs' for two main reasons to be explored further below. First, the AKP's policies are connected to other wars on drugs around the world. Thus, from this global perspective a common language would be revealing. Second, the language and tactics of war are prevalent in the case of Turkey.

9. For a history of drug trafficking in Turkey, see Gingeras 2014, in which he locates heroin as central to state formation in the country.

10. The international agreements Turkey signed are the 1961 Single Convention on Narcotic Drugs, the 1971 Convention on Psychotropic Substances and the 1988 United Nations Convention against Illicit Traffic in Narcotic Drugs and Psychotropic Substances. According to the United Nations Office on Drugs and Crime, the 1961 convention 'is the cornerstone of the global drug control regime. It establishes a global drug control system, placing manufacturing, possession, trade and use restrictions on specific psycho-active substances'. The latter two expand the scope of this convention and require countries to fight the illicit drug trade both individually and in cooperation with others. See Cockayne and Walker 2015: 3.

11. Robins 2016.

12. The Susurluk Scandal in 1996, in which a senior police chief, an ultranationalist, organized crime leader (Abdullah Çatlı) and a member of parliament were identified together in a car accident, exposed that high-level bureaucrats and organized crime groups cooperate in managing drug trafficking through Turkey. The state-sponsored local militia are also composed of local Kurdish populations, organized as village guards against the PKK.

13. Robins 2016: 160. The story Robins tells about narcotics and the PKK is quite different from the dominant state discourses in Turkey, which accuse the PKK as being the main actor in narcotics trafficking. Robins argues that the narcotics trafficking in the Kurdish region is organized by the village guards. The traffickers in the region use bribes to pay off officials in the area, or they threaten to harm the families of officials. He also suggests that, although the PKK was not the main actor, it was also part of this process because of its power in the region during the 1980s and 1990s.

14. Gingeras 2014.

15. Robins 2016.

16. The first of these documents and action plans are the *2006–2012 Policy and Strategy Document on Narcotic Drugs and the Fight against Addiction* and the *2007–2009 Action Plan for the Policy and Strategy Document on Narcotic Drugs and the Fight against Addiction*. After 2015, following the 2014 revisions in drug policies, these documents have been called 'Rapid Action Plans' rather than simply 'Action Plans'.

17. On the efforts for dealing with drug-related issues, see 'Rewards for informants, color codes for suspects to help war on drugs', *Daily Sabah*, 27 June 2018.

18. 'Türkiye Uyuşturucu Raporu 2019', http://www.narkotik.pol.tr/kurumlar/narkotik.pol.tr/TUB%C4%BoM/Ulusal%20Yay%C4%B1nlar/2019-TURKIYE-UYUSTURUCU-RAPORU.pdf.

19. For a few examples of such operations, see 'Mahalle Boyu Operasyon', *Radikal*, 24 February 2006; 'Ankara'da 2500 polis ile uyuşturucu operasyonu', *Yeni Şafak*, 14 February 2017; 'Bursa'da dört mahallede eş zamanlı huzur operasyonu', *Hürriyet*, 11 November 2016.

20. Alan Denetimi Projesi.

21. 'Türkiye Uyuşturucu Raporu 2019', p. 41, italics added.
22. See http://www.narkotik.pol.tr/.
23. 'Türkiye Uyuşturucu Raporu 2019', p. 42.
24. 'Open Door' is a literal translation of *Açık Kapı*.
25. See the website for the project: https://www.acikkapi.gov.tr/.
26. The education project is titled NARKOREHBER.
27. Article 58 of the constitution; Law No. 2313 on the Control of Narcotic Drugs; Anti-Trafficking Law No. 5607; Turkish Penal Code no. 5237; Penal Procedures Law No. 5271; Law No. 3298 on Narcotic Drugs.
28. See Mullings 2003.
29. Alexander 2010.
30. Bourgois 2015.
31. Müller 2015.
32. See Dölek 2015; Hülagü 2015; Berksoy 2016; Uysal 2010; Gönen 2016; Balta Paker 2012.
33. See, for instance, Yonucu 2011, 2014; Gönen 2016; Günay 2018.
34. Yonucu 2014.
35. Günay 2018.
36. Cockayne and Walker 2015. See also McCoy and Block 1992.
37. See '2018–2023 Uyuşturucu ile Mücadele Strateji Belgesi ve Eylem Planı'; see also Benoit Gomis (2014) 'Turkey declares new war on drugs, ignoring pitfalls and global trends', *World Politics Review*, 3 October.

References

Alexander, M. (2010) *The New Jim Crow: Mass Incarceration in the Age of Colorblindness*. New York, NY: The New Press.

Balta Paker, E. (2012) *Küresel Güvenlik Kompleksi*. Istanbul: İletişim.

Berksoy, B. (2016) '"Güvenlik Devleti", Gözetim-Polislik Ağları ve 2000'li Yıllarda Türkiye'de Üniversite Kampüslerine Yansımaları: Kürt Özgürlük Hareketi Özelinde Bir Değerlendirme', *Praksis 40*: 121–52.

Bourgois, P. (2015) 'Insecurity, the war on drugs, and crimes of the state: symbolic violence in the Americas' in J. Auyero, P. Bourgois and N. Scheper-Hughes (eds), *Violence at the Urban Margins*. Oxford: Oxford University Press, pp. 305–21.

Cockayne, J. and S. Walker (2015) 'What comes after the war on drugs – flexibility, fragmentation, or principled pluralism? A policy report 2015.' Tokyo: United Nations University.

Cohen, S. and A. Scull (1983) *Social Control and the State*. New York, NY: Palgrave Macmillan.

Dölek, Ç. (2015) 'Privatization of security as a state-led and class-driven process: the case of Turkey', *Science and Society 79* (3): 414–41.

Gingeras, R. (2014) *Heroin, Organized Crime, and the Making of Modern Turkey*. Oxford and New York, NY: Oxford University Press.

Gönen, Z. (2016) *The Politics of Crime in Turkey: Neoliberalism, Police, and the Urban Poor*. London and New York, NY: I. B. Tauris.

Günay, O. (2018) 'Drugs, crime, sex, and Sufis: ethics and politics of everyday life in Kurdish Istanbul'. Paper presented at the workshop 'Warzones as Displacement in the Middle East: Kurdish Case', Princeton University, 9 November.

Hall, S. et al. (1978) *Policing the Crisis: Mugging, the State, and Law and Order*. New York, NY: Holmes and Meier.

Hobsbawm, E. (1965) *Primitive Rebels.* New York, NY: Norton & Company.

Hobsbawm, E. (2000) *Bandits.* New York, NY: The New Press.

Hülagü, F. (2015) 'Turkey's security sector reform in crisis: what caused it?', *Research Turkey IV* (8): 67–78, http://researchturkey.org/?p=9682.

McCoy, A. and A. A. Block (1992) *The War on Drugs: Studies in the Failure of US Narcotics Policy.* Boulder, CO: Westview Press.

Müller, M. M. (2015) 'Punitive entanglements: "the war on gangs" and the making of a transnational penal apparatus in the Americas', *Geopolitics 20*: 696–727.

Mullings, L. (2003) 'After drugs and the "war on drugs": reclaiming the power to make history in Harlem, New York' in J. Scheider and I. Susser (eds), *Wounded Cities.* Oxford and New York, NY: Berg, pp. 173–202.

Öztürk, S. (2000) *Solun Hapishane Tarihi.* Istanbul: Yar Yayınları.

Robins, P. (2016) *Middle East Drug Bazaar: Production, Prevention and Consumption.* Oxford: Oxford University Press.

Spitzer, S. (1975) 'Toward a Marxian theory of deviance', *Social Problems 22* (5): 638–51.

Taylor, I. R., P. Walton and J. Young (1973) *The New Criminology: For a Social Theory of Deviance.* New York, NY: Routledge.

Türkiye Barolar Birliği İnsan Hakları Merkezi (2017) *İnsan Hakları Raporu 2016–2017.* Ankara: Türkiye Barolar Birliği Yayınları, http://tbbyayinlari.barobirlik.org.tr/TBBBooks/610.pdf.

Uysal, A. (2010) 'Riot police and policing protest in Turkey' in L. Khalili and S. Jillian (eds), *Policing and Prisons in the Middle East: Formations of Coercion.* London: C. Hurst and Company, pp. 191–206.

Yonucu, D. (2011) 'Capitalism, desperation and urgency: how working-class youth cope with the capitalist present', *Red Thread 3*: 1–11.

Yonucu, D. (2014) 'Kapitalizm, suçlulaştırma ve siyaset', *Birikim 297*: 29–36.

15 | 'THE LAW OF THE CITY?'[1]: SOCIAL WAR, URBAN WARFARE AND DISPOSSESSION ON THE MARGIN

Çağlar Dölek

Introduction

> Altındağ has always experienced emergency rule; now, it is time for Ankara to live through it.[2]

> The tradition of the oppressed teaches us that the 'emergency situation' in which we live is the rule. We must arrive at a concept of history which corresponds to this.[3]

This chapter intends to contribute to this volume's central assertion on 'the re-making of the neoliberal state' in Turkey via a critical exposition of the violent urban order fabricated through police power in the 2010s. Grounded in a condensed historical critique of neoliberal police reform in the country, it attempts to reveal the organic links between the 'social war',[4] rooted in the violence of capital accumulation, dispossession and marginalization of proletarian life, with the urban warfare waged against political dissent, and especially against the Kurdish movement in Turkey. The chapter thereby argues that we need to take into account this organic relation to understand the violent character and generalized contradictions of the 'new order' fabricated through police power in Turkey.

This chapter incorporates data from fieldwork conducted in the Altındağ slums in Ankara in 2015 (February–May) and 2016 (January–August).[5] As a historical social space of the marginalized sectors of the Ankara working classes, Altındağ has long been stigmatized as a 'no-go' area due to its concentration of 'social crime',[6] practices that are characterized by a range of pilfering, from coal and wood picking to petty theft including shoplifting and pickpocketing, and by minor property theft by domestic servants, porters and other sectors of the informally working masses.[7] The twenty-fifth largest mega-slum in the world in the early 2000s,[8] it resembles the *favelas* of Brazil or *villa miserias* of Argentina. The very character of social marginality, however, has been transformed since the 1990s in Altındağ. Conditioned within the broader neoliberal processes of dispossession, criminalization and marginalization, the area has harboured organized and para-militarized forms of crime and illicit networks involving, for example, street gangs, the drug economy and armed clashes. We might argue, therefore, that the Altındağ slums have gone through a contested process of 'advanced marginality'[9] during the contradictory neoliberal transformation of Turkey.

This chapter argues that the changing character of social marginality in the Altındağ slums during the AKP years does not represent an isolated case. On the contrary, it signals a paradigmatic transformation concerning the urban margins of Turkey's cities on two grounds. First, it denotes the interpenetration of a social war that has increasingly characterized proletarian life on the margin, and an urban warfare that determines the form of the state's presence in the lives of the dispossessed. Second, policing strategies formulated amidst this twin warfare on the margin have become crystallized and generalized, reflecting the dominant form of police order in the 2010s. That is why one of my respondents made the assessment quoted above while elaborating on the state of emergency declared after the coup attempt in July 2016. Recalling the historical memory of the area, the respondent exposed the inherent tendency for generalization of the emergency situation that is 'the rule' in the lives of the dispossessed.

Relying on critical anthropological and criminological scholarship, the chapter hereby reads 'the margin' as the 'constitutive outside'[10] of the dominant order fashioned through police power in everyday life. It is 'a necessary entailment of the state'[11] that shapes the political and ideological projects determining the making of police power. The margin also refers to a dynamic historical social space, within which alternative forms of popular organization and regulation emerge on the basis of 'the pressing needs of populations to secure political and economic survival'. As a 'dynamic site of practice', therefore, the margin represents a decisive spatio-temporal moment for a constant rebounding of order and law making on the part of the state.[12] In short, the urban margin represents a constitutive moment of police order, a fundamental point of reference through which the police attempt to restructure themselves on spatial, organizational, legal and political grounds, and through which they intend to give shape to social relations and spaces at large. The contested role of the AKP's police during the 2010s is a significant exemplar for such an exposition.

The making of police power from the margin

The narco police have employed an incredible tactic to bring a drug gang down in Çinçin and Hıdırlıktepe, which are known as crime-ridden neighbourhoods in [Altındağ,] Ankara. A movie set was built in Ankara Citadel, which has a view over the neighbourhoods, with the cover of 'shooting a documentary film'. The inhabitants got to know the police chief as director and the policemen as the crew for three months. Shooting hundreds of scenes of drug dealing in the neighbourhoods, the police have brought the gang down.[13]

The 'narcotic film' shot by the Ankara police in December 2010 seems to present an extraordinarily imaginative strategy of 'crime fighting' in the Altındağ slums. Fabricating a film set as part of a broader strategy of 'proactive policing', the Ankara police mobilized an extensive surveillance apparatus that put Bentham's panopticon to shame. As the reader learns from the news report, a major police raid was undertaken by heavily armed special operation teams against the drug gang on the basis of 'the evidentiary scenes' gathered through the shooting of this bogus documentary. The story comes to an end with the arrest of 24 people along with the ringleader of the drug gang.

Notwithstanding its extraordinary character, this incident is not exceptional but reflects a striking example of the extensive repertoire of policing strategies formulated during the neoliberal transformation of the country. Similar police operations undertaken in old *gecekondu*[14] neighbourhoods have become routine practice over the last two decades. These operations are characterized by the involvement of special operation teams with police helicopters and armoured vehicles, reflecting the paramilitary and professionally reorganized nature of the Turkish police. The spectacle of power and violence performed through such operations has received widespread media coverage, with every detail of the police raids broadcast. Historically conditioned by the ever-deepening urban contradictions of Turkey's neoliberal transformation, the police have played a contested role in this process; this role needs critical examination with reference to a number of controversial issues underlying the currently normalized police order. Such a critical exposition would reveal how policing strategies as formulated amidst the twin warfare on the margin have become crystallized and generalized, culminating in the currently dominant form of police order in the 2010s.

Urban renewal amidst the twin warfare

It has long been argued in the vast *gecekondu* literature that Turkish capitalism has not produced 'ghetto-like' social marginalization processes to any great extent. Neighbourhoods in the Altındağ area, such as Çinçin Bağları, have been cited as isolated cases in this regard.[15] In fact, there are a number of crucial reasons for this historical experience. First and foremost, the peculiar informal dynamics of *gecekondu* formation has meant that the urban poor have been incorporated into the existing socio-economic and political order from 1960s onwards. That is, *gecekondu* has always been part of a 'populist coalition' politically constructed throughout the history of capitalist urbanization in Turkish social formation. Coupled with the informal solidarity networks reproduced through family and kinship ties, the *gecekondu* regime in Turkey has seemed to protect the urban poor from deep processes of social and political exclusion on a massive scale.[16]

The last four decades of neoliberal urbanism, however, have radically transformed the character of urban living in Turkey. In parallel with global trends, Turkey's neoliberal urbanism has been characterized by the mass commodification of the city, gentrification, and associated dynamics of socio-spatial segregation and exclusion. In this context, certain *gecekondu* areas of large urban centres have become slum areas, characterized by chronic or *new* poverty that has been interpenetrated with various sorts of common criminality. That is, Turkish metropolises have experienced the formation of novel socio-spatial processes of social exclusion and marginalization, with various petty crimes combined with chronic poverty.[17]

In the process, the *gecekondu* neighbourhoods have also become the main site of urban renewal projects largely engineered by TOKİ. Reflecting Turkey's embrace of the ideological paradigm of 'revanchist urbanism'[18] and its associated neoliberal strategy of 'zero-tolerance policing',[19] neoliberal urbanism has been closely intertwined with the politics of crime and policing. That is, regeneration projects have been incorporated into a particular marginalizing gaze at the urban margins that has been instrumental in the police involvement in urban transformation processes during the AKP years. Denoting an administrative form of capitalist state power in the production of state space,[20] the police have thus assumed a central role in neoliberal urbanism in Turkey.

While this central role already existed in the 2000s, it was in the 2010s that discourses rooted in social war and urban warfare increasingly merged to inform urban renewal processes. In November 2012, for instance, the provincial security directorates in 16 cities, including Istanbul, Ankara, İzmir, Diyarbakır and Adana, applied to the Ministry of Environment and Urbanization with a request to make certain *gecekondu* regions the primary areas of demolition as part of the ongoing urban regeneration projects. Categorizing *gecekondu* neighbourhoods as 'crime zones' characterized by 'terror, drug-dealing and public disorder',[21] the police have intended to give shape to the urban landscape to ensure the materialization of their 'security' project through urban renewal processes.

This 'security' project has thus depended on an ideological presentation of urban renewal as a 'magical formula' for resolving the increasingly dense problems of urban criminality, perceived or otherwise. For instance, İdris Güllüce, Minister of Environment and Urbanization at the time, repeated this commonly used argument in the following words: 'This is scientific detection: it is known that crime rates decrease after urban renewal in neighbourhoods that have become centres of crime.'[22] Glossing over the social relations of dispossession and associated processes of spatial dislocations, this discourse has increasingly been formulated through an intimate connection between social war and urban warfare, which has been decisive in the transposition of violent policing strategies that were primarily employed in Kurdish cities to urban centres in the western part of the country. Especially in the 2010s, the war on drugs became 'a fully fledged wartime mobilization [*seferberlik*]'[23] that depoliticized urban social problems and contradictions, subjecting marginalized populations to increasingly para-militarized police power. In this way, the war on drugs has been performed as a spectacle of conquest of the urban margins. For instance, large-scale police operations against drug gangs in Altındağ were presented as 'Operation Qandil', making a direct connection between the spatial containment of a marginalized part of Ankara with a desire for the pacification of the PKK headquarters in the Qandil Mountains in northern Iraq.[24]

Policing formulated in this way has been instrumental in the displacement of the urban poor and in the spatial restructuring of class relations in the country. In the case of Altındağ, for instance, it was ironic to observe that, after the destruction of the old *gecekondu* neighbourhoods in Çinçin, middle-class urban professionals were deployed as the new residents of the area. Indicating the final conquest of police power in the neighbourhood, the news headlines read: 'Three hundred police officers with their families' have begun living in the area following the urban renewal projects. The reporting on this settlement was even more striking: 'They [the police] have settled in the neighbourhood that they had not been able to enter' for decades.[25]

In this regard, contrary to the dominant presentations, urban renewal as a police project has deepened the marginalization of proletarian life along the lines of a racialized process of social exclusion and political stigmatization. It is through this process that police power has been reorganized on spatial as well as ideological and political grounds. The Alevi- and Kurdish-populated neighbourhoods in Istanbul, for instance, have been the main point of reference for the Turkish police to strategize tactics and formulate long-term policies concerning their organizational restructuring as well as their legal, political and financial empowerment.[26] The Altındağ experience, therefore, seems generalized to all the *gecekondu* neighbourhoods as they undergo ever-deepening processes of marginalization. As one of the respondents stated during the field research: 'Altındağ is a training ground for the Ankara police. They employ the young, newly recruited officers during large-scale operations to develop experience. It is only after this period of training that they can begin their patrols in other parts of the city.'[27] The culmination of policing strategies has been decisive for the crystallization of police power on the margin. Accordingly, a historically normalized emergency rule in Altındağ has been politically productive for the making of police power, and for fabricating an urban order in accordance with the transformation of social relations of power.

282 | ÇAĞLAR DÖLEK

Neoliberal urbanism has also had dialectical repercussions in the spatial powers and organization of the police. The involvement of the police in urban renewal has also been accompanied by the advent and systematic deployment of novel technologies of urban governance, such as Mobile Electronic System Integration (*Mobil Elektronik Sistem Entegrasyonu* or MOBESE), General Information Check (*Genel Bilgi Taraması* or GBT), Geographic Information System (*Coğrafi Bilgi Taraması* or CBT) and Population Registration System (*Merkezi Nüfus İdaresi Sistemi* or MERNIS), as well as new 'crime-mapping' techniques. Largely instigated during the first decade of AKP rule, an all-encompassing surveillance and control mechanism over urban space has therefore been adopted by the police. This extensive network of technologically sophisticated surveillance apparatus was informed by the US-originated ideologies of spatial control as exemplified by 'situational crime prevention', 'broken windows policing' and 'qualify of life policing'.[28]

The spatial imagination of police power is thus haunted by a political project for the pacification of alternative spaces of social and collective organization. *Police power thus represents a spatial problem* in the processes of the production of state space that is founded on a foundational state violence in producing dominant spatial forms, while simultaneously undermining or eliminating alternative spatial forms and practices.[29] Seen in this way, the conquest of the margin has also been a spatial problem for the police, who are concerned with dismantling the social spaces of *gecekondu* topography. For one thing, the political geography of policing in urban space generally reflects the official politics of urban planning. In other words, police power rests on the production of urban space through a particular spatial delineation of social relations that follows the political and economic priorities as determined by urban planners. The historically spontaneous *gecekondu* topography, however, is fundamentally at odds with the formalizing logic of police power. In the case of Ankara, for instance, urban plans have historically reflected a radical modernist outlook that included grid street plans, public squares and *sublime* buildings. This was spatially instrumental in governing everyday social relations through standardized and uniform structures that were functional for constant surveillance and spatial control. This strategy was politically productive in the broader political geography of policing in the city because it enabled the police to engineer public order through the enactment of boundaries and the restriction of access to particular spatial zones.

In stark contrast to these state spaces, the *gecekondu* neighbourhoods are characterized by an interwoven network of shanty houses with randomly structured narrow side streets and blind alleys. This layout, therefore, becomes a fundamental obstacle for the police to exert its power spatially over the neighbourhoods. The aforementioned police request presented the social organization of *gecekondu* space as the primary reason for urban renewal. As the following news article reported:

> The [police] reports submitted to the Ministry contained interesting material. Accordingly, the reports directed attention to the following: because of the low-layered structure and attached ordering of [*gecekondu*] houses, the criminals run away by skipping from house to house; that the narrow streets make it difficult for the police to intervene in social events [protests]; and the lighting is insufficient [in *gecekondu* neighbourhoods]. It is only through urban renewal that an effective fight against crime can be ensured in these areas, where families from the same social status generally live.[30]

Thus formulated, the dismantling of *gecekondu* spaces has always incorporated a strategic ambiguity in defining the contours of crime, disorder and political dissent. That is, the political categories of the criminal (policing) and the enemy (war) have been increasingly incorporated into a twin policing strategy for the pacification of the urban margins. Reflecting this strategic ambiguity, the destruction of the Çinçin *gecekondus* in the late 2000s was praised as a major achievement in urban renewal, and as 'a model' for the rest of the county. In fact, after the large-scale military destruction of Kurdish areas such as Cizre in Şırnak, Nusaybin in Mardin and Sur in Diyarbakır, urban renewal *à la* Çinçin was presented as a decisive strategy by the police. The political rationale and the spatial strategy were strikingly similar, reflecting the organic connection between social warfare and urban warfare that determines the making of police power in contemporary Turkey.[31]

On the other hand, the massive mobilization of police power through urban renewal processes has occurred with the transposition of strategies for urban warfare against the Kurdish movement into a large-scale campaign against any kind of 'suitable enemy' for the deployment of police power. Whereas this transposition has become normalized in the post-Gezi period, the establishment and proliferation of *kalekols* – high-security police stations – need particular attention. As heavily armed military stations established especially during the Peace Process in the Kurdish provinces,[32] *kalekols* have been transposed to the western part of the country as a new spectacle of militarized policing at the heart of urban living. The first *kalekol* was established in the Başakşehir district in Istanbul in May 2017. Conceived as a 'security centre', the *kalekol* in Başakşehir is heavily armoured to 'quickly respond' to any acts of social and political dissent that might emerge in the surrounding districts, including Avcılar, Küçükçekmece, Esenyurt, Esenler, Bağcılar and Arnavutköy.[33] In just one year, new *kalekols* were constructed in the following districts: Ataşehir, Gaziosmanpaşa, Sultangazi, Okmeydanı and Sancaktepe.[34] According to news reports, the AKP government plans to introduce *kalekols* in politically 'risky' neighbourhoods in Ankara, Izmir, Aydın, Adana and Mersin provinces as well.[35] This transposition, therefore, reveals how the war waged against the Kurdish movement has continued to inform policing strategies in the rest of the country, reflecting Turkey's adoption of 'new military urbanism'[36] to manage the ever-deepening social, political and urban contradictions of a violent order in the making.

At this point, it is important to underline that this large-scale mobilization of police power has also been rooted in the recent memory of a 'spatio-temporal crisis' of police order in the early 2010s. The TEKEL resistance in 2009–10 and the Gezi protests in 2013 were historically significant points of reference for the police in this regard. The TEKEL resistance marked the end of a protracted period of silence with regard to labour struggles that characterized the 2000s, and it paved the way for a series of spontaneous workers' protests in the years to come.[37] The suppression of the TEKEL resistance on 1 April 2010 resembled the spectacle of a conquest in Ankara, something that would become normalized in subsequent years. Orchestrated using helicopters, armoured vehicles and hundreds of riot police, the violent police intervention was depicted as follows by Sami Evren, then chair of the Confederation of Public Employees' Trade Unions (*Kamu Emekçileri Sendikaları Konfederasyonu* or KESK): 'It seems like there is a coup in Ankara.'[38]

With its dazzling multitude taking to the streets against the neoliberal-cum-Islamic authoritarian regime of the AKP, the Gezi protests were radical in the sense that they represented a spontaneous transgression of police order on a massive scale, which resulted in a temporary paralysis of police power in many parts of the country. This paralysis reflected the demonstrable inability of the police to deal with the massive, spontaneous and dispersed mobilization of the masses. The Gezi resistance, therefore, was a politically transformative moment of crisis for the police. Thus, in the post-Gezi period, the central strategy of the police has been the violent prevention of any kind of collective mobilization, as exemplified by the Kobane protests in 2014, the protests against the Soma massacre in 2015, and numerous other protests by social and political agents of dissent in the country.

Extensive police power has been spatially mobilized, especially during the period of the state of emergency between July 2016 and June 2018, and has become 'normalized'. For instance, the police have already routinized their intrusive and spectacular presence in everyday life through numerous deployments of large-scale operations in recent years. Table 15.1 provides a summary of the five large-scale operations undertaken just in 2019.

While these numbers demonstrate the spectacular presence of the police in everyday life, the declared reasons for such large-scale

TABLE 15.1 Operations Trust–Peace Turkey in 2019

Operation	Date	No. of police involved	No. of checkpoints	No. of people questioned
Operation Trust–Peace Turkey I	16/02/2019	58,528	4,623	575,163
Operation Trust–Peace Turkey II	19/03/2019	66,503	21,738	634,841
Operation Trust–Peace Turkey IV	14/10/2019	67,848	16,566	565,662
Operation Trust–Peace Turkey V	26/10/2019	62,144	5,621	672,876
Operation Trust-Peace Turkey VI	09/11/2019	69,246	5,646	699,602

Note: No report was published on Operation Turkey III.

Source: Compiled from the website of the Department of Public Order Police. See http://www.asayis.pol.tr/uygulamalar.

operations are illustrative of the twin warfare in question. Representing an ambiguous amalgam of a wide range of issues, the Department of Public Order Police presents the following as the motivations behind the Operation Trust–Peace deployments: ensuring public order and police visibility; preventing potential crimes related to terror, public order and narcotics; and apprehending criminals in relation to terror, public order and narcotics. On the other hand, the spatio-temporal dynamics of police order function as 'boundary work' in everyday social relations, creating and maintaining boundary lines through checkpoints, raids, aerial patrols and associated technologies.[39] This boundary work was originally defined in the context of neo-colonialist urban warfare in the Kurdish provinces and then transposed into the western parts of the country, reproducing the intimate connection between the two ongoing forms of warfare.

The social reality of crime and insecurity

Arguably, the social war that has increasingly characterized the urban margins has arisen on the basis of the actual formation of illicit economies or affairs (*gayrimeşru*). Therefore not only the Altındağ area in Ankara but also many other 'relegated' neighbourhoods experience the fundamental issue of an illicit economy and associated social, political and economic problems.[40] Producing a surplus population in large numbers, this generalized reality is conditioned in a system of wageless life as 'the main mode of existence' for the labouring masses on the urban margins of the global South.[41] This reality, therefore, represents an important aspect of proletarian life and subsistence, conditioning the character of the ongoing social war and associated strategies of policing in contemporary Turkey.

At this point, therefore, we need to understand the dialectical relationship between criminalization and the social reality of crime and insecurity. That is, crime should be understood 'only as a relation between ... crime and control'.[42] To view these as distinct phenomena means being trapped by the empiricist project of positivist social science, and thereby reproducing dominant state discourses in fabricating political categories of the poor, the indigent and the criminal. Devoid of social and political context, the criminal becomes a 'suitable enemy'[43] for the deployment of state violence in various forms. For a dialectical relationship between work, poverty and crime, we need to view them as moments in social relations of dispossession, as moments through which capital reasserts its power over labour while consolidating the regime of private property, albeit in many contested forms and through many controversial practices.

What is particularly important here is that the neoliberal politics of the police in Turkey, as elsewhere, has appeared due to the paradigmatic exploitation of the deepening problem of crime in poor neighbourhoods. Glossing over the social relations of oppression and exploitation, the neoliberal discourse on crime has been instrumental in normalizing a violent state presence in the lives of the dispossessed. Scholars such as Christian Parenti have argued that crime has the function of social control by both justifying a police presence, together with an increase in their powers and violence, and closing all possible political alternatives:

> A look at the real impacts of street crime begins to reveal that crime and the fear of crime are forms of social control. Strong-arm robbery, rape, homicide, and general thuggery in poor communities leave people scared, divided, cynical, and politically confused; ultimately these acts drive the victims of capitalism, racism, and sexism into the arms of a racist, probusiness, sexist state. In short, crime justifies state violence and even creates popular demand for state repression. Thus, it helps to liquidate or at least neutralize a whole class of potential rebels. Crime also short-circuits the social cohesion necessary for radical mobilization.[44]

Crime as social control, therefore, functions as a fundamental policing strategy for the generalized legitimation of the empowerment and the violent presence of the police on the urban margins. The spatial strategy of the police is mainly concerned with the solidification of 'the boundaries of perceived criminality' or the creation of 'frozen zones' where crime and associated public order problems are contained.[45] In the case of Altındağ, as part of urban renewal projects, the Altındağ District Police Department was deployed in Çinçin. Contrary to the dominant discourse on urban renewal as a remedy to crime, even after the demolition of *gecekondus* and the spatial deployment of the police, the drug problem has not been resolved; rather, it has been displaced to other neighbourhoods in Altındağ. It is ironic to observe that, after a decade of urban renewal, the Ankara police continue to undertake large-scale police operations against neighbourhoods located just a few blocks away from the district police department.[46]

We also need to shine a spotlight on a controversial dimension of this issue that is central to understanding the contested character of policing in the contemporary metropolis. What can be called 'police–criminal collusion'[47] has increasingly been debated, especially in terms of the establishment and operation of the narcotics police in poor neighbourhoods. Although this collusion seems to be not as systematic as it is in other national contexts, most notably Latin America, organized crime has a long historical trajectory in the making of the modern state and the police in Turkey.[48]

The lived experiences from Altındağ are illustrative in this regard. The following respondent described the actual functioning of the recurrent police operations undertaken against the drug gangs in the area:

> They undertake police operations from time to time with heavily armed robocops, special teams, helicopters and other things. They make these operations not to eliminate drugs here. They come and arrest 16-, 17-year-old poor boys, and send them to jail for ten years. But those people who are at the top of this drug business are informed beforehand and they can save their bacon. What is happening then? The very next day, another young boy begins selling drugs in the place cleared by the police.[49]

As I highlighted above, Altındağ has become a permanent space for police operations that seem to do nothing to solve the problem in question. This violent and intrusive police presence in the lives of the dispossessed is illustrated by another respondent:

> There are no police undertaking their duty at all [in Altındağ]. Because there are no police properly functioning, there are drug dealers and all sorts of other problems. The policemen come here only to bother me and other innocent people, not to solve the issues of crime, drugs, etc. If the police do their job, everybody would like them. But, because they are not fulfilling their duty here, nobody likes them.[50]

In fact, such views have become more and more pronounced in the marginalized social spaces of Turkey's cities. Among others, the legal case that began following the murder of the revolutionary activist Hasan Ferit Gedik by a drug gang in the Gülsuyu neighbourhood in Istanbul reveals the somewhat tacit collaboration between the police and drug networks at the local level.[51] In addition, the mobilization of marginalized Roma people in Keşan, Edirne, a province located in the north-west part of the country, provides a vivid illustration. On the basis of allegations about collusion between the police and the drug gangs, people took to the streets of Keşan with the slogan 'Down with the police station!'[52]

Conclusion

This chapter has mainly argued that the new police order has arisen on the basis of a twin warfare rooted in the violence of Turkish capitalism and the Turkish state throughout the 2010s. This signals the interpenetration of a social war that has increasingly characterized proletarian life on the margin, and an urban warfare that determines the form of the state's presence in the lives of the dispossessed. The contested culmination of policing strategies amidst this twin warfare has been decisive for the making of police power on the margin and its crystallization into the currently dominant police order. It is thus indispensable to develop a critical comprehension of the urban margins to understand the crystallized tendencies concerning both the violent character and the generalized contradictions of policing in contemporary Turkey.

The AKP's police has been increasingly characterized by extra-legal violence against all forms of political dissent and against marginalized populations. Contrary to liberal arguments, however, what is relevant here is not the 'excessive' or 'disproportionate' use of force by the police. Rather, it is the generalized expression of the selective deployment of police violence as 'ordinary punishment, and therefore as a form of retributive justice'[53] in the current context of gendered and racialized class rule.[54] In other words, police power functions as a primary means through which the existing hierarchies of class, race and gender are reinforced on a daily basis. As an inherently contradictory and contested form of political power, however, police power is also characterized by popular frustrations and contestations. Exemplified by the aforementioned slogan of the marginalized Roma people, this popular frustration reminds us that the proletarian demand for public security represents a world-historical contradiction that underlies the social organization of the modern bourgeois police in its 'public' form. It exposes 'the precarious position'[55] or 'the schizophrenic image'[56] assumed by the police in everyday relations with the subordinate classes. Dispossessed of the public provision of security, therefore, the marginalized neighbourhoods of contemporary Turkish cities arguably represent social spaces of 'a generalized withdrawal of legitimacy from the institution of policing *per se*'.[57] Rooted in the complex socio-spatial and political processes of stigmatization and marginalization, this crystallized tendency is deeply embedded in the normalized violence against marginalized populations that represents the current form of state presence in the lives of the dispossessed.

Notes

1. This title is inspired by the collection of rap songs, #*Susamam* (I can't stay silent), released by dissident rappers in Turkey on 5 September 2019. Representing a powerful critique and exposition of the AKP's violent order in its many facets, the collection had been watched on YouTube by over 30 million people as of November 2019.

2. Conversations with U., summer 2016, various localities in Altındağ, Ankara.

3. Benjamin 1968 [1937]: 257.

4. *À la* Engels 2008 [1892]: 132. In his original exposition, Engels used the notion of 'social war' to critique the structural processes of dispossession that create the conditions of radical dependence of the proletariat on the impersonal imperatives of the market. This social war lies at the heart of the social constitution of the poor and its political administration. In the words of Engels: 'Since capital, the direct or indirect control of the means of subsistence and production, is the weapon with which this social warfare is carried on, it is clear that all the disadvantages of such a state must fall

upon the poor ... If the worker can get no work he may steal, if he is not afraid of the police, or starve, in which case the police will take care that he does so in a quiet and inoffensive manner' (Engels 2008 [1892]: 25).

5. This fieldwork was conducted as part of my PhD research on the social history of policing, law and crime in Ankara. See Dölek 2019.

6. See Lea 1999.

7. For instance, in her monograph entitled *Hüznün Çoşkusu Altındağ* [*Altındağ: The Vigor of the Sorrow*], feminist author and trade unionist Yaşar Seyman describes Çinçin Bağları in Altındağ as 'the criminal record document of Ankara'. See Seyman 1986: 82.

8. Davis 2006: 28.

9. See Wacquant 2008.

10. *À la* Butler 1993: 3.

11. Das and Poole 2004: 4.

12. Ibid.: 8.

13. 'Narkotik bir film', *Hürriyet*, 30 December 2010.

14. *Gecekondu* literarily means 'built overnight', denoting the spatio-temporal dynamics of the making of informal settlements in the capitalist

urbanization trajectory of Turkish social formation. It originally emerged as part of the makeshift economy of the urban poor, but it has been constantly redefined in the midst of the always conflictual dynamics of the socio-spatial formation of use value and the commodification of public lands throughout the history of the republic. As an attempt to come to terms with one of the most contested issues in Turkey's experience with capitalist modernity, there has been a distinct field of *gecekondu* studies in Turkey since the 1950s, which, over time, has received an extensive volume of contributions from numerous disciplines, including urban studies, sociology, political science, anthropology and economics. For a critical examination of changing scholarly representations of the *gecekondu* phenomenon, see the rigorous survey by Erman 2001.

15. Erdoğan 2007: 39.

16. See Buğra 2001; Işık and Pınarcıoğlu 2001; Şengül 2009. While this sociological emphasis on the contested incorporation of *gecekondu* settlements is important, we also need to understand the historically indispensable and irreducible role assumed by the police in the pacification of the *gecekondu* settlements as one of the core issues that have haunted the making of urban modernity in Turkey. It was only in and through the consolidation of police power that the once spontaneous and makeshift character of *gecekondu* settlements became incorporated into the existing order, although in contradictory forms. The manner of Altındağ's integration was characterized by the deep-rooted social and spatial trajectory of marginalization and segregation, which were both the product of and a constitutive element in the making of the police in Turkey's national capital since the early decades of the republic. See Dölek 2019.

17. See Adaman and Keyder 2006; Buğra and Keyder 2003; Yılmaz 2008; Yonucu 2008.

18. See Smith 2001; Gündoğdu and Gough 2009.

19. See Gönen 2016; Gönen and Yonucu 2011.

20. See Neocleous 2000; Lefebvre 1992.

21. 'Önce bizi yıkın', *Hürriyet*, 12 November 2012; 'Taş atan çocuklar için kentsel dönüşüm', NTV, 11 December 2011.

22. 'Kentsel dönüşüm suç oranını azaltıyor', *EnsonHaber*, 3 August 2015.

23. See Gönen (Chapter 14).

24. See 'Kandil operasyonu', *Milliyet*, 17 July 2013; 'Uyuşturucu çetesine 2 bin polisle baskın', *Yeni Şafak*, 17 July 2013.

25. 'Giremedikleri mahalleye yerleştiler', *Cumhuriyet*, 15 August 2012.

26. See Yonucu 2018a, 2018b.

27. Conversations with A., summer 2016, Yenidoğan-Altındağ, Ankara.

28. See Berksoy 2010; Gönen 2016; Topak 2013.

29. À la Lefebvre 1992.

30. 'Önce bizi yıkın', *Hürriyet*, 12 November 2012.

31. See 'Hendek kazılan yerlere Çinçin modeli', Memurlar.Net, 9 January 2016.

32. See 'Çözüm süreci 'kalekol'luk oldu', *Diken*, 27 April 2014; 'Kalekol yapımı ve Barış Süreci hakkında önerge', *GazeteKars*, 1 May 2014; İ. Aktan (2014) 'Çözüm süreci kronolojisi', *Bianet*, 26 November.

33. See 'İstanbul'da ilk kalekol açıldı', *Hürriyet*, 25 May 2017.

34. 'İstanbul "modern kalelerle" daha güvenli', *Anadolu Ajansı*, 19 April 2018.

35. 'Terörle mücadele yurt çapına yayılıyor', *Sözcü*, 11 January 2016.

36. See Graham 2011.

37. See the Working-class Protests reports regularly updated by the Labour Studies Group since 2014: https://emekcalisma.org/category/raporlar/.

38. 'TEKEL işçilerine Ankara'da sert polis müdahalesi', BBC Türkçe, 2 April 2010.

39. See Tahir 2019; Kaplan and Miller 2019.

40. See 'Ankara'nın 'öteki' semtleri', BBC Türkçe, 18 July 2013; 'Damgalı mahalleler', Aljazeera Turk, 1 December 2014; 'İstanbul'a suç gece kondu', *Aksiyon*, 14 March 2015; 'Gülsuyu: Mafya 1990'larda girdi', BBC Türkçe, 4 October 2013; 'Türkiye'nin San Andreas'ı: Çinçin Bağları', *Radikal*, 19 March 2015.

41. Denning 2010: 86.

42. Hall et al. 1978: 185.

43. Christie 1986.

44. Parenti 2000.

45. This is indeed a fundamental dimension of modern policing since its inception. See, for instance, Varga 2013: 90.

46. 'Ankara'da dev operasyon', *Hürriyet*, 20 June 2017; 'Ankara'nin Çinçin ve Yenidoğan mahallelerinde bin

polisle operasyon', *YeniAkit*, 23 March 2016; 'Altındağ'da 553 polisle operasyon', *Hürriyet*, 14 September 2019.

47. See Auyero and Sobering 2019.

48. See Gingeras 2014.

49. Interview with V., 4 March 2015, Örnek neighbourhood, Altındağ-Ankara.

50. Interview with Y., 25 March 2015, Örnek neighbourhood, Altındağ-Ankara.

51. See 'Polis ve çete zanlısının "sohbeti" tapelerde', *Bianet*, 14 September 2014.

52. See 'Keşan halkı: "Kahrolsun karakol"', Meydan.org, 6 February 2018.

53. Fassin 2019: 555.

54. For a critical analysis of gendered state violence, see Hülagü (Chapter 13). For a critique of the racialized character of the police violence, see Yonucu 2018a, 2018b; Gönen 2016.

55. Wood 2003: 9.

56. Robinson and Scaglion 1987: 114.

57. Reiner 2000: 49.

References

Adaman, F. and Ç. Keyder (2006) *Avrupa Komisyonu Araştırma Raporu: Türkiye'de Büyük Kentlerin Gecekondu ve Çöküntü Mahallelerinde Yaşanan Yoksulluk ve Sosyal Dışlanma*, https://ec.europa.eu/employment_social/social_inclusion/docs/2006/study_turkey_tr.pdf.

Auyero, J. and K. Sobering (2019) *The Ambivalent State: Police–Criminal Collusions at the Urban Margins*. New York, NY: Oxford University Press.

Benjamin, W. (1968 [1937]) *Illuminations*. Translated by Harry Kohn. New York, NY: Schocken Books.

Berksoy, B. (2010) 'The police organization in Turkey in the post-1980 period and the re-construction of the social formation' in L. Khalili

and J. Schwedler (eds), *Policing and Prisons in the Middle East: Formations of Coercion*. London: C. Hurst and Company, pp. 137–55.

Buğra, A. (2001) 'Ekonomik kriz karşısında Türkiye'nin geleneksel refah rejimi', *Toplum ve Bilim 89*: 22–30.

Buğra, A. and Ç. Keyder (2003) *Yeni Yoksulluk ve Türkiye'nin Değişen Refah Rejimi*. Ankara: United Nations Development Programme.

Butler, J. (1993) *Bodies That Matter: On the Discursive Limits of 'Sex'*. New York, NY and London: Routledge.

Christie, N. (1986) 'Suitable enemies' in H. Bianchi and R. van Swaaningen (eds), *Abolitionism: Towards a Non-repressive Approach to Crime*. Amsterdam: Free University Press, pp. 42–54.

Das, V. and D. Poole (2004) 'State and its margins: comparative ethnographies' in V. Das and D. Poole (eds), *Anthropology in the Margins of the State*. New York, NY: Oxford University Press, pp. 3–34.

Davis, M. (2006) *Planet of Slums*. London and New York, NY: Verso.

Denning, M. (2010) 'Wageless life', *New Left Review 66*: 79–97.

Dölek, Ç. (2019) 'Thieves, *kabadayıs*, and revolutionaries on the margin: a social history of the police in the Altındağ slums in Ankara, Turkey (1920s–1970s)'. PhD thesis, Carleton University, Ottawa.

Engels, F. (2008 [1892]) *The Condition of the Working-class in England in 1844*. New York, NY: Cosimo.

Erdoğan, N. (ed.) (2007) *Yoksulluk Halleri*. İstanbul: İletişim.

Erman, T. (2001) 'The politics of squatter (*gecekondu*) studies in Turkey: the changing representations of rural migrants in the academic discourse,' *Urban Studies 38* (7): 983–1002.

Fassin, D. (2019) 'Police are the punishment', *Public Culture 31* (3): 539–61.

Gingeras, R. (2014) *Heroin, Organized Crime, and the Making of Modern Turkey*. Oxford and New York, NY: Oxford University Press.

Gönen, Z. (2016) *The Politics of the Crime in Turkey: Neoliberalism, Police, and the Urban Poor*. London and New York, NY: I. B. Tauris.

Gönen, Z. and D. Yonucu (2011) 'Legitimizing violence and segregation: neoliberal discourses on crime and criminalization of urban poor populations in Turkey' in A. Bourke, T. Dafnos and M. Kis (eds), *Lumpen-city: Discourses of Marginality / Marginalizing Discourses*. Ottawa: Red Quill Press, pp. 75–103.

Graham, S. (2011) *The New Military Urbanism*. London and New York, NY: Verso.

Gündoğdu, İ. and J. Gough (2009) 'Class cleansing in Istanbul's world city project' in L. Porter and K. Shaw (eds), *Whose Urban Renaissance? An International Comparison of Urban Regeneration Strategies*. Abingdon: Routledge, pp. 16–24.

Hall, S. et al. (1978) *Policing the Crisis: Mugging, the State, and Law and Order*. London and Basingstoke: Macmillan.

Işık, O. and M. Pınarcıoğlu (2001) *Nöbetleşe Yoksulluk – Sultanbeyli Örneği*. İstanbul: İletişim.

Kaplan, C. and A. Miller (2019) 'Drones as "atmospheric policing": from US border enforcement to the LAPD', *Public Culture 31* (3): 419–45.

Lea, J. (1999) 'Social crime revisited', *Theoretical Criminology 3* (3): 307–27.

Lefebvre, H. (1992) *The Production of Space*. Oxford: Wiley-Blackwell.

Neocleous, M. (2000) *The Fabrication of Social Order: A Critical Theory of Police Power*. London: Pluto Press.

Parenti, C. (2000) 'Crime as social control', *Social Justice 27* (3): 43–9.

Reiner, R. (2000) *The Politics of the Police*. New York, NY: Oxford University Press.

Robinson, C. D. and R. Scaglion (1987) 'The origin and evolution of the police function in society: notes towards a theory', *Law and Society Review 21* (1): 109–54.

Şengül, T. (2009) *Kentsel Çelişki ve Siyaset*. 2nd edition. Ankara: İmge.

Seyman, Y. (1986) *Hüznün coşkusu Altındağ*. İstanbul: Gür Yayınları.

Smith, N. (2001) 'Global social cleansing: postliberal revanchism and the export of zero tolerance', *Social Justice 28* (3): 68–74.

Tahir, M. (2019) 'Violence work and the police order', *Public Culture 31* (3): 409–18.

Topak, Ö. (2013) 'Governing Turkey's information society', *Current Sociology 61* (5–6): 565–83.

Varga, J. J. (2013) *Hell's Kitchen and the Battle for Urban Space: Class Struggle and Progressive Reform in New York City, 1894–1914*. New York, NY: NYU Press.

Wacquant, L. (2008) *Urban Outcasts: A Comparative Sociology of Advanced Marginality*. Cambridge and Malden, MA: Polity Press.

Wood, J. C. (2003) 'Self-policing and the policing of the self: violence, protection and the civilizing bargain in Britain', *Crime, History and Societies 7* (1): 1–19.

Yılmaz, B. (2008) 'Türkiye'de sınıl-altı', *Toplum ve Bilim 113*: 127–45.

Yonucu, D. (2008) 'A story of a squatter neighbourhood: from the place of the "dangerous classes" to the "place of danger"', *Berkley Journal of Sociology 52*: 50–72.

Yonucu, D. (2018a) 'The absent present law: an ethnographic study of legal violence in Turkey', *Social and Legal Studies 27* (6): 716–33.

Yonucu, D. (2018b) 'Urban vigilantism: a study of anti-terror law, politics and policing in Istanbul', *International Journal of Urban and Regional Research 42* (3): 408–22.

INDEX

www.ingramcontent.com/pod-product-compliance
Lightning Source LLC
Chambersburg PA
CBHW060147280326
41932CB00012B/1665